exploit a tribal conflict as a struggle against the "bourgeoisie.") They show that Communism grows not by an intrinsic "revolutionary" appeal, but by its ability to obscure its aims and identify itself with other groups, goals and popular symbols. The French Communists, Mrs. Kirkpatrick points out, have attempted to capture Victor Hugo, and the American Communists have staked a claim to Tom Paine and Abraham Lincoln. The Communists, it is demonstrated, are masters of *real politik,* and should be the enemy and the adversary, rather than the bogeyman, of freedom-loving people and their political leaders.

The editor, Mrs. Jeane J. Kirkpatrick, is presently a member of the Political Science faculty at Trinity College, Senior Analyst in Operations and Policy Research Inc., Washington, D.C., and a consultant for various government agencies. Mrs. Kirkpatrick received her A.B. from Barnard College, and her M.A. from Columbia University, where she is now completing her Ph.D. Mrs. Kirkpatrick has written articles for *The New Leader, The New Republic, Western World,* and co-edited, with her husband Evron M. Kirkpatrick, *Elections U.S.A.* (1956).

THE STRATEGY OF DECEPTION

THE STRATEGY OF DECEPTION:

A study in world-wide Communist tactics

EDITED BY JEANE J. KIRKPATRICK

■

Farrar, Straus and Company
New York

23481

FOREWORD

Work on this collection of essays was begun by the late S. M. Levitas, who for more than thirty years was executive editor of *The New Leader*. When the pressures of ill health made it impossible for him to carry the volume to completion, the essays which had been solicited by Mr. Levitas were passed on to me with the understanding that I should supplement them, edit them, provide an introduction, and otherwise do whatever was required to prepare a book which would carry out the original intent of the understanding. I have tried to execute this commission faithfully.

J. J. K.

CONTENTS

4 Old Tactics in the New World

5 Conflict and Consensus in the United Nations

INTRODUCTION: THE POLITICS
OF DECEPTION

Jeane J. Kirkpatrick

This is a book of essays on the Communist movement outside the U.S.S.R. Its subject is the means by which Communist parties attempt, and sometimes succeed, in capturing power. All the essays are concerned with Communist parties in action. Those which deal with theory are concerned with theory in action, with its uses and consequences. In brief, these essays are case studies, designed to provide an operational description of characteristic instruments and procedures utilized by Communist parties in their efforts to come to power. They are case studies in *political* conflict.

Communist parties, which we carelessly call Communism, achieve political power through political contests. This fact, which appears almost to be a tautology, is repeatedly, and in some cases systematically, overlooked and obscured. Its implications are of extreme importance. To assert that Communists achieve power by competition at the political level implies first, that they are not swept into power on the tides of historical inevitability; second, that except where they gain control through military occupation, the success of Communist parties is determined by the political skill of Communist leaders in exploiting their opportunities; and third, that when we discuss the expansion of Communist power, we are dealing not with an amorphous historical force but with the activities of identifiable men in specific situations.

Communists themselves long ago made the transition from historical determinism to political voluntarism *on the operational level.* Since this transition is of basic importance to understanding the Communist movement it seems worthwhile to examine it briefly.

It is by now well known to historians and social scientists outside the circle of Communist orthodoxy that the class struggle described by Marx and thought by him to be the motor of historical change, has failed to develop as predicted. In the most industrially advanced nations, the working classes have not been kept at a subsistence level, the middle classes have not been pauperized, the cycles of prosperity and depression have not become shorter, nor the depressions more severe. The "inevitably" catastrophic development of capitalism failed to occur. History succumbed to economism. Powerful trade unions developed which proved able to extract concessions in wages and security from employers and the state. Instead of becoming progressively more miserable and desperate, the working classes of the highly industrialized nations enjoy a level of prosperity unprecedented in history and, incidentally, unequaled in Communist countries. The capitalists themselves refused the self-defeating roles assigned them by Marx and declined to fight to the last ditch for the last possible cent of profit, which, as embodiments of the capitalist ethic, they should have done. The state in the industrially advanced nations was not transformed into an instrument of fascist repression. Instead, it undertook to eliminate through regulation the most important abuses of the capitalist system, and, in some countries—such as the U.K., the Scandinavian countries, and France—to eliminate important sectors of the system itself. Social legislation governing the terms and conditions of employment, collective bargaining, securities and trust regulation, graduated income taxes, and social security systems are but a few of the "reformist" devices with which history has confounded Marx's predictions.

Lenin's efforts to salvage Marx's doctrine of historical determinism and class struggle on the scientific level by stretching the conception of class to include whole nations was as unsuccessful as scientific theory as it was successful as propaganda. In fact, of course, the doctrine of inevitable class struggle as expounded by Marx was simply a mistaken prediction, which would have long since become only a datum of intellectual history had it not been embodied in the official ideology of a world power. Its failure on the level of science—as opposed to that of propaganda—deprives the notion of Communism's inevitable triumph of any scientific or historical basis, and converts into a purely mystical doctrine the Communists' claim to have penetrated the laws of history. All this is well known, but its implications are regularly ignored.

The failure of Marx's central hypothesis concerning the future of political systems did not inhibit the growth of the political movement acting in his name. Neither did the growth of that movement constitute any confirmation of the Marxist hypothesis. As early as the Bolshevik Revolution itself, Lenin emancipated Communists from the encumbrance of Marx's error. The first major step in the transition from economic determinism to political voluntarism was taken at the crucial moment in the Russian Revolution when it appeared possible for the Bolsheviks to seize power. At this moment, Lenin decided that Russia could "bypass" the capitalist stage of development. This action, discussed in some detail by Benedict Kautsky in his essay in this volume, was the first clear-cut decision by a Communist leader that leadership and state power could circumvent or transcend the laws of history. Determinism was tacitly abandoned in favor of human intelligence, will, and power. Marx had suggested that Communists could assist history; Lenin proposed they outwit it.

A second major step in sloughing off dialectical materialism was taken in response to the *fact* that the underdeveloped and colonial areas appeared to offer a promising area for Communist expansion. By encouraging the formation of Communist parties in colonial, largely prefeudal areas, Lenin emancipated the Communist movement from Marx's laws of economic development. According to Marx, Communist movements were a specific, inevitable product of capitalism. Lenin proposed to create them by political decision. Lenin believed that he had integrated prefeudal societies into the theoretical structure of Marxism through his highly revisionist doctrine of imperialism, which introduced the concept of seduction into dialectical materialism and transferred the class struggle from the national to the international level. In fact, he had merely politicized the doctrine of the class struggle. It is nonetheless true that Lenin's essay on imperialism was the last major effort of a Bolshevik leader to revise Marxist doctrines in the light of practice.

Once the movement had assimilated the crucial decision of Lenin that state power could be used to circumvent whole stages of historical development, that is, once the transition from historical determinism to political voluntarism was made *on the operational level,* the capture of state power everywhere became the actual goal of the Communist movement. The presence, or absence, of an industrial proletariat and a capitalist class became irrelevant to the class struggle after it had been operationally redefined to mean the struggle of a Communist party against any non-Communist government, or internationalized to mean the struggle of the Communist bloc against non-Communist nations.

Economic determinism was sloughed off in response to concrete historical situations in which Communist leaders were confronted with the possibility of extending their power in situations which did not conform to the "laws of history" which should have brought Communism to power. In each such conflict, the requirements of presumably inflexible laws of historical development have been ignored and the opportunity to seize or maximize power has been grasped. Inside the Soviet Union, terror and propaganda have been relied on to produce changes that should have occurred inevitably once the structure of ownership had been altered. The decision to deny nationality groups and "autonomous" republics the right to secede, the decision to impose revolution by military occupation in Eastern Europe, to seize power by *coup d'état* in Czechoslovakia are but a few examples. The aggressive pursuit of power in societies which lack capitalists and industrial workers as well as a class struggle is perhaps the most dramatic example of Communist leaders' indifference to Marx and Engels' doctrine of the historic role of Communism.

If human behavior conformed to the rationalist's model, the Bolsheviks' willingness to subordinate doctrine to the exigencies of the power struggle would constitute evidence that Communist leaders were pragmatic rather than dogmatic, that they had submitted basic items of Marxism to the test of history and revised them in the light of experience. Of course, no such thing has occurred. Practice has been adapted to actual historical developments and to the Communist leaders' desire to maximize their power; basic doctrine has been maintained intact. Communist leaders are *both* pragmatic and dogmatic. Adaptation to historical experience has been named "tactics," and a substantial literature on tactics has been developed to guide the actual operations of Communist parties. This literature on tactics constitutes the most impressive existing guide to the capture of political power in a wide range of contexts. It is eminently realistic, pragmatic, and cynical. Its analyses and prescriptions are ideologically neutral: the tactics they recommend could be utilized with equal success by any minority engaged in the uninhibited pursuit of state power. Much of this literature deals with the pursuit of goals which, according to classical Marxism, could not conceivably be achieved. Apostasy for the sake of expanded power is called tactical flexibility.

In the name of tactical flexibility "socialism" is imposed on pre-feudal societies; Communist parties serve as "vanguard of the proletariat" in nations with no proletariat, no capitalists, no industry; military conquest, subversion, and *coups d'état* are substituted for proletarian revolutions; tiny elites of intellectual freebooters are substituted for the working masses.

All the while, classical Marxism is invoked to surround the quest for power with an aura of morality and science. It is occasionally augmented, but, for the most part, it is simply invoked. Its basic postulates are examined neither in the light of history nor of Bolshevik practice. It is left intact: a body of propositions about the development of history which has been disproved by history. It nonetheless serves valuable functions for the Communist movement. (1) It provides the movement with ultimate goals which serve as moral justification of the movement. (2) It frees the Communist elite of moral inhibitions to the unhampered pursuit of power. (3) It justifies unceasing hostility against all persons and organizations outside the movement and sanctions aggression as moral and inevitable. (4) It provides grounds for believing in the ultimate and inevitable triumph of the movement.

Instead of there being the much vaunted "unity of theory and practice" in Communist practice, there is an absolute split between theory and practice. Unlike the central doctrines of a supernatural religion, those of Marx and Engels concern historical facts and are testable in history and by history. As we have seen, many have already been contradicted by actual developments, and have been discredited by non-Communists as theory and by Communists as a guide to action. The effort to preserve them intact, to avoid relating them to concrete historical realities while permitting concrete historical realities to guide day-to-day political behavior, necessitates a colossal dissociation of theory and practice. Maintaining it requires a habit of irrationalism, and makes irrationalism a necessity to the Communist movement and Communist leaders. It is hardly necessary to point out that maintaining this type of dissociation leads to extreme defensiveness, rigidity, and hostility toward any threat to the valued doctrine. But it does not necessarily affect efficiency.

Democrats are tempted to believe that the dogmatic, unscientific character of official Communist ideology is a potential source of weakness which will eventually render the Communist movement and Communist governments less sensitive to reality, and less efficient in the long run than governments guided by a pragmatic philosophy. These latter, it is believed, draw strength from regularly submitting their policies to the test of experience. This view overlooks the fact that, at the level of political conflict, the Communists are consummate pragmatists and masters of *Realpolitik*, as unhampered by dogmatic ideological considerations as by ethical inhibitions. It also misjudges the function of official ideology.

It has proved exceedingly difficult for non-Communists to assimilate the fact and implications of the irrelevance of the Marxist philosophy of historical development to the conduct of the Communist movement. *In fact,* the Communist movement has no economic base; and no specified relationship to any economic class. *In fact,* Communist parties have no predictable, determinate, or integral ties to any particular social or economic group. Once Marx and Engels' doctrine of historical determinism had been abandoned, and the class struggle operationally defined to mean the struggle between Communist parties and non-Communists, Communists were free to look for support in any quarter, and to declare enemies all those who opposed their accession to power. This they regularly do. In the essays in this volume on Communism in India, Burma, France, Italy, Africa, and elsewhere, the reader will find instance after instance of the indeterminate relations between Communists and other groups. Tribal membership, regional interests, language, personal rivalries, nationalism, color, and other factors often serve as the basis for dividing enemies from friends as do relations to the means of production. In the underdeveloped areas, we see again and again the efforts of Westernized Communist leaders to find or create a social base for a tiny party. Their efforts are concentrated on whichever group is most alienated from existing authority, or least integrated into the existing structure of authority. In China, this proved to be intellectuals and peasants; in India, certain regional and caste groups; in the United States, certain portions of the middle class; in Britain, certain ethnic minorities; in France, industrial workers and the intelligentsia; in Africa, certain tribes. And so forth. Communist parties do not reliably draw their support from the poorest class or classes in any given nation. They may or may not, depending on the degree to which these classes are or may be politicized and alienated. In short, they seek supporters wherever they think supporters are to be found.

The extent to which economic categories have become irrelevant to the Communist struggle for power is obscured by Communist leaders' universal habit of describing the political conflicts in which they are involved in the language of classical Marxism. A tribal conflict may be billed as a struggle against the bourgeoisie.

Clarity about the relation of Communist parties to the class structure has important practical consequences. The fact that Communist parties represent no particular class, but are simply an elite competing for political power, seems very difficult to assimilate. The notion that Communists are somehow engaged in the struggle between rich and poor, haves and have nots, workers and employers, oppressed and oppressors leads to the persistent notion that Communism is *somehow* more democratic and progressive than its undemocratic rivals. And this notion in turn leads to a lingering, half-conscious inhibition among many democrats to judge the Communist party by the same criteria it judges competing undemocratic elites. The notion persists that Communists are somehow morally superior to other elites which use amoral means to gain power and impose repressive, minority dictatorships.

Alienation from existing authority—not economic role—is the principal determinant of a group's susceptibility to Communism. The most depressed classes in a society may or may not be the most alienated. In the noncapitalist countries of Asia, Africa, and the Middle East, educated minorities who have felt the full impact of Western industrial civilization and of Western colonialism are usually most alienated from traditional authority, values, and social organization. They are the carriers of the famous "revolution of rising expectations." They are bearers of social change. They are the groups most likely to be anti-Western as well as Westernized, to be most conscious and resentful of the colonial period. The poorest, least privileged classes in these countries are often profoundly traditionalist. Their expectations have been undisturbed for centuries. Their political worlds are dominated by traditional loyalties and traditional rivalries. Through skillful exploitation of traditional conflicts, and extravagant promises of good things to come, they can sometimes be involved in struggles at the level of nation-state politics. But in spite of rhetoric to the contrary, Communism in the underdeveloped areas is not fed by the restless hopes and resentments of the masses. The relation of indigenous Communists to native masses is manipulative and exploitative.

There is no significant predictable difference between the supporters of Communist elites and other nondemocratic elites. There is also no difference in the way they come to power. In no nation ruled by the Communists have they been elected to head the government, or even swept into power by a mass revolt which was overtly Communist in character. Where they have won the support of large numbers of peasants, as in China, and the Philippines during the Hukbalahap uprising, they have done so by promising land to the peasants (which promises they betray as soon as their power has been consolidated), conducting guerrilla warfare against opponents and the government, and infiltrating the government. In countries with a tradition of national unity, an established sense of national identity and a central government capable of administering its laws, the Communists have come to power only through military occupation (Poland, Rumania, Bulgaria, Albania, and Eastern Germany), or by *coup d'état* (Russia and Czechoslovakia). In areas with no tradition of national unity and central government, they have relied on guerrilla war and terrorism to exploit the weakness of the government (China, Viet Minh). The means by which Communist parties have come to power do not suggest either democracy or progress.

The important difference between Communist elites and other antidemocratic elites is found in the way Communist elites use power, once they have achieved it. Many antidemocratic elites are interested in maintaining the traditional social structure and culture. Franco, for example, has not attempted to undermine the social power of the Catholic Church in Spain, nor that of the large landowners. Like many military dictators in Latin America and elsewhere he has not attempted to alter significantly the cultural, social, or economic status quo. This means, of course, that he has not undertaken reforms to correct traditional inequities. But since the needs, expectations, values, and cognitive structures of most people in any society reflect traditional culture and roles, it is a fact that maintaining a culture requires less repression than does the effort radically to alter it by administrative decision. The traditional social structure may impose hardships and poverty, but its norms are internalized. Traditional autocrats and oligarchs can rely largely on subjective needs and habits to keep masses of people performing traditional roles. Typically, they utilize coercion only to protect their own power. For the traditional autocrat the political sphere, that is, the arena relevant to the contest for control of government, is quite narrowly defined. Like the European or American liberal he does not see society as coterminous with the state.

In practice, Communist elites are more repressive than traditional dictatorships because they aim at revolutionizing society, culture, and personality. Therefore, they perceive the totality of social structure and culture as involved in the political struggle. Attachment to traditional culture is likely to be interpreted as political opposition. And political opposition is not tolerated.

The most important consequence of treating society and culture as parts of the political sphere is that it multiplies many times the number of potential points of conflict between citizens and political authority. It greatly increases the issues in which the authority and the coercive power of the state are involved. Norms established by the state must be enforced by state power if the authority of the state is to be maintained. Therefore, the larger the number of subjects on which a state acts, the larger the number of issues on which it must be prepared to coerce. In the "Labor Universities" and army barracks of Red China, people are politically liable for what they say in their sleep, because the government of Communist China has staked a claim to the subjective lives of its citizens as well as to their behavior. This is, of course, the reason for its massive efforts at thought reform. In the Soviet Union, literature, styles of painting, architecture, and music are still as in the Stalinist era—official concerns of the state. Linguistics, philosophy, psychology, biology, as well as social science and history are areas in which the authority and coercive power of the state are engaged.

To summarize, Communist leaders' determination to revolutionize society and culture leads them to attempt to control by regulation a very wide range of activities normally governed by custom and personal preference. Where the state regulates, it stands ready to coerce. Extension of regulation and coercion into all spheres of society is the meaning of totalitarianism. Since regulation in social and cultural areas is uniquely difficult to enforce, it requires more police, more surveillance, more terror. This is the reason that totalitarian regimes are uniquely repressive.

Despite the fact that Communist parties have no reliable relation to the masses, do not come to power through mass action (either legal or illegal), do not submit industry to the control of the masses or organize production for the benefit of the masses, and do not rule at the pleasure of the masses, a vast area of myth, misunderstanding, and confusion supports the notion that there is some sort of mystical affinity of Communism and "the people."

This confusion, which often exists only on the half articulate level of assumptions, is extraordinarily durable. Its sources are several. One is the semantic confusion fostered by the Communists themselves through their systematically perverse use of language. By calling "autonomous" that which is powerless, "federated" that which is unitary, "democratic" that which is autocratic, "united" that which is schismatic, "popular" that which is imposed by terror, "peaceful" that which incites war—in brief, by systematically corrupting language to obscure reality, the Communists have made inroads into our sense of political reality. Language is, after all, the only medium in which we can think. It is exceedingly difficult to eliminate all the traditional connotations of words—to associate words like "For a Lasting Peace and a People's Democracy" with neither peace nor popular movements nor democracy.

A related form of semantic subversion, practiced by Communist parties everywhere is the effort to capture prestigious symbols, slogans, and traditions. Communist parties in the underdeveloped world attempt to identify themselves with the slogans of nationalism and anticolonialism. Communists in France attempt to identify themselves with the symbols of the resistance, the French Revolution, and the tradition of the "Left." French Communists have attempted to capture Victor Hugo, as American Communists staked a claim to Tom Paine and Abraham Lincoln.

Communism does not grow by disseminating and winning sup-

port for its own values. Neither members nor followers are regularly recruited through the appeal of Communist values. Communism grows by identifying itself with the prestige symbols of competing movements and so blurring issues, stakes, and alignments. In his seminal work, *World Politics and Personal Insecurity*, Harold Lasswell pointed out that the spread of a revolution is often checked when opposing groups adopt key symbols of the revolution. This he termed restriction by partial incorporation. The carriers of Communist revolutions reverse this process, and attempt to advance their revolution by tactical incorporation of the symbols of opposing groups.

If Communist parties spoke of collectivization to peasants, of internationalism to the new nations, of inexorable conflict to pacifists, of ideological conformity to intellectuals, of state capitalism to the working classes, and of dictatorship to the middle classes— in short, *if Communist parties attempted to recruit support through the appeal of their own values, the lines of conflict would be clearly drawn.* Communism, whose values have sharply limited appeal, would be readily defeated. The Communist movement is a Trojan horse because it systematically conceals its identity—in its propaganda and organizational tactics.

Another inhibition to clarity about the character and habits of the Communist movement grows out of internal inconsistencies of the movement, rather than an effort to deceive. The dissociation of theory and practice discussed earlier, and the effort to bring the two into harmony on the verbal level, introduces confusion into the Communists' self-conception which is communicated to the non-Communist world. Surprisingly often, non-Communists accept at face value the Communist's own formulation of his role, when in fact there is about as much reason for accepting the Communist's conception of his identity and role as there was for accepting a divine right king's view of his credentials.

A third source of persistent confusion about the Communist movement and Communist parties results from projecting our own expectations, needs and values, and cognitive habits. The programs of democratic political parties are influenced to varying degrees by the aspirations and expected responses of voters outside the party. But their general orientation and basic programs are determined by the values of leaders and members. Tactical flexibility of democratic parties is sharply limited by commitments to values other than power. Honest projection of the party's identity is itself a value which prevents parties from adapting programs that falsify basic aspects of their identity. The tendency to project habits and values has repeatedly led the non-Communist world to mistake a Communist party's temporary tactical position for its identifying characteristics, and temporary lulls in the Cold War for peace. A nationalist posture assumed to gain specific tactical ends is taken as evidence that a Communist party is basically nationalistic. An antiwar position taken in response to Soviet foreign policy requirements is mistaken for genuine pacifism. When the Communists negotiate agreements to gain time or a respite we feel that we have achieved peace.

Still another of the reasons we attribute a class character to Communist parties throughout the world is our habit of thinking about political alignments in terms of economic classes. It is paradoxical that the officially voluntaristic Western nations attach greater importance to economic and social factors than do the officially deterministic Communists. In the underdeveloped countries Communist leaders often behave as if they regarded social and economic structure as irrelevant to the struggle for power, while representatives of the United States and Western Europe often behave as if the basic economy held the key to the outcome of the political struggle. There is a double irony in the fact that when we concentrate on the development of an economic infrastructure in an underdeveloped country *to halt the spread of Communism,* we are projecting to the local Communist movement an economic character which it claims but does not have, because of beliefs we have but do not claim.

To these sources of confusion must be added another. Until the last decade or two the study of politics has been crippled by a kind of formalism which persistently mistook form for reality. It encouraged appraising the Soviet Union in terms of its written constitution, and the Communist movement in terms of classical Marxism. It reinforced the tendency to accept any given tactical posture of a Communist party as a definition of the aims of the party, and to mistake a Communist party for a garden variety political party because it called itself one. Because the Communist movement is fundamentally different from political organizations to which we are accustomed, because it deals regularly in deception and obfuscation, because its representatives decline traditional roles and ignore traditional rules, sophisticated functional analysis is all the more necessary.

Authors of the essays in this volume share a bias in favor of reality. They ask concrete questions, and offer concrete answers. They attempt to translate vague concepts like "The Chinese Revolution" into the ideas, feelings, and activities of specific people in specific places. They are interested in the actual composition of the "vanguard of the proletariat" and the actual relations between it and actual working classes. They are interested in how power is used, as well as whose name is invoked by those using it; in what actually happens in the U.N. as well as what should happen.

Two of the essays treat subjects concerning the whole of the Communist movement. The rest examine aspects of the movement in limited areas. Five are concerned with the theory and practice of Communist parties in the underdeveloped areas; five deal with European Communist parties; two describe the activities of Communists in the Americas; and one discusses the collision of the American and Soviet orientations in the United Nations.

Perhaps a word is in order about the political commitments of the authors. Collectively, they cover the spectrum of *democratic* policies. Several have been active in democratic socialist movements and trade union activities for decades. Several of the Americans can be broadly categorized as liberals—and Democrats: a few are conservatives and Republicans. All are committed to democratic government. Each has won distinction and recognition for scholarship and/or participation in the field of politics. Each is a distinguished man, with a deep commitment to human freedom. It is a pleasure to have been associated with them in this project.

Jeane J. Kirkpatrick
Trinity College
Washington, D.C.

1

Reflections on Theory and Practice

THE DEATH OF THE CLASS STRUGGLE

Abba P. Lerner

■ In the following essay, Professor Abba P. Lerner examines the doctrine of the class struggle as a theory which purports to explain observed facts, and as a faith invulnerable to facts. As we observed earlier, the theory of the class struggle is a theory about history which can be tested in history. Lerner submits it to these tests. He then examines the "astounding practical success" of this mistaken theory that is always invoked by the Communists to explain any conflict in which they find themselves—anywhere, any time, with anyone. ■

The reader of this volume will have repeated opportunities to observe the flexibility of the Communist doctrine of the class struggle. It can be made to comprehend the struggle of a "national bourgeoisie" for independence, the struggle of a regional movement for autonomy, a tribal or racial conflict, a campaign against a trade union movement, a fight to the death with a Socialist party.

Abba P. Lerner, a professor of economics at Roosevelt College, has written widely on political and economic subjects. His books include The Economics of Control, The Economics of Employment, and Essays in Economic Analysis. His essay here is controversial, stimulating, and incisive. ■

By this title is meant not the death of the class struggle, but rather the death of the theory that human history can be explained in terms of class struggle, and only in such terms. But in another sense the view that class struggle is the key to a true understanding of the nature and the development of social organization is more a faith than a theory. A theory is an explanation of observed facts which one must be ready to modify or to reject if it fails to explain the facts. A faith is an explanation which survives all evidence to the contrary, the faithful either denying the facts or reinterpreting the dogma, even if this requires giving the text a meaning which is the exact opposite of what it says.

The line between theory and faith is not always as clear as it should be. All theories tend to develop a life of their own, people trying to hold on to them even when the facts cause doubt or difficulty. It is often said that nothing is more fatal to a theory than a fact with which it cannot be squared; but this too is theory. In many cases theories are held on to in the hope that the disturbing facts may finally prove to be illusory. At other times the disturbing facts are merely ignored or forgotten. The human mind, it appears, hates a vacuum and prefers a poor theory to none at all. To get rid of an unsatisfactory theory a new theory is required which fits the facts better. Disproven or unsatisfactory theories therefore tend to survive inconvenient facts as long as no better theories rise to supplant them.

The faith which is known as the theory of the class struggle, however, shows greater than average vitality. Much more purely a *faith* than most theories, it is not at all dependent upon its ability to explain the facts. The basic scripture of this faith is the *Communist Manifesto* published by Marx and Engels in 1848 which has as its primary dogma that the whole of history is the history of the class struggle. Acceptance of this dogma simplifies history and makes it easily understandable to the believer. For the actual world a model is substituted which does not consist of people but of *classes*. Although a class comprises millions or hundreds of millions of individuals, each of whom is very difficult if not impossible to understand thoroughly, it is assumed that we do know how the class itself behaves. A class necessarily pursues its own interests. Thus the vastness of history shrinks, and the ordinary man discovers that his eyes are perfectly capable of viewing the entire process.

Moreover, in this simplified version, there are generally only two actors on the historical stage at any given time: an exploiting and an exploited class. The latter, disliking to be exploited or repressed, struggles against the former, overthrows its enemy, and in turn becomes the exploiter of another class lower in the class scale. The classes are arranged like rungs in a ladder, the lower always being exploited by the higher.

This phenomenon repeats itself in a series of struggles in which the exploited becomes the exploiter of the class below, until finally the bottom class is reached, the proletariat or working class which, having no other class to exploit, establishes the classless society.

In the classless society, man no longer exploits man—only nature. There is brotherhood and a superabundance of everything. All the great evils of society—war, discord, unemployment, poverty, etc., disappear automatically. Furthermore, this process is the inevitable outcome of the class struggle.

Now there is nothing wrong with constructing a simplified model to explain complicated phenomena. Indeed, it is only with the help of such devices that the human mind can understand anything of a universe that is much too complicated for any single brain. *Only* models of limited aspects, or limited parts, of the universe can be perceived by men. Fortunately these models have been sufficiently effective in explaining various aspects of the universe to enable human beings to survive and prosper on this planet. A theory may, however, be too simple to be useful.

As a model of human history, the theory of the class struggle is superior to an even simpler construct, namely, a harmonious humanity living without conflict. Sometimes the high priests of the theory of the class struggle seem to suggest that all other attempts to explain history reduce to this even more ridiculous proposition. Probably no one has ever held the view of a completely harmonious history, but if it ever was seriously propounded, the theory of the class struggle is so small an improvement upon it that it is difficult to understand how it came to be regarded as such a great contribution to human understanding.

It is not that the picture of a series of struggles leading to a final climactic conflict and then to peace and beauty is not of itself a very attractive one. Indeed it always puts me in mind of my mother's coffeepot. When I was a little boy one of my tasks used to be to turn off the gas before the coffeepot boiled over. I was fascinated by the way a large number of tiny bubbles first appeared on the surface of the water and then explosively combined into larger and larger bubbles until there were only a small number of them, and finally only one large, beautifully hemispheric bubble which covered the whole of the coffeepot. I would try to turn off the gas before this last bubble also burst.

At the time I saw this phenomenon as a cosmological analogy. I was attending elementary school in London and the bubbles suggested to me the way the British Empire was spreading over the map. With the completion of the Cape-to-Cairo railroad, the pink area would reach to the foot of Africa and finally would cover all the land surfaces of the globe. Justice, peace, and civilization would then have been disseminated by the Empire to the entire planet.

This particular bubble appears to have burst for almost everybody. It took the suppression of the Hungarian revolt by the Soviet army in 1956 to burst the bubble of history seen exclusively as class struggle.

But what disappeared with the events in Hungary in 1956 was only the *theory* of the class struggle. The dogma survives as a militant faith maintained by the armed forces of the Soviet Union and China and their satellites. The Communists in the rest of the world also go on believing. Theirs is a *pure* faith and therefore completely invulnerable to mere experience.

But that the theory should have died at last is less surprising than that it survived as long as it did. What kept it alive? A closer examination shows that much of the attractiveness of this theory lay in its development into a system which purported to explain very nearly everything.

If human history is indeed the history of the class struggle, and history is inexorably proceeding toward the classless society, then in this development the "primary" or "basic" determinant is the "relations of production" or the "mode of production." Immediately one becomes involved in such questions as: who owns the instruments of production? in what way is each product shared? how are the workers maintained? who decides how the various products are to be used? All the rest of history is declared to be "superstructure" and in a somewhat mysterious or metaphysical sense "derived from" developments in the mode of production. The attitudes of people, opinions, beliefs, ways of thinking, modes of life—indeed, all culture is nothing but a superstructure which can somehow or other be derived from or explained by a knowledge of the basic or "primary" element.

Out of this view develops a second thesis: under capitalism the economic position of the proletariat continually deteriorates until finally it becomes clear to all (and not only to Karl Marx and his friends) that the working class has nothing to lose but its chains.

In addition, as the workers' material situation worsens, the "crises of capitalism," which is Marx's expression for business depressions, intensify, causing additional misery and hastening the overthrow of the bourgeois state by the proletarian revolution.

Moreover, as the working class prepares for this final culmination of prehistory (true *human* history will begin with the establishment of the classless society) it loses all national and racial feelings or prejudices and unites together in an international movement. National and racial feelings are only inventions of the bourgeoisie, or if not mere inventions, attitudes that are strengthened and manipulated by them through the use of propaganda.

Inevitably the conflict between capitalists and workers sharpens. The economic development brings it about that society becomes more and more divided into a small group of very large capitalists and a vast number of impoverished proletarians, the middle class tending to disappear.

And where, according to the theory would these proletarian revolutions happen? Obviously, since they were to be the work of the proletariat, they would be initiated in the more advanced countries where the proletariat is numerous and organized into powerful trade unions, and not in backward agricultural countries. Only to the degree that countries became industrialized would they develop the kind of people able to carry through the social revolution. The advanced countries, having achieved their social revolutions, would then help the backward countries to reach the classless society.

Now with the revolution achieved, the state would begin to "wither away." For the state, in this theory, is nothing more than the instrument of force by which one class maintains its ascendancy over another. With the destruction of the exploiters, police and army become unnecessary. No longer is there any private property to be protected against the poor. Nor need people be coerced into doing what must be accomplished in the social interest. All being of one class, there are no longer any conflicts of interest. Without the slightest force or compulsion, society begins to operate more and more efficiently. Brotherly love, human understanding, and natural, voluntary cooperation for the common good take over.

Finally, it should be noted, the revolutionary overthrow of the bourgeoisie was not to be the work of any single political party. Many working class parties were to cooperate with each other to accomplish the common interest of the working class. The "mode of production," and not the program of any particular party, would bring about the growth and organization of the proletariat.

The mere enunciation of this system is enough to give one pause, for its predictions are wrong on every count. It is not true that the workers have become worse off; on the contrary, their material position has been continually improving in all capitalist countries. It is also untrue that the "crises" or business cycles have become more and more severe. The crises have varied in the extent of their seriousness, and now there is good reason to believe that enough has been learned to prevent any depression from becoming catastrophic. Nationalism, instead of disappearing with the rise of the working class, seems more rampant today than ever. The middle class has not shrunk in size; on the contrary it has become more and more powerful in the capitalist countries, and indeed in nations like the United States almost everybody considers himself middle class. The conquest of power by Communists (called proletarian revolutions by believers in the theory of class struggle) has not taken place in countries where the proletariat was strong, but in agrarian countries like Russia and China. Nor was it advanced technology but the peasants' desire for land that produced these revolutions. The proletariat did not come to power in advanced, industrial countries like Germany, Britain, and the United States. As for the satellite countries, neither proletariat nor peasantry brought Communism to them, but the power of the Soviet Union and the threat of its armies. Moreover, there have been no visible signs of the withering away of the state in the Communist countries. On the contrary, the power of the state has grown to an almost unbelievable extent. And instead of there being many political parties in every case where the revolution has occurred, only a single party now exists. In these states neither rival party nor faction is tolerated.

This record of being wrong on every single point becomes even more remarkable when one remembers that the institution built on this dogma is the most powerful tyranny the world has ever known, and controls one third of the world's population. It would seem that there must be some element of truth in the doctrine to explain its astounding success. But look as hard as one can, the only true propositions one can discover in this mass of fabrication are so puerile and obvious they seem scarcely worth repeating. Yes, there is conflict in society and this insight is an advance over the assumption that society is a harmonious whole. But the mere assertion that conflict exists does not help very much in understanding the nature of the different groups and organizations which come into conflict in society, nor the sorts of conflicts in which they participate. Indeed the theory of the class struggle limits the study of conflicts to those which occur between classes.

An examination of the tensions which exist within classes is regarded by the adherents of the class struggle theory as a wicked and bourgeois heresy.

True, also, is the assertion of proponents of the class struggle theory that change (sometimes called progress) takes place in the universe. We could consider this a genuine advance if anyone could be found willing to assert that there is *no* change in the world. However, the proposition scarcely seems an important contribution to the social sciences.

A somewhat more sophisticated idea credited to Marx is that people's beliefs are influenced by their wishes and their interests. This, the concept of ideology, appears also to have been held by Shakespeare. Closely related to this idea is the theory that people's ideas of morality are not static but vary with time and place. Though the position is sound, its usefulness is impaired by the way it is used in the doctrine of the class struggle which goes on to declare that moral ideas are only a part of the "Superstructure" whose nature at any time and place can be explained as determined wholly by the "mode of production."

Yet despite the erroneousness and puerility of the theory, people in free countries still speak of Marx's monumental contributions to the social sciences. An article in *Dissent* by Ben Seligman lists at great length Marx's errors, and yet passionately lauds his greatness and the vastness of his contribution. Equally astonishing is Joan Robinson's view that although Marx didn't come up with the right answers, he asked important questions.

The truth is that the theory of the class struggle is not a scientific theory and cannot be tested as such. Karl Marx, the creator of the theory, was not primarily historian, social scientist, political scientist, or economist. He was above all a revolutionary and his purpose was to show how to effectively organize a revolution. The theory of the class struggle admirably serves this purpose by mobilizing powerful passions and sentiments in the service of revolutionary conspiracy. Human hostilities are concentrated by the theory into hatred of an exploiting class, which is blamed for poverty, depression, wars, and indeed almost every evil to be found in the world.

Anti-Semitism has been called "the socialism of the middle class." With equal justification one might say that the theory of the class struggle is the "anti-Semitism of the proletariat." Like anti-Semitism, it concentrates hate on a group which is regarded as being the source of all evil and whose elimination would permit the natural development of the good society.

The manipulators of the theory of the class struggle are not in the least particular as to what kinds of prejudices or passions they mobilize. They made use of sentimental attachment to imaginary precapitalist societies presumed to be based on hallowed tradition and brotherly love, employing these sentiments to generate contempt for "the cash nexus," the inhuman, nonsentimental decisions based on cold calculations of gain made by miserly money changers. Here the rhetoric is not original but is borrowed from an aristocracy that feared and hated the rising industrialists and businessmen whose greatest crime was their efficiency. Equally useful to the revolutionaries is man's basic desire to protect his property. So hatred of the capitalist is further enforced by the argument that property rightfully belonging to the workers is being stolen deviously by the capitalist. The labor theory of value is the "scientific" expression of this notion. To all the other revolutionary passions is added the worker's demand that his lawful property, stolen from him by the capitalist, be returned. Moreover, the theory of the class struggle assists the organizers of the revolutionary conspiracy to draw supporters away from movements designed to improve the lot of people. Such movements are denounced as "reformism" which, since it does not conform with the theory of the class struggle, must be dishonest and illusory.

When it comes to reformism, the manipulators of the theory of the class struggle are particularly violent in their attacks. Not only do they wish to harness the supporters of the reformist movement to their chariot, but in addition they fear that reform, by reducing the misery of the people, will hinder recruitment for the proletarian revolution. Their *argument* is that reform is unworkable, that it is invented by the enemy to distract from the necessary social revolution, and that the only cure for society is the destruction of the oppressing class and the establishment of the good society.

Exactly what the good society is, however, remains obscure. The theory of the class struggle helps concentrate all attention on the organization of the social revolution. All concern with what will happen when the revolutionaries take power is denounced as utopianism, utopians being people who discuss ideal societies or utopias without considering the means by which these ideals can be established. Those members of the conspiracy who continue to ask embarrassing questions about the future are given more work to do to distract them.

In this way the theory of the class struggle has served as a protection against rival organizations. Attempts to improve conditions in the near future have been denounced as "reformism"; efforts to take a somewhat longer view have been called "utopianism." Cleverly, the manipulators of the theory of the class struggle have mobilized hatred not only against the capitalist class but also against rival parties. Reformists and utopians have been proclaimed the agents, conscious or unconscious, of the enemy capitalist class.

One has only to read Marx and the Marxists to see how an atmosphere of hatred is created. Those with whom they disagree are attacked in the most violent language, language which finally leads to the liquidation and murder of opponents whenever the revolutionaries take power.

This lack of restraint in the attack on and suppression of rivals is further helped by that portion of the theory of the class struggle which asserts that moral ideas are only a superstructure built on the mode of production. This doctrine enables the leaders of the conspiracy to remove, or at least weaken, any moral scruples which their supporters might have. The conspirators now feel that whatever they do to serve the revolution is *ispo facto* right. They identify themselves with History written with a capital H. They are on the side of History and so are bound to conquer. Moreover, History is associated with God and morality, and the adherents of the doctrine of the class struggle can always be sure that they are always on the side of justice. The revolutionary is provided with the moral authority to carry out the greatest crimes, certain that in the long run History will vindicate all cruelties. Morality is thus identified with the historical process, and such assistance to History is given the honorific title "Progressiveness." Evil or sin is identified with fighting against, retarding, or interfering with History, and is known as "Reaction."

But not only are the excesses of the revolutionaries justified historically; they are also "scientifically" valid. Science has shown, it is maintained, that the program being used is the only way in which the ideal society can be established and all the evils of the present world eliminated. To be upset about the inevitable is sentimental. One might as well rail against the workings of the solar system.

It is interesting to note that this complete abnegation of all social responsibility does not in the least prevent the utmost extremes of moral indignation from being mobilized against anyone whom the runners of the revolutionary movement want to condemn. It is as if the opponent, having by his opposition shown himself to be working against History, has outlawed himself from the universe. Furthermore, his actions are inconceivably wicked because they interfere with the task of History.

This duality, which would of course constitute a fatal flaw in the theory judged as science, only increases its effectiveness as an instrument for the achievement and consolidation of the power of the leaders of the revolutionary conspiracy. Nor does this necessarily mean that the leaders are hypocritical. The leaders find it perfectly possible to believe their opponents wicked men who must be destroyed and that they themselves are nothing but the morally neutral instruments of History. This is far from the strangest belief that faith has enabled men to believe.

In this way History is identified with the revolutionary conspiracy, and both History and the conspiracy with the good. With such a view in control, critical thought ceases and authority becomes more and more centralized.

The essential device for facilitating such complete centralization of authority is to be found in that "dialectical materialism" which is the philosophical aspect of the theory of the class struggle. By a series of sophistries, anything can be transformed into its opposite; so the dialecticians maintain that the logical inconsistencies in their arguments are actually contradictions in the capitalist society itself. Logical thinking having now been destroyed, and all propositions having become equally cogent and noncogent, an authority to lay down and enforce the true interpretation of the dialectic becomes mandatory.

In this procedure the central authority is assisted by such notions as "objectively counterrevolutionary." Anybody who disagrees with the interpretation given by the authority is thereby hampering the activity of the organization or the party; he is interfering with the progress of History, and preventing, or at least retarding, the establishing of the good society. Consequently, since his actions are maintaining a situation which causes war and poverty and hatred of man for man and nation for nation, he must be treated with the utmost ferocity. He is "objectively counterrevolutionary," and it now becomes the moral duty of every adherent of the faith to help in his liquidation.

It is the application of this technique that involves the declaration from time to time of what is the correct policy or line that the conspirators must follow. Inevitably the line is decided by authority from above and any questioning of its correctness (it may be the opposite of yesterday's line) must be considered not as a difference of opinion but as the work of the devil.

Distilled also from the theory of the class struggle is the idea of class thought, a potent weapon for the consolidation of the central authority. If no other argument can be found against someone with whom the central authority disagrees, his view is declared to be not that of the proletariat or working class but a deviation produced by some bourgeois element in the offending critic's history which has interfered with his ability to think pure working-class thoughts. The ultimate authority is naturally the central committee, or the big boss who controls the committee, that is, the highest authority of the conspiratorial movement.

A perfect parallel to this theory of class thought can be found in the Nazi idea that it is not the individual but the race, and of course the *right* race, which somehow feels or thinks the higher truth. The Fuehrer is the judge of what the higher truth is. Any class theory of thought belongs to the same category, to the same realm of scientific acceptability as the theory that it is only the chosen race or the pure blood that can feel the truth and think purely. "Class think" is not different from "blood think."

A corollary of the theory of the class struggle is that only the working class can think straight since its thought alone is not infected by ideologies. But since only the "pure" members of the class express the essence of the class, the working class becomes synonymous with the central authority which rules upon which members of the conspiracy have had their thought contaminated. Thus the masters of the revolutionary conspiracy gain an immunity from logic.

So, as it turns out, the theory of the class struggle, though a very poor theory, is an extremely efficient and successful device for organizing and mobilizing the Communist conspiracy. It can be used to attract disaffected individuals of all varieties and turn them into instruments of the organizers of the revolution. It can help to control the consciences of the adherents of the revolutionary conspiracy, making them feel that all crimes committed in the name of the cause are acts of the highest virtue. Finally, it can assist in centralizing authority by subjecting the minds, as well as the consciences, of the adherents of the conspiracy to the control of the party boss.

It is this combination of a powerful faith with an even more powerful organization that explains the great difficulty that Communists have in breaking with their religion. A man committed to the Communist conspiracy has chosen a certain way of life. To break with the organization means that he will lose his friends and very often his livelihood as well. Lost also will be his identification with history, the future, mankind, morality. But beyond even these external pressures are the internal ones, the difficulties of escaping from a rigid system of thought.

Escape from the religion can occur in either of two ways. There may be a sudden shock or conversion, but this generally happens only if the believer can fall into another autocratic system. Complete emancipation is extremely difficult and involves a gradual shedding of layer after layer of the Communist system. At first the individual, becoming aware of the evils and unreasonableness of the system, does not blame the system itself. Instead he denounces the local bosses for not properly executing the doctrines of the faith. At last he takes the next step, which is to lay the blame on the topmost boss whose death he expects will lead to the purification of the party.

It now becomes obvious to him that something must have been very wrong to have made a Stalin possible. He decides that the error was Lenin's, but not Trotsky's, or vice versa. Eventually, however, he is forced to the conclusion that the path taken was wrong from the beginning, starting from Marx himself. He sees that the evils of totalitarianism are the natural fruit of the theory of the class struggle and the system of dialectical thinking. This final lesson is learned only when the individual in question realizes that every attempt to eliminate the centralized control which fosters Stalinism poisons the organization it is intended to cure. Attempts at democratic Communism were made in Yugoslavia and then given up when it became evident that democracy threatened the various groups (it is heretical to call them a class) who benefited from centralization. The bureaucrats and party bosses would not countenance the elimination of their privileges and the authorities had to restore the despotism. A man like Djilas could not be tolerated in Yugoslavia. In recent years we have also seen the retreat in China from the democracy promised in the "Doctrine of the Hundred Flowers," the restoration of Stalinism under Khrushchev, the continual pressure to make Poland more tyrannical.

All attempts to establish some form of democracy or "socialist"

legality appear to be fraudulent. Mr. Khrushchev's decentralization, for example, seems to mean nothing more than that he has
been more successful in planting his supporters in the larger central committee than in the smaller executive committee. His vas-
sals are spread more widely over the country than are the henchmen of his rivals, and so by giving his clique more power he con-
solidates his dictatorship.

The belief that the death of Stalin and the collapse of his cult
would lead to the establishment of democracy and human decency in government now is seen to be akin to the pathetic faith
of the downtrodden Russian peasants of the last century that, as
soon as the Czar learned what was going on in the country, everything would be put right; or the not very different daydream that
all that was required to create the good society in Russia was the
removal of the Czar. In short, the idea that the tyranny established by the manipulators of the theory of the class struggle would
turn into a free society once some evil man was removed is nothing but a variation on the ancient myth that lies at the center of
the theory of the class struggle: heaven is the reward for the overthrow of the bourgeoisie. Only when an adherent of the theory of
the class struggle understands that a tyranny built on the theory
cannot survive any significant democratization does he realize that
the theory is no more scientific than the proposition that if all the
Jews in the world were murdered everything would be fine.

As I have said, the suppression of the Hungarian revolution of
1956 destroyed the theory of the class struggle. Now it is possible to alter the opening phrase of the *Communist Manifesto*
which reads: "A spectre is haunting Europe—the spectre of communism. . . ." to "A spectre is haunting the Communist world—
the spectre of democracy."

In the above, I have identified the theory of the class struggle
with the Communist movement, since it is this movement that
has utilized the theory to seize and maintain power. I have not
considered social democratic parties which also consider themselves to be followers of Karl Marx, and hence adherents of the

class-struggle theory. The social democrats, however, are too much imbued with humanitarian and democratic ideals to take the doctrine seriously. They remember that they are human themselves and are not prepared to murder all who disagree with them in the name of History. Their humanistic appreciation of western civilization, their recognition that it is possible to err sometimes, their acceptance of the principles of democracy, all these disqualify them from being conspirators. It is for this reason that the Communists insist that the social democrats have been contaminated by bourgeois ideology.

It is even probable that Karl Marx himself was so "contaminated" by Western civilization that he would not have been tolerated as a citizen of a Communist state. After all, he did insist that the social revolution would not be the work of a single party. Such "factionalism" is obviously "objectively counter revolutionary." In a sense, therefore, the social democrats can be considered the followers of Karl Marx, or Karl Marx can be said to have been a kind of social democrat. But then he was as wrong about the way in which the theory of the class struggle would develop as he was about everything else.

What does the death of the theory of the class struggle mean for those who are interested in the human ideal which led so many to turn to the theory in the first place—the ideal of establishing a unified society based on justice and freedom for all. Now we can see that there is a series of elementary lessons that men must learn all over again.

1. One must not look for progress through the mobilization of hate and fear. Although hatred and fear may be used effectively by a group seizing power, any regime established in such a manner will continue to use cruelty and oppression to maintain its hold. Nor will it matter whether the regime has seized power for narrow selfish interests or for the good of all.

2. The good society cannot be brought about by purely negative actions, such as the elimination of an "exploiting class." There is no Santa Claus ready to establish the good society once

the naughty devil has been killed. Genuine progress comes not from destroying an enemy but from engaging in the much more complicated task of *building* the good society.

3. Before one can build, one must have a notion of what one is seeking to construct. The theory of the class struggle ridiculed and condemned this idea as "utopian" and "reformist." It also condemned as "reactionary" any consideration of the conservation of beneficial arrangements already achieved.

4. In addition to knowing where one wants to go, he must also know where he is starting from. It is not very useful to name a destination when there is no way to reach it. This means that we must take into account the existing constellation of forces that have a bearing on the possibility of bringing about social improvements. It does not help much to repeat the proposition that conflict exists, and it is worse than futile to try to fit into a two-class-conflict model the complex set of conflicts and interests of pressure groups and subgroups, or ignorance, prejudices, superstitions, inefficiency and inertia, and other elements that can make all the difference as to how and whether a suggested improvement or innovation would be carried into effect. If utopians can be described as people who discuss the nature of places where it would be nice to be, without considering whether or how one can get there from where we are, Marxists must be described as people who concentrate on destroying what we have without considering what we will get in its place. With the death of the class struggle it becomes obvious that sensible behavior calls for a marriage of both of these considerations.

5. In getting from here to there, from the total present situation with all its complications and difficulties to the good society with the maximization of freedom and plenty, one should not invent additional gratuitous difficulties to the task by stipulating certain "principles," laying down what economic instrumentalities may or may not be used. The dogma that only public enterprise may be used in the good society and not private enterprise is no more justifiable than the dogma that only private enterprise may be used and not public enterprise. Instead of prejudging the different

forms of enterprise by one or the other of these dogmas, every kind of enterprise can be tested, in the time and place where it is to be applied, to see whether it serves better than other forms of organization in bringing about the desired ends.

6. The best test of the different kinds of economic organization is the test by competition. Competition permits that instrument to survive that can pay higher wages for the same price and quality of output, or which can provide cheaper and better products while paying the same wages. With the acceptance of this test it becomes meaningless to speak of capitalism and socialism as alternatives, since in practice all societies have had to make their prejudices subservient to this ultimate pragmatic test by effectiveness for the ends desired.

All so-called capitalistic economies are shot through with socialistic forms of enterprise, and all so-called socialistic countries are permeated with capitalistic institutions and forms of organization. The conscious recognition of this development and the consistent application of the pragmatic test so as to minimize decision by prejudice needs a new name, for it would be neither capitalist nor socialist. My own pet name for this is "democratic functionalism," the touchstone of competition being applied to discover which form functions most effectively for the democratic purpose of getting people whatever it is they want most.

Those under the spell of the theory of the class struggle were accustomed to speak of socialism as a stage leading from capitalism to the ideal society of communism where it will be possible, since it will be a state of economic plenty, to have everyone contributing according to his ability and receiving according to his needs. But it is just as reasonable, though rather less usual, to say that *capitalism* could be a stage leading from socialism to the land of plenty. The restoration of some elements of private enterprise in Russia in the New Economic Policy of 1921 permitted a great increase in productivity from the extreme poverty to which Russia had been reduced by Communism and civil war, and thus was an important step toward the state of plenty—if that goal should ever be attained.

In the last few years, marginal cost accounting and concepts which correspond to the rate of interest have been discussed more freely in Russia, Yugoslavia, and Poland, and there is talk of their being used more widely in the future in the management of the economies of these countries. If this is done it would contribute importantly to efficiency and increased output and would constitute another case of capitalism, or capitalistic instruments, leading toward that state of economic plenty which is sometimes confusingly called Communism but which is more appropriately called anarchism (because there would be no property of any kind, private or public, and no state or its police would be needed to prevent anyone from taking anything he wanted).

7. "Things" are not more "basic" than "ideas." There is no more justification for declaring that the mode of production or the technical conditions of production are "primary" or "basic" or the determining factors "in the last resort," and that human institutions, customs, beliefs, ideas, and mores are only "superstructure," than there is justification for declaring the exact opposite and saying that ideas are what come first and the material means of production and the techniques can be derived from these. If one looks at the development of society as a whole he can only say that there is continuous and almost indefinitely complicated interaction of all elements with each other. If one is looking at a particular problem it is sometimes convenient to pick out some elements as "causes" of other elements because something may possibly be done about the "causes" which have the desired effects on the "results." In such partial examination it will sometimes be the material conditions of production that are the causes of attitudes or customs, and sometimes it will be the other way round. There is no basis either for a so-called "materialism" that gives a universal priority to things or for so-called "idealism" that gives a universal priority to ideas. The theory of the class struggle stresses the priority of things over ideas. The apparent basis for this seems to be a confusion with quite another meaning of the word "priority"—the meaning of "earlier in time"—and the consideration that the existence of the planet to say nothing of the sun and

the stars) appears to have preceded the development on it of living creatures who alone have ideas. But this normal view of the origin of life and thought on our planet in no way affects the recognition that in some cases "things" like the mode of production, either in a technical sense or in the sense of how the product is shared among the different people involved is determined by ideas or attitudes, rather than the other way round.

An interesting example is to be found in the problem of reducing the inequalities of income or of wealth of different people that are at the base of many dissatisfactions with the existing social order. A great deal has been done in many countries (especially in those usually called capitalistic countries) to reduce inequalities. This has been done by progressive taxation, by the regulation of prices charged by monopolies, by the provision of minimum incomes and wages, and in other ways. What has become clear in the course of this development is that the limiting factor to the degree of economic equality that can be achieved is to be found in the so-called "superstructure"—in the realm of people's ideas, attitudes, and mores. A certain degree of inequality is necessary for the economic system if it is to function effectively. This necessary inequality, which may be called "functional inequality," depends on the degree to which people have been educated to work effectively without obtaining great differences in pay for work that is harder or more unpleasant or more demanding in responsibility.

In more primitive countries—one might say in less socialistic countries, where people have been less educated to the acceptance of equality—greater inequalities of reward are necessary. Thus Russia, for example, is much less socialistic than Britain in that much greater inequalities of pay for different kinds of work seem to be necessary there than in Britain. (If these greater inequalities are not functional inequalities, i.e., if they are not necessary for the functioning of the economic system, then Russia is less socialistic than Britain in another and perhaps more important sense.) In any case, here is an example where, for a particular problem, the relations of production, which the theory of the class struggle declares to be always more "basic" or "fundamental" or determining things "in the last resort," are clearly dependent on elements in the "superstructure." This is only a special case. There is no general short cut or magic key to tell us what is "basic" in general. In the complex relationships of human society and its development everything depends on everything else.

8. Genuine progress can only be gradual. This is because there is no Santa Claus waiting to build as soon as we destroy, because before we can get anywhere we must figure out where it is we want to go, because we have to find out not only what kinds of society would work if established, but also what ways there are of building such societies with the materials, including the human material, with which we have to work, because the complex of conflicts of interests, of pressure groups and subgroups, of inefficiency, ignorance, prejudices and inertia, cannot be fitted into a simple dichotomy of two-dimensional class conflicts, because the "superstructure" of ideas, attitudes, mores is no less "basic" than anything else and cannot be neglected, because in many cases improvements are delayed by the necessity of having *people* adjusted to the new ways before these would work in the way they are planned to work. In short, because all the magic tricks of the spell of the theory of the class struggle are dangerous illusions that lead not to the promised land but to totalitarian tyranny called people's democracy and to the threat of planetary annihilation called the declaration of love of peace.

9. The final lesson is similar in some ways to the lesson taught by Voltaire in *Candide*. Voltaire was there showing Candide's escape from the doctrine that all is for the best in the best of all possible worlds—a doctrine that justified and called for the acceptance of all existing horrors. With the death of the class struggle its victims can escape from the doctrine that all would be for the best in the best of all possible worlds when the classless society burst upon the scene—a doctrine that justified the *imposition* of any horrors in the name of the magically assured infinite good that would come thereafter. Voltaire's solution was the return to private decency, to cultivate one's own garden together with one's friends.

The escape from the theory of the class struggle shows us that we need not limit ourselves to the cultivation of our private gardens. We *can* work for the betterment of the greater society. But we can succeed in this only if we stop relying on magic and only to the extent that we know what we want to build, only in the degree that we understand what we have to build with, and no more rapidly than, with our natural shortsightedness, we can see what we are achieving.

THE RISE OF THE PROFESSIONAL REVOLUTIONARIES

Benedict Kautsky

■ The structure and character of the Communist movement and of national Communist parties reflect the decisive influence of Lenin. The relation between what Lenin did and what Marx said is in many ways identical with the relationship between the Soviet Union and the Marxist utopia. One need not subscribe to the Marxist analysis of history to observe that the "Leninist Deviation" introduced into the Communist movement elements that diametrically contradict Marx's own views on the one hand, and the popular image of Communism on the other. The relation of Lenin to Marxism is important, first, because Marx and Marxism enjoy great prestige in large areas of the world, and, second, because understanding Communism requires separating myth from fact, claim from reality, and lie from truth. Some of the myths, claims, and lies concern the relation of Communism to Marxism. In the following chapter, Benedict Kautsky, a second generation Marxist dialectician, explores the character and consequences of the Leninist contribution. ■

LENIN'S LEGACY

Few such important and complex historical phenomena have been as carefully planned as was Communism by Lenin. This fact, generally admitted by adherents and enemies alike, is all the more startling in view of what Communism has become. For Lenin believed he had created, or at least laid the foundations of, a socialist-democratic society. The aspiration and the reality contrast sharply. Today the Communist state is a dictatorship in which a few persons wield absolute power, and in which even the majority of the ruling elite live in continual dread.

Dictatorships and despotism have not been infrequent in history; for thousands of years autocracy has been the normal system of government in the Orient. The Communist dictatorship, however, differs from most despotisms in that it is not content with the obedience of its subjects, but demands articulate professions of loyalty. In this it is similar to the Holy Inquisition and unlike the Roman Empire.

Four preceptors were chiefly responsible for Lenin's political education: Karl Marx, Friedrich Engels, Karl Kautsky, and Georgi Plechanov. Two of them, Marx and Engels, were dead before Lenin appeared on the political scene. Marx died at a time when the workers' movement was subjected to severe persecutions, and, moreover, divided by the emergence of anarchism. Engels lived to see the revival of the labor movement, but subsequent developments did not justify the optimism which this aroused in him. He and his friend August Bebel expected that the Social Democrats would achieve a majority in the German Reichstag before the end of the nineteenth century, but the rise of the working class turned out to be exceedingly painful and slow. Lenin's knowledge of Marxist theory was acquired principally from Kautsky and Plechanov, from the former on political and economic questions, from Plechanov on questions of philosophy. Lenin ended in sharp conflict with both. He split with Plechanov during the first Russian revolution (1905), and with Kautsky after the outbreak of the First World War, both becoming his bitter enemies. Plechanov died in the chaos created by the Bolshevik coup of November 1917. Karl Kautsky survived Lenin by a decade and a half, living long enough to witness the great purges of the thirties, and the essential fulfillment of his predictions concerning the development of Communism away from its democratic-Marxist beginnings.

Nevertheless, he was spared witnessing Leninism's ultimate consequence: the Nazi-Soviet Pact.

Until his break with Kautsky and Plechanov, Lenin considered himself a Marxist social democrat. Only after the Bolshevik seizure of power did it occur to him that it might be more useful, both for him and for his party, to pose as Marx and Engels' *direct* descendant. Indeed, during his later years he seems to have viewed everything Marx and Engels wrote after the *Communist Manifesto* as a mere elaboration of its basic ideas or else as so many damnable deviations—though he never said this quite that bluntly. He therefore preferred to change the name of his party to conform with that of the Communist League, so as to distinguish it more clearly from the Social Democratic party.

In fact, Lenin had other teachers besides these Marxists, although he never referred to them with much emphasis or detail. These were Russian socialists and anarchists: Chernyshevski and Tkatchew, Bakunin and Nechayev were as much his intellectual ancestors as Marx and Marx's disciples. It can be argued convincingly that on questions of practical policy Lenin was often more influenced by his Russian than by his Marxist teachers. His ambivalence toward Russian and Western European culture and society are equally obvious.

CZARISM'S DUAL FACE

This ambivalence was characteristic of Russia and Russians of Lenin's period, and was not merely an intellectual quality, but an aspect of personality which reflected the dual nature of the Czarist society—a fact not clearly recognized by the Marxists, and to which there is hardly a reference in Lenin's writings. Indeed it is doubtful whether Lenin was actually aware of this dichotomy or that Czarism represented a phenomenon without parallel in history.

Toward the end of the first millennium, powers influencing

Russia from the north and from the south drove her into the orbit of European civilization. Under the influence of the Normans on the one hand, and of Constantinople on the other, the basic elements of the Western Middle Ages, i.e., feudalism and Christianity, were brought to Russia. But Russia's absorption in European culture was interrupted by the invasion of the Mongols who brought with them Oriental despotism, with its extreme centralism and its characteristic concentration of power at the court of an autocratic ruler. After the expulsion of the Mongols, Russia was left with a centralized despotism modeled after the Oriental example, plus a characteristic element of European feudalism: serfdom.

In neighboring Poland, Hungary, and Prussia, serfdom became the basis of a system of government in which the lower nobility exercised control, degrading the monarchy to the role of a mere tool; the Russian Czars, however quickly destroyed the power of the nobility. In adopting Western technology and in introducing Western communications techniques, Peter the Great added another alien element to the strange and unique amalgam of Eastern and Western culture that characterized the Russia of this period. But whereas in Western Europe industrial technology immediately enriched the rising bourgeoisie, it did not in Russia, since Peter relied chiefly on his bureaucracy and on the native nobility for the technical development of the country and only in the last instance on members of the Western European middle class, whom he attracted to Russia by granting them privileges hitherto reserved for the native nobility. Unlike any other European nation, industrialization in Russia began with bonded labor drawn from the peasantry.

Technological development and closer contact with the highly developed economies of Western Europe had unforeseen consequences. It became evident that forced labor and modern technology are not in the long run compatible. The rapid growth of industry during the nineteenth century made it clear that skilled workers and foremen could not be recruited exclusively from abroad. Continuing industrialization required large numbers of persons with an academic background. This need produced an educational revolution which, in its turn, affected the despotic nature of the Czarist system.

Here were the germs of a conflict which has decisively influenced Russia's political life to this day. The followers and advocates of autocracy warned the rulers not to continue on the path of modernization, realizing that this process was likely to release forces that would tend to undermine the Czarist system. Yet to renounce modern technology was tantamount to renouncing power and expansion. Already in the nineteenth century technical progress had revolutionized war and military strategy, and a nation could count itself among the great powers only if it were ready to make use of contemporary technology. The Czarist government realized this bitter truth during the Crimean War when it failed to rout enemy troops besieging Sebastopol. In abolishing serfdom in 1861, Alexander II was merely drawing an inevitable conclusion. Nevertheless, the manner in which the liberation of the peasants was effected showed he had no intention of basically altering Czarist despotism. The reform was merely a means toward the end of modernizing the economy to enhance Czarist power. The core of the Czarist autocracy remained unchanged. In fact, the liberation of the serfs strengthened the economic position of the nobility, since the indemnities the peasants had to pay for their liberation were so high that they restored the solvency of the noblemen who had incurred debts under the system of bondage.

A special feature of this reform was the preservation of the *mir*, i.e., the organization of villages along primitive Communist lines which the Czarist government used as an administrative device useful for taxation and recruitment. The purpose of preserving the mir was to enable the government to hold the entire community responsible for the payment of indemnities. The consequences for the Russian economy, as well as for the development of Russian socialism, were momentous.

Economically, the preservation of the mir seriously handicapped the development of agriculture and industry. The Russian peasant was now free to move to the cities if he chose and to look for work in the rising industry. But he still shared responsibility for the payments levied against the community from which he came and had no prospect of freeing himself from this obligation. This system entailed complex bureaucratic regulations, in addition to being a heavy burden for peasants who migrated to the cities. On the other hand, the native community was a drag on the ambitious and successful peasants. The weaker elements of the mir, draining the energies of the community as a whole, forced those farmers who had managed to adjust themselves to the new financial economy to carry all of the social obligations. Nevertheless, the continued existence of common landownership did not prevent the formation of class distinctions in the villages. As everywhere else, the rise of a financial economy proved to be the deadly enemy of primitive agrarian Communism. All the existing difficulties notwithstanding, thriftier peasants managed to accumulate money which they used to exploit the economically weaker elements in the rural communities. Most effective in this process were loans granted to those among the peasantry who were unable to meet their tax obligations. Thus the "kulak," the village usurer, was born, a figure well-known throughout the Orient.

In Russia this development caused considerable concern, particularly among the early Socialists. Originally the Socialists had believed it possible to base a unique type of socialist economy on the Mir. Marx was consulted about this by his Russian friends; his views were somewhat ambiguous, although he obviously was not enthusiastic about preserving the mir, Engels, on the other hand, took a more definite stand: he simply denied the possibility of maintaining the mir within the framework of modern society. Time increasingly proved the accuracy of Engels' view, although traces of the original "narodniki" concept remained. On occasion, even the Communists have reverted to this tradition in setting up the kolkhozes, as well as in their use of the Czarist principle of collective community responsibility for raising taxes.

From the point of view of agrarian development the liberation in 1861 of the peasants turned out to be a failure. Although the situation of the peasantry had not been good, there had at least been a fairly equal distribution of burdens. Now, however, more and more peasants sank to the level of a rural proletariat. Famines became frequent while at the same time Russia was increasing her grain exports enough to become the temporary leader on the international grain market. It is quite literally true that these exports were based on the hunger of the peasants who were forced to sell grain in order to meet tax obligations.

On the other hand, when one views the technological development in the cities and the consequent growth of Czarist power, the liberation of the serfs no longer seems a failure. Industry, flourishing at an almost American pace, was creating the basis for an urban middle class. Simultaneously with this industrial development a renewed expansion began into the Near and Far East, highly indicative of the dual role of the Czarist regime. Czarism always supported a progressive type of government and economic life in Asia, despite its role as a pillar of reaction in Europe and Russia. Its "Western" nature sufficed to make it appear progressive, particularly when compared with Oriental despotisms and the tribal organization of the Siberian peoples.

Marx and Engels were entirely unaware of this dual role of Czarism and saw Czarism merely as the deadly enemy of the European revolution, the very incarnation of reaction. This is particularly evident in their evaluation of the Pan-Slavic movement which they regarded purely as a Czarist tool, overlooking the democratic and revolutionary element that inspired the Slavic peasant movements of Europe in their fight against the authority of the Polish, Hungarian, or Prussian noblemen.[1] Above all, they misjudged the danger which this instrument of Russian foreign policy was to the Czarist system itself, not realizing that whenever Russia attempted to make use of Pan-Slavism to further her European expansion, the Russian autocracy exposed itself to attack. Such exposure occurred in the Russo-Turkish war of 1878, and later during the First World War. Another example is Stalin's short-lived attempt at Pan-Slavism in which he grotesquely included

[1] Stalin's interest in Pan-Slavism is revealed in Milovan Djilas' most recent book, *Secret Conservations with Stalin*.

not only the Poles but also the Hungarians and Rumanians. Tito's defection finished this effort.

MARXISM IN RUSSIA

Following the failure in the eighties of anarchist methods, Marxism became the dominant form of Russian socialism. Only the Social Revolutionaries remained non-Marxist: its doctrine followed the teachings of the narodniki and in time attained the largest following among all Russian parties, as became apparent in 1917. Yet even this group was somewhat under Marxist influence which reached far into the ranks of the middle class. This striking phenomenon may be traced, among other things, to the decisive role which the Marxist doctrine assigns to the industrial development of modern nations. It is a basic concept of Marxism that socialism will come about as a result of the expansion of capitalism; that due to its own inherent laws capitalism is forced to generate its own "gravediggers," the proletariat, which, growing stronger and stronger, will finally overpower the capitalist system. An indispensable prerequisite for the complete unfolding of capitalism is the overcoming by it of all obstacles put into its path by earlier social orders. Only when these precapitalist vestiges of absolutism and feudalism have been eliminated by a series of middle-class revolutions can capitalism reach its fullest development. Maximization of profit is the motivating force of the capitalist system. To achieve this, some freedom of movement is allowed to the working class.

It is this freedom of movement which ultimately endows the proletariat with the strength to overthrow capitalism and replace it with socialism. Therefore it is in the interest of the working class to support the middle classes, wherever they are fighting for recognition, and to further bourgeois revolution. This theory was fully accepted by the Russian Social Democrats. Lenin, too, unquestioningly agreed with it, abandoning it gradually only after his seizure of power in 1917 when the rule of his party became more important to him than Marxist theory.

In the basic questions of the application of Marxism to the political struggle Lenin did not differ with the Social Democrats. There were, however, considerable and, as it turned out, basic differences between Lenin and the other Social Democrats on questions of day-to-day strategy. While the latter, faithful to the Marxist theory, were prepared temporarily to come to terms with the middle class in order to attack Czarism on certain specific issues, Lenin maintained at a very early stage that the Russian bourgeoisie were essentially different from the Western European middle classes and did not possess the qualifications for a revolutionary role. It may be argued that history has justified Lenin. Right or wrong, Lenin's views contradicted basic Marxist theory, but Lenin never dared face the questions raised by this contradiction.

WAS MARX'S CONCEPT OF REVOLUTION APPLICABLE TO RUSSIA?

Until 1917, Lenin never wavered in his belief that Russia was not ready for a proletarian revolution.[2]

But if, as he thought, the bourgeoisie did not represent a potential ally of the working class, another class had to take this place. Lenin found it in the peasantry. Therewith Lenin reverted to the ideas of the narodniki.

There can be no question that Lenin assessed the revolutionary energies of the peasantry more correctly than his comrades in the other Social Democratic groups: in this respect he was indeed in close agreement with the Social Revolutionaries, although he always denied this affinity. Logically, however, a joint revolution of workers and peasants has to take a different course from a bourgeois revolution, even if led by the workers. On this point,

[2] On the eve of his arrival in St. Petersburg he wrote: "Our revolution is a middle-class revolution" (*Pravda*, April 3/4, 1917: *Selected Works* in 2 vol. Foreign Language Literature Publications, Moscow 1947, vol. I, p. 894). The following quotations are taken from the same edition.

Lenin differed not only with his party comrades but deviated decisively also from Marx; here he was—to use an expression that has once more become fashionable in our time—a "revisionist," in fact the first after Eduard Bernstein.

The fact that Lenin himself was unaware of this is immaterial for a historical investigation. Nor need we be concerned here as to whether Lenin was honest, as there can be no doubt that he was convinced that he was an orthodox Marxist acting in the best interests of the working class.

More than once in his life, Lenin proved he was uniquely capable of linking heterogeneous views in a seemingly logical context. The fact was that his thesis of the alliance of workers and peasants in a future revolution raised the question whether in the Russian situation a bourgeois revolution would precede the proletarian. As history since 1905 has taught us, Marx's predictions have been controverted everywhere by the pattern of revolutionary development, beginning as it did in Russia, then spreading to Asia, Africa, and South America. None of these countries has seen a middle-class revolution of the Western European type, for the simple reason that none has had more than the scantiest beginnings of an industrial middle class. What is called a "bourgeoisie" is recruited from the commercial and financial strata, i.e., from a financial economy already in existence in pre-capitalist societies (although not affecting the basic barter nature of these societies). Consequently, in the underdeveloped areas under discussion, a proletariat in the modern sense is almost nonexistent, although it is usually somewhat stronger than the industrial bourgeoisie, since government-controlled sectors of the economy—especially in the fields of communications, industry, and mining—have often fathered an indigenous working class, without creating a middle class of comparable strength. Whenever a highly developed financial economy and modern technology have penetrated pre-capitalist societies, bringing with them improved health standards which markedly increase the population (this has happened often since the eighteenth century, as a result of European colonialism), problems arise which can be solved only by industrialism. Thus, there is a superficial appearance of technological development resembling the rise of Western European capitalism. Since this development tends to skip steps which occurred gradually in the evolution of Western Europe, the illusion is created that a process analogous to the development of nineteenth-century Europe and North America is occurring.

The influence of Lenin's theoretical hypothesis makes it all the easier to overlook the fact that this is an utterly different historical process from the rise of capitalism, and that it has only one feature in common with it—i.e., the adoption of modern technology. The Western European middle class is older than the capitalist system, and was ready to administer the system as soon as it was created. In the noncapitalist areas today, however, the exact opposite occurs: first comes industry and only later the bourgeoisie and working class are born. The entire undertaking is carried out by a group which we shall designate here by the Russian term "intelligentsia."

This category embraces far more than what we normally call the "intellectuals"; it embraces the entire government bureaucracy, including those engaged in the government-controlled sectors, of the economy and the military. The chief difference between the present development of the "underdeveloped areas" and the earlier development of Western capitalism lies in the motives of the directing class. While the main motive for the development of Western European capitalism was economic, the ruling elite of the newly rising nations seeks, like nineteenth-century Czarism, to create an industrial economy for political reasons.

No one has furthered this development more than Lenin, although his understanding of what was involved was more instinctive than intellectual. Until his death he remained convinced that he had been faithful to the political theories of Marx and Engels. The thought never occurred to him that either in Russia or in the underdeveloped countries outside of Russia, the development of industry might proceed in a way unforeseen by Marx or Engels.

When modern technology was grafted upon Oriental despotism, and in areas which had not even progressed toward any stable form of government organization, but where society was still based on the patterns of kinship and tribes, the result differed basically from the development of capitalism out of medieval feudalism. Marx did know from his studies that the Oriental system of government differed fundamentally from European feudalism, but had no clear idea of what forms their integration with the industrialized Western world would take. Lenin simply brushed aside the question of differentiation between the various precapitalist social and economic systems. To him and his Communist adherents everything that existed before the capitalist system was "feudalism." This is the reason that we are now witnessing the grotesque drama of the Chinese Leninists' falsifying the "empire of Heaven," a bureaucratic despotism *par excellence*, to make it appear a feudal society, complete with large estates, and the institution of serfdom, so that they may apply Marx's concepts of the English and French middle-class revolutions to present-day Chinese conditions. The Communist analysts are in this way preventing themselves from gaining a genuine comprehension of the conditions they have set out to change. This is exactly what happened again and again to Lenin and explains why the results of his "October revolution" were quite different from what he expected, even in his own time. But this did not induce him to find out whether and where he might have erred; he was far too sure of himself to face the possibility of any such error. Mistakes therefore were attributed not to conditions but to human beings against whom he turned his wrath.

WAS LENIN A MARXIST?

In view of all these considerations it appears justified to raise the question whether Lenin can correctly be called a Marxist at all, despite his believing himself the legitimate heir of Marx. Lenin, of course, had a comprehensive knowledge of the writings of Marx and Engels and had completely absorbed their thinking and terminology. There cannot be the slightest doubt about his ability to use Marxist methods of analysis wherever he was not directly involved as an active politician. Thus, his writings on Russian agricultural problems reveal not only his thorough knowledge of the subject but, at the same time, his ability to interpret events in the spirit of Marxist analysis. However, those writings, in which we may consider Lenin as essentially disinterested, are rare and cannot really be considered as decisive contributions to the historic era which bears Lenin's name.

As has just been demonstrated, Lenin was reluctant to adjust his opinions to existing conditions but tried to do the exact opposite. In so doing, he violated the foremost principle of Marxism which aims at exploring reality and the adjustment of political action in accordance with the latter. It is true that Lenin often changed his strategy but without revising his theoretical formulations to make them consistent with his actions.

Lenin's approach differed from that of Marx and Engels not only in his concept of revolutionary objectives but also in questions of basic social analysis. His own writings demonstrate that he deviated from Marxist theory on fundamental issues. Even if one admits that he was driven by a genuine revolutionary impatience and therefore preferred to rely on Marx and Engels' earlier writings, which reflected the period of their illegal activities, Lenin's views will be found not even to be in accord with those of the *early* Marx and Engels. His pamphlet, *What Is to Be Done*, written in 1902, contained all those ideas that were to bring about the split in the Russian Social Democratic movement into Bolsheviki and Mensheviki and included statements which Marx would never have written and whose author he would never have recognized as a genuine follower. They are precisely of the kind which once caused Marx to exclaim, "*Quant à moi, je ne suis pas marxiste!*"

One of Lenin's most decisive passages reads:

We said that *there could not exist* a Social Democratic consciousness among the workers. . . . This consciousness could only have been provided from without. As the history of all countries shows, the working class, on its own account, is only able to produce a trade-union type of consciousness, i.e. it may by itself realize the necessity for combining in unions, to fight against the employers, to force the government to pass labor legislation, etc. It is not true that trade unionism—as is so often assumed—necessarily precludes political activity. Trade unions have always furthered a certain (even though not a Social Democratic type of) political propaganda, engaging in a certain amount of political struggle. The theory of Socialism, however, grew out of the philosophical, historical and economic theories which were evolved by the educated representatives of the propertied classes, the intellectuals. Marx and Engels, the founders of modern scientific Socialism themselves, belonged to the bourgeois intelligentsia, as far as their social background is concerned. Similarly in Russia the theory of Social Democracy developed quite independently from the spontaneous growth of the labor movement, as a natural and inevitable result of the ideas of the revolutionary Socialist intelligentsia.[3]

This quotation could easily be supplemented by a number of others from the same work, e.g.:

. . . the kind of talk became the fashion, according to which one ought to push the "average" into the foreground, the worker from the crowd rather than the "elite" of labor, that "political activities must always faithfully follow the economic development," etc., exercising a powerful attraction on the young people who were joining the movement. In most cases, they knew about Marxism only from occasional fragments of the official version. What this meant was the complete predominance of spontaneity over actual consciousness. . . . (*loc. cit.* p. 104).

Which proves that *any* admiration for the spontaneity of the working class movement, any diminution of the role of the "concious element," of the specific role of the Social Democratic movement is tantamount to an increase in the influence of the bourgeois ideology upon labor—*regardless of whether those, who weaken this role, desire such an effect, or not* (*loc. cit.*, p. 206).

Thus, *any* weakening of the Socialist ideology, *any deviation* from it, is tantamount to a strengthening of the bourgeois ideology. There is much talk about spontaneity. Yet the *spontaneous* development of the labor movement leads to its subordination under the

[3] *Loc. cit.*, vol. I, p. 199. Italics (also in the following quotations) are Lenin's.

bourgeois ideology . . . because a spontaneous labor movement means trade unionism, and trade unionism equals the ideological enslavement of the workers by the bourgeoisie. Our job, therefore, the task of the Social Democratic movement, is to *fight spontaneity*, by *counteracting* the spontaneous urges of trade unionism inside the labor movement which impel it to seek the protection of the bourgeoisie, leading it instead into the haven of revolutionary Social Democracy. Therefore it is *tantamount to a complete renunciation of Socialism* to maintain . . . that even the greatest efforts of its most enthusiastic ideological leaders could not deflect the labor movement from the path traced by the interaction of material factors and the physical environment. . . . (*loc. cit.*, p. 208).

These passages make it perfectly obvious that Lenin had a complete misconception of Marx and Engels' ideas concerning the class struggle. It is not our aim to discuss here whether the Marxist theory of class warfare is or is not correct; but if one does subscribe to it—and Lenin consistently maintained that he did—one is forced to note that Lenin's views flagrantly contradict the theory.

Lenin assumes that there are two levels in the development of a consciousness within the class struggle of the proletariat. The working class itself is merely capable of evolving "trade unionism," i.e., the awareness of the necessity of a fight for better material conditions. Actual consciousness, however, and connected therewith the awareness of the necessity of a political struggle for a new social order, does not develop within the working class itself, but has to be brought to it "from without," i.e., by the "educated representatives of the propertied classes."

Lenin intentionally neglects to discuss the reasons that these representatives of the bourgeois class decide to side with the proletariat, contrary to the interests of their own class. Here—if viewed from the perspective of the Marxist theory of the class struggle—we are faced with two fallacies which completely distort the essential nature of Marxism. In the first place, Marx considered it an impossibility for one class to comprehend and, what is more, recognize the interests of another. It is at all times up to the particular class itself to realize its own interests and therewith to achieve the full consciousness of itself. Marx and Engels themselves were always aware that they had reached socialism only through their contact with the labor movement. But, what is more, the term "class" does not fit the intellectuals at all, nor were they ever considered as a class either by Marx or by any Marxist, with the sole exception of Lenin. In fact, here we have a deviation from Marxism on Lenin's part which must be considered as the most serious among his theoretical writings, signaling the strong influence of Czarist conditions upon his thought. Under the Czarist system, similar to the Oriental despotism, officialdom and the military assume the role of a special class—a class which Lenin, moreover, sometimes confuses with the bourgeoisie.

Lenin turned the realization of the predominant role of the intellectuals in the evolution of the socialist theory into an outright claim for leadership; only under the leadership of the intellectuals can the working class achieve class consciousness and therewith the ability to evolve a Social Democratic policy. Here, Lenin is very far indeed from the attitude of Marx, who in 1850 had asked the workers to mature, over fifty years of civil and national wars, in order to become fit for leadership. Nevertheless, Marx and Engels were keenly aware of the significance of their own work for the development of socialism; they would not otherwise have given the type of socialism they were developing the name of "scientific" socialism.

But no matter how highly they may have valued their own role —they would never have dreamed of asserting that it was up to them to teach the working class a consciousness of their social position, including the need for class warfare—or, more than that, that it was up to them to prescribe its objectives. They were at all times aware of the limited influence of the intellectuals—without, incidentally, ever idolizing the proletariat. Their concept of their own role was that they were facilitating labor's way toward socialism. They were placing their philosophical, economic, and political knowledge in the service of labor, knowing full well that it would depend on the workers themselves as well as on conditions, as they developed, to what extent labor would ultimately utilize the results of their studies. Throughout their lives they were free from

Lenin's illusion that one could, or even ought to, impose this kind of knowledge upon the working class.

Marx and Engels' disciple, Karl Kautsky, whom Lenin invoked in this connection in his polemics against the so-called "Economists," thoroughly agreed with Marx and Lenin on this point. He believed that the working class needed the cooperation of the intellectuals and the insights of scientific socialism to formulate its objectives and political arguments. But Kautsky never thought that this role entitled the intellectuals to a position of leadership.

There is no need today for analyzing Lenin's controversy against the "Economists"; history has by-passed it, and its only relevance, from the viewpoint of the history of ideas, is in the fact that it highlights Lenin's early detachment from the spirit of Marxism on important points. He was far more influenced by the realities of Russian life which surrounded him, than by the observations of Marx, who as early as his controversy against Proudhon in 1846, had come to realize the importance of trade unions which he later called the "gladiator of the working class." In Russia the unions were never able to play a decisive role, because the political fight against Czarism repressed any politically significant act of the working class and because underground work is hardly the natural climate for a trade union movement. On the other hand, the role of the intellectuals in the Russian revolutionary movement was far more outstanding than in any other European country.

The unpleasant connotation which the term "trade unionism" has in Lenin's writings merely proves his utter lack of understanding for the more mature role of the labor movement within a capitalist, democratic environment. The history of the English as well as the American labor unions shows that the exact opposite of Lenin's concept was true; in both these countries a political movement was able to develop "spontaneously" out of mere labor union beginnings, i.e., without being influenced by the intellectuals. In Britain the trade union movement is consciously Socialist, while in the United States it abandoned its early political neutrality to become a very important factor on the political scene.

Another important evidence of Lenin's misunderstanding of

Marx's views about classes was his failure to understand that proletarian character is not an inborn condition clinging to a man all his life, but the result of the type of activity he performs in the productive process.

This misapprehension played a major role in Communist legislation and practical policies following the seizure of power (recalling the medieval corporate system or the Indian caste system). Whether a person was qualified to fill a public office in the Soviet state did not depend on his talents or achievements but on his parentage. The descendants of aristocratic or middle class families were rejected. The children and grandchildren from such an environment were even forbidden to attend secondary schools and universities. There is only a short step from this practice to the Nazi or Communist system of making entire families legally responsible for the actions of their members and the shooting of hostages, which was advocated by Lenin himself.[4]

THE PROFESSIONAL REVOLUTIONARY

Lenin's conviction that the incapacity of the working class to provide its own leadership, and his conception of the crucial role of intellectuals in stimulating class consciousness and class warfare led directly to his conception of *party* and the "professional revolutionary." The political party, organized along the lines of the "cadre" principle, was one of Lenin's unshakable ideas. His fight against "spontaneous" working class action was of a piece with his conception of party, as the last chapters of *What Is to Be Done* make clear. For him the revolution depended on the "professional revolutionaries" in whose hands the political leadership of the Russian Social Democratic movement was to be concentrated. This is an utterly non-Marxist concept, clearly revealing the in-

[4] *Loc. cit.*, vol. 2, p. 601: "Without such measures one cannot wage war." ("All-out in the Fight Against Denikin!")

fluence on Lenin of the Russian anarchists—Nechayev defeating Marx.

The full personality of the professional revolutionary emerges only when we place it in context of Lenin's statements about the role of the intellectual in the Russian Social Democratic movement. While it is true that Lenin, from the outset, stressed the ability of the worker to play the role of the professional revolutionary once he had received the necessary indoctrination and personally seized every occasion to place workers in this role, nevertheless, the cadre of his own party consisted almost entirely of intellectuals, including a good number of those elements which Marx had sharply denounced in his controversy against Bakunin, i.e., down-and-out students, doctors without patients, lawyers without clients—in short, intellectuals who for some reason or other had been forced out of their professional careers. Lenin, as well as Bakunin and Nechayev correctly considered these suitable raw material for a tightly centralized revolutionary organization.

It would be a serious mistake to underestimate the importance of organizational problems for the subsequent development of Russian socialism. Controversies about these issues have always been of far-reaching importance in the international labor movement. The controversy between Marx and Lassalle was less concerned with theoretical questions, in which Marx considered Lassalle as his disciple (although not an exactly orthodox one), than with Lassalle's attempt to organize his "General German Workers Association" along Bonapartist lines, i.e., with decisive power concentrated in the hands of the president. Marx had discussed this problem in considerable detail in his letter to Schweitzer, and it is unlikely that Lenin should not have been familiar with this letter. Nevertheless, the procedure he chose conflicted with Marx's views and conformed to those of Lassalle.

Much of the history of Bolshevism and the world can be traced directly to Lenin's conception of party. Its first major consequence was to split the Russian Social Democrats.

THE SCHISM

It is not within the scope of this study to survey every detail of the split which occurred within the Russian Social Democratic party during the London conference of 1903, thanks to Lenin's conduct. Suffice it here to recall that the rift occurred over questions of organization.

If one strips the crucial debates of all their ideological and political trimmings, the issue was basically to what extent democratic principles should be applied inside the party. Lenin defended the principle of tight centralization, of a concentration of power in an all-mighty Central Committee which, in effect, would be responsible to no one. The idea of elected officers and a democratic control over party finances had already been rejected by Lenin in his *What Is to Be Done* as an unbearable interference in the conspiratorial fight against Czarism. There is probably no clearer formulation of this attitude than Lenin's when he wrote that he tried to create within the Social Democratic ranks a perfect counterpart to the organization of the Russian government, i.e., a strictly military, tightly centralized setup subject to a single will.

Communist propaganda has subsequently tried to minimize the importance of the organizational questions, explaining the rift as the result of Lenin's insistence, in London, on pursuing an "orthodox Marxist" line in the face of the "opportunism" of his opponents. But this version is in no way related to the facts. In London the Mensheviks were in the minority, being at least as radical in their Marxism as Lenin; not one of them had, in fact, identified himself with Bernstein's revisionism. As shown above, it was Lenin who acted as a "revisionist" in matters of theory, although, to use the Communist jargon, his was a "Leftist deviation."

The Mensheviks insisted on Marxist principles even in questions of policy and organizational matters. They, too, were aware that the fight against Czarism required illegal activities and that internal party democracy, therefore, had to be subject to severe limitations. But they felt that it should exist within these limits.

It seems certain that Lenin would have effected the break and realized his organizational principles within his own group, even if he had found himself in the minority in 1903. The unfortunate vote at the London Conference, however, enabled him to pose later as the sole legitimate leader of the Russian Social Democratic movement, although it became manifest again and again (finally during the elections for the National Constituent Assembly in 1917) that he had the support of only a minority, both within the party and, more important, among the people as a whole.

It should not be assumed that the threat to the Russian labor movement, caused by Lenin's victory, passed unnoticed at the time. We shall here quote only two warnings which carry especial weight, since they came from persons who in 1917 counted themselves among Lenin's companions-in-arms, i.e., Rosa Luxemburg and Leon Trotsky. Rosa Luxemburg, as early as 1904, warned against Lenin's ultra-centralism, especially the "barracks atmosphere" which it reflected and its threat to the free development of the revolutionary labor movement. This, she cautioned, was particularly serious, since Russia was on the eve of a revolutionary upheaval. Trotsky's warning, made in 1905, anticipated the coming developments to an amazing extent:

> The party organization replaces the party itself; then, the Central Committee replaces the organization and, finally, the dictator replaces the Central Committee.

LENIN'S AMORALITY

These warnings failed to stop Lenin in his course. During the following years he managed to create the kind of organization of which he had "dreamed" in 1902. Even during those years when his party organization, at least to the casual observer, seemed to function normally, he was in fact already its dictator and could indulge his despotic leanings within its framework. Nor did it bother him that in this way he frequently lost touch with the actual labor movement; behind the Marxist mask there appeared the ghost of Nechayev, the anarchist author of the principle of individual terror, who had scorned the suggestion of being fettered by "bourgeois morality."

Lenin demonstrated again and again his inability to tolerate controversy or competition without converting it into a life and death struggle in which victory was the only moral obligation. As early as 1907 he made clear his belief that battles within the working class—as well as interclass struggles—should be fought by every available means, with annihilation regarded as their goal. The occasion was his appearance before a party tribunal in 1907 while the party was temporarily reunited. The tribunal had been set up by a central committee without a Bolshevik majority. In a pamphlet Lenin had accused thirty-one Mensheviks of having contacted the Cadet party prior to the Duma elections for the purpose of "selling the labor vote to the Cadets." The central committee viewed this accusation as conduct "inadmissible for a party comrade." In his defense Lenin stated that he had never intended to accuse the Mensheviks of selling the labor vote "for money." "Anyone making such an accusation should be turned over to the courts for libel, rather than for creating confusion in the ranks of the working class. . . ." He went on, "But if I have stated in the respective passage that the thirty-one wanted to transfer the labor vote to the Cadets in exchange for a Social Democratic seat in the Duma, this, on the other hand, is a typical example of a loyal type of controversy, such as is permissible among party comrades."

In what way does this presentation differ from the one I have chosen? The difference is one of innuendo and tone. In the aforementioned presentation, the perusal of the text appears to be designed to arouse hatred, disgust and contempt against the people who have committed similar actions. The purpose of such a presentation is not to convince the opponent but to carry confusion into his ranks, not to correct his errors, but to destroy and eradicate his organization. This type of presentation is indeed apt to arouse the worst possible opinions, the worst suspicion against the opponent and—contrary to the persuasive, corrective type of argument—produces indeed "confusion in the ranks of the working class."

"So, you do admit that such an argument is inadmissible?" you ask me. "Yes," I answer, "with one minor qualification: it is inadmissible among the members of a united party." That, however, is the crux of the matter. The whole incorrectness and even unscrupulousness of the accusation of the Central Committee against me lies in the fact that the Central Committee conceals the lack of a united party at the time the pamphlet was written. . . . It is unscrupulous to make an accusation against "a party member's inadmissible appearance in the press" at a time when the party was split.

A split means the breakup of all organizational ties, transferring the battle of opinions from within the organization to an outside level, and from the level of the attempt of correcting and convincing the comrades to one of destroying their organization and of inciting the labor rank and file and the people as a whole against the dissident organization.

What is inadmissible among the members of a united party, is admissible, and even required for the elements of a divided party. One certainly should not write about party comrades in a language designed to arouse hatred, disgust, contempt, etc. within the working masses, against those who think differently. One may and in fact should, however, write in this way if one faces a divided organization.

Why should one proceed in this manner? Because the fact of the division involves the obligation to prevent the masses from following the secessionary leadership. The objection is made that I have carried confusion into that section of the Petersburg proletariat leaning towards the Mensheviks after they had seceded on the eve of the elections. However, I shall act in this manner, whenever there has been a split. I have indeed been able to shatter the ranks of those workers who had trusted and followed the Mensheviks in launching my sharp, insulting attacks, prior to the Petersburg election. That was exactly my purpose. That in fact was my duty as a member of the Petersburg organization, engaged in fighting the left-bloc campaign. . . . I have fought a battle of annihilation against these political enemies and I shall do the same if there should be a continuation or repetition of the split. . . .

From the point of view of the organization a split means the discontinuation of all organizational ties, i.e., a transition from the attempt of convincing the comrades within the organization to a war of annihilation against the organization of the enemy and his influence among the working class. Even from the psychological viewpoint it is evident that the breaking of all organizational ties among comrades involves the highest possible degree of mutual anger, of hostility and hate.

Lenin maintained these views to his end. In his pamphlet: *Left-wing Communism, An Infantile Disorder* (1920) he wrote again:

One must . . . be prepared for all and any sacrifice, even, if necessary, be ready to resort to every possible trick, ruse, illegal method, to conceal and falsify the truth in order to infiltrate the unions, to remain within them and to perform Communist activities inside the unions at all costs. (*Loc. cit.*, vol. 2. p. 701.)

The Communists have followed this prescription to this very day. The morality here set forth has governed and continues to govern Communist relations with all other groups, including all working class organizations not under this control. Lenin was the first to elevate invective into a principle of political controversy. Lenin was not concerned to convince the opponent by arguments based on the truth but to arouse "hatred, disgust and contempt" against him.

In promulgating these principles Lenin revealed himself as the faithful disciple of Nechayev, the man who had come from Russia to present himself to Bakunin as the alleged spokesman of a vast anarchist organization and in turn had received a written endorsement which he used after his return to Russia as proof that he was Bakunin's authorized representative. Convinced of his mission, he felt entitled to decide arbitrarily about the life and death of his adherents; thus one of his followers was executed after asking some indiscreet questions about the existence of the alleged extensive organization.

Bolshevik morality, including its readiness to resort to banditry (expropriations) to finance its activities, attracted criminal elements, and the whole range of revolutionary activities became shot through with paid agents and semicriminals.

The more tightly centralized the organization, whose active elements are not subject to the scrutiny of intraparty democracy, the more easily it may happen that the entire group may come under the influence of bribed and corrupt elements in questions of principle. Only the centralistic organization set up by Lassalle enabled Schweitzer to guide his party for years along pro-Bismarckian lines. And it was only Lenin's supercentralism which enabled the police spy Malinovsky to rise to the position of chairman of the Bolshevist delegation in the Duma and to become a member of the party's Central Committee, and which enabled Lenin to make the pact with Ludendorff and the imperial German government following the outbreak of the Russian Revolution of March 1917.[5]

COUP D'ETAT

By the outbreak of the revolution in March 1917, the basic character of the Bolshevik party was already formed. Lenin's conception of party organization of the labor movement and working class, and of the revolutionary amorality, virtually precluded the possibility that he would work toward establishing a democratic form of government in Russia in collaboration with the other Social Democratic groups or the other democratic parties, which would give Socialist labor an opportunity for a free development. What he proclaimed was the dictatorship of the proletariat as represented by his own party.

Forgotten were his own statements, according to which Russian

[5] The documentary evidence of Lenin's receipt of 50 million gold marks from the German government was established in an article by George Katkow, "German Foreign Office Documents on Financial Support to the Bolsheviks in 1917" (*International Affairs*, London, April 1956). Evidence known prior to this revelation has been assembled by David Shub in his *Lenin*, New York, Doubleday & Co., 1948.

conditions required that a middle class revolution should precede a revolution of the proletariat; forsaken was his own prophetic warning, made in 1905:

> And in replying to the Anarchist assertions that we are delaying the Socialist revolution, we say: we are not delaying it, we rather are taking the first step towards it, on the only possible and correct way—which is the way that leads over the democratic republic. Those who try to achieve Socialism by means other than political democracy, are bound to come to conclusions which are reactionary and absurd in economic as well as political respects.[6]
>
> An assembly of the representatives of the people is absolutely essential for establishing a republic, an assembly that is supported by all the people, to be based on universal, equal, direct suffrage and the secret ballot, acting as a constituent assembly.[7]

By now Lenin supported Trotsky's demand for an immediate dictatorship, even if exercised by a minority. He acted now without restraint; any catchword promising success was readily accepted, whether it happened to be in agreement with his theories and earlier views or not. Immediate peace, the factories to the workers, the land to the peasants, all the power to the soviets—but at the same time elections for a legislative national assembly, immediate seizure of power by the proletariat, world revolution by transforming the war among nations into a revolutionary civil war —the slogans of Bolshevist propaganda promised all this and more in the summer of 1917.

At first, this strategy of Lenin's did not meet with full approval inside his own party. Among the Bolsheviks there were some who could not as easily forsake their past. There were others who questioned the possibility of immediate success. Also, ties with the other Socialist groups were not yet definitely severed, in spite of Lenin's separatist tactics. Consequently, some Bolsheviks hesitated to participate in the dogged fight, which he unleashed especially against the Mensheviks, in view of the strong tendencies then cur-

6 *Two Tactics, loc. cit.,* vol. 1, p. 430.
7 *Loc. cit.,* p. 427.

rent among the workers to disregard group interests for the sake of unity among all Socialist groups. In this period of mass movements, when the other political parties were trying to find as broad a support among the population as possible, Lenin emphasized the necessity of strengthening his cadres. The failure of the July uprising, his first attempt to seize power, provided him the opportunity to create an illegal organization amid the unrestrained freedom of revolutionary Russia, benefiting from the generosity of the Provisional Government which neglected to indict him for treason.

Soon Lenin's organization was the only well-organized, disciplined group in the midst of general chaos which spread rapidly after the failure of the unfortunate Kerensky offensive and rapidly engulfed all aspects of economic, government, and military life.

In rejecting any objections, whether raised by others or possibly even besetting his own mind, Lenin pointed to the imminent world revolution which would solve all problems.

Lenin's *coup d'état* in November 1917 was executed along the lines of a well-prepared Oriental palace revolt or the uprising of a South American officers' junta. The population did not participate in any way. The Socialist government had no adequate means to counteract Lenin's well-organized armed groups, all democratic parties having considered it an important element of freedom to keep armed forces out of the political controversies to the greatest possible extent. The idea of creating armed units to serve political parties was totally alien to them.

It therefore proved an easy job for Lenin and Trotsky to seize power. Yet the question, what to do with the power he now held, was posed not only by his opponents but by his adherents as well. He had given his answer to both as late as October 1917 in his pamphlet *Can the Bolsheviks Maintain the Power of Government?*" which contained the prophetic words: "If the Czar has been able to rule Russia with 130,000 members of the aristocracy and the lower nobility, the Bolshevik party with its 240,000 members should do at least equally well."

In the pamphlet *The Impending Disaster*, written between September 10 and 14, 1917, Lenin listed what he felt were the most important steps to be taken by the Bolshevik government:

1. Consolidation of all banks into one single bank, to be controlled by the government or nationalization of all private banks;

2. Nationalization of the syndicates, i.e., the largest monopolistic organizations of the capitalists (sugar, oil, coal, mine syndicates, etc.);

3. Abolition of secret business operations;

4. Compulsory establishment of syndicates for industrialists, businessmen and other employers (i.e., their compulsory enrollment in such associations);

5. Compulsory enrollment of the people in consumers' cooperatives, or at least the promoting of this type of organization and control.[8]

As will be shown later on, Lenin's concept of a Socialist society was inspired by the example of German monopoly capitalism:

> And now one should try to substitute a *revolutionary-democratic* state for the Capitalist society of the *Junkers*, the Capitalist society of the land-owners, in other words, a state which by revolutionary means abolishes *all* privileges which does not shrink from realizing complete democracy by revolutionary means. You shall see that monopoly capitalism, run by the state, within a truly revolutionary and democratic society unquestionably, inevitably, means a step forward, if not several steps, on the road towards Socialism.[9]

And to avoid any misunderstanding concerning the extent of freedom, which the people should derive from this "complete democracy" under such a type of Socialism, he went on to say:

> In Germany the *Junkers* (big land-owners) and the Capitalists have instituted compulsory universal labor, which necessarily acts as a military prison for the workers. But let us consider the same institution and its implications within a revolutionary and democratic state. Universal compulsory labor, as introduced by the So-

---

[8] *Loc. cit.*, vol. II, p. 96.
[9] *Loc. cit.*, p. 123.

viets of the Workers, Soldiers and Peasants, and as regulated and managed by them, is *not yet* Capitalism. It is an important *step* towards socialism. . . .[10]

The following passage from Lenin's *State and Revolution*, written about this time, shows how he visualized the transition to a Socialist society. It should be remembered that this work was for quite awhile considered as the catechism of the Communist movement until its views about the imminent decay of the state, and the "equalization" of the income of the state functionaries—later bitingly ridiculed under Stalin and Khrushchev—appeared to clash too drastically with Soviet practices. Lenin wrote:

> Capitalist civilization has *produced* mass production, factories, railroads, postal services, telephone companies, etc., *in this manner* simplifying most of the functions of the governments and reducing them to such simple operations of registration and control, that they have become accessible to anyone who is not an illiterate.[11]

And lest one think these sentences should be attributed to the excitement of the impending battle, when Lenin's energies were solely bent upon the day-by-day tactical problems rather than the more distant future, one ought to read the following sentences, written by Lenin in 1921 in his pamphlet *About Taxes in Kind*, in justification of his New Economic Policy:

> So as to further clarify the problem, we shall begin by mentioning a concrete example of State Capitalism. Everybody knows what example I have in mind—i.e., Germany. Here we find the last word in modern high-Capitalistic technology and planned organization, subject to the *imperialism of the Junkers and the bourgeoisie*. If one throws out the underlined words and substitutes for the military, Junker-bourgeois, imperialist state *another type of state*, one of a different social brand, different class content, i.e., the Soviet state, that is to say: a proletarian state, one obtains the *sum total* of the conditions equalling socialism. . . . And if in Germany the revolution is not yet about to "break out," it is our duty mean-

[10] *Loc. cit.*, p. 125 f.
[11] *Loc. cit.*, p. 190.

while to *study* the State-Capitalism of the Germans, to copy it as *thoroughly* as we can, to shun no *dictatorial* methods in order to speed up this transplanting of Western civilization in barbarian Russia, without ever hesitating to use barbarian methods in the battle against barbarism.[12]

These passages provide a reliable picture of what Lenin, to the end of his life, envisaged as the Socialist content of the Soviet dictatorship: i.e., a state capitalism along German lines, with the members of the Communist party replacing the Junkers and big capitalists. In his entire concept there is not a trace of the evolutionary process which had been so carefully outlined by Marx; it is enough to change the form of government to transform society. Lenin was satisfied to give the label of "proletarian" to his party, made up—according to his own wishes—of professional revolutionist intellectuals, to meet all the prerequisites for a Socialist society. He blithely rejected the idea that the working class needed to acquire the ability to take over the government in an evolutionary struggle lasting over many decades. Nowhere in his comments on achieving socialism is there reference to true economic democracy or labor's share in management; all activities everywhere are directed from above in a centralized structure mirroring organization of the party. "Socialism is Soviet power plus electrification"—this was the formula in which Lenin eventually crystallized his views. Lenin's Socialism is power plus technology—with no room left for the human being.

The *coup d'état* was but the first in a long succession of actions that moved the Bolsheviks and the Russian Revolution further and further from the goal Lenin continued to proclaim: democratic Socialism.

As early as in December 1917 he established the Cheka, the secret police which, though often changing its name, has basically retained its character, i.e., that of the strongest pillar of the Soviet dictatorship. He destroyed parliament and thereby started the civil war; but step by step he also managed to deprive the soviets of their influence in city and rural areas, turning the elections into a

[12] *Loc. cit.*, p. 829 f.

pure farce by his suppression and persecution of other parties. Soon, he had robbed the workers of their influence in the factories, subjecting them to the yoke of a work discipline more severe than anything they had known under Czarism. At the same time, he began to extort food from the peasants by a system of rigorous requisitions, thus saving the members of the Bolshevik party, the newly founded Red Army, the Cheka, and government officials from starvation. All this he advertised as the heroic period of Communism in which a new world was about to be born, only to throw all these policies unflinchingly overboard, rejecting them as "wartime Communism," when the uprising of the Kronstadt sailors and workers convinced him that this system would not lead to the desired goals. Nevertheless he was ready to resort to the utmost brutality against his most faithful comrades-in-arms of 1917, thus drowning in blood the last attempt to save the great democratic and Socialist traditions of the Russian Revolution in open battle.

The New Economic Policy put an end to the requisitions, gave small craftsmen and shopkeepers some freedom and opened up certain opportunities for foreign investment in the Russian economy. But those who had hoped for a change in the political system were in for a disappointment; it was this period of the NEP, when the concentration camps were opened on the Solovietsky islands and the Menshevik republic in Georgia was attacked. Therewith Lenin betrayed the principle of national self-determination, one of the few ideals he had actually applied during the Revolution, and thus opened the way for a policy of expansion which ever since has been a characteristic of Soviet policy, just as in Czarist times.

Some observers, convinced of the basic difference between Stalin and Lenin, have emphasized Lenin's warnings against Stalin in the former's testament. While these warnings were made, there is nothing either in this document or in any of his other written or spoken statements to show that Lenin had planned any fundamental changes in the Soviet system. Despite his comments on the excessive growth of the Soviet bureaucracy, made during his last years, he undertook no measures to eradicate this evil which he himself had fostered. He made no effort to replace the all-powerful control of the state with genuine self-government. In practice, his only solution consisted in setting up a new department for the supervision of the already existing government agencies, the "Workers' and Peasants' Supervisory Board."

Lenin is, therefore, the author and originator of a system still prevailing in the Soviet Union today, as well as everywhere else in the Communist world. He is, in particular, the founder of the all-mighty party which has survived every change so far. It was Lenin himself who equated the "dictatorship of individuals" (i.e., his own) with the "dictatorship of the revolutionary classes."[13] The party remains the primary support and tool of this dictatorship, and the slogan which in 1945 circulated in the Soviet zone of Germany, "The party is always right," still has full validity throughout the Soviet orbit.

The nature of this party has been analyzed with profound insight by a former leading member in Milovan Djilas' book, *The New Class*. A group of originally devoted, courageous revolutionaries developed into a political machine, made up of selfish careerists and held together by the special privileges they enjoy and by their common fear of retribution should they fall from power—a fear only too justified in view of the fate of the Hungarian secret police in October 1956.

We are already familiar with the primary aim of these leaders since Lenin's days: i.e., the expansion of the economy for the benefit of the power of the state, domestically as well as on the international level. This is the historic function of Communism.

[13] *Loc. cit.*, vol. I, p. 384.

2

The Vanguard in Search
of the Masses

SOVIET INDUSTRIALIZATION AND THE UNDERDEVELOPED AREAS

E. P. W. da Costa

■ Around the fact of the U.S.S.R.'s rapid progress in industrializing its economy and raising the level of its technology there has developed a myth which serves to lure and to justify. According to this myth (1) the Soviet Union possesses an extremely advanced industrial economy; (2) this economy was achieved by uniquely rapid industrialization since the Bolshevik Revolution; and (3) the Soviet experience in industrializing is uniquely relevant to the problems of underdeveloped nations aspiring to rapid industrial progress. Leaders of underdeveloped areas are invited to regard the U.S.S.R. as a model and to achieve the same success with the same methods.

It is an appealing myth, because it purports to provide a guide to, and guarantee of, success in a terribly difficult undertaking. While it is not exactly based on facts, it is at least surrounded by them. The Soviet Union has made dramatic technical and industrial advances. The Bolsheviks did inherit an economy which lagged behind that of Western Europe (though not as far behind as is often believed). And the underdeveloped nations will certainly encounter some of the problems which were met and solved by Soviet technicians. Assiduously fed by Soviet propagandists and inflated Soviet statistics, the myth exaggerates what is good and ignores what is repellent or equivocal in the Soviet record. It makes efficient use of Sputniks but neglects whole segments of the population—numbering literally millions—who were sacrificed to forced industrialization. It emphasizes the advantages of cen-

tralized economic planning in securing rational economic development, but ignores its tendency to produce waste, low quality, and
irresponsibility. E. P. W. da Costa is Editor of The Eastern Economist and Managing Director of the Indian Institute of Public
Opinion and of the Marketing Research Corporation of India. His
publications include The Economic Progress of Russia: 1860-1948;
Indian Industry, Today and Tomorrow; and numerous articles
which have appeared in newspapers and magazines. ■

INTRODUCTION

There is a widespread belief, and not only in Southeast Asia, that
the spectacular performance of Soviet industry in the last twenty-
five years makes the Soviet pattern of industrialization more attractive than any other for underdeveloped countries. There is no
denying that in terms of industrial growth there are few parallels
to the Soviet achievements. It is, however, not often appreciated
that this advance has been achieved at the expense of the nonin-
dustrial sectors of the Soviet economy, and agriculture in particular. It is the purpose of this essay to weigh as accurately as possible
the Soviet performance and its cost, and to assess the utility of the
Soviet pattern as a model for the industrialization of underdeveloped countries.

The subject has been approached under three broad heads.
First, I have undertaken a statistical assessment of Soviet rates of
growth in terms which those living in underdeveloped countries
can accept as being objective and outside the powerful currents
of the cold war. Unfortunately, few economic or statistical controversies are so heavily colored with personal feeling as this one.
This is not only true in Asia or Africa; the controversy has penetrated deeply into the heart of the Western world. Western
scholars seem to us to be sharply divided about the Soviet Union's
industrial record. While a very large number of anti-Communist
writers tend to raise an alarm about the overwhelming capacity of

Soviet industry, there are many others who tend to belittle it by demonstrating or attempting to demonstrate the inadequacies of Soviet official statistics for purposes of comparison. It is therefore necessary here to define the penumbra of statistical uncertainty which surrounds but does not, one hopes, eclipse the hard facts.

The second section discusses the burdens which the Soviet approach to industrialization has placed on the economy as a whole and on agriculture in particular. Here the argument deals largely with the cost of collectivization, both in terms of reduction of agricultural productivity from what it otherwise would have been, and also in terms of the heavy rate of capital formation exacted from the agricultural sector in order to be thrown into socialized industry. While the theory of making agricultural collectivization support industry springs from Soviet practice, the best illustration of the theory in practice is found in the People's Republic of China where the process of collectivization is essentially an instrument of ruthless taxation rather than the step toward more rational organization of primary production that it is often claimed to be. The classic "Hundred Flowers" speech of Mr. Mao Tsetung contains proof enough that the burden on the Chinese agricultural sector could not be sustained by other underdeveloped countries which lack a tradition of heavy exploitation of agriculture.

In a postscript a modest attempt is made to relate Japanese and Indian experience to that of China and the Soviet Union and to indicate that industrial progress that has been achieved by the U.S.S.R. at a devastating price can in fact be largely achieved in a free or moderately planned economy, without the terrible hardships imposed by the Soviet method. It is also argued that approximately the same industrial achievements can be secured at the same time that agriculture can be released from its traditional backwardness and enabled to become the instrument of capital formation for itself and, to a not inconsiderable extent, for industry, too, as demand is created for the products of new industries.

Democrats oppose the sacrifice of agriculture and agricultural populations as undesirable and unnecessary, and advocate that industry and agriculture march together, each contributing revenue to the other through free demand for each other's products. It can never be in the best interests of the underdeveloped countries to crush their rural population to better the standard of living of the towns. The moral is therefore plain. It is that the techniques of forced industrialization, while being spectacular in the areas where massive resources have been employed, are on the whole disadvantageous to national welfare and hamper the intrinsic capacity of an economy to grow spontaneously in all sectors at the same time. Soviet industry is like a perpetual prize fighter; it achieves its spectacular successes by knocking out the springs of spontaneous and cooperative effort in other sectors, and sometimes in other countries, which have to distort their national economies in order to dovetail their production to conform to the supreme goals of Soviet industry. Satellitism, in its economic component, is in fact the fruit of Soviet industrialization; but it is not often recognized that it extends to the Soviet Union itself, where industry dominates and exploits the primary and tertiary sectors of the economy.

1. SOVIET PERFORMANCE

In Industry

It is a historical fact that in less than thirty years the Soviet Union transformed itself into an advanced industrial economy. But it is no less true that while the pace of progress in basic and heavy industries was breath-taking, no comparable advance occurred in the consumer-goods industries. The statistics of Soviet performance tell their own story, and these are presented in three tables.

These statistics, however, provide no over-all measure of Soviet industrial performance in terms of output. Estimates of Soviet industrial output as a whole in 1928 and in 1955 are, however, available in three different indexes. One is the official Soviet index of industrial output, which was 1,900 in 1955 as compared to the 1928 base of 100. Second, according to an index constructed by Mr. Hodgman of Harvard University, Soviet industrial output in 1955 was 1,085 as compared to the 1928 base of 100. Third, there is the index prepared by the Joint Economic Committee of the U. S. Congress, which lowers the 1955 level to 750 as compared to the same 1928 base. In these three estimates the annual average rate of growth of Soviet industrial production was worked out as 11.5 per cent, 9.2 per cent, and 7.7 per cent, respectively, as against, for example, 3.6 per cent in the comparable period in the case of American industrial production. That Soviet industry as a whole (including manufacturing, mining, and electric power generation) produced only about a third of the total quantity of goods produced by American industry in 1955 does not detract from the magnitude of Soviet achievement in specific industries of basic importance. This is brought out in Table I.

The official U.S.S.R. estimates indicate that, between 1955 and 1960, Soviet output in industry increased at 10.5 per cent per annum (compound). It is indeed remarkable for Soviet industry, if the official figures are correct, to maintain a steady rate of rise over such a long stretch of time. Unfortunately, the official figures tend to exaggerate the gains achieved in Soviet industry. This particular aspect has been significantly explained in the research work of a well-known Soviet economist, Mr. S. G. Strumilin, who has clearly demonstrated that the official Soviet indexes are based upon gross output and not on output. In the table below, prepared by Mr. Strumilin, who is the Dean of Soviet economists, data in regard to official index for gross output is set against Strumilin's index of net output between 1928 and 1956. It will be seen that Strumilin's estimate of the rate of industrial growth is approximately half the rate of growth shown by the official figures. Strumilin's estimate is corroborated by Hodgman's series, though the figures released by the Joint Economic Committee of the U. S. Congress tend to decrease the growth rate by slightly more than half.

TABLE I

| *Strumilin's Estimates of Industrial Output:* | | | | *Index of Growth 1928 = 100* | |
	(Billions of rubles) gross	1926-27 net	Net as percentage of gross	Official index of gross output	Strumilin's index of net output
1928	21.5	10.1	47	100	100
1932	43.3	19.4	45	202	192
1937	95.5	39.8	42	446	394
1940	138.9	69.3	50	646	686
1945	127.5	46.9	37	593	464
1950	240.6	81.1	34	1,119	803
1955	444.8	136.1	31	2,069	1,347
1956	492.4	147.7	30	2,288	1,462

Another index of Soviet industrial growth is provided by a breakdown by sectors of the total national product, that is, the nation's total output of goods and services. According to this breakdown, the agricultural sector accounted for 42 per cent and the industrial sector for 28 per cent of the Soviet Union's net national product in 1928; the respective sectoral contributions in 1961 were 20 per cent and 53 per cent of that country's national product. Incidentally, the corresponding figures for the United States were 9 per cent (agricultural sector) and 34 per cent (industrial sector) of that country's national income in 1928 and *4 per cent and 31 per cent, respectively, in 1961.* It is thus clear that the relative importance of industry in the Soviet economy exceeded that of industry in the U.S. economy in 1961.

So much about industry in general. Let us turn now to the Soviet performance in that dominant subsector: basic and heavy industries. The figures in Table I show that in less than thirty years the Soviet Union has established a broad base in basic and heavy industries—a base which will make possible an even more impressive edifice of absolute production in the future. Such a development may be inferred from the long-term trend of high growth rates of production in individual industries. Depending on the respective growth rates of U.S. and Soviet industry, it may be that in ten to fifty years' time, the absolute outputs of individual industries will reach levels equaling their U.S. counterparts.

First, it may also be seen from the figures in Table I that the Soviet output of steel (which is basic to all other heavy and light industries) in 1928 was just 8 per cent of the U.S. output in that year; but it was 43 per cent of that of the U.S. in 1955. Second, the Soviet output of petroleum in 1928 was just under 10 per cent of the U.S. output in that year; but it was 21 per cent of the latter in 1955. Third, the Soviet generation of electric power was just under 5 per cent of the U.S. generation in 1928; but it represented 20 per cent of the latter in 1955. Fourth, the Soviet output of cement was just under 6 per cent of the U.S. output in 1928; but it was 44 per cent of the latter in 1955. Fifth, the Soviet output of sawn timber was just under 16 per cent of the U.S. output in 1928; but it was 76 per cent of the latter in 1955. And lastly, the Soviet output of coal was just under 7 per cent of the U.S. output in 1928; but it was 87 per cent of the latter in 1955.

Yet despite this remarkable industrial growth, there has been no spectacular increase in the output of consumer-goods industries. For example, the bulk of Soviet steel output appears to be allocated to the production of military goods or to other basic industries conducive to the further growth of heavy industries. Since the growth rate in the sector of consumer-goods industries has not even approximated that of heavy industries, the inference is conclusive that war-oriented industries have been draining away a large part of the real resources created by heavy industrialization. What that part is nobody knows, for a thick blanket of secrecy envelopes the Soviet Union's armament industries.

In Agriculture

Paradoxically, the phenomenal growth of Soviet industry in the period under study must be attributed more to the fact of socialization (collectivization) of agriculture than to the fact of socialization of industries as such. According to official Soviet statistics, the socialist sector accounted for 82 per cent of the total industrial output in 1928 as against 100 per cent in 1938. On the other hand, the socialist sector accounted for just 3 per cent of the total agricultural output in 1928, whereas it accounted for nearly 97 per cent in 1937. There was an organic connection between collectivized agriculture and rapid industrialization; the former contributed importantly to the latter by making possible a high rate of industrial investment. Other factors, such as restricted consumption brought about by the turnover tax and by socialized trading which accounted for the entire retail turnover in 1937, played a role. But agricultural collectivization was decisive in sustaining the tempo of heavy industrialization.

The performance of collectivized agriculture in the period 1928-55 thus acquires particular relevance. A picture of performance in this sector is, however, not available in terms of a weighted index of agricultural output based on 1928. As the official Soviet index with its base 1950=100 is not suitable for the present study, absolute figures of production of principal crops in the two years—1928 and 1955—are given below:

TABLE II

Crops	1928 (In million metric tons)	1955 (In million metric tons)	Percentage increase in 1955 over 1928
Grain	73.3	100.0	36.4
Potatoes	46.4	67.0	44.4
Cotton (ungrained)	0.8	3.9	387.5

In the same period the areas under these crops have increased as below:

Crops	1928 (In million hectares)	1955 (In million hectares)	Percentage increase in 1955 over 1928
Grain	92.2	126.4	37.1
Potatoes	5.7	9.1	59.6
Cotton	0.97	2.20	126.8

The above figures, by themselves, are an eloquent proof that up to 1955 Soviet agricultural performance, measured in terms of unit-area yield, had not improved under conditions of collectivization. An increase of about 36 per cent in grain output in the period 1928-55 had come about through an area increase of 37 per cent and not through any increase in productivity. In the case of potatoes, the position was worse because an area increase of 60 per cent in the period had resulted in only a 44 per cent increase in output. The only exception was cotton, which had registered an output increase of 388 per cent for an area increase of just 127 per cent. This performance of cotton is explained by the fact that the small area under that crop could be, and actually had been, dealt with on a special basis, and provided with adequate irrigation and fertilizer.

Since grain crops and potatoes together constituted 98 million hectares out of a total crop area of 113 million hectares in 1928, and 136 million hectares out of 186 million hectares in 1955, the output of food crops alone is more than sufficient as an index of Soviet agricultural performance. Here, too, if allowance is made for the fact that the small area—less than 3 per cent of the total crop area—reserved for private cultivation as kitchen plots accounted for 10 per cent of Soviet agricultural output, it is seen that by 1955 an increase of only about 26 per cent in the output of food crops (grains and potatoes) had resulted from a 35 per cent increase in the area devoted to those crops in the state and collective farms.

It would thus appear that the productivity of land under conditions of collectivization had actually declined from the 1928 level. As a matter of fact, the performance of collectivized agriculture was still worse in terms of per capita production. That the output of grains and potatoes had remained static at 0.75 tons per capita in 1955 as in 1928 despite an area increase of about 35 per cent in the period is a further eloquent commentary on the state of collectivized agriculture in the Soviet Union. Incidentally, this thirty-year experience of collective farming proves conclusively that it is not a more rational or efficient organization of primary production than peasant farming.

This virtual stagnation in Soviet agriculture—in terms of unit-area yield and per capita production—resulted from inadequate reinvestment in agriculture. No doubt there was some input of capital into agriculture by way of reclamation, irrigation, mechanization, fertilizer application, and so on. But this investment was just sufficient to maintain per capita production at the same level as in 1928, and not sufficient to arrest the decline in per hectare productivity. In other words, the rate of investment in agriculture up to 1955 was too low to bring about a substantial increase in total as well as per capita food output *through an improvement in productivity*. The resources for industry were, thus, found by the ruthless exploitation of Soviet agriculture.

The developments in Soviet farming since the mid-fifties abundantly bear out this conclusion. The inadequacy of this investment in agriculture was recognized by the Soviet authorities in 1953, when they devised rather drastic measures to set this sector of their economy in order. Among the most important steps that have been taken since 1953 to improve productivity in Soviet agriculture are: (1) institutional changes introduced to decentralize decisions on crop patterns; (2) provision of incentives to collective farmers in the form of higher prices and substantially— even drastically in some cases—reduced compulsory delivery quotas for their products; and (3) provision to collective farms of machinery, fertilizers, and other aids to agricultural production at subsidized rates. These changes, in fact, amounted to introducing into Soviet agriculture some of the essential elements of free agricultural economies. For instance, to make available larger funds to collective farmers for investment on their lands the statutorily fixed prices for compulsory delivery quotas have been twice raised, first in 1953 and then in 1958. The price increases allowed in 1953 were quite heavy—about 2½ times over the levels prevailing in 1952. The 1958 revision, of course, was much smaller, amounting to about 20 per cent above the 1956 levels.

Though these changes in the pattern of Soviet agriculture gave material incentives to collective farmers and helped to step up output in subsequent years, they failed to stimulate Soviet agriculture permanently. Since 1958 Soviet agriculture has again tended to stagnate. The recent utterances of the top Soviet leaders, not excluding Mr. Khrushchev, are a clear indication that all is not yet well with the Soviet agriculture, despite the fact that the rate of investment in this sector, both on state account and owing to plowing back of profits from collective farms, had been stepped up quite appreciably in the late fifties.

In the Over-all Economy

The consequences of Soviet industrialization for national income are buried in a controversy so deep that it is difficult to obtain a firm figure on which argument can proceed. There is fairly general agreement that the rate of gross investment in the Soviet Union constituted as much as 27 per cent of gross national product in terms of current prices. The corresponding figure for the United States was 19 per cent, of which 15 per cent was private and 4 per cent government. Official Soviet statistics claim a rate of growth of national income of between 14 and 16 per cent. These figures cannot be accepted at their face value because the concept of national income and the technique of computation are different from those accepted in the Free World. This point needs elaboration. The income accruing from many services is omitted from the Communist concept of national income, and since this sector shows a lower rate of rise, its exclusion serves to inflate the rate of growth. Concerning the technique of computation, it must be emphasized that the official Soviet index uses 1926-27 prices as a base for arriving at the weights to be assigned to different sectors. This gives an upward bias to the index. Because of economic diversification, new commodities are incorporated in the index from time to time. But the new commodities are incorporated in the national income at the prevailing prices in the years they were first produced, which are invariably higher because of the upward trend in prices since 1926-27. After making reasonable allowance for these factors, Gregory Grossman estimated that the rate of national income growth of the U.S.S.R. was between 6½ to 7 per cent before World War II, and approximately the same in the postwar years. Other authorities, including the U. S. Congress Joint Economic Committee's Report, put the figure at 4 per cent as the annual average rate of increase in the Soviet Union's gross national product from 1928 to 1955 as against the United States' 3 per cent in the comparable period.

Can underdeveloped countries maintain an average annual growth rate of between 4 per cent and 6.5 per cent without the political, social, and economic consequences entailed by the Soviet system? An answer to this question is vital if one is to argue that the Soviet methods of industrialization need not be pursued to secure similar results. The record of India offers some evidence that such a rate of growth can be maintained over a substantial period. From 1950-51 to 1960-61 India's annual rate of growth of net domestic product at factor cost was 4.3 per cent and this was fairly evenly distributed: agriculture rose 3.5 per cent; mining and manufacturing 4.3 per cent; commerce, transport, and communications 4.8 per cent; and professional and other services 6.6 per cent.

The Indian achievement constitutes a prima facie case that Soviet methods are unnecessary for economic development in underdeveloped areas at the lower limit proposed. Japan maintained a still higher rate for a much longer period, and incidentally, faced recovery problems after 1945 comparable to those of the Soviet Union. The best calculations indicate that the average growth rate of Japan from 1914 to 1937 was about 6.7 per cent. That is, for more than two decades Japan's progress equaled the best years of Soviet performance. The fact that these methods have been consistent with both democracy and a species of totalitarianism might be read to imply that the real strength of the Japanese economy does not depend on Japan's political system. From 1890 to 1941, war certainly played a part in Japanese economic development, but the peacetime record of Japanese industry has not been inferior.

The Japanese and Indian rates of economic growth provide concrete evidence that the Soviet approach to industrialization is not the only one of proved success. The question remains whether the Soviet method has any unique strength from the point of view of the underdeveloped countries. It is possible that elimination of political opposition and the single-minded pursuit of a plan constitute sources of strength. Given human fallibility, this strength must be balanced against the ability of a competitive market place to expose errors by converting them into cumulative losses. Misdirection of resources is an evil common to all economic systems, because they depend in the last analysis on the human capacity to make correct decisions. Given reasonably comparable conditions, a strong case can be made to support the contention that a system of free markets assists rather than retards economic progress.

2. THE PRICE OF SOVIET INDUSTRIALIZATION

Rate of Capital Formation and its Financing

Why do underdeveloped countries develop so slowly? Clearly, because they have neither the capital to finance, nor the technical skill to organize, large-scale production on competitive lines. Usually this vicious circle is described in simple terms. Because income is low, saving is low; because saving is low, investment is low; because investment is low, income is low, and so on. How can the vicious circle be broken? The superstition exists that the Soviet Union has found via its plans the perfect way.

The view that the socialist system practiced in Russia can stimulate capital formation far more effectively than free economies is based on the argument that if an investment at, say, 12 per cent of national income, is decreed by a rigid plan, development is secured before consumption. In other words, in such a system the rate of saving can be made a function of the planned rate of investment, whereas in free economies—at any rate in those that exist at the present time—investment cannot exceed saving substantially without introducing an element of inflation.

It should be recognized, however, that the Soviet system operates by lowering consumer demand. It is the process of consumer rationing, and not the socialist planning of investments, that speeds capital formation. It is perfectly possible for a free economy to institute rationing when supplies are short—as in wartime —and obtain precisely the same results as in the U.S.S.R., and accomplish these without comprehensive regimentation of every section of the economy. In India, during World War II, a rate of saving of over 15 per cent was so obtained, demonstrating that this method can succeed even in an underdeveloped economy. In other words, those who consider that the problem of raising capital formation has been solved by the Soviet Union in some unique and incomparable way are fundamentally mistaken. The success of the Soviet Union arises not from its arbitrary fixing of a level of planned investment or even by its totalitarian methods (though these are naturally of assistance), but by the submission of the public to consumption controls which drastically decrease the availability of goods. This system of consumer controls is ultimately dependent on the ability of the government to coerce or persuade citizens to accept a policy of deferring present consumption in order to increase capital accumulation and speed economic progress.

Two illustrations are given to show that this process of raising the rate of saving and investment, which worked itself out in Japan in relatively free conditions and is working itself out democratically in India, does not necessarily imply or require an arbitrary prefixing of investment or a denial to the population of necessary consumption goods. G. C. Allen, in a recent book, *Japan's Economic Recovery*, has pointed out that in the period in which Japan was developing her capital-goods industry as rapidly as any other country of the world, her agriculture was not only not deprived of resources but showed a rate of progress which, while maintaining domestic consumption, was able to provide its own capital formation for internal agricultural development. The example of India, during the fifties, illustrates the same point in a somewhat different context. Thus Japan and India have enabled industry and agriculture to advance together, while in the Soviet Union, and more recently in the People's Republic of China, agriculture has been denied the fruits of its output so that the process of heavy industrialization might proceed unchecked. The development of industrialization in Japan and India suggest that the hardships imposed by the process of industrialization in the Soviet Union and China are unnecessary.

Capital Goods and Consumer Goods

One of the most significant aspects of Soviet industrialization is, as we indicated above, the extent to which it has required that the people postpone indefinitely the enjoyment of consumer goods so that resources can be concentrated on the development of capital and producer goods. Since capital goods constitute the necessary base for consumer-goods industries, rapid industrialization requires that consumer satisfaction be subordinated to capital development in the short run. It is the *extent* rather than the fact of this subordination that is notable in the Soviet case. Notable too is the extent to which the industrial base has, over twenty-five or thirty years, been devoted to the development of armaments industries rather than durable consumer-goods industries. Examination of the steel and petroleum industries—to take but two examples— demonstrates that only an insignificant portion of increased production in these fields has been devoted to satisfying consumer needs for automobiles, washing machines, refrigerators, and similar commodities. It is sometimes argued that such products are durable "luxury" goods which the Soviet Union can ill afford in the light of its over-all industrial situation. This argument, however, at least implies a distinction between these "luxury" consumer goods and "essential" consumer goods, and suggests that the success of the system in providing for the needs of its citizens cannot appropriately be judged by the provision of consumer "luxuries." But if durable consumer goods cannot be made available to the vast masses of the Soviet population as they are to masses of Americans, one might justly expect that the high tempo of Soviet industrialization would have at least made available essential consumer goods for mass consumption on about the same scale as in the United States. This, of course, has not happened either in percentage terms or in per capita terms. The Soviet Union lags far behind the U.S. (and to a less dramatic extent, behind Western Europe) in almost every important phase of per capita consumer production and consumption. How, then, does it come about that the Soviet Union is considered a nation with an exceedingly advanced technology, particularly by the underdeveloped peoples? The answer is found in isolated but exceedingly well-publicized Soviet achievements.

The general picture of technological backwardness reflected in the figures from 1928 to 1955 has to some extent been reversed by the spectacular developments of Soviet science in the last four or five years. It is a fact that, so far as popular psychology in the underdeveloped countries is concerned, the impression left by the Sputniks, and by the great feats associated with the names of Major Yuri Gagarin and Major Gherman Titov have largely eliminated the feeling that the Soviet Union was technologically backward. The basis of this judgment was that the Soviet Union was first in the field of every great satellite achievement. While no credit should be denied to the Soviet space scientists and cosmonauts, the impression that spacemanship goes hand in hand with equal technological excellence everywhere is mistaken.

The index of Soviet industrialization is found not only in spacemanship but in a whole range of producer and consumer goods. Table II, which shows the growth of some essential consumer-goods industries in the Soviet Union from 1913 to 1961, indicates that there has indeed been spectacular progress. On the other hand, in certain essential fields such as cotton fabrics, wool fabrics, footwear, meat, sugar, vegetable oils, and paper, the Soviet Union in per capita consumption in 1961 lags far behind the United States. The footwear figure is still 2.2 per capita against a figure of over 3.3 in the United States; cotton fabrics are 29.5 meters against well over 83 meters in the United States. Wool fabrics are less than half, paper less than a tenth; vegetable oils less than half, and dairy products and meat less than half. There is no area of per capita production where the United States has not surpassed the Soviet Union. In other words, the tremendous technological advances which the Soviet Union has made in the last few years should not be interpreted by the underdeveloped countries to mean that Soviet industrialization has achieved for its people anything like the affluent society of the United States or the level of affluence of Western Europe.

It is quite true that many of the figures to which reference has been made are completely unpublicized and unknown, whereas the great feats in space have been dramatized. It is, therefore, quite difficult for the average man in the underdeveloped countries to get a true estimate of comparative industrial progress. On the whole, however, the free economy of the United States remains a much more successful provider of high consumption standards than the Soviet Union. Indeed, the Soviet leaders regard the U.S. as a model of affluence. The greatest imitator of the high consumption stage of industrialization is, in fact, Nikita Khrushchev, whose future plans are all slanted toward equaling United States levels of consumer-goods production. One should remember here that imitation is the sincerest form of flattery.

It must also be remembered that even while Khrushchev has been anxiously seeking to abolish United States ascendancy everywhere, he has been able to do little for Russian agriculture. Russian agricultural stagnation and the tremendous efficiency of American agriculture continue to provide the deepest contrast between the technology of America and that of the U.S.S.R.

Over-all, per capita consumption in the Soviet Union is only about one-fifth to one-seventh as great as personal consumption in the United States. Approximately the same findings have been obtained on comparative living standards by a crude comparison of real wages of nonagricultural workers in the two countries. It is again broadly estimated that per capita consumption or standard of living in the Soviet Union in general has only recently risen above the 1928 level, probably because the food and housing components have not registered appreciable qualitative improvement. This is partly confirmed by the trend of average real wages of Soviet urban workers; the relevant index for 1955 shows 82-119 before taxes as compared to the 1928 base of 100. This was because, while average money earnings had increased by 10.7 times during the period, cost of living had increased by 9-13 times. However, the real wages of a small class of workers—the Stakhanovites—should have undoubtedly been greater than they were. As money wages of other workers had not increased to the same extent as those of Stakhanovites, the real wages of the former should have been less than the 1955 index of 82-119. In other words, the higher real wages enjoyed by that privileged group of workers were obtained at the expense of the larger section of the industrial working class. If the Soviet system has considered it necessary to maintain this inequality in the matter of real wages in the urban and industrial sector, the inequality of wages between industrial workers and rural workers who are far less privileged can be easily inferred. The real wages of collective farm workers can thus be seen as comparatively lower than those of industrial workers in general.

Quite apart from the problem of real wages of industrial and agricultural workers is the burden of the turnover tax* on the entire Russian population. As a means of financing development, the turnover tax is probably the most oppressive instrument ever devised. The function of the tax is to provide the government with

---

* The turnover tax is a type of sales tax levied on a great many consumer goods at the source of production. It is collected on goods in relatively constant demand, including grain, alcohol, sugar, meat, cotton textiles, oil, and vegetable oil. In the mid-thirties, funds raised by the turnover tax amounted to roughly 70 per cent of the total budget, and have since declined to slightly under 50 per cent of the total income. The profits tax, which accounts for the second largest source of Soviet tax revenues, is also an indirect tax, ultimately paid by the consumer. Soviet reliance on indirect taxes on essential commodities of mass consumption apparently stems from their belief that this is the safest means of ensuring the reinvestment of a large portion of the national income in capital goods, and of mass regulating purchasing power. It is another irony of the Soviet system that indirect taxation, once denounced by Lenin as "the most unfair form of taxation," should be the keystone of the Soviet tax structure. (V. I. Lenin, "To the Rural Poor," *Selected Works*, Cooperative Publishing Society of Foreign Workers in the U.S.S.R., Moscow, 1934, Vol. II, p. 283.—Ed.)

the resources it requires while, at the same time, distorting the structure of consumption. Over and above this is the factor of price-fixing which is done in a manner that takes less account of the total welfare of the community than do orthodox principles of public finance. Between them, the turnover tax and the price mechanism of the Soviet Union ensure that the consumption needs of the Soviet population are not only not satisfied fully, but that real wages in terms of productivity and purchasing power are kept down for the population as a whole. From this point of view the Soviet industrial economy, however advanced it may be otherwise, is not as progressive as are other advanced industrial economies. Furthermore, as we have shown above, improvements in the economic welfare of the urban and industrial sections of the population have been bought at the expense of the rural and agricultural sector.

The Price Paid by Agriculture

In discussing the depressed condition of Soviet agriculture during the twenty-five years of hectic industrialization, a distinction has to be drawn between the price, if any, paid by the agricultural population and that paid by the agricultural economy. In a general sense industrialization was, of course, a boon to the agrarian economy inasmuch as it provided employment to vast numbers of surplus rural labor; in 1928 the agricultural population including handicraftsmen represented 74 per cent (123 million) of the total population, and in 1955 was just 42 per cent (84 million).

This boon was, however, secured at heavy cost by the technique of collectivization which crystallized a labor surplus and made it available to industry. The cost was nothing less than the lives of tens of thousands of landlords and kulaks, who were "liquidated" in the thirties. (Incidentally, this kind of price was also paid more recently in China where the entire process of land reform and collectivization involved the physical liquidation of between one and two million "landlords.") What is currently of no less importance is the price that the collective and state farm workers continue to pay by receiving less than a just share of the agricultural income.

The price paid by the agricultural economy, on the other hand, has been a retarded development. In a way, this too spells a lower standard of living for the agricultural population since it means not increasing the total income of this primary sector to a level to which a more balanced and democratic plan of development could certainly have raised it. In the absence of democratic solicitude for peasant welfare, Soviet agriculture has been subjected to an authoritarian and cruel method of development.

To say, however, that agriculture development was retarded does not, of course, mean either that some expansion has not taken place or some capital investments have not been made. The latter in particular provides the clue to the way agriculture was treated until the mid-fifties and is brought out in the table on the facing page.

It will be seen from these figures that investment in Soviet agriculture during the entire 1928-55 period constituted only one-seventh of all investments in the economy. Industry, on the other hand, accounted for more than half, and all other sectors for less than one-third of all investments during that period. In the end year 1955 (for which figures are not given separately in Table III) agriculture accounted for about 15 per cent, industry for about 50 per cent, and other sectors for about 35 per cent of all investments. In the first year 1928-29 (for which, again, figures are not given separately in Table III) agriculture accounted for one-tenth, industry for three-fourths, and other sectors for just under a sixth of all investments. (Incidentally, a comparison of the Soviet Second Plan's sectoral investments with those of India's Second Plan would be revealing. Under the Soviet Second Plan, agriculture accounted for 12 per cent, industry for 69 per cent, and other sectors for 19 per cent of all investments. Under India's Second Plan, on the other hand, agriculture accounted for 24 per cent, industry 36 per cent, and other sectors for 40 per cent of all investments in the public and private sectors together.)

The imbalance, thus seen, in sectoral investments in the Soviet

TABLE III

Investments in Billion Rubles
(in 1953 prices)

1	In agriculture (a) 2	In industry 3	In all other sectors 4	Total 5
First Plan period (beginning 1928)	6 (9.4)	49 (76.6)	9 (14.0)	64 (100)
Second Plan period	18 (12.0)	104 (69.3)	28 (18.7)	150 (100)
Third Plan period	24 (15.9)	87 (57.6)	40 (26.5)	151 (100)
War period	23 (15.5)	82 (55.6)	43 (28.9)	148 (100)
Fourth Plan period	51 (14.3)	186 (52.3)	119 (33.4)	356 (100)
Fifth Plan period ending 1955	99 (14.4)	357 (52.0)	231 (33.6)	687 (100)
Total for 1928-55	221 (14.2)	865 (55.6)	470 (30.2)	1,556 (100)

N.B.: Figures in parentheses are percentages of the totals in column 4.

(a) Cover investments by collective farms themselves and estimated state investments in state farms, machine-tractor stations, irrigation, etc. Figures may err somewhat on the high side.

Union needs to be set against the fact that gross agricultural product, as of 1955, amounted to three-fourths of gross industrial product. By and large, this imbalance is still continuing despite the fact that the relative share of agriculture in the total investment in the economy has increased somewhat from 12 per cent in the Second Plan period to 14.4 per cent in the Fifth Plan period (and somewhat further since then). A better insight into the extent to which Soviet agriculture is starved of adequate investment or contributes a surplus to the over-all pool of investible resources is, however, necessary if the certain ruthless exploitation to which the agricultural economy has been subjected is to be broadly measured.

A gross investment of the order of 169 billion rubles (in 1953 prices) in the entire economy in 1955 represented 28.5 per cent of gross national product (in 1953 prices). From this it can be calculated that gross national product was approximately 593 billion rubles in 1955. The agricultural sector's contribution to this gross national product was 172 billion rubles, while that of the industrial sector was 243 billion rubles. The gross investment in agriculture in that year was 25 billion rubles in 1953 prices as against a gross investment of 85 billion rubles in industry. Thus investment in the agricultural sector constituted 14.5 per cent of the gross agricultural product, whereas the investment in the industrial sector represented 35 per cent of the gross industrial product. Such a high rate of industrial investment could have been possible only because of a far lower rate of agricultural investment.

Suppose a more balanced structure of sectoral investments had been in operation, more or less as in India, with agriculture accounting for 25 per cent and industry for 33⅓ per cent of all investments. In that case, investment in the agricultural sector would have represented 24.4 per cent of the gross agricultural product and investment in the industrial sector would have constituted 23 per cent of the gross industrial product. Actually, however, the distortion or imbalance in the structure of sectoral investments means that Soviet agriculture has released for the industrial sector an investible surplus of about 10 per cent (24.4 per cent *minus* 14.5 per cent) of the gross agricultural product.

This means that the total burden on agriculture including reinvestment from its own resources must have been exceedingly heavy. It would thus appear that instead of industry releasing an investible surplus for agriculture (which in any underdeveloped economy has a very low margin—lower than in the secondary or the tertiary sector—for saving and investment on account of low farm incomes), a substantial surplus has been squeezed out of agriculture for investment in industry in the Soviet Union. This is precisely what is happening in Communist China where up to

20 per cent (including reinvestment) of the gross agricultural product is being squeezed out by way of taxes and discriminatory prices, as against 3 per cent or less by way of land revenue in India. In China, where the Soviet model has been followed, the surplus forced out of agriculture would not have been possible without collectivization and concomitant regimentation of the peasantry. The Soviet peasantry did not cheerfully pay the price. Neither has the Chinese peasantry. "It is doubtful," as Mr. Wolf Ladejinsky, an expert on agriculture and land reform, has said, "whether it [the Communist dictatorship] will find an answer to the only questions that matter: how to insure the loyalty of the peasants, and how to raise agricultural production with a peasantry lacking the incentive to produce." "The dogma persists," Mr. Ladejinsky continues, "that only Communist-controlled, collectivized agriculture can insure the progress of industrial development. . . . This dogma can survive only through continuous recourse to force. On the collectivized fields of Soviet Russia the Communists have practiced this for 27 years, and the struggle is still on."

Distributive Injustice

It is now possible to draw together the strands of the argument which has been developed in the preceding pages. It has been shown that the rate of industrial growth in the Soviet Union is among the highest in the world, and that over a period of time it is possible that this rate of growth will surpass all other performances in the industrial sector. On the other hand, the cost exacted increases with each acceleration of the pace of industry. In the First Five-Year Plan of the Soviet Union the price was doubly heavy; not only because of heavy industrialization in itself, but also because the Soviet Union built units so large that it was not possible for many years to use them up to capacity. The distribution of resources between capital and producer goods and consumer goods has never been appropriate, when account is taken of the fact that workers must be given incentives as well as distant goals to stimulate them to further efforts. In the Soviet Union incentives were provided by creating a privileged Stakhanovite group inside the privileged group of industrial workers; even so, there has been a far smaller improvement in the standard of living of industrial workers than the massive industrial program of the country would suggest. The withdrawal of comparable rewards from other workers, mostly those in agriculture and the non-secondary occupations, by the regulation of prices has meant that the real productivity of workers has never been sufficiently compensated. Even where personal incomes have risen (as they have over a large portion of the country) a substantial part went to compulsory saving, and by a pricing system designed to reduce the wages of workers below their average net productivity.

The point that the Soviet industrial system has been unfair not merely to agricultural workers but to the great majority of industrial workers is not often recognized; yet this constitutes one of the most cogent arguments in favor of a free economy with collective bargaining as a means for securing to the worker his fair share of gains in productivity. It can be shown in the United States and, indeed, in many other countries, including India, that the average rewards to organized labor are in conformity with productivity over a period of time. Where there are lags, as there are bound to be in particular industries, the machinery of collective bargaining with the possibility of workers resorting to a strike is generally sufficient to secure for the worker what might comprehensively be described as a "fair" deal. In the Soviet Union spectacular developments in industry have often been built on the exploitation of the worker who has no collective right to strike for higher wages. This is a strange development in a system designed to structure the whole economy to benefit the proletariat, which, under capitalism, in strict Marxist theory, is condemned to a progressively lower standard of living as population grows. One of the most important facts about Soviet industrialization is this: that distribution is less equitable and that the worker has fared less well than under free enterprise, or restricted enterprise in capitalist or democratic socialist countries. It is, in fact, in the field of production, and *not in the field of distribution,* that Soviet industry has excelled.

Postscript: *Japan and India*

A word should be added at this point on the alternatives to the Communist method of industrialization. It was mentioned, in passing, that over the long period, Japan offered a pattern of industrialization in no way inferior in performance to that of the Soviet Union and in the short period (from 1952 onward) performance in the Indian Union showed that totalitarianism is not necessary for a high rate of industrial growth. The basic strength of Japan's industrialization lay in efficient organization. Japan's great deficiency in raw materials was made good by a supremely efficient export drive which enabled her to win the foreign exchange necessary for rapid industrialization. At the same time, the rate of internal saving was so high that domestic resources were available even earlier. The Zaibatsu employed centralized banking as part of an industrial organization to exploit free financial resources. All in all, one might look upon the performance of Japanese industry, particularly in the period 1913 to 1924 when Japan's rate of economic progress is generally admitted to have been of the order of 7 per cent per year, as being supremely efficient. Judged by its capacity to advance and to overcome stupendous natural obstacles, the Communist system cannot be deemed exceptional. One matter of great interest in this connection is the way in which Japan's economic growth was harnessed to agriculture.*

* *Cf.* G. C. Allen's *Japan's Economic Recovery,* page 51, where the following observation is made:

Japan's economic progress in the modern era is commonly associated with the rise of industry and the appearance of a large foreign trade in manufactured and semi-manufactured products. Yet, as in other countries that have passed through an industrial revolution, the growth of the secondary industries was accompanied by far-reaching changes in agriculture. The nature of the industrial development cannot be understood without reference to these changes, since the present condition of manufacturing

In the case of India, the rate of industrial growth in organized industry in the last decade has been roughly 8 per cent per year which, at least until 1955, was somewhat higher than that of the People's Republic of China. Larger claims have subsequently been made for the People's Republic of China, but enough has been said about the reasons for advance in industry to show that it does not provide an acceptable model for the Indian Union or any other underdeveloped country which is unwilling to sacrifice its rural population or its political freedom. The exploitation of Chinese agriculture by a high rate of taxation and forced levies has meant that China has more capacity for investment per capita than the Indian Union. But what has been gained in industrialization is lost in agriculture, and it may well be argued that no underdeveloped country in Southeast Asia would be prepared to accept the level of agricultural taxation or forced levies now enforced in the People's Republic.

3. CONCLUSION

We have argued that while there have been spectacular achievements in Soviet industry and grounds for believing that Soviet performance can be maintained at an extremely high level, the burdens imposed on the entire economy are not commensurate with the advantages obtained. This is not only because of totalitarian methods which, in addition to being oppressive, are often wasteful, but also because the satisfaction of consumers' demand both in agriculture and industry implies that resources be made available not by a process of abstinence, but by a process of fulfillment. It is the strength of the free economies that they thus do not need to place an unjust burden on any section of the community whilst the process of industrialization is under way. Agriculture, industry,

---

trades, their organization, the structure of wages, and the pattern of industrial relations, has been powerfully influenced by the circumstances of the rural economy.

and tertiary occupations grow together in a manner which gives every section of the community a stake in progress, with the result that industrialization creates no internal political strains such as those in the satellite countries and in the People's Republic of China. Mao's "Let a thousand flowers bloom" speech of February 1957 is the most eloquent commentary on the burdens of heavy industrialization on the agricultural population.

Soviet industrialization is a process which must necessarily be spectacular in the area on which resources are concentrated, though even here the fruits of industrial performance are very poorly distributed. But it cannot be anything but tyrannical in the area of agriculture. Tertiary occupations appear to stand betwixt and between; but, by and large, the rate of development by these occupations is lower than it would be in a free economy such as that of Britain or of the United States.

While, therefore, underdeveloped countries might from time to time look with envy on the spectacular rate of industrial growth in the Union of Soviet Socialist Republics and the People's Republic of China, they need to take into account the burden on the rest of the economy—a burden about which far too little has been said in current literature on the problem of economic growth in these countries. It is, however, clear, as the example of Poland will show, that there are strict limits on the capacity of industry to exploit agriculture even under totalitarian conditions. There is, therefore, an added political liability in the destruction of participation of those engaged in agriculture and some tertiary occupations in national development while heavy industrialization is under way. Thus there are not only good economic reasons for underdeveloped economies to avoid Soviet methods; there are also clear political limits beyond which they cannot be employed.

A final word should be said about these political limits. In most of the countries of Southeast Asia and Africa, the arrival of the people to political sovereignty has had a spiritual, as well as a material, component. The right to vote against the ruling party is conceived as a high political benefit of the revolutions which have transferred power from civil servants or bureaucrats to the representatives of the people. In this sense the Soviet pattern of economic development which transfers authority to bureaucrats from the people is conceived as a retrograde measure nullifying its political counterpart; that is, it negates the spiritual character of the revolution which was designed to liberate and not to enslave the people. Thus it is that, notwithstanding the tremendous attractions of a rapid rate of industrial growth to the underdeveloped regions of Southeast Asia or Africa, the Communist party still finds it difficult to secure working majorities even in countries like Indonesia which are torn by factions and provide large scope for subversive activities. The arguments against the Soviet system of industrialization are both spiritual and material. The Soviet Union denies to large populations their fundamental political rights and also deprives many of a share of the benefits of industrialization. The system provides no benefits great enough to warrant the loss of basic liberties and a sense of participation in rising standards of living. At present, the battle of ideas is contained within the limits of sacrifice—political and economic—which the people of the underdeveloped countries are prepared to make. That is the decisive point and, in the opinion of those who have lived through the revolutions in Southeast Asia, it may well be the decisive factor in the rejection of the Soviet way of life in the uncommitted world.

STUDENTS, INTELLECTUALS AND "THE CHINESE REVOLUTION"

Richard L. Walker

■ Once we have freed ourselves of the assumption that Communist parties are necessarily or even regularly composed of and supported by the working classes or even the poorest people, the question arises, Who then are its leaders and followers? This question must be answered empirically for each country. In the following essay, Richard Walker, a well-known expert on China and Chinese Communism, examines the "important—in some ways decisive—role" of Chinese students and intellectuals in the Communist movement in China.

This group, which is the catalyst of social change in many underdeveloped areas, adopted the typically Western values of national independence, unity, and equality. In the name of these values it opposed Western domination and privilege on the one hand, and traditional indigenous authority on the other. Their distance from the traditionalist masses, and the problems of administering the government, left Chinese intellectuals and students particularly susceptible to Utopian politics. Utopian politics thrives in abstraction: it lives off slogans and impatience. The world of Utopian politics is a world of possibility: disciplined only by logic, limited only by imagination and intellect. Compared to values and symbols organically related to a concrete culture, the values and symbols of Utopian politics are highly susceptible to manipulation by demagogues.

In China, the Communist party successfully captured the symbols of nationalism and progress, and the support of a large portion of Chinese intellectuals and students. Most of those whom it did not capture, it neutralized. The importance of this propaganda victory to the loss of mainland China can hardly be overestimated.

In the following essay, Professor Walker, head of the Department for International Studies at the University of South Carolina, makes a plea for recognizing the crucial importance of intellectuals in underdeveloped countries, and for more critical analysis of massive abstractions by intellectuals—Western and non-Western. Professor Walker has written widely on China and Chinese Communism. His books include China Under Communism (1955) and The Continuing Struggle. He is also a regular contributor to a number of scholarly and political journals. ∎

Let us hold our heads low today. A small country on our border has paid the ultimate penalty for its temerity to aspire for independence. Tibet is dead and much else could die with Tibet if we do not now heed the warning.

Thus cautioned the *Hindustan Times,* organ of the Congress party in India, March 30, 1959. The "Rape of Tibet" here referred to was the act that brought to a culmination the disillusionment of Asian intellectuals with the Communist regime in China and with Communism in general. Prior to this attack on India, there were many other events which contributed to the growing doubts of Asian political and intellectual leaders. Among them were: the drastic antirightist movement which followed Mao Tse-tung's encouragement of criticism of his regime in the spring of 1957; the militarization of the Chinese countryside and accompanying forced resettlement of students and intellectuals; the crackdown on all religious groups; the attack on the Chinese family represented by the people's communes in 1958; the serious and open rift in the Sino-Soviet alliance in 1959, and finally, the Sino-Indian border dispute.

Yet there remains in China and other Asian countries an emotional and romantic attachment to the "New China" and "The

Chinese Revolution" which the West must understand and reckon with. Even the confessions in 1957 of the leaders of all eight minor parties in the "United Front" (China's intellectuals) have failed to shake this commitment to Mao's China.

The world's negative reaction to some of China's policies and actions probably does not cause mainland China's leaders as much concern as liberals in general might hope. These Communist leaders have continued to trade on the short memory of the past. They know that their achievements in China are of a nature which appeal to the masses, particularly among the literate, in underdeveloped and former colonial areas of the world. Their successes encourage a glossing over of past history and of the less desirable aspects of Communist rule in China.

The goals which have had the greatest appeal to the underdeveloped areas are national unity, equality with the West, and national independence. These goals are usually conceived of as linked together mystically in the term "The Revolution." Such goals as higher living standards, human rights, democracy, or industrialization have had less attraction in areas where Western power or domination had gone unchallenged for a long time. Although after "the Rape of Tibet," leaders in India, Burma, and Ceylon began to ponder the price in human terms of the Communist path to either revolution or development, one cannot underestimate Communist China's simultaneous growth in strength and confidence vis-à-vis the West. Indeed, Mao and his cohorts may be quite accurate in calculating that the people's communes in 1958 or the "Rape of Tibet" in 1959 or food shortages in the 1960's will not weigh too heavily in the long-run future.

The Chinese Communists have frequently stated that their pattern for the seizure and consolidation of power and economic development is the classical model for underdeveloped and formerly colonial areas. For this reason alone the lessons of China are important for all of the world, but in the years ahead they are likely to prove especially significant for the newly independent countries where the Chinese have offered guidance and urged acceptance of their regime. The three keys to success, according to Mao, are the

Leninist party, armed struggle, and correct policy on the united front.[1]

There have been many interpretations of the long road by which the Communists came to power in China. Some interpretations stress the role of warfare, some stress internal economic and political forces, some the role of the Soviet Union or Stalin's "grand strategy," and still others, the policies of the United States. These diverse interpretations have led to protracted and often petty arguments among the outside observers of modern China. Far too little attention has been paid to the important—and in some cases, decisive—role of the students and intellectuals.

Since Mao and his colleagues believe in China's future as a revolutionary model for the "backward countries" (to use Lenin's term),[2] it is important that attention be drawn to the unique role of the intellectuals and students in these underdeveloped areas and their crucial function in united front strategems. Given the existence of chronic mass poverty and limited opportunity among two-thirds of the earth's people, the "intellectual" within such societies is frequently defined simply as one who can read and write. Because literacy is a prerequisite for any significant administrative position, the intellectuals have been involved in the processes of government, and have been the chief communicators within their societies. Those few who have had the opportunity for education abroad, although often strangers to their own people, are looked up to as leaders in their nations' development. Although some intellectuals have preferred to remain uninvolved in the great ideological currents which have swept the earth since the end of the First World War, most are sensitive to the past humiliations of their country and are desirous of national independence and stature in the modern world.

In their attempts to accommodate their own traditional modes

1 On Communist China as a model see the very prescient article by A. M. Halpern, "The Foreign Policy Uses of the Chinese Revolutionary Model," *The China Quarterly* (London), No. 7, July-September 1961, pp. 1-16.
2 Lenin, "Preliminary Draft of Theses on the National and Colonial Questions," *Selected Works*, Foreign Languages Publishing House, Moscow, Vol. II, Part 2, p. 469.

of life with the new technological civilization, the literate few in the underdeveloped lands are generally fragmented in their political views. The only unifying element among them has been nationalistic fervor. The intellectuals—and particularly those with Western training—have naturally transmitted their ardent nationalistic ideals to the students. Because of their opportunities for the new learning and their extreme nationalism, the students on many occasions have served as tools for organized group expression led by intellectual reformers and activists. Thus the intellectuals and students have tended to be a key group in the political life of societies striving to adjust to the technological age. It must be noted that these efforts of students and intellectuals have been on the whole located in the large ports and urban centers influenced by the West. Too often "the people" of these cultures whom the intellectuals claim to represent are an inchoate mass, totally unaware of the sweeping demands and claims made for them by the articulate minority.

It was to this group—certainly not an economically definable class in the Marxist sense—that Lenin and his fellow leaders of the Comintern turned to organize the Communist movement in China and the colonial countries. Although agonizing attempts were made to fit (or distort) Marxism and the Marxist class analysis to the Chinese scene, the appeal that guaranteed the most unified and enthusiastic response from the intellectuals was nationalism and anti-imperialism. The preoccupation of Chinese intellectuals and students with these highly emotive goals led them to enter into three United Fronts with Communism, although many did not accept the Communist system and ideology as valid for China.

A United Front in a land like China was of a special nature in that the basis for unity bore relatively little relationship neither to specific social or economic policies nor to the politics of trade unions or political party activities. In many respects what existed in China was neither a United Front from above nor below in the classical Communist application of the term to Europe. It was actually a national front of all those who agreed on complete national independence and anti-imperialism, and the active leaders were the intellectuals and students—a group which has always defied categorization within the Marxist class framework.

An indication of how strong the resentment of Western imperial privilege was in China is the fact that many Chinese intellectuals and students were willing to come back despite the sacrifice of their integrity for a second and third attempt at a United Front with the Communists. They expressed the final tragedy of their lack of freedom during the "Hundred Flowers Campaign" in 1957 by the following phrase, "the intellectuals are in agony." [3]

Although one can generalize about the position of the intellectuals in all the underdeveloped lands, it is necessary to stress the special importance attached to students and intellectuals in China. There was, of course, the strong Chinese tradition which linked political power to the *shen-shih*, or gentry. This elite group had derived its position essentially from its relative monopoly of learning in a very difficult written language and from its ability to deal with politics within the framework of the Confucian tradition which was embodied in that language. For almost two thousand years prior to the twentieth century, the literati, including students, had occupied a unique position in Chinese politics. This position did not depend on wealth in property or possessions but rather on their qualifications as scholars, on their intellectual standing and resultant position in the bureaucracy, frequently bringing about wealth and property. Thus, within the Chinese tradition, the intellectuals were almost a class apart, and by definition also the political leaders. The policies of the Chinese Communists have consistently reflected the importance they attach to the intellectual and the unique role of the literati in China. [4]

[3] For an eloquent treatment of the fate of the intellectuals under the regime of Mao Tse-tung, with original documents, see Roderick MacFarquhar, *The Hundred Flowers*, New York, Praeger, 1961.

[4] The definitive work on the Chinese gentry, stressing the fact that their wealth was dependent on their position, is Chang Chung-li, *The Chinese Gentry*, Seattle, University of Washington Press, 1955. On Communist appreciation of the intellectuals, see *Peking's United Front*, China Viewpoints, Hong Kong, 1957.

The gradual impact of the West, the breakup of China's traditional unity, the increased power of regional warlords in the late
nineteenth century, and particularly the defeat of China by a
Westernized Japan in 1894-1895, contributed to the response of
students and intellectuals to the restoration of China to its leading
role in Asia. The Chinese, whose very culture made them chauvinistic, were ready for the nationalistic movement, and by the turn
of the century thousands had joined in denouncing the vested
interests—local and international—which divided their country.
Those who were the purveyors of Western science, technology, and
political ideas rose to new positions of stature and influence. The
early years of the century were characterized by the search for new
principles of authority to replace the discredited and weakened
structure of the Confucian state. Scientism, anarchism, pragma-
tism, and other new systems of thought circulated among the Chinese intellectuals.

The man who eventually precipitated the Chinese Revolution,
Dr. Sun Yat-sen, had received financial and moral support from
many of the foreign-trained intellectuals, especially the students in
Japan. His Revolution of 1911, however, brought none of the
achievements which he had promised. The phantom "Chinese"
republic set up in Peking only invited further pressures from
abroad, and the consolidation of power of regional military leaders (backed by foreign states) seemed to prepare for the eventual
breakup of China. All of this occasioned disillusionment, bitterness, and an attitude approaching desperation among the new intellectuals in China. Many among them began to write and agitate
from points of safety within the international settlements. In response to the fragmentation and humiliation of their country, the
demands and goals of the intellectuals became more uncompromising, their willingness to resort to violence was reinforced, and their
actions pointed toward a complete revolutionary overthrow of
former social and political patterns.

There was no general agreement among these Chinese intellectuals as to revolutionary method. Many who had maintained close

contacts with the countries where they had received advanced education advocated solutions to China's problems that reflected the political ideas of those foreign countries. But by the end of World War I they were practically unanimous in asserting that China needed a new and thoroughgoing revolution which would bring national unity and strength as well as the complete elimination of foreign privileges in their land. Anything less would be tantamount to betrayal.

The key importance of Chinese intellectuals and students and the power of their position in the modern period became patently clear at the Paris Peace Conference in 1919 in China's reaction to the West's concessions to Japan. The intellectual body led nationwide demonstrations, known from the date of their inception as the May Fourth Movement, to which, within a month, practically all the major cities in China had responded. Chinese negotiators at Paris, who had actually given good account of themselves but had been presented with a *fait accompli*, were denounced by Chinese intellectuals as national traitors. The movement in its active form involved not only student strikes and protest marches, but elicited support in form of sympathetic labor walkouts and cooperation by industrialists and businessmen. It was, in many respects, the first full-fledged manifestation of how powerful a force nationalism had become in modern China.

But the May Fourth Movement, a term which later came to characterize the general intellectual and social ferment from 1917 to 1921, also demonstrated how crucial the leadership of the new intellectuals was to be in modern China. It brought into the foreground an uncompromising enthusiasm and even "radicalism" on the part of the Chinese youth, dramatized the disillusionment with the Western powers and illustrated the opportunities for political agitation. Despite later Communist claims to leadership in the May Fourth Movement, it was essentially a spontaneous response, and not under the management of any political group or groups. The period symbolized by the term "May Fourth Movement" was characterized by a literary and cultural renaissance which served also to reveal the importance of the intellectuals. There was a climate of intellectual and cultural enthusiasm and expectancy which persisted for more than two decades.[5]

It was at this point that Lenin and the Soviet leaders turned to China and addressed themselves primarily to the new intellectual leadership. The timing and nature of their action disclosed their awareness of the dynamics of the Chinese scene and of the position of the literati in the power structure of the future. The Russian Revolution of 1917 had already stirred some interest among the Chinese, only months after the May Fourth Movement, when Lenin's vice-commissar of foreign affairs, Lev Karakhan, announced that the Soviet government unilaterally gave back to China all territories, rights, and privileges seized by the Czarist government. The response was enormous. Enthusiastic groups in Peking and Shanghai found Marxism and its application in Russia a new principle of authority for China; they could not be expected to be overly critical in their assessment of Soviet promises and how they were carried out.

The Soviets quickly attached conditions to their former "unconditional" offer (in fact, they denied the existence of the original text, even though copies showed up). They signed a secret treaty with Mongolia on November 5, 1921, detaching that area from China. But despite other similar items in Chinese relations with the new Soviet state, representatives from Moscow received a rousing welcome from many students and intellectual leaders in Peking during the early twenties. This was the group to which Lenin, and later Stalin, looked, to bring about a Communist seizure of

[5] Chow Tse-tsung, *The May Fourth Movement, Intellectual Revolution in Modern China,* Harvard University Press, 1960. Chow's work is necessary background for an understanding of the many currents which have persisted into the present. It lays the ghost of most of the recent Communist claims that Mao was one of the key leaders of the movement, and does so convincingly. A good companion volume is Kiang Wen-han, *The Chinese Student Movement,* King's Crown Press, Morningside Heights, New York, 1948. Its fourth chapter on united-front tactics for the second united front in China stresses some of the Communist tactics which were being repeated while the book was being written. See also Li Chien-Nung, *The Political History of China,* translated by Ssu-yu Teng and Jeremy Ingalls, Van Nostrand, 1956, pp. 436-505; and Chiang Monlin, *Tides from the West,* Yale University Press, 1947.

power in China. There was much talk and disagreement later as to the role of the almost nonexistent Chinese proletariat and of the peasantry, particularly during the period of the Stalin-Trotsky feud. But from the outset, Communism has been led by a group of intellectuals, and the further direction of the movement remains in their hands. Talk of self-conscious economic classes in China was little more than tactical verbiage by which these Moscow-inspired intellectuals justified their drive to power.

In his approach to the Chinese intellectuals Lenin appealed to the same emotions they had expressed in the May Fourth Movement. Moscow's leaders presented Communism primarily in terms of an anti-imperialist movement and promised that through Communist leadership China could become strong and independent. Lenin's pat theory of imperialism offered to many Chinese a simple and understandable explanation of Western behavior both at Paris and at the Washington Conference of 1921-1922. It explained Western privileges in China, and later it offered a seemingly convincing means of viewing Japanese aggression against China. Within the Leninist framework the Chinese Communists could join in a united front with the bourgeoisie and other patriotic groups in the revolution against imperialism. But Lenin was careful to state that "under modern international conditions there is no salvation for dependent and weak nations except in a union of Soviet republics" [6] (1920). A United Front in China or in other colonial areas was regarded by Moscow from the outset only as a temporary expedient which would enable the group of Communist-indoctrinated leaders to take over at a later date. A most important doctrinal facet for such countries as China was the presentation of a two-camp conception of the world with the Soviet Union as the leader of the anti-imperialist forces.

[6] Lenin, *Selected Works*, Vol. II, Part 2, p. 469. Soviet strategy is discussed in David Dallin, *Soviet Russia and the Far East*, Yale University Press, 1948; Robert C. North, *Moscow and Chinese Communists*, Stanford University Press, 1953; Conrad Brandt, *Stalin's Failure in China*, Harvard University Press, 1958; and Benjamin I. Schwartz, *Chinese Communism and the Rise of Mao*, Harvard University Press, 1951. Schwartz stresses the leadership of the Communist movement by the intellectuals.

The development and application of Marxist theory played an important part in the leftward swing of many Chinese in the 1920's and the next two decades. But perhaps equally important was the leadership offered by the Soviet Union and the application in China of Leninist organizational and propaganda techniques that had proved so successful in Russia. It was Stalin who had provided the organization and assistance for the reunification of China under Chiang Kai-shek, Sun Yat-sen's successor, during the first united front, 1923-1927. And it was that first United Front which was to set the bitter tone of division and strife in China for more than three decades. The Chinese people were to be the losers.

Despite the maneuvering of Soviet policies and shifts in the military fortunes of the Nationalist and Communist factions which followed the breakup of the first front in 1927, the Communist leadership gave constant attention to the organization of the young intellectuals in China. The more these groups came into conflict with the established government, the more uncompromising their demands became, and the more willing they were to follow the Communist leadership, which was the most unrestrained political group in its denunciation of the government.

Civil war, continued foreign privilege, appalling poverty, and economic dislocation inspired an impressive literature of protest during the 1930's, especially in Shanghai and Peiping, which also took a turn to the left, especially after the Japanese takeover in Manchuria in 1931. Writers, artists, professors, and students more and more encouraged developments that aided the Communist cause in China, particularly during the agitation from 1932 to 1937. And this period led to the creation of the second front in the fight against Japan and in the 1945-1949 mass movement against civil war and dissatisfaction with the Nationalists. In these two periods the slogans shouted by students, their methods of organization, the terms of denunciation, and the exploitation of contacts with Western leftist and liberal groups are all markedly similar. But the intellectual climates of the two periods were quite different; and in the second the absence of belief among students and intellectuals in the Nationalist government made possible their ultimate submission to Communist united-front tactics.

During the period just before the formation of a second united front in 1937, the Chinese intellectuals were almost as fragmented as they had been during the May Fourth Movement. There was a general atmosphere of irritation over the continuing civil war between Nationalists and Communists in the face of Japanese encroachments. Some leading scholars like Weng Wen-hao, the geologist, joined the Nationalist government, breaking a tacit compact among many elder scholars not to get embroiled in politics. Others joined pro-Communist groups such as the League of Leftist Writers, not sharing the cautious optimism that had begun to pervade the Nationalist capital of Nanking by 1935 following the major achievements by the Kuomintang government. But many of the leading intellectuals preferred a total isolation, regarding themselves as a liberal third force though they lacked both the party and the military organization of their Nationalist and Communist contenders.[7]

Again in 1935, the combined forces of nationalism and anti-imperialism made possible a united front, this time directed against the Japanese. The Communists, not hampered by the formal responsibilities of a legitimate government, were able to make better use of student enthusiasm and the aroused patriotism of the Chinese. They made meaningless declarations of war upon the Japanese, and their call in 1935 for the cessation of civil war and an anti-Japanese united front was destined to find support among many academics, who, no matter how divorced from politics, still thought in terms of the mystique of "The Chinese Revolution" which would bring power, unity, and elimination of foreign privilege in the Middle Kingdom. These intellectuals, through their Western contacts, related the developments in China to the worldwide drive for a united front.

Notwithstanding the Communists' anti-Japanese program in the initial years of resistance following the Japanese attack on July 7, 1937, the forces of patriotism supported the Nationalist govern-

[7] See Carsun Chang, *The Third Force in China*, New York, 1952.

ment. But the long war, which eliminated the best of the Nationalist forces, at length produced lowered morale, corruption, inflation, dislocation, and growing Nationalist-Communist friction.[8] Despite American efforts to prevent it, the civil war broke out again after World War II, and by this time Communist appeals to the students and intellectuals proved strong enough that by early 1949 many were willing to enter a third United Front.[9] The Communist regime which was proclaimed on October 1, 1949, was presented as an alliance of "democratic parties" under the leadership of the Communists.

Chow Ching-wen, one of the major leaders of the new "People's Republic," and a member of one of the minor parties, escaped to Hong Kong eight years later to tell of the agony of the intellectuals. He notes, "Looking back upon those days, the democratic parties and groups seemed incredibly naïve and innocent. But in contrast to the measures the Nationalist government was taking to suppress the people, the bait set out by the Communists seemed attractive indeed." [10] Chow goes on to state, "But I was powerless to do anything for my people in the eight years I was supposedly a member of the regime. I discovered too late that I had been deceived by the CC (Chinese Communists)." [11]

How had the forces loosed by Lenin in China been able to deceive so many Chinese intellectuals? One reason was the Communists' singleness of purpose and organizational ability. Another reason has been discussed by the British economist E. S. Kirby. In a chapter entitled "The Deep Roots of Chinese Marxism" in his *Introduction to the Economic History of China,* he observes, "It may be asserted that in the field of intellectual endeavor, the fate of China was decided—as between Communism and Nationalism

---

[8] The importance of the early decimation of Nationalist forces in the early Japanese attacks for later developments is stressed by F. F. Liu in his important A *Military History of Modern China, 1924-1949,* Princeton University Press, 1956, pp. 143 ff.

[9] A brief outline of the three United Fronts is given by Chow Ching-wen in his *Ten Years of Storm,* Holt, Rinehart and Winston, New York, 1960, pp. 22-49.

[10] Chow Ching-wen, pp. 36-37.

[11] *Ibid.,* p. 41.

—not just recently, but about twenty years ago. It was in the early 1930's that Kuomintang Nationalism failed, in the judgment of the educated and active Chinese, to give ideological satisfaction or mental stimulation." [12] Kirby points out the importance of the interrelations between Chinese and Western intellectuals and the response of many of the Chinese to Marxist interpretations of events in China as well as in the West. He also underscores the importance of intellectual currents as a weighty factor in developments in China.

There can be little argument about the powerful, though not official, position of the Chinese intellectuals and students. Mao's government still sees fit to maintain the fiction that they and their minor parties participate in the mainland regime. But there is another aspect of the United Front strategy and its relation to intellectuals and students which deserves attention in analyzing the Chinese situation as a model for other underdeveloped lands. This is the concept of "The Revolution" which assumed an almost mystical and sacred quality in the language of the new literati. The lessons to be learned from China's use of this term relate crucially to the demands and expectations of intellectuals in other areas of the world today. The mystique of "The Revolution" proved of decisive importance in the deception of the Cuban intellectuals some ten years after the Communists came to power in China, and the Chinese pattern was repeated in the way in which outside observers of Cuba were deceived. The relation of the concept of "The Revolution" to the operation of the united front should be recognized by Western interpreters whose opinions are more widely studied by intellectuals of underdeveloped areas than is usually appreciated.

Lenin had warned in 1920 that the Communists should constantly "explain and expose among the broadest masses of the toilers of all the countries and particularly of the backward countries, the deception systematically practiced by the imperialist powers in

[12] E. S. Kirby, *Introduction to the Economic History of China*, George Allen and Unwin, London, 1954, Chapter III.

creating under the guise of politically independent states, states which are wholly dependent upon them economically, financially and militarily." [13] Thus, within the Communist program, no revolution could be complete until it brought a break with the past and with the Western capitalist countries. Today, the doctrine of incomplete national revolution is being pushed forcefully in areas of the Middle East, Africa, and Latin America, especially among student and intellectual groups, in the same manner which proved so effective in China. In fact, in these areas, Chinese Communist representatives now assert overtly the importance of their experience as the pattern. Many parallels can be drawn between the writings of *pensadores* and the activities of the students in present-day Latin America, and those features in the 1930's in China.

A glance at a bookshelf devoted to modern Chinese history will uncover an astonishing number of titles containing the expression *Chung-kuo-ke-ming*, "The Chinese Revolution." Yet for each author the phrase carries an entirely different meaning: its content is emotional as well as intellectual, general and specific, long-run and short-run, Marxist and nationalist. What immediately becomes apparent from examining these volumes is that there are many categories encompassed by the term.

To begin with, the phrase "The Chinese Revolution" usually includes many diverse historical forces and changes, some triggered by the arrival of Western technology in China, others that were already on the Chinese scene. The phrase includes the overthrow of an alien dynasty as well as the traditional Chinese political system, the Nationalist seizure of power in 1927, the development of industry and commerce, changes in the educational system, improvements in transportation and communication, an emerging new social status for women, as well as the phenomenal growth of the Chinese population. In other words, the term has been used to describe the over-all and rapid transformation of Chinese society, politics, and even the Chinese landscape.

Second, the phrase "The Chinese Revolution" has usually em-

13 Lenin, *op. cit.*, p. 469.

braced a set of different goals which seemed to offer direction for this transformation in Chinese society. These goals, many of them importations from the West, proved rather intoxicating ideals when combined and seemed to offer a simple solution for the pressing problems of modern China. From their training in the West, the Chinese students derived an appreciation of the power gained by Germany and Italy through unification. In their study at Western universities they also discovered the goals and ideals of the French philosophies. The developing vogue of Marxist literature following the Bolshevik Revolution provided yet another source of knowledge.

The new Chinese literati, particularly the students during the May Fourth Movement, drawing on what they had learned abroad, raised a set of goals which soon became near absolutes in their concept of "The Chinese Revolution." As indicated above, these included: (1) *unity*. This meant an orderly national administration with a single national army and an end to civil war with the government commanding the loyalty of all the Chinese people. Unity was expected to aid in the achievement of a second goal: (2) *sovereignty*. This meant equality with the nations of the West, the elimination of all vestiges of imperial privilege and especially the hated unequal treaties. It also meant the restoration of dignity and respect for China in world councils. (3) *Democracy* was yet another goal linked with the others. To some intellectuals it meant the liberal Enlightenment, to others it came to stand for a Marxist version of socialism. Still another aim raised in the name of the Chinese Revolution was: (4) *stability*. Looking back on the disruptions of the past century, many Chinese intellectuals legitimately contended that political and economic stability was a prior condition for the fulfillment of their goals.

Inevitably there was also a strong emotional dimension in the notion of "The Chinese Revolution." Moreover, the whole concept acquired an aura of inevitability; the goals became as inexorable as the changes to which they were linked. Both Chinese and Westerners used this term "The Chinese Revolution" as a substitute for rigorous analysis and talked convincingly about "The Unfinished Revolution in China," to quote the title of a 1946 pro-Chinese Communist interpretation of events.[14]

This conceptual vagueness caused many intellectuals who should have given rational consideration to the possible improvement of China to find themselves emotionally involved in destructive criticism. Some who urged caution at critical moments were roundly denounced by the younger firebrands, who held up absolutes as a basis for judgment. For example, Hu Shih and Dr. John Leighton Stuart were both singled out for denunciation by Chinese student groups when they urged moderation and pointed to the dangers of destructive agitation in the fall of 1947.

Although influenced by their Western education, probably not many Chinese intellectuals pondered Edmund Burke's warnings on the French Revolution. Burke had pointed out that against the absolute goals of the French radicals (goals such as the Chinese were to raise a century and a half later in the name of "The Chinese Revolution") no government could look for security or stability in its "length of continuance." With regard to the intellectuals who held such absolute goals, Burke said, "In the groves of *their* academy, at the end of every vista, you see nothing but the gallows." The English defender of the American revolt pointed out that only a completely authoritarian control could provide a bulwark against the instabilities and dissatisfactions attending a revolution conducted in such absolute terms. Given the attitudes stemming from the early days of the Chinese student movement, it would have been optimistic to expect that students under the direction of Communist intellectuals would listen to such voices of caution.

The experience of the Chinese Nationalist government in the years 1927-1937 is in many ways illustrative of Burke's comments. Sun Yat-sen, who had understood Comintern intentions and denied the suitability of Marxism for China, had nevertheless in his agreement of 1923 justified the Chinese Communist party's use

14 Israel Epstein, *The Unfinished Revolution in China*, Little, Brown, 1947.

of the term "The Chinese Revolution." [15] Because the Chinese Communists conceived of "The Revolution" as a complete process leading to a socialist state in alliance with the Soviet Union, they were in the forefront in pointing out that the goals were being compromised. In fact, they accused any regime compromising on these absolute goals of betraying the cause to which so great an emotional attachment had been given. In the years 1927-1937 this was a major factor contributing to the destructive criticism of the Nationalist government—a criticism which came from those very people who might have been making formative contributions to China's future. This was also the period that Marxism was sending roots deep into the nonpolitical aspects of the Chinese intellectual scene in their interpretations of Chinese history (Kuo Mo-jo), literature (Lu Hsun, Mao Tun), and drama (Ts'ao Yu). The very considerable achievements of the Nationalists were undermined not only by the havoc wrought by the Japanese but by student and leftist political agitation and continued demands based on absolute goals.

A few examples should suffice to illustrate the point. The Nanking government reached agreements with the Western powers which resulted in its recognition. But some of these very Western powers had extraterritorial rights in China, rights which the Nationalists had neither the power nor the position to contest in their early years. Although Nanking had made gains such as complete tariff autonomy by 1930, given the Communist demand for unconditional sovereignty, its agreements with the former imperialist powers were denounced as a "betrayal."

Or again, once the Communists had been excluded from positions under the Nationalist regime, they could claim that the government was not democratic and, further, that without their participation there could be no unity. On these two scores also, the government of the Kuomintang, based on the theory of political tutelage and democratic centralism, was betraying "The Chinese

---

[15] For a good treatment of Sun Yat-sen and his views on Communism, see Leng Shao-chuan and Norman D. Palmer, *Sun Yat-sen and Communism*, Praeger, 1960.

Revolution." In addition to the charges of the Marxists, many ardent Chinese nationalists felt that too many compromises had been made with goals they had attached to the social changes occurring in China.

Well-organized Communist propaganda during the 1927-1937 period held some appeal for the ardent Nationalists. The Communist regime, which maintained its own army, territorial base, and claims to sovereignty, promised achievement to the Chinese people where the Nationalists had compromised. The Communists did not have the responsibility of dealing with the foreign powers and could count on a favorable presentation in the international leftist press. When they declared war on the Japanese following the Manchurian incident, student groups, impressed by this call to arms, understandably did not pause and consider that there was little chance that the Communist regime would have to bear the consequences.[16] But strong Communist leadership against Japanese imperialism, together with their demand for a new United Front, served particularly after 1935 to give the student movement a further push to the left. It should be noted that in 1935 when the Nationalists, responding to Japanese pressure and to the Chinese demands for military resistance, instituted military training in the schools, the very student agitators who demanded war with Japan protested against this measure. Many students, after their dissatisfaction with the first decade of Nationalist government, increasingly channeled their doubts into harsh criticism. After eight years of war this criticism had gradually turned into an acceptance of the Communist interpretation of "The Chinese Revolution."

Such dissatisfaction was bound to transmit itself in powerful terms to the West, for the only really effective contact between China and the West had existed between the intellectuals and the West. Thus, for example, Mme. Sun Yat-sen addressed a plea to American friends in January 1935 in the following terms: "I appeal to you to do all within your power to see that not a single American gun nor a single American penny should be used to help the Nanking Government and its henchmen in crushing the

16 See Kiang Wen-han, *The Chinese Student Movement*, pp. 103 ff.

legitimate human aspirations of the broad Chinese masses. No support of any kind should be extended to the Nanking Government whose historical role is the naked and successive betrayals of the Chinese National cause." [17] Many Western scholars also began to talk in terms of the "betrayal," or *The Tragedy of the Chinese Revolution.*[18]

In other words, the only way a government could operate in the face of such a theory of revolution was by exercising almost total control. But the more the Nationalists tried to control the writings and activities of the intellectuals, the louder were the cries of "betrayal" and the greater the disillusionment with the Nationalist cause. The Nanking regime never really had the organization, the appealing doctrine, or the means to enforce its claim that it embodied "The Chinese Revolution." In fact, in many ways Nationalist doctrine contributed to the feeling that The Revolution was still incomplete. It was no sheer accident that every small child who recited (and on Taiwan today still recites) Sun Yat-sen's "Will" in school repeated the sentence: "The work of The Revolution is not yet done." At an early date, then, a basis for lack of stability and lack of support was laid for a government which sorely needed both.

The Chinese intellectuals made their mistakes of this nature. For example, there was the assumption—frequently expressed—that unity, sovereignty, and some form of stable government (usually thought of in terms of democracy) would provide a panacea for all the nation's problems. This misconception distracted attention from badly needed research and work on pressing problems and encouraged the belittling of some of the real efforts being made by the Nanking government. It was often implied that such

[17] Message printed in *China Today*, monthly publication of the American Friends of the Chinese People, New York, March 1935.
[18] This was the title of Harold Isaacs' Trotskyite polemic against Stalin's stupidities in China policy and against the Nationalist success under Chiang. Secker and Warburg, London, 1938. In subsequent revised editions (for example, Stanford University Press, 1951) the introduction by Leon Trotsky has been deleted as have many of the Trotsky-inspired polemics, but the theses of the work remain the same.

problems as population, agrarian development, and language reform would be solved with the achievement of The Revolution.

Not only did the imprecision of the phrase "The Chinese Revolution" lead to fuzzy thinking, but it also fitted in with the academic jargon coming from the West, especially after the literature of the Russian Revolution began to pour into academic circles. Chinese intellectuals thus drew support from the writings of Western students of China who used the phrase in just as loose and uncritical a manner as they did. In terms of intellectual effort, scholars both in China and in the West frequently attempted to draw specific and accurate conclusions from a vague, emotionally defined term.

"The Chinese Revolution" offered a neat explanation and excuse for United States policy in China after World War II. Only a few months after the Nationalist collapse, a respected American historian of China wrote, "As used today by people who ought to know better, there is a slick element of self-flattery in blaming the revolution in China on the administration in Washington. It assumes that we Americans can really call the tune if we want to, even among 475 million people in the inaccessible rice paddies of a subcontinent ten thousand miles away. . . . Chiang Kai-shek sat on top of the Chinese revolution as long as he could, fighting it with arms rather than reforms, but no amount of American aid could have kept him there forever, nor could even a nation of MacArthurs put him back today." [19] What is "The Chinese Revolution" in this case? An inexorable force? A set of goals for China? A state of mind?

The trend toward ill-defined phrases has continued down to the present day, and the basis for future instability is being prepared by romantic intellectuals in the underdeveloped areas of the world and their friends in the West through their attachment to the mystique of "The Revolution." A political scientist recently read a much-applauded paper before a learned society in the United States in which he commented on the "ideological tone of the

[19] John K. Fairbank, "China," *Atlantic Monthly*, November 1950, pp. 21-22.

Asiatic Revolution." Despite the smooth flow of academic verbiage, one wonders whether his was much of a contribution to a national approach for dealing with contemporary societies.

Obviously intellectual currents, especially those created by intellectuals of the former Western countries, are important. The tragic experiences of the Chinese students and intellectuals with United Fronts are cases in point. Vague relating of undeniably great historical changes in the underdeveloped lands of the world with the term "The Revolution" has undermined stability and prevented urgently needed actions by indescriminate use of the slogan "The Revolution." The Communists involve and exploit through united fronts the students and intellectuals in backward lands.

Lenin and his successors realized only too well the latent power of the students and intellectuals in countries like China. Developments around the world clearly illustrate that the China experience is being applied elsewhere. The lesson of China would seem to be that military security and economic development can well prove ephemeral unless the organization of the idealism and enthusiasm of students and intellectuals is in the hands of those who understand the nature of Communist deception.

NATIONALISTS, SOCIALISTS AND COMMUNISTS IN INDIA

Asoka Mehta

■ India is, in many ways, a prototype of the "new nations" which have moved from colonial domination to independence since World War II, and which are confronted with the multiple problems of building a nation, engineering a social and economic revolution, caring for a burgeoning, poverty-stricken population, and all the while conducting the "normal" functions of government. From the British, India inherited a national administrative organization, national postal and railway systems, a university education system, and a "Westernized" elite with experience in staffing a civil service and organizing the country for political action. In short, from the British the Indians inherited the basic human, bureaucratic, and technical systems which both precipitate and accompany what we call "industrialization." They also inherited the problems arising from drastic social upheaval: a society in which traditional values were eroded but still strong enough to command wide spread loyalty, in which traditional authority was undermined but strong enough to impede acceptance of a new authority structure, in which traditional class and caste ties were weakened but strong enough to be divisive, in which national consciousness was strong enough to provide unity against a colonial ruler but not strong enough to prevent the recrudescence of regional, linguistic, and religious particularism once the alien ruler had departed.

In addition to the almost staggering range of problems accompanying rapid industrialization, urbanization, overpopulation, poverty, and resurgent regionalism, the Indian government has also had to cope with an aggressive, expansionist Communist neighbor —the Chinese People's Republic, and a strong domestic Communist party.

Like its problems and its government, Indian political parties are a blend of western and traditional practices and ideologies. Although the Congress party has dominated both national and state governments since independence, India does have effective party competition. There are four parties, including the Congress, with sufficiently dispersed support to be considered "national" parties, and more than seventy small parties which are local in character but which nonetheless participate in national elections.

Of the four major parties, only two—the Congress and the Praja Socialists—are committed to the present constitution. The Communist party along with several lesser Marxist parties are totalitarian, and the Hindu Jan Sangh and several lesser Hindu parties are antistate and regional in orientation. The intrinsic problems of governing India are exacerbated and complicated by the existence of disloyal opposition groups with no stake in the preservation of orderly government.

The struggle for independence exercised a decisive influence on the character of the Congress party and the terms of political discourse in India. Organized and directed by a small group of Westernized university graduates from India's coastal cities, the Congress party early became a truly national movement united by its opposition to an external enemy and its dedication to a national goal. Its national, anticolonial, and Westernized character were all consistent with the adoption of a strongly statist and socialist orientation, which was already apparent in the early thirties. Because its leaders imbibed the same socialist doctrines that were current among their British and Continental contemporaries at that time, because of hostility to "liberal" colonialist governments, and because rapid modernization of Indian social and economic structures obviously required the use of state power, socialism spread quickly among the Indian leaders of the independence movement.

The socialist bent of these leaders further reinforced their anti-capitalist bias.

Since the other main forces in Indian political life—the Hindu and the Gandhian—looked backward to some form of village communalism, the identification of nationalism, industrialization, and socialism was firmly established in the Congress party. The establishment of the Congress Socialist party, the Praja Socialist, the growth of the Communist party and the proliferation of small Marxist-oriented sects, as well as the orientation of many Congress leaders and members, meant that much of the debate about politics, policies, and government would be carried on in the language of socialism and Marxism. Since India is an excellent example of a nation whose development and structure cannot be fitted into the categories of classical Marxism, the gap between political reality and political discourse is often wide. India has not moved through the "necessary" stages of history from feudalism to capitalism to socialism. Its most important social cleavages are not between industrial bourgeoisie and proletariat but between traditional caste, linguistic and regional groups. In fact, India constitutes an intriguing example of the indeterminate relation between social, economic, and political structures.

With flexibility characteristic of Communist movements, the Indian Communist party has adapted itself to the actual conflicts which divide Indian society. As we shall see, its most important successes have resulted from the skillful exploitation of ancient rivalries and loyalties. In the little former princely state of Tripana, the CPI once won an absolute majority by campaigning for the restoration of the maharajah. In Hyderabad, its championing of the Telegana movement enabled it to foment civil chaos, establish a guerrilla base, and organize hundreds of village "soviets." An alliance with the low caste Izhavas contributed importantly to its success in Kerala where Christians reguarly vote Congress. In Andhra, its principal support comes from the Kamma caste, comprised chiefly of prosperous peasants. And so forth.

The CPI's exploitation of regional and linguistic separatist movements diminished somewhat after the Soviet Union took a more friendly view of the Nehru government. However, the CPI continues to demonstrate its skill at exploiting conflicts in Indian society without regard to their "class" content.

Asoka Mehta's account of the ebb and flow of Communist strength in India makes crystal clear the flexibility of the CPI in seeking alliances, championing causes, and adopting programs. In the approximately forty years of its existence, the Indian party has radically shifted its position on virtually every important issue in Indian political life. Most of these shifts have occurred in response to decisions of the Kremlin, to whom the CPI has more than once sacrificed not only the interests of the nation but those of the Indian party itself.

In four decades, the CPI has supported national independence and opposed it; supported the Congress party and denounced it as "social fascist" and a "running dog of imperialism"; opposed Indian participation in World War II and supported it; fomented civil violence and been the most ardent proponent of civil obedience; endorsed the unity of all Socialists and denounced other Socialist parties as class traitors; supported regional and linguistic separatism and opposed it; attacked Gandhi and his movement and praised them; and so forth. There is virtually no man, no movement, no issue on which the Indian party has not switched sides, demonstrating its conditional attachment to all programs, including nationalism. That the Indian Communist party is neither "national" nor "nationalistic" is proved by its history and its habit of obedience to the Soviet line, including its opposition to the "Quit India" movement and independence during World War II and its indifference to Chinese aggression against Indian territory.

Asoka Mehta's account makes it disturbingly clear, however, that the CPI's record of equivocation, disruption, and indifference to Indian interests has not stopped the spread of Communism in India. Mehta's account also provides insight into why and how it has continued to grow. Indian Communism has profited when and where it has been able to identify itself with ideals espoused by other groups. It has suffered when mistaken calculations or the exigencies of international politics have isolated it. It has prospered not through appeal to specifically Communist doctrines and programs but through identification with causes in which it has no intrinsic interest, to which it has no reliable commitment. The CPI's greatest electoral successes have occurred when it has been able to form alliances and United Fronts with other Indian parties and groups, such as its 1935 alliance with the Congress Socialist party, its 1952 campaign in Madras and Travancore-Cochin in a "left" United Front, and its 1957 alliance with the Praja Socialists in Bombay and West Bengal. All this is to say that there exists in India, as in many other nations, an inverse relation between the clarity of the CPI's identity and its capacity for growth. The hope of Communism in India is not the appeal of Communism to Indians but the opportunity and ingenuity of Indian Communists in obscuring their identity and goals.

Asoka Mehta is a leading exponent of democratic socialism in India and Asia. Mr. Mehta has served two terms in the Indian Parliament and has been active in the nationalist struggle for freedom in India and in the socialist movement since his student days. Arrested and imprisoned several times for his political activities, Mr. Mehta is widely known, in Asia and in the democratic socialist and free trade-union movements everywhere, as a courageous and determined friend of freedom. ■

COMMUNISM IN INDIA: AN OVERVIEW

Communism is a strong and growing force in India. In Kerala state, one of the constituent units of the federal union of India, the Communist party was voted to power, the first instance of its kind in the world. In both houses of the Indian Parliament the Communists continue to provide, through three general elections, the main opposition. In two other states—Andhra Pradesh and West Bengal—the Communists are strongly entrenched, though still far from seats of power.

The Communist movement in India has grown from tiny beginnings in 1924 into a massive force that obtained over ten million votes, out of 103 million votes polled, in the recent 1962 elections. In thirty-eight years the movement has passed through the gyrations that have characterised the Communist movement the world over.

The Early Years: Isolation and Popular Front.

Immediately after the Russian Revolution, some Indian revolutionaries who had fled to Europe contacted the Bolsheviks and were converted to the new creed. From abroad they tried to organize the new party in India. The chief of these mentors was M. N. Roy.

The Communists became involved in conspiracy cases, first at Kanpur and then at Meerut, and the severe sentences meted out to them won them public sympathy. The Meerut conspiracy cases involved the trial of thirty-one Communists and trade unionists on charges of engaging in a conspiracy to deprive the King-Emperor of his sovereignty over India. Those arrested included practically the whole leadership of the CPI. Eight defendents were members of the All India Congress Committee; one was a former president of the All India Trade Union Congress. The cases gained the sympathy of all Indian nationalists, including Gandhi himself. Dr. M. A. Ansari and Jawaharlal Nehru served on the defense committee. The trial, which dragged on for three years, resulted in long prison sentences, most of which were reduced on appeal. All had been released by 1933. The trial made martyrs of the Communists and assumed sufficient symbolic importance that Harold Laski compared it to the Sacco-Vanzetti, the Dreyfus, and the Reichstag Fire trials. Till 1928, the Communists were active inside the Indian National Congress. I remember that as a young student when I first went to the Congress House in Bombay to participate in the boycott of the Simon Commission sent out from Britain, the leaders of the Congress Committee were leading Communists, like R. S. Nimbkar.

Soon after, with the new ultraleftist twist given to the Communist policy by the Sixth Congress of the International, the Communists not merely left the Indian National Congress but began fighting it. They concentrated on trade-union work and instigated prolonged strikes, particularly in the distressed textile industry in Bombay. In 1928, the Sixth Comintern Congress adopted, after a long struggle, a new colonial thesis which denounced bourgeois nationalist movements as reformist, and called on the Communist party to oppose, rather than support, them. Although the Indian Communist party hesitated for some time to break all its ties to the independence movement, it did so after the tenth plenum of the ECCI, held in Moscow, July 3-19, 1929, which unequivocally supported an ultraleftist platform. It was also this meeting which finalized the Comintern's break with M. N. Roy.

During the same period, the Indian National Congress was developing its mass base. In 1928, Vallabhbhai Patel led a powerful peasant struggle, known to history as the Bardoli *satyagraha*. The nation-wide boycott of the all-White Simon Commission sent out from London gave an edge to the youth movement organized in the Youth League. In 1930, Mahatma Gandhi launched his salt *satyagraha** which drew even women into the freedom struggle. The Congress achieved a new position of preeminence and the country surged with hope and pride. In 1932, the mass struggle was resumed, tens of thousands trekked to prison, and a new generation of freedom fighters was born.

The Communists had opposed the movement, denounced it as bourgeois deception, and did not hesitate to tear down the tricolor flag unfurled as a symbol of the nation's will to be independent. These antics of the Communists estranged them from

---

* Salt was a state monopoly under the British. Mahatma Gandhi asked people near the seacoast to break the Salt Law and manufacture salt for themselves.

the people, an isolation that was further aggravated by the Com munists themselves, who split the trade-union movement in pur, suance of the policy of the Profintern at that time.

By 1934, the Communists had lost much of their influence. The Meerut trials had disrupted party membership by imprison- ing most of its leaders. Furthermore, in July 1934, the CPI was declared illegal, along with the Red Trade Union Congress, the Workers' Publishing House, the Young Communist League of Bombay and Madras, and other subsidiary organizations. I remem- ber a Communist telling me after we had formed the Congress Socialist party, a Socialist group inside the Congress, that only then did it become possible to talk about Socialism, because be- fore this the people were in no mood to listen to such talk! The initial reaction of the Communists to the formation of the CSP, however, was one of outright hostility. The Communists charac- terized the CSP as "social fascist" and as "a left maneuver of the bourgeoisie," and did everything they could to destroy it.

By 1935, the Communist policy was revised in conformity with the decisions of the Seventh Congress of the International. The earlier policy was dismissed as sectarian and a new policy of closer association with the Congress and even more with the CSP was adopted.

In January 1936, the Congress Socialist party adopted a reso- lution to admit Communists to membership in the CSP on indi- vidual application. The initiative in forming this alliance was taken by the Socialists and was rather slowly responded to by the Communists. Once the decision was made that Communists should apply for membership, new organizational means were es- tablished to enable Communists to fully exploit the United Front. Notable among these was the system of CPI "fractions" through which Communists in the CSP, trade unions, and peas- ant organizations worked as disciplined units to attain CPI goals within these organizations. Less than a year later, in early 1937, the National Executive of the CSP noted the disruptive tactics of Communist fractions in the CSP and threatened disciplinary ac- tion.

Trade-union unity was restored. Seven years of political isolation had brought Communists little popular support but had
trained the cadres.

As in Europe and the U.S.A., the thirties was a "red" decade in
India. The young intellectuals swept into the national movement
in 1930-34, were profoundly impressed by the Front Populaire.
The visit to India of able and ardent advocates of the line like Sir
Stafford Cripps gave the impression deeper impact. The steady
flow of books brought out by the Left Book Club ushered in an
intellectual transformation. Pandit Nehru's open championship
of Socialism made it a major issue of debate inside the Congress.
The dramatic disputes over Socialism between him and his colleagues began with a famous correspondence exchanged between
two terms of prison with Mahatma Gandhi, and gave to Socialism
a popular interest it never had before. The Left Book Club gave
the interest an orientation not unfavorable to the Communists.

The then prevailing situation was well brought out by a statement adopted by the Executive Committee of the CSP in August
1937, from which long extracts are given here:

> The Party faced opposition at the outset from the "Red" group
> which went to the length of describing it as a left manoeuvre of
> the bourgeoisie, and certain leading lights of which even called it
> social fascist. On our side, however, we refused consistently to join
> in any campaign of mutual recrimination. In fact, even in the face
> of these attacks from that group, we negotiated a united front
> agreement with the "Red" T.U.C. Subsequently, more markedly
> after the Seventh World Congress of the Comintern, the attitude
> of the "Red" group towards our Party changed, as a result of which,
> but yet largely on our own initiative, we succeeded in establishing
> friendly relations with them.
>
> When these steps were taken, it was on the understanding that
> the "Red" group looked upon us as a Marxist Socialist Party and
> were prepared to treat with us as such as also on the clear assump-
> tion that they would not attempt to carry on fraction work within
> our Party either through its members or through those whom it
> could influence. . . .
>
> We find, however, that the "Red" group has not adhered to these
> positions. At its Delhi meeting, our Executive found that there

were evidences of fraction work in the Party conducted on their behalf and it sounded warning to the Party branches. Now comes an amazing "Statement on the C.S.P." from the "Red" group. This statement categorically gives up the position that the C.S.P. is a Marxist Socialist Party and it says that they cannot let a rival Marxist party exist. This conception of rivalry is a most unfortunate and unintelligent appreciation of the position. The former, and undoubtedly correct, position was that there were two Marxist parties existing side by side, working with closest co-operation and working with a definite object—the evolution of the Marxist Socialist Party of the country uniting within it the entire leadership of the left forces in the country. To talk of rivalry is not only petty but also to misunderstand the development of the socialist movement in the country.

The statement goes on to say that the C.S.P. is the growing organisational expression of Left Unity and that its future lies in its development into a mass party not with the rigid discipline of a one class party but with an organisational structure which corresponds to the unification of all Left forces. It also demands that it must open its doors to all active anti-imperialists who accept the aim of Socialism and are therefore willing to carry out the programme of Left unity with all its implications. This is a conception of the C.S.P. which goes contrary to what the C.S.P. considers itself to be as also to the conception on which friendly relations were established.

The anxiety to establish friendly relations, the equating of Socialism with Marxist Socialism as then understood, the simple devices of describing and proscribing fraction work, all show how the dice were being loaded in favor of the Communists. Nehru popularized Socialism in the nationalist ranks; the Socialists yearned for acceptance by the Communists and sought a common visage for Socialism. What wonder if many a young nationalist preferred to become a pukka Communist rather than an occasionally critical fellow traveler!

By 1937, the isolation of the Communists was broken; they were not only in the midstream of the nationalist movement but, ideologically speaking, among the most looked up to part of it.

The Communists' work inside the CSP was so successful that: (1) their influence prevented their expulsion although their activities were known through experience and corroborated by captured documents; (2) they very nearly succeeded in capturing the National Executive of the CSP at the Labore Conference; (3) their access to the CSP's national audience enabled the party to greatly increase its membership and prestige; and that (4) the CSP provided the CPI with access to the Congress party and the Congress' mass following.

In 1937, the Congress had won 707 out of 1,585 seats to the Provincial Legislatures and formed ministries in eight out of eleven provinces of British India. The formation of governments provided a great divide between the Right and the Left in the Congress, and in the Congress party's Left Wing the Communists found the needed rehabilitation.

The break between Subhas Chandra Bose and Mahatma Gandhi further confused the ranks of the Congress and the formation of the Left Consolidation Committee by Bose gave a wider sphere of influence to the Communists who, with the Socialist elements, had undertaken to work among the peasantry in addition to their usual trade-union activities. When Gandhi made an issue of confidence of the election of Subhas Chandra Bose, a left-of-center leader, as Congress president, the Communists supported Gandhi and Congress unity, and without obvious embarrassment set about to study and emphasize "every positive side of Gandhism"—the movement they had previously denounced as "social fascism."

Jayaprakash Narayan, General Secretary of the CSP, wrote in a brochure, "Socialist Unity and the C.S.P.," published in 1941:

> It might be asked why, if it did not believe in unity, did the Communist Party agree to send its members into the C.S.P. For two obvious reasons. It might be recalled that for some time it refused to have anything to do with us. But when it was ordered by the International to change its policy and to enter the Congress it found itself faced with a serious problem. It had no contacts with the Congress and, of course, it must at once become the leader of the national forces. It was here that it found in the Congress Socialist Party an ideal instrument. The C.S.P. held a strategic

position within the Congress. The Communists were anxious to get into the Provincial Congress Committees, the Executive, the All India Congress Committee, possibly the Working Committee. With their own resources it was impossible to get anywhere near them. They were not four anna (i.e., primary) members yet. Here was the C.S.P. with its members even in the highest committees. "Three cheers for the C.S.P. Let us join it." They did, and the C.S.P. votes sent them as high as the All India Congress Committee and the Provincial Executives. In addition, being an open party, the C.S.P. afforded a splendid platform for self-advertisement to these, till then, practically unknown Communists. What was the other reason for their entering the Party? It has been pointed out that from their point of view no socialist party apart from the Communist Party had any right to exist. The growth of the C.S.P. into an independent party was a danger to their monopoly. Therefore, they took advantage of the opportunity to enter the Party so as to capture or break it up. But, in order to gain admittance, they had to accept the slogan of socialist unity, for otherwise there was no reason why the C.S.P. should have let them come in. So, behind the smokescreen of unity, they worked out their plans.

The foregoing has made clear that the whole idea of unity with a party like the Communist Party was misconceived and fundamental difficulties were not understood. But apart from the manner in which unity was brought about was itself a grievous mistake. It was very wrong to have admitted members of other parties into our Party. This was against sound principles of organisation. The experiment should never be repeated. It cannot but lead to internal confusion and conflict. It should be kept in mind that nowhere in the world has an attempt to unite two parties been made by allowing the infiltration of members of one into the other. The C.S.P. tried it and found it to be a disastrous experiment.

Earlier in the brochure, Jayaprakash Narayan describes his former spirit of accommodation:

It was during this period that the General Secretary of the Party (that is, Jayaprakash Narayan himself), by way of reorganisation, handed over to the Communists the whole of Andhra Party.

The consequences of these actions were not undone by the expulsion of the Communists from the CSP (in March, 1940).

M. R. Masani, a close colleague of Jayaprakash Narayan, in his book, *The Communist Party of India*, writes:

> The C.S.P. expelled all Communists from its organisation. This decision was taken in the nick of time. A little delay, and the Communists would have broken the (Congress) Socialist Party. As it was, while parting, the Communists carried with them almost intact three of the best organised State branches of that Party—in Andhra, Tamilnad and Kerala in South India.

And these have proved to be stubborn pockets of strength for the Communists.

By the time Communists were expelled by the CSP, they had captured and/or converted large numbers of Socialists, including some members of the Executive and large numbers of rank and filers who had secretly joined the CPI, and did not make their memberships known until the time Communists were expelled.

Imperial Solidarity and the People's War

With the declaration of World War II, the Communists broke with their allies. "With the advent of war," wrote Jayaprakash Narayan, "the Communist Party discerned the approach of the revolution. At that point it did not want that any other party should be about to dispute the leadership of the coming historic event! It desired to appear before the masses—workers, peasants, students—as the *sole* revolutionary party in the country. The natural corollary of this thesis of megalomania was that other parties must perish, i.e., their hold over the masses must be destroyed."

The Communists organized strikes, denounced individual civil disobedience initiated by the Congress, and furiously attacked the CSP and Subhas Bose's Forward Bloc. With the German attack on the Soviet Union, the Communists hesitated briefly, then acclaimed as a People's War the war they had until then resisted as an imperialist war. They supported the proposals that Sir Stafford Cripps brought to India on behalf of the Churchill Cabinet and castigated the Congress for not subordinating the claim for independence to the overriding military needs.

As the Congress moved toward the massive "Quit India" movement launched in August 1942, in which the Socialists emerged as the outstanding organizers, the Communists moved closer to the British government in support of the war. Following Hitler's attack on the U.S.S.R., international Communist authorities demanded that the CPI support the war unconditionally. The inner core of Indian Communist leaders, including S. A. Dange, Muzaffer Ahmed, S. S. Mirajkar, and others, were at that time imprisoned at the Deoli Detention Camp, where they had been sent as a consequence of their campaign of mass strikes and violence in 1939-40. This group swung quickly behind all-out support of the "People's War," with or without guarantees of Indian freedom. At the same time, leading Communists outside prison stated their determination to convert the "imperialist war" into a revolutionary war and to intensify the struggle against the British. This segment of the party, more sensitive to Indian political realities, did not fall into line on all-out support of the British until mid-1942. Both Indian and British Communists were encouraged to believe that the leftist elements of the Congress would give "defense of the Soviet Union" priority over independence. Those fighting for independence were denounced and not rarely betrayed to the British police. Members of the Azad Hind Fouz (Free Indian Army, organized by Subhas Bose in the South East Asia) were reviled as traitors. These activities once again estranged the Communists from the people and led, by 1945, to their ejection from the national movement. They, however, gained three advantages to compensate for their isolation and popular losses.

First, the Communist party's members were severely tested when the *volte face* policy, so unacceptable to the Indian nationalist opinion, was executed. Second, during the phase of support of the war, the Communists gained an *entrée* to upper-class circles where before they had lacked contact. Many such persons, particularly socially prominent women, sought to bolster their unpopular position by adopting the radical justification provided by the

Communists. Lastly, the Communists supported the Muslim League and thus obtained a foothold among the Muslim masses (which later proved of little value).

The CPI also profited from the British decision in July 1942 to legalize the CPI. This decision permitted the Communists to work freely and openly in the peasant association and student associations in which it gained ascendancy, and the trade unions in which it greatly increased its influence without gained control. At the same time, the CPI announced its intention to become a "mass" party, and, chiefly by lowering its standards of admission, its membership increased from fewer than 5,000 in 1942 to more than 25,000 in 1945. Organizational work concentrated on the grass-roots level. Despite these gains, the Communists suffered severely from their alienation from the Congress party and the independence movement.

In the elections of 1946, the last to be held on restricted franchise under the British, the Congress polled over 12.7 million votes and won 929 seats to the Provincial legislatures. The Muslim League received 4.5 million votes and won 427 seats. The Communist party also contested the elections and polled approximately 650,000 votes and won 8 seats. In Labour constituencies, where only trade-union members were entitled to vote, the Congress polled 304,981 votes and won 20 seats, while the Communists received 108,895 votes and got 7 seats. The Communist party's main support was in Madras state, which then included Andhra and a part of Kerala; 369,785 votes were cast in that state. But in Labour constituencies of the state, the Communist vote (36,832) was higher than that of the Congress (35,920). This was no mean achievement for the Communists at a time when they were estranged from public opinion, and were fighting against the Congress and the League at the crest of their influence.

Commenting on the election results, I wrote as follows in July 1946:

The Congress must not dismiss the Communists because they won only eight seats; *their votes were the third biggest in the coun-*

try. If there was proportional representation the Communists would have got 51 instead of eight seats.

The challenge of the Communist Party is sure to gather strength. It can be met only by developing the Congress along Socialist lines. [Italics in the original.]

Independence: New Problems and New Prospects

In 1947 came independence and with it the partition of the country. The Communists initially hailed independence and supported Pandit Nehru's government struggle against the havoc wrought by partition. Soon the cold war broke out in Europe, and the Communists in India, as all over Southeast Asia, took up arms and sought to organize insurrectionary movements. 1948 and 1949 were marked by efforts at fomenting chaos. Communist strike calls failed to evoke much response, but party militants fought hard, in and out of prisons. Their campaigns involved sabotage, incendiarism, looting and murder, and kept the Communists on the front pages of the newspapers for months.

Following a speech in which Nehru himself accused the Communist party of a deliberate effort to foment chaos and undermine orderly government, state governments launched a campaign of repression against the CPI. The party was outlawed in West Bengal, Mysore, Indore, Bhopal, and Chandernagor. Its newspapers were suppressed in West Bengal, Kerala, and Andhra, and scores of party leaders were arrested throughout India. Raids on party headquarters produced many documents proving that preparations for violent revolt were underway. See *Communist Violence in India* (New Delhi: Ministry of Home Affairs, Government of India, 1949) for an account of CPI activities and plans during this period.

It was in Hyderabad state, where the Nizam was resisting integration of the state into the Indian Union, that the Communist campaign of violent revolt was most successful. Communists championed the Telengana movement, organized in the area contiguous to Andhra and linked to it by ties of common language and culture. The retreating Razakars (fanatical supporters of the

Nizam) handed over arms and equipment to the Communists. Several hundred village "soviets" and a full-scale guerrilla army were organized, and for months after the government of India's police action had brought Hyderabad securely into the Indian Union, the Communists gave serious trouble to the military governor of Hyderabad.

Through these violent skirmishes, the Communists once again toughened their cadres but lost a considerable part of public good will. The series of mistakes beginning with support of the British government's war efforts and ending with violent opposition to the nascent Indian Union would have cost the Indian Communists heavily if just in 1948-50 the Communists had not won spectacular victories in China.

By 1950 the Communists realized the need for a revision in policy. India's new Constitution was nearly complete. The first general elections on the basis of adult franchise were in the offing. A four-man commission went to Moscow to receive guidance and instruction. When they returned, the insurrectionary policies were abandoned and preparations were made to contest the forthcoming elections.

"As the time for polling in the General Elections approached," observes M. R. Masani in his book, "startling signs of the Party's sudden opulence became visible. In the State of Andhra, this took the form of a fleet of cars and jeeps used for campaigning purposes and later the purchase of an expensive rotary printing press for starting a daily in Telagu language. It was widely asserted that, except for the ruling Congress Party, the Communist Party had more funds available for the election campaign than any other in India." The sources of the sudden opulence were the same foreign patrons who had brought finances in the past and who provide far larger funds today.

Communist prospects received a substantial boost when an influential group broke away from the Congress on the eve of the elections and formed with the Communists in the Madras state (which then included both Andhra and parts of Kerala) the Kisan Mazdoor Praja party. After the elections, the KMPP merged with the Socialist party to form the Praja Socialist party and abruptly broke its ties with the Communists. But the mischief had already been done.

In the general elections of 1952, the Communists polled 5,370,361 votes (5.06 per cent) for the House of the People and 6,062,-943 (5.84 per cent) for the state assemblies. They, with their close associates, won 26 seats (5.31 per cent) to the Parliament and 173 seats (5.27 per cent) to the state assemblies. Significantly, 2,591,923 votes were polled in Madras state and 1,086,111 in Hyderabad state, the bulk of them having been polled in Telengana, the Telugu-speaking part of the state.

Though the Communist vote was much smaller than that of the Socialist party (11,126,344), the Communists increased the number of seats they held in the Parliament and their prestige soared. For the first few months after the elections, the Indian press and public made considerable fuss over the new phenomenon of the comrades perched uncomfortably in their parliamentary saddles.

The novelty of Communists in Parliament, however, began to wear off. After an initial period of walkouts and histrionics, the Communists, too, settled down to parliamentary routines. Outside, of course, they pooh-poohed parliamentary institutions and continued to press for mass action to bring about a people's democracy in India.

After the death of Stalin, many changes began to occur. It appeared that a period of liberalization had begun: many roads to socialism were being opened and even the parliamentary path was not ruled out. The "de-Stalinzation" campaign also had a sobering effect. One found the Communist members in Parliament in a mood to discuss new policies.

Simultaneously, after Pandit Nehru's visit to China, he came out with proposals for an ambitious Second Plan which good harvest and other favorable aspects of the First Plan made attractive to the people. In a major debate on economic policy, the Parliament resolved, almost unanimously, to shape the nation's future on a socialist pattern. At its annual session, the Congress adopted socialism as its objective. Suddenly socialism became the accepted goal of the nation.

These changes had substantial effects on the Communists. When fresh elections were held in Andhra on the issue of its being constituted as a separate state, the Congress was swept to the polls. Congress victories amazed even its own leaders. I remember in the Parliament our crowding round the newsboard as the election results poured in: one could almost hear the hissing air that came out of the deflated Communist balloon. The Communists won just 15 seats, only a third of what they had held before. Despite this debacle, the total Communist vote remained fairly high. But in constituency after constituency the Congress had outpolled them, and Communist candidates were snowed under by the unusually heavy endorsement of the Congress.

The Andhra elections marked a low watermark of Communist influence. I remember Communist members of the Parliament shuddering at the prospects of general elections in that atmosphere. There was a mood of optimism in the country in which the Communists felt disoriented.

Then came the Report of States Reorganization Commission. It recommended reorganization of states on linguistic basis. Students of southeast Europe know how frustrating such an effort can be. In India, too, the issue precipitated great turmoil, resulting in riots in many places. The year 1956 was filled with shrill controversy on claims and counterclaims for disputed areas. The most acrid controversy was in Bombay City. This period of trouble proved God-sent to the Communists. The Congress, which necessarily bore the brunt of responsibility, was weakened; opposition parties gained and Communist gains were greatest.

In the meantime, the Praja Socialist party had passed through many vicissitudes. In 1953, Prime Minister Nehru had invited it to join with the Congress in administering the country. Some leaders of the party were prepared to respond on certain conditions because of what they felt to be "the political compulsions of backward economy." Other leaders considered such a move a near betrayal of socialism. The only concrete result of the Prime Minister's offer was to split the Praja Socialist party.

Another cause of this split was an episode in which police fired on a crowd of troublemakers in Travancore (later merged in Kerala state) where the Praja Socialist party held power as a minority government tolerated by the Congress. The Socialists had been most critical of the Congress about frequent police violence in areas under its administration; and a similar lapse on the part of the PSP government caused a crisis in its ranks. The split separated over a fourth of the members from the party. The long process of mutual recrimination weakened both the sections.

Almost on the heel of the split, the widely respected Chairman of the PSP, Acharya Narendra Deva, died. Simultaneously, the doyen of the Socialists, Jayaprakash Narayan, abandoned party politics. These repeated blows weakened the PSP, and the splinter Socialist party started weakly. The agitation on linguistic reorganization of the states provoked further controversies in the ranks of the Socialists.

Victory and Defeat in Kerala

Reversing the policy that the Socialists had pursued since 1940, in the general elections of 1957, the PSP entered into electoral understanding with the Communist party in the two important states of Bombay and West Bengal. At least in West Bengal the Communists gained considerably by this agreement.

In the general elections of 1957, the Congress improved its vote but lost a number of seats, particularly in the state assemblies of Bombay and West Bengal. The PSP retained its previous vote of nearly 11 million, while the splinter Socialist party polled 2.5 million votes. The Communists increased their vote by more than 3 million votes, achieving a total vote of over 10 million. The Communists, however, emerged as the main opposition to the Congress in two states, West Bengal and Andhra Pradesh (the new state formed by the merger of Telangana with the Andhra state). Public attention was riveted on the Communists, however, because in the state of Kerala the party emerged as the majority party in the state legislature. The Communists had at last arrived in one out of the fourteen states of the Indian Union.

How did the Communists win a majority (of two seats) in Kerala? On the eve of the general elections, I had asked Ajoy Ghose, the general secretary of the Communist party, to assess the elections. He was clear about all other states, but singularly evasive about Kerala: "Anything can happen in Kerala," he said. The unexpected did happen. The Communists won a majority of seats on a minority of votes—the Communist vote was just 35 per cent. In a three-cornered contest—the Communists, Congress, and the PSP and a couple of small local parties—this was enough. As the unity of democratic forces had routed the Communists in Andhra in 1955, in Kerala the sharp divisions in the ranks of the democratic forces opened wide the gates of power to the Communists.

Again, the Communists emerged as the principal (though small) opposition group in the Parliament and for the first time managed to get one or more representative in *every* state legislature in India. While their traditional pockets of strength remained unshaken (barring the truncated state of Madras—from which Andhra had been separated in 1955 and parts of Kerala were transferred to the state of Kerala in 1956—where the Communists were routed), the party extended its influence to all the states and emerged for the first time as a nation-wide party, a status till then enjoyed only by the Congress and, to a lesser extent, the Praja Socialist party.

The formation of government in Kerala proved a mixed blessing for the Communist party. The opportunity to lead the only non-Congress government in the country gave the party a boost in prestige and imparted significance to its claim of being the only real alternative to the Congress. But the administration of the state proved difficult. Kerala has so far proved to be the grave of many reputations. The stubborn problems of poverty and unemployment in this most densely inhabited and highly educated part of India are not easy to resolve. The Communists failed to increase food production, implement land reforms, augment employment, or eliminate corruption. And their interference with the executive and the judiciary, and systematic attacks on opposition members weakened the fabric of law and order and brought them nation-wide opprobrium.

The Communist government sanctioned firing on industrial workers on a number of occasions, arrested hundreds of persons, combated students' strikes, and faced a judicial inquiry on a charge of corruption. The Communists acquired funds estimated at between $500,000 to $1,000,000 during their twenty-seven months' regime in Kerala.

The misrule of the Communists in Kerala led to a coalition of democratic forces. The presence of a large, well-organized Christian population in the southern part of Kerala provided an additional organizational prop. Together, these forces launched a Liberation Struggle that brought the Communist administration to a virtual standstill. Finally, the President of the Republic dismissed the Communist ministry and ordered fresh elections. United democratic forces easily defeated the Communist party which, nonetheless, increased its vote, as did the democratic alliance, by a million votes.

The Communists faced another major problem when the Chinese invaded India. Initially, the Communists hedged against taking a position on Chinese aggression and faced a division of their own ranks between the so-called "nationalists" and the pro-China elements. The emerging rift between the Soviet Union and China made the position of the Indian Communists somewhat easier. The government of India was eager to have Russian support, or at least neutrality, in the Sino-Indian dispute. So the Communists were spared an agonizing reappraisal about their relations with the Communists abroad. Sino-Soviet tensions and their own close ties with Moscow enabled the Indian Communists largely to come round to support the Indian nation's stand against China. The pro-China elements in the Communist party of India have naturally been strong in areas that skirt China, such as the Punjab and West Bengal.

In the Himalayan region of India the Communists tried to gain strong footholds. The government of India found it necessary to enact special legislation to circumscribe their activities in these strategic areas.

1962: *The Election and the Prospect*

The third general elections indicate that although Communist growth has been checked, even the Chinese aggression on India has not weakened the Communist position in their traditional strongholds.

The following table shows the fluctuation of the Communist poll in the three national elections:

Lok Sabha			State Assemblies		
1952	1957	1962	1952	1957	1962
3,484,401	10,754,075	10,586,603	4,552,537	8,821,941	8,925,000*
		Seats Won			
16	27	29	106	161	188

* This figure does not include the votes polled in Kerala and Orissa where the elections took place earlier.

The figures for 1962 are misleading because in some states, particularly Hyderabad and Travancore-Cochin, the Communists fought the election as independents, or under other labels. Votes cast for them under these circumstances were not recorded as votes for the Communists. However, the fact remains that while the party made substantial gains between 1952 and 1957, it made little progress from 1957 to 1962. The states where the Communist party has improved its position are: Andhra Pradesh, Mysore, Punjab, Bihar, Rajasthan, Uttar Pradesh, and West Bengal. It has suffered losses in Assam, Gujarat, Madras, Maharashtra, and Madhya Pradesh.

The following table shows seats won by the party to the Lok

Sabha and the state assemblies of different States in 1957 and 1962:

States	Lok Sabha			State Assembly	
	1957	1962		1957	1962
Andhra Pradesh	2	7	(300)	15	51
Assam	—	—	(105)	4	—
Bihar	—	1	(318)	7	12
Gujarat	—	—	(154)	—	—
Kerala	9	6	(126)	—	—
Madhya Pradesh	—	—	(288)	2	1
Madras	2	2	(206)	4	2
Maharashtra	3	—	(264)	13	6
Mysore	—	—	(208)	—	3
Orissa	1	—		6	9
Punjab	1	—	(154)	1	5
Rajasthan	—	—	(176)	9	14
Uttar Pradesh	1	2	(430)	46	50
West Bengal	6	9	(252)	—	—
Tripura	1	2			

(The figures in parenthesis show the total number of seats in the state legislative assembly.)

In Andhra Pradesh in the mid-term elections of 1955, the Communists had got a disproportionately small number of seats compared to the vote they had polled. In 1962, the imbalance has been corrected. In fact, the actual vote has gone down. Only in West Bengal has the vote gone up spectacularly by half a million, though the actual representation in the state assembly has not changed proportionately. In all other states the variations in the votes were minor.

In West Bengal, the Communist share of the total vote in 1952, 1957, and 1962 was 10.8, 17.8, and 23.9 per cent, respectively. A quickening tempo is apparent. The bell seems to have started tolling for democracy in that state, as in Kerala.

The Communists have been quietly consolidating their trade-union base. In 1958, it was rumored that the Communists had received from the usual mysterious sources $600,000 for trade-union work. While the Communists lost their seats in the industrial cities of Bombay and Coimbatore, they improved and consolidated their position in the textile cities of Indore and Kanpur and the steel city of Jamshedpur. The Communist target continues to be the steel-coal belt with its sprawling complex of steel plants and heavy engineering concerns. As a Union minister put it, "Whoever holds this belt has more power than those who control two states."

India is engaged in the early stages of industrialization and economic development. She faces the usual difficulties of inflation, shortages, unemployment, higher taxes, controls, etc. There are the familiar stresses and strains and the inevitable disillusionment. These naturally help the Communists.

In 1962 the democratic socialists, in the Congress and the PSP, lost in the elections, the latter more heavily. The resulting gains have not gone to the Communists but to reactionary parties like the Swatantra and the Jan Sangh. These developments are inducing the Communists to develop a new strategy.

They denounce the reactionary parties (while working with them when it suits them as in the Punjab legislature) and offer support to the Congress. The Communists support the Five Year Plan while opposing many of the new taxes and the discipline of any planning. They praise the Prime Minister in season and out and put all the blame for difficulties and failures on his so-called right-wing colleagues. They pose as the true custodian of Nehru's purposes. There are powerful elements in the Congress, round Mr. V. K. Krishna Menon, that are only too anxious to oblige.*

The Communists will thus be working on two fronts, in opposition to the Congress governments and also as allies of the Congress in the effort to soften and loosen the fabric of that organization. The growth of the right-wing forces and the weakening of the democratic left as an alternative to the Congress are likely to make the Prime Minister not only move somewhat to the left but be less concerned about dangers from the Communists.

After fourteen years of freedom, various groups and sections of Indian society aspire to self-determination. The urge for such expression complicates the politics of India. Economic development

* After this essay was completed, fresh Chinese attacks on the Indian border led first to the demotion and finally to the exclusion of Mr. Krishna Menon from the Cabinet.

results in the breakdown of the traditional order, and it brings into the open inadequacies of employment, social security, and educational opportunities. The more that is attempted, the more must be done—that is the inevitable predicament of a poor country, with heavy pressure of population on land, attempting economic transformation. In such a milieu, Communist strength cannot be wholly checked.

There will be flow and ebb in the Communist strength, and every flow will carry it a step further. But there are still built-in reserves available in the Indian democracy. If the West continues its partnership in the economic growth of India, and if the democratic forces within are encouraged to work together, the Communist challenge can be transformed into a spur for quicker, informed action.

As in the world, the fast increasing Communist strength menaces—but cannot overthrow—the democratic world, so in India will the Communist strength grow without overwhelming Indian democracy. The tragedy of China need not recur in India. That is the hope and the task of democrats in India and abroad.

NATIONALISM AND COMMUNISM IN BURMA

F. N. Trager

■ In Burma we see again how Lenin's doctrine of imperialism served as a bridge between nationalism and Communism. Through this doctrine which confirmed nationalist leaders' darkest suspicions about the motivation and consequences of colonialism, anti-capitalism was integrated into Burmese nationalism on the ideological level. It became a part of what Frank Trager terms the "nationalist amalgam" which dominated the Burmese ideological climate during the years immediately before and after independence was achieved. In the following chapter, Trager traces the process of "ideological clarification" that set in once Burmese nationalists were confronted with the responsibilities of government.

Frank Trager, Professor of International Affairs at New York University, is a well-known specialist on Southeast Asia. Professor Trager has lived and traveled widely in Asia. He has been employed by a number of U.S. government agencies and from 1951 to 1953 served as Director of the "Point Four" program in Burma. His publications on Southeast Asia include Marxism in Southeast Asia; Burma (three volumes); Building a Welfare State in Burma; Burma's Role in the United Nations, 1948-1955; and a large number of articles on Southeast Asian affairs. ■

MARXIST AND NATIONALIST POLITICS IN BURMA

Burma in the twentieth century typifies a battle which will continue to be fought for some time to come in Asia and other parts of the ex-colonial world. Its history is marked by the struggle, first for independence from colonialism, then for a free choice of the path toward political, economic, and social development. Former comrades-in-arms under the all-encompassing banner of Burmese nationalism came quickly to the realization of basic differences before and after the attainment of the goal of independence on January 4, 1948. "Marxists" became aware that they had little in common with each other except the Marxist label and that that label was questionable. Fourteen years of Burmese independence have meant fourteen years of diminishing civil strife, greater clarification for the Burmese and for the outside world of where Burma stands in the ideological struggles of today. But the creation of solid institutional bases for sustained political and economic growth within a commitment to democracy and socialism has remained a difficult problem. The second advent of a General Ne Win government on March 2, 1962—this time by a military coup —points up the still-unsolved Burmese problems in the building of a stable, secure nation.

1. IMPERIALISM AND THE NATIONALIST AMALGAM

Burma's present-day situation can perhaps best be understood by taking a backward glance at its history. Western writings on Burma during the period referred to as the Age of Exploration (or, according to Asians the Age of Exploitation) attest to Burma's ability to produce, trade, and acquire the marks or respected display. As an independent monarchy in the dynasties of the eleventh, sixteenth, and eighteenth centuries, Burma had boundaries which exceeded those of today. It has, like most countries, its share of national *amour propre*, and tends to remember and glorify these periods of dynastic unity and power. Indeed, the vigorous eighteenth-century dynasty was able (between 1765 and 1769) to defeat four invading armies of the great Chinese emperor Chien Lung. But in glorifying its past successes, Burma has tended to overlook the internal causes which led up to its defeat by the increasingly imperialistic Great Britain, in the three Anglo-Burmese wars of the nineteenth century. The power and rule of the monarchy was gradually dissipated in the wars of 1824-1826, 1852, and 1885. The differences between the duration of each of these wars —two years, eleven months, and fourteen days, respectively—reflect the failure of Burma to come to terms with the science and technology of the industrial revolution and with the requirements for national transformation. By contrast, Thailand in the eighteenth century, although decisively defeated by the Burmese in the last of fourteen wars, found, in the present Chakri dynasty which came to power at the end of the eighteenth century, the diplomatic and other means to preserve its independence despite the advances of English and French imperialism on the Southeast Asian mainland in the nineteenth century.

There remained in Burma what Harvey, a contemporary historian, has called "the immemorial nationalism of the Burmese." [1] It was this nationalism which necessitated a "pacifying" effort by the British after the third Anglo-Burmese war. Several factors strengthened and organized this nationalist feeling into what became a successful independence movement for Burma. Buddhism, the prevailing religion of the country, was the first of these factors. Buddhists resented the way in which British practices lowered the status of their faith. They also resented the substitution of British law, with its emphasis on something called justice, right and wrong, for their customary law with its principles of compromise and of problems in the villages. Under colonial rule, British law often seemed to give preference in decisions to those who were

---

[1] G. E. Harvey, *British Rule in Burma, 1824-1942*. London: Faber and Faber, 1946, p. 90.

non-Burman. In a striking passage, Furnivall sums up this British period which contributed so much to Burmese nationalism:

> The effect of British rule was to remove the abuses of the Burmese political and social system, and endow the people with the privileges of economic freedom and the rule of equal law. But . . . this undermined all the stable elements in social life; it reduced the hereditary leaders of the people to the common rank, broke up the political organization into villages, transformed the village from a social unit into a crowd of individuals; it cut at the roots of the national religion and converted education from a social force into an instrument of individual ambition. The changes, however, were gradual, and the people, while quick to profit by their new freedom, were slow to recognize what they had lost . . . economic forces, subject to no restraint but law, upset the balance of the native economy, sapped its foundations of religious life and institutions, ousted native arts, crafts, and industries, and killed the social pastimes and recreations.[2]

Lest this sound too negative, it must be also borne in mind that Burma's nationalism was maintained by gradual contact with western institutions and was generally influenced by western society. For example, in obvious imitation of Western organizations such as the Young Men's Christian Associations, the Burmese shortly after the turn of the century similarly organized Young Men's Buddhist Associations. As they became acquainted with western law the Burmese became lawyers; they sought, especially after World War I, some place in the judiciary, the civil service, and the various councils which advised the British Governor of Burma. Western conceptions of an independent judiciary, of due process, and of parliamentary constitutional democracy were retained when Burma became independent. When India, through its National Congress, clamored for, and received, limited forms of home rule in 1919, the Burmese by similar exercise secured it in 1923. When advances were made during the next ten to twelve years, leading to the passage of the British Act for India (1935), giving

[2] J. S. Furnivall, *Colonial Policy and Practice: A Comparative Study of Burma and Netherlands India* (Cambridge University Press: 1948), pp. xi-xii.

India, albeit grudgingly, additional forms of self-rule, there was a similar act passed in Burma at the same time, which took effect in 1937. Western education was not only a conduit to economic opportunity; it also provided the content for nationalist schools and for nationalist student strikes. A free public educational system from elementary through graduate and professional schools on Western models has been instituted since independence. What is significant is that in one way or another, from the final annexation of what remained of free Burma in 1885 to the event of independence on January 4, 1948, Burmese nationalists, utilizing both indigenous and foreign institutions, toiled unremittingly toward the re-establishment of Burmese freedom.

One of the infusions in this rising tide of nationalism was "Marxism." A kind of generic Marxism appears in Burma very early, particularly after the seventh meeting of the Comintern in 1935. Some Burmese had had some acquaintance with the writings of the Fabians, the British Laborites, and other Socialist groups in England, but by and large, they absorbed the generalities of the Leninist anti-imperialist Marxist version. The long-ruling Prime Minister of Burma, U Nu, translated some parts of Marx in the mid-1930's, and he and his colleagues at the University of Rangoon organized Marxist study groups, left-wing book clubs and publishing companies. But on the whole, although their generalized "agit-prop" purposes were clear, they evidenced little of the tightly knit party organization typical of Marxism-Leninism elsewhere. They had little interest in the niceties of Marxist argument, and were indifferent to such intellectual exercises as what Marx *et al.* "really meant" or "what is living and what is dead in Marxism." It is significant that prior to independence and excepting party documents, there were few articles or books published in English or Burmese which were devoted to an exposition of Marxist doctrine. They were satisfied primarily by having found in Marxism-Leninism a rationalization for their already existing anti-imperialist points of view.

As events pressed on to World War II these young nationalist Marxists, who called themselves the Thakins (a Burmese word meaning "master" which was commonly demanded in addressing the British, like the Indian "sahib"), to indicate that they considered themselves the equals of the British, adopted a policy on the war resembling Lenin's "Zimmerwald" position. They determined to use the occasion of an imperialist war for national liberation. Almost without exception, when war broke out in 1939, the Thakin movement threatened to turn on the British unless definite promises were forthcoming from London concerning Burmese freedom. This the British refused. The Burmese then turned to Japan, who promised them liberation, and with the exception of less than a half-dozen members of the Thakin movement, Burma remained committed to this point of view even after the Nazi invasion of the Soviet Union. There was, in other words, no pre-World War II Communist party in Burma which conformed to the zigzags of the Comintern "line."

Some of the Thakins during the early war years called themselves Communists, others Socialists; together the major persons among them were members of the National or Burma Revolutionary party, the leader of which was a respected Socialist, Thakin Mya. This party group had above-and-below-ground elements after 1939. During these same years there is evidence that a few Thakins (Soe, Ba Tin, Ba Hein, Thein Pe) began to think of themselves and to act as orthodox Communists, but not until 1942-43 was an identifiable Communist party as such organized, which included the present BCP leader, Thakin Than Tun. Ba Hein is now dead; Thein Pe, known today as Thein Pe Myint, is a left-wing "opposition" leader and prominent writer who remains on good personal terms with his fellow writer U Nu. (For Soe, see below.) The Communists of this period are among the Communist and crypto-Communist leaders of today: Thakins Soe, Than Tun, Ba Tin, (H. Goshal), Lwin, Chit Maung and Bo (military leader) Zeya, Yan Aung, and Ye Htut. Some of these— especially Thakins Soe and Thein Pe—immediately accepted the international Communist line after the Nazi invasion of Russia in 1941, but so did some non-Communist Fabians (e.g., journalist and teacher "Deedok" Ba Choe), who were prepared to give support to the Allies in an antifascist struggle. Others, led by Than Tun, continued to work together with the Socialists and participated in Japan's Burmese puppet-government in 1942-43. Only when the main body of the Thakins became convinced in 1943 that Japanese offers and promises of independence were spurious did they decide to turn on the Japanese and once again make common cause with the British. [3] The decision to resist the Japanese resulted in the formation, in August 1944, of a coalition group called the Anti-Fascist Organization (AFO). The Communists, the Burma Revolutionary party, army leaders, and others met to organize this resistance group, later known as the Anti-Fascist Peoples' Freedom League (AFPFL).

In joining forces, neither the British not the Burmese had illusions of agreement on the basic issue of independence. The Thakins, however, were more aware of British opposition than the British were aware of the reality and extent of the Burmese nationalist movement. Returning to Burma in October 1945, under the terms of the White Paper of May 17, 1945, the British attempted to reinstate their civil government without understanding the change in climate. The White Paper called for the exercise of "emergency powers" (given by the Act of 1935 to the English-appointed governor) until 1948. Only in 1948 would London consider restoring to Burma its prewar status; and then, after another period of delay, Burma might be granted some additional measures of home rule or perhaps dominion status.

The Burmese nationalists-Marxists rejected the British attempts to impose this prewar status. From October 1945 to September 1946, there was organized civil disruption until the new Governor, Sir Hubert Rance, restored order by dealing with General Aung San and recognizing the Anti-Fascist Peoples' Freedom League.[4] The British Labor party had taken approximately eleven months

[3] U Nu, *Burma Under the Japanese* (J. S. Furnivall, ed. and trans.), New York: St. Martin's Press, 1954. See for a firsthand account of these early episodes and the wartime political decisions.

[4] General Aung San—the George Washington of Burmese independence—had been a student leader of the 1936 strike; underground and later aboveground commander of the Burmese Independence Army and succeeding mili-

to arrive at this decision; but when it did, it acted quickly. Prime Minister Attlee announced plans to hold a conference in London with a Burmese delegation to discuss the future of Burma. Accordingly, a politically mixed Burmese group, headed by Bogyoke Aung San, arrived in London in early January 1947. Conversations were begun at No. 10 Downing Street on the thirteenth. Two weeks later, Attlee and Aung San completed their discussions with the signing of an Agreement; the Act of 1935 was to be set aside; the minority groups in Burma would be consulted; a constituent assembly would be elected within the year to draw up a constitution for Burma; and, most important of all, the Burmese people were to have the choice between remaining within or leaving the British Commonwealth.

There was little doubt as to the outcome for Burma. The right-wing and somewhat discredited prewar leaders decided against competing in the elections for the constituent assembly. The Communists contested for seats in twenty-five districts, located in what they regarded as stronghold areas, and won in only six. The AFPFL won 171 of the 182 elective constituencies. The constituent assembly, meeting in June 1947, never hesitated. On June 17th it voted for separation from the Commonwealth and for the creation of an independent, constitutional republic based on a bicameral parliamentary system. But following close to the joyfully received news of the constituent assembly's decision to form an independent Union of Burma came the tragedy of July 19th. General Aung San, leader of the battle for independence, Thakin Mya, and several of their colleagues were assassinated by the henchmen of U Saw. An opportunist and right-wing Prime

---

tary formations. He rose to pre-eminence during the Japanese period. He was the political architect of the campaign which led to Burma's independence. See Frank N. Trager and Associates, *Burma,* 3 vols. (New Haven: Human Relations Area Files, Inc., 1956), Vol. III, pp. 959-1201. See also Clement R. Attlee, *As It Happened* (New York: Viking Press, 1954), pp. 263-266, for a brief and friendly account; admitting the "earlier mistakes" of the British unwillingness to negotiate with General Aung San; and especially, Maung Maung, *Aung San of Burma* (The Hague: Martinus Nijhoff, 1962, forthcoming).

Minister of the prewar period, U Saw was a disgruntled member of the London delegation who had refused to sign the Attlee-Aung San Agreement.

Thakin Nu (known later as U Nu) replaced Aung San as Prime Minister. The constituent assembly's constitution for the Union of Burma was adopted on September 24, 1947, and on October 17, 1947, the Prime Ministers of Burma and England, Nu and Attlee, agreed to the final treaty of independence, which called for a transfer of power on January 4, 1948.

THE STRUGGLE FOR POWER: THE BREAKUP OF THE NATIONAL-MARXIST AMALGAM

Led by Aung San, the Thakins had won the day. In August 1944 their Nationalist-Marxist amalgam had been formed into a typical people's or United Front organization. First called the Anti-Fascist Organization and later renamed the Anti-Fascist Peoples' Freedom League (AFPFL), this coalition included the Socialist and Communist parties and various economic, ethnic, youth, and women's organizations. Almost from the very organization of the AFPFL, differences between the Communists and the non-Communists began to be apparent. At first in 1944-1945 while the war was still on, the Communist faction, led by Than Tun and Thein Pe (who in 1948 refused to go underground with Than Tun and the BCP) was prepared to make concessions to the British (as allies of the Soviet Union) which the Socialists, led by Aung San and Thakin Mya, thought damaging to Burma's strategy for independence. Later, in 1946 and 1947, when the Socialists were winning their battle for independence with the British, especially with the victorious Labour Party in England, the Communists did everything in their power to embarrass the AFPFL, offering public opposition to the steps taken by it to achieve the final victory. One faction of the Communist party, led by Thakin Soe (subsequently known as the Red Flag Communists), went underground in 1946, and since then has engaged in insurgent activity.[5] Difficulties with the remaining Communist faction (later called the White Flags, led by Than Tun), increased when Aung San, Thakin Mya, and other socialist leaders, displaced a Communist from the key post of Secretary-General of the AFPFL with one of their own number. The struggle for power became even more bitter when, in October 1946, the AFPFL entered the Governor's Executive Council and took over the government. Though the Communists were awarded one seat (Thein Pe) in this governing council, they bid for more while simultaneously attacking the majority leadership with increased intensity. Finally on October 10, 1946, the AFPFL leadership democratically ejected the Communist party from the coalition. At the time of the expulsion, Aung San spoke against the Communists at length, accusing them of engaging in subversive activities inside the League and out. He stated that the Communists had never had any faith in democratic processes and were moved only by the consuming ambition to gain absolute power. In his speech, Aung San further accused the Burma Communist party of substituting Moscow's directives for conscience. From that time forward a clear-cut conflict has existed between the AFPFL, and its successor organizations after the split in 1958, and the Burma Communist Party.

Though the Communists opposed the 1947 Aung San-Nu-Attlee agreement leading to independence, they made a momentary show of cooperation after the assassinations in July 1947. U Nu, thereupon, throughout the rest of 1947 and in early 1948, made a series of moves to reforge the wartime unity of the Socialists, Communists, and other factions within the AFPFL. None of these efforts could have succeeded, which U Nu and his colleagues did not know at the time. For, as a result of the reorganization of the Cominform in September 1947, Moscow had determined to

[5] Thakin Soe broke with Than Tun over the control of the Communist Party, since he claimed priority over Than Tun as a resistance leader. Soe and his faction have frequently been called Trotskyites. There is not the faintest resemblance between his faction and any known Trotsky group. He is a Marxist dogmatist not unlike Daniel De Leon; an isolated radical who has been able to command a small and fanatical following.

direct a series of blows at Southern Asia. In order to bring about an understanding of its reversion to a "left" strategy (most clearly represented by the Comintern in its so-called Third Period, 1928-1935), Moscow had dispatched to Asia various Communist couriers and indigenous Communist party leaders who had been resident in the U.S.S.R. during the previous years (e.g., S. Dange to India, Musso to Indonesia, etc.). From November 1947 through March 1948 a series of meetings were held in India (in Bombay and Calcutta) during which time the Indian Communist party (CPI) served both as the host for Communist party representatives from European and Southern Asian countries, and as the vehicle through which the new "left" line was transmitted throughout Southern Asia.[6] Than Tun and H. Goshal of Burma were present at these meetings in India and dutifully adopted the new Cominform line, which called for revolution, armed struggle, and "national liberation," even in those countries which had already won their independence.

This change in policy and line of action was puzzling, even to some Communists. In Burma, Thein Pe (who had by this time been demoted from the Central Committee of the party) was bewildered by the turn of events. In a letter written to Comrade Dange of the Communist party of India in October, 1950, he looked back at the events of 1948 and described his reactions to them:

> The Party at first welcomed it (the Nu-Attlee Agreement and independence). . . . The Party participated in the independence celebrations. Than Tun himself witnessed the transfer of power in the presence of the President of the Union of Burma.
>
> Then came the interview given by Goshal[7] at Calcutta to the special correspondent of the *People's Age* which appeared in the issue of January 4, 1948. It was the new line which was entirely

[6] For a discussion of these conferences, see Frank N. Trager, editor, *Marxism in Southeast Asia* (Stanford University Press, 1959), pp. 263-273.

[7] Goshal, alias Comrade Ba Tin, born in Bengal, brought up and educated in Burma. He attended the Bombay meetings of the Communist party of India as a member of the Central Committee of the Communist party (Burma); he is still in 1962 the theoretician of the party and one of its top leaders.

different from the then official party line. He gave it out as the Party line on his own initiative and responsibility. It was a serious crime that he committed. But when he came back he got his line adopted by the Central Committee. He continued to be the Politburo Member.

When I got that issue of the *People's Age* I could see that it was another swing. I recognized it as an attempt to transplant the CPI line into Burma. I submitted my criticism to the Central Committee which never considered it. I was, at that time, supposed to be a Party member, but I was not given any responsibility nor assigned to any cell in spite of my repeated requests.

Than Tun went to the second congress of the CPI [Calcutta, 1948]. You can recall his speech there. How warlike it was! Two blows to be returned for one blow of the Government! Do as the CPC does to the Kuomintang! We have guerrilla fighters, etc. The Socialist Party was worried with Goshal's interview and Than Tun's speech and reports they got from the police. The Socialists did not like the prospect of a civil war. A Socialist leader, at the instructions of his Party, contacted me and urged me to bring about reconciliation. I could only report it to Than Tun and ask for a meeting between the Party and the Socialists. Than Tun did not reply.[8]

Thus, on signal from Moscow, through the vehicle of the CPI, the Communists in India, Burma, Malaya, and Indonesia followed the left strategy of the Cominform and went into armed struggle. (A similar policy had already been initiated in Indo-China and the Philippines. But in the former the Communists took guidance from the French Communist party, which, as in the 1930's, heralded before others a change in line.) In India and Indonesia, Nehru on the one hand and Sukarno and Hatta on the other were quickly able to suppress the Communist uprising. In Burma and Malaya, however, the uprisings continued, at first in great force and finally diminishing to sporadic action, up to the present.

[8] Letter in English reproduced in Thein Pe Myint *Political Memoirs* (in Burmese) (Rangoon: Shwepyidan Press, 1957). See also John S. Thomsin in F. N. Trager, editor, *Marxism in Southeast Asia, op. cit.*, pp. 38-39. Note: CPC—Communist party (China).

No story out of independent Burma has been told more often in the Western press than that of the multicolored insurgents, and no story has been more important to the Burmese. Each group of insurgents adopted some colored flag or arm band as a mark of recognition. Basically, there were two major groups of rebels—one Communist, the other ethnic. The Communists were not always united: they were followers of either Thakins Soe or Than Tun, or were disgruntled ex-soldiers from a servicemen's organization called the People's Volunteer Organization (PVO). At various times the Communist factions united and then broke apart. The ethnic rebels were led mainly by a minority called the Karens (long favored by the British, an object of Christian missionary attention since the early nineteenth century and historically at odds with the majority group, called the Burmans) and constituted as serious an element in the insurrection as the Communists because of their military and intellectual leadership. The Karen rebels, known as the Karen National Defense Organization (KNDO) occasionally united (and still do) with the Communists and with the remnants of the Kuomintang, the KMT's, or Chinese Nationalists.

These Chinese Nationalist troops escaped from Mao into Burma via Yunnan. From 1950 to 1954, they did their best to take control of the northeastern reaches of Burma and otherwise to harass the central government in Rangoon. Originally a force of twelve to seventeen hundred troops led by General Li Mi, they were gradually reinforced by local and over-the-border recruits and supplied with American and other equipment and cadre leadership from the Republic of China on Taiwan. Their number increased to twelve hundred by 1952-1953. Not only did they refuse to lay down their arms or be quietly repatriated, but they used Burma's territory as a base for futile raids across the border into Communist China—thereby inviting Communist China's retaliation against Burma. By 1953, their encroachments on Burmese territory, their pillaging and terrorizing of the villages and countryside of the area had become so serious that Burma made a formal, and on the whole successful, appeal to the United Nations for aid in dealing with the problem.[9]

As the Prime Minister U Nu has said of these precarious years, "We were two inches from the edge of the precipice." For a time the writ of law of the Central Government did not extend much beyond the perimeter of Rangoon. Gradually, the Burmese army, which was rebuilt by Chief of Staff General Ne Win with the help of the militia, extended central power throughout the country. In 1961—after a temporary letdown of security throughout the country—U Nu (still Prime Minister) reported that there were about 3,000 Karens and 1,500 Communists among the various insurgent forces.[10]

The Communist insurrections and others have been a dangerous drain on the country's resources. "It is not possible to furnish a complete list of the damage and loss incurred on account of the insurrection," U Nu has pointed out.

But according to statistics that could be gathered up to the end of 1955, loss of civilian lives in Burma amount to 22,077; loss of life of soldiers, armed personnel and other government servants

[9] The United States had been approached to use its good offices before Burma went to the U.N. but did not respond effectively. After the 1953-54 U.N. appeals, the U.S., together with Thailand, used "good offices" to evacuate about 5,000-6,000 of these KMT troops, including families. A similar number were evacuated in 1960. Remaining small bands, now officially disavowed by Taiwan, have taken to banditry and smuggling in the corner of Burma where it joins Thailand, Laos, and Yunnan. They continue to make trouble in the area, uniting with dissident elements among the Shans and Kachins, and otherwise obstructing the central government in Rangoon. They are still an invitation to danger from Peking. Present estimates place their number at about 750. See U Nu, *Speech to Parliament*, August 15, 1961. This speech was printed serially in the *Burma Weekly Bulletin* from August 24, 1961, *et seq.*

[10] These figures are based on frequent but incomplete releases and statements from high officials. See for example: U Nu, *Ibid.*; also *The Guardian*, April 1, 1961; *The Burma Weekly Bulletin*, July 20, 1961. A more detailed and at the time more hopeful picture of armed encounters, casualties on both sides and surrenders for the period November 1958-December 1959, i.e., during the first regime of Prime Minister General Ne Win, will be found in *Is Trust Vindicated* (Rangoon: Government Printing, 1960), pp. 19-58. Since the second Ne Win government took power, increased pressure on remaining Communist and ethnic insurgents, including these KMT remnants, may be expected.

amounts to 5,693; the extent of damage and destruction caused to railway lines, government buildings and other public property runs to kyats 250 million [one kyat = 21 cents], and the extent of damage and destruction of properties owned by civilians comes to more than kyats 448 million.[11]

As well as the damage to life and property which the Communists have inflicted, their corruption of minds should be noted as another obstacle in Burma's path to genuine and durable democracy.

Since the change of policy following Stalin's death in 1953, both the insurgent Communist groups led by Than Tun and their aboveground counterparts in the Burma Worker's party have occupied themselves in calling for a "negotiated peace" between the government and the Communists—the last one was reported in the Burmese press on January 22, 1961. Periodically, the government has issued amnesty orders, calling upon the rebels to give up the "cult of the gun" and take the "path of legality" (repeated in Parliament in November, 1961). The partial success of these appeals is shown by figures available to the end of 1956, which claimed a grand total of 28,000 surrenders, of which 5,000-5,600 were assumed to be Communists.

But internal security in Burma still depends on safeguards against insurrectionary activity, infiltration from Communist China, and political subversion. Communist and Karen rebels, including the more recent insurgency of other dissident ethnic groups among the Shans and Kachins (aided respectively by the KMT's and probably the Chinese Communists) can still blow up a train or water main or track. They can still severely inhibit the efforts of the government to bring law and order to some remaining parts of the countryside. But the rebel attempts have become more and more circumscribed. Some day the government's armed forces will locate, kill, or capture the remaining hard-core leaders of the rebellions. When they do there will be an end to insurrection. This may not be far off because of the announced determination of the new Ne Win regime. Then Burma will face the task

11 U Nu, Speech in the Chamber of Deputies, September 27, 1957 (Rangoon: Government Printing Office, 1957), p. 51.

of wiping out what has become during the past years a profession of armed banditry or dacoity, in many instances hidden behind a political, insurrectionary mask.

The political insurrections in Burma have been, as we have seen, costly. Politically they have failed for the three following reasons, all interrelated. First, the insurrectionists never forged a sustained, unified attack upon the government, and their dissentient opinion, as well as the counterattack of the government, kept them divided. The Communists especially tried to imitate the Chinese and create in Burma a counterpart of "Yenan." This they never succeeded in doing, though in various villages in the dry zone they were able to force support from villagers. They never succeeded in establishing a base of operations contiguous with Communist China.

Second, during the early years of the rebellion, that is, from 1948 to 1953, the Sino-Soviet axis was occupied with bigger political game than the Burmese. These were the years in which Mao consolidated power in China and in which the Chinese Communists were primarily concerned with North Korea and North Vietnam. The amount of tangible Sino-Soviet aid to the Burmese Communists—other than propaganda and ill-will expressed toward the Burmese government—was not large. When the Sino-Soviet "line" changed again in 1954-1955, the Burmese central government, like the rest of newly independent Afro-Asia, was genially cultivated and tendered the kind of "outstretched hand of friendliness" which Stalin had used during the Peoples' Front years of 1935-1939. Local Communist parties that were engaged in insurrectionary activity in Burma and elsewhere were not then the object of "B & K" smiles.

Third, and perhaps most important, the AFPFL government was able for several reasons of its own to sustain itself during periods of attacks from the insurrectionists. It did this by carrying on the ordinary business of government; by reorganizing the trade-union and peasant movements; and by working hard at the enterprises that the Communists are normally credited with doing. The central government launched its *Pyidawtha*, or welfare state plan, and, aided by the Korean war boom, found itself almost to the end of 1953 in a sellers' market for its raw materials and agricultural products. Its finances were in good order, with favorable balances of trade making foreign exchange available for necessary imports. The armed forces carried on a psychological warfare campaign against the Communists, following up military gains in the village areas with civil organization. One interesting aspect of the government's psychological campaign was its success in setting up rehabilitation camps, where surrendered rebels were fed and housed with their families while being prepared to re-enter civilian life with a new trade. Of course, the government suffered setbacks, but its progress toward ultimate victory was unmistakable. Essential to its success was the fact that the Communists in Burma were not fighting against an imperialist opponent but against genuine nationalists, socialists, and others who had fought for and brought independence to Burma.

3. THE SOVIET UNION, COMMUNIST CHINA, AND BURMA

The Communist Party rising in Burma during the 1940's never hesitated to take guidance from Moscow and (after 1947) from the Cominform, which originally operated through the Communist party of India. When Lenin turned to the East at the second Comintern meeting of 1920, India became the first target for Communist operations in Asia. Subsequently, China became the more immediate and major goal. Both India and Indonesia retained relative important positions in the plans of the Comintern. Burma was largely ignored in the twenties and thirties even by the Indian Communists. In this context, therefore, Moscow's real interest and role in Burma began after the organization of the Cominform in 1947. In the same year, Communists from Burma were invited to a British Empire Communist gathering in London sponsored by the Communist party of Great Britain (CPGB). In similar fashion, contact between the BCP and Yugoslavia (then a member in good standing of the Cominform) was established. Moscow had not put out much literature on Burma during the immediate postwar years. Its Cominform policy came to be reflected in a "secret" document brought back by Goshal from Bombay and Calcutta meetings in 1947 and 1948.

In this document we can follow the "line"—Burma, like India, was accused of having a "fake independence." U Nu, his government and the Socialists, were said to be acting as "the tools of imperialism." The Nu-Attlee Agreement was a "treaty of slavery and humiliation," dictated by the British. This same document, *On the Present Situation in Burma and our Tasks*, criticizes the local Communists in Burma (as in India) for having been "reformist" and for having been willing to support the provisional and independent government of Burma. ("Browderism" was the name for this sin of reformism in Asia. This appears to be the only attempt to introduce American terms in the ongoing Communist internal factional warfare.) Now, after the Cominform and Indian meetings, the document called for the "creation of a fighting force" capable of achieving "the final seizure for power," loyal only to "the teachings of Communism and hatred of social democratic reformism." Reflecting this international Communist line, through 1953 *Pravda* kept up a series of attacks on "the right-wing socialist traitors" in Burma who have "recruited from the dregs of society" in order to organize "repressions against the working class . . . and the movement of peasants."

But during these years, one consequence of the success of the Chinese Communists on the mainland was the gradual shift of guidance for the Burma Communist party and other Southern Asian Communist parties from Moscow to Peking. The BCP is known to have addressed communications to Red China and in turn to have been guided by the Chinese Communists.[12] As a re-

[12] Thuriya Than Maung, "Burma and the Red Star," in *The New Burma Weekly*, IV (Jan. 31, 1959), 165-167. Thuriya Than Maung is an ex-Communist, who joined the BCP armed revolution in 1949 and served as the chairman of the Mandalay BCP until 1955, when he became disillusioned with the Communists and left the party. Most recently, at the beginning of January 1962, a Communist student front in Rangoon celebrating its sixth anniversary by burning effigies of Khrushchev and Mikoyan as "reactionaries."

sult, ever since February 1951, Chinese Communists have been active in the training of Burmese Communist cadres both in Burma and at Kunming, China.

The U Nu government was not unaware of these events, and was then as always in fear of its big neighbor to the north. Burma was the first government in Asia to recognize the People's Republic of China (PRC) and has steadfastly urged Peking's entry into the United Nations.[13] These essentially protective devices have been regarded as necessary, in part to counterbalance not only the domestic Communists, but also the very real danger created by the warlike activities of the Kuomintang troops in Burma, which served as a continuing invitation for some kind of retaliatory measure by Peking. But, most of all, Burma's relations to the PRC have been dictated by her now realized desire to secure a treaty with Peking which would demarcate her borders with mainland China.

This is too long and too complicated a story to treat here in detail.[14] Suffice it to say that from 1949 onward Burma made overtures to get such a treaty with Peking. Armed clashes between Burmese and Chinese troops took place in mid-1953 and again in 1956. At a time when the PRC had alarmed many Asians (and others) by suppressing Tibetan autonomy and by its determination to press southward into India, its leaders elected to achieve a more favorable impression by concluding a fair border treaty with Burma. Serious negotiations were begun in 1959 and concluded by a treaty in 1960. In October 1961, a protocol was signed by the two governments completing, in record time, the task of delimiting the border (except for a small sector on the India-China-Burma confluence).

Earlier, in a review of foreign policy, U Nu had described the period up to 1954 as one in which Burmese relations with the

---

13 *Statement* by Ambassador U On Sein, 1073rd Plenary Meeting, XVI UNGA, December 7, 1961.

14 See, Maung Maung, "The Burma-China Border," *India Quarterly*, Vol. XVI, No. 4, October-December 1960, pp. 358-364; and Frank N. Trager, *Burma and the United States*, published by the Council on Foreign Relations in 1962.

new Chinese government "remained uncertain for a number of years" and mentions that the "Soviet Union apparently decided to treat us as 'on probation.'" [15] The change in Sino-Soviet policy after the death of Stalin and the concurrent depression of the export rice market at the end of the Korean war boom made Burma agreeable to a series of barter-and-credit aid programs offered by the bloc. The ensuing "aid" experience with the U.S.S.R., especially between 1955 and 1957, did not work out to the satisfaction of Burma. However, the trade and credit agreements with China, like the border settlement, appear to have given both countries what they sought at the time. As a result, Sino-Burmese diplomatic relations today are characterized by frequent cultural exchanges and expressions of mutual satisfaction. The PRC's pursuit of a "peaceful" policy with Burma as with Cambodia has strengthened its hand in mainland Southeast Asia. Whether it has removed the underlying fear and suspicion of the Chinese, historically existing in Burma, is doubtful. The present relations between the two countries have not yet influenced the course of Burma's internal policy and ideological development.

4. IDEOLOGY AND PRACTICE IN BURMA

The Nationalist-Marxist amalgam which succeeded in re-establishing the independence of Burma never had been a well-defined ideology. Its adherents had been unified in the AFPFL primarily by their agreement on the object of attack, the colonial regime, and by their voiced aspiration for a free Burma. The Nationalist-Marxists were to a large extent activists. That is, they were, among other things, trade-union and peasant organizers, students, and soldiers. They called themselves Socialists, Communists, or Marxists because Marxism seemed to rationalize their anti-imperialist and anticapitalist outlook. (One must remember that in

[15] *Premier Reports to the People* (Rangoon: Government Printing, 1957), pp. 35-36, 41.

Burma and throughout Southern Asia the capitalists were usually foreigners whose profits were largely repatriated.) Originally, the "Marxists" were all Burmese patriots with no overseas attachments. This common origin tended to obscure the need for the inevitable differentiation which has everywhere taken place among those who adopt a "Marxist" philosophy of revolutionary theory and practice. It also created dangerous illusions among some Burmese leaders who believed that they could "win back" or otherwise convert their erstwhile comrades who were "deluded" by those whom U Nu charitably called the "Pied Pipers." These latter cause "foolish children . . . [to] listen to their aunt rather than to their mother." [16] U Nu himself spent precious years seeking to re-establish "Marxist" unity. But, in time and in a conventional and traditional fashion, the split between the Socialists and non-Communists on the one side and Communists on the other came about by their rival attitudes toward the road to power and the nature of power. The Socialists and other nationalists gravitated, at first hesitatingly, toward democracy both as means and end; the Communists, as always, were totalitarian. Neither the Burmese Socialists nor the Communists have produced a literature for and about their revolution, though a few books, articles, and many speeches are available to trace their evolution. The Socialists in this amalgam learned through the experience of the pre-insurrectionary and insurrectionary years that they had to "break with" the Communists if they and Burma were to survive in a constitutional, parliamentary democracy. They had to rid themselves of the staunchly held *Burmese* view which romanticized the "*Burmese* Nationalism" sufficiently to embrace the Communists. Somehow many Burmese Communists felt they were more "Burmese" than "Communist" and that relations between Socialists and Communists would be "different" in Burma from those elsewhere. These illusory, sentimental views gradually gave way before the bitter experience of trying to achieve a small, stable nation.

As indicated, the non-Communist AFPFL had to expel the Communist party from the AFPFL in 1946 and take up arms

[16] *Burma Under the Japanese, op. cit.*, p. ix.

against them in 1948. Once again, in 1950, they faced a similar challenge from a group of crypto-Communists still holding membership in the AFPFL. This group had not gone underground in 1948. In and out of the Parliament these crypto-Communists fought within the AFPFL and against U Nu's government on the issue of foreign policy, refusing to support the government's affirmative votes in the U.N. on the major 1950 Korean resolutions and demanding support for the Sino-Soviet line.[17] They broke away from the AFPFL and formed the Burma's Workers' and Peasants' party (BWPP), now called the Burma Workers' party (BWP). Since then, this opposition group has been a consistent, legal, above-ground Communist party, always expressing whatever is the current international Communist line. In addition to its support to the insurgents' cries for a "negotiated peace," the BWP is constantly reiterating current and traditional Communist party domestic slogans. At its last Congress (held in Rangoon from December 27, 1957 to January 2, 1958), it listed a number of its policies. Among other things, the BWP is determined to fight the AFPFL (and its successors), which they consider the organ of imperialism; to ally their party with Workers' parties all over the world; to nationalize all paddy fields and foreign enterprise; to assist capitalist nationals in competition with foreign investors (while at the same time preventing them from abusing their position); to put foreign trade under state control; and, to strive for more economic and cultural cooperation with the Communist Bloc.[18]

[17] *Security Council OR, Supplement for June, July and August 1950*, Document S/1950. *United Nations, OR of the Fifth General Assembly*, First Committee, Summary Recordings of Meetings, 353rd Meeting, October 4, 1950. See Frank N. Trager (and others), *Burma's Role in the United Nations 1948-1955*, Institute of Pacific Relations (New York: 1956), pp. 6-8.

[18] Alex Josey, "The Political Significance of the Burma Workers' Party," *Pacific Affairs*, XXXI (December 1958), pp. 374-375. In addition to the above, the BWP adopts the typical attitude toward any joint venture scheme involving western capital, or any plan involving Western aid. Conversely, every opportunity is taken to laud the U.S.S.R. and Communist China. When the Burma-China border problem was under discussion, Chou En-lai's proposals for negotiations were loudly greeted. When it became apparent that part of the Kachin state would be lost by Burma, the BWP and the Burmese Communist press were forced to maintain a discreet silence.

The AFPFL had no difficulty in weathering the 1950 split, and, if anything, it prompted the Socialist leadership of the League to define its own ideology and to organize the Asian Socialist Conference. The Asian Socialist Conference was formed in January 1953 and forced the Burmese Socialists to think through their position on the major issues of the day. Although there is very little written documentation of the Asian Socialist Conference, there is enough, together with what figures such as Asoka Mehta of India and Sjahrir of Indonesia have supplied, to support the view that the Asian Socialists, including the Burmese, are ideologically and practically committed to a program of democratic socialism. It was in the context of the Asian Socialist Conference meetings between 1953 and 1956 that the Burmese Socialists redefined their views on imperialism, having concluded that "ruthless" Soviet imperialism was more dangerous than the old-style Western imperialism, precisely because the former came under the guide of Communism. U Kyaw Nyein at Kalaw, Burma, in 1954, and U Ba Swe at Bombay, India, in 1956, criticizing the Hungarian suppression, were the chief spokesmen for this reorientation.[19] All the Burmese leaders other than the Communists and their allies had already endorsed the "Principles and Objectives of Socialism," adopted in 1953 by the Asian Socialist Conference, which rejected Communism and accepted and defined "democratic socialism." [20]

Just before a second and major AFPFL split in April 1958 (see below), Prime Minister U Nu, speaking for the entire Cabinet, and fully supported by his usual party opponent, U Kyaw Nyein, not only advocated strong adherence to the ideology of democratic socialism but also indicated a break with "Marxism," which he defined as synonymous with Communism.[21] It is quite probable

---

[19] Kyaw Nyein, "To Prefer Is Not to Choose," *Socialist Asia*, Vol. III (June 1954), pp. 9-11; and Ba Swe, "Asian Socialists Look Ahead," *Socialist Call*, Vol. XXV (January-February 1957), p. 20.

[20] See *Report of the First Asian Socialist Conference*, Rangoon, 1953, which reprints the resolutions of the Conference in the Appendix, pp. 91-110.

[21] *Towards a Socialist State*. Speech, January 29, 1958. Third All Burma Congress of the AFPFL (Rangoon: Government Printing Office, 1958), 68

that some leading socialists in Burma do not entirely agree with U Nu's definitions and wish to regard themselves as democrats, socialists, and even Marxists, but all of them, as far as one can tell, accept his utter rejection of Communism. The Nationalist-Marxist amalgam had thus become divided, whatever labels are used, into those still supporting Communism, and those preferring democratic socialism.

A further major development in Burmese politics occurred in April 1958, when the incessant arguments, personality differences, and personal feuds among AFPFL leaders bust into the open, accompanied by strong invective. The differences, basically nonideological in nature, resulted from an accumulation of petty quarrels over the twenty years when the same group of men had worked together for Burmese independence. Differences which had been overlooked during times of common trouble became increasingly important with the growth in peace and security afforded by AFPFL successes. In April, headlines appeared which shattered the illusion of unity and comradeship among AFPFL leaders. The debate was of such a personal nature, however, that for a time allegiances shifted back and forth as rank and file members debated loyalties. After this battle the AFPFL leadership split into two factions. U Nu, supporting Deputy Prime Minister Thakin Tin, was aligned against former Prime Minister U Ba Swe and Deputy Prime Minister U Kyaw Nyein: the factions referred to themselves as the "Clean AFPFL" and the "Stable AFPFL," respectively. As a result of the split, the U Kyaw Nyein group called for a vote of confidence in June 1958. U Nu barely managed to retain his majority by a margin of eight votes (including the support of the crypto-Communist BWP and other minority groups). An impasse was reached in August when U Nu postponed the budgetary session of Parliament, knowing that he could not be sure of his customary slim majority. By September 1958, a stalemate had forced U Nu to announce that he had asked General Ne Win, chief of the armed forces, to take over the govern-

pp. This is the longest document of its kind since World War II by any Socialist in Burma.

ment on a "caretaker" basis (for a six-month period demanded by the Constitution), until new elections could be held. After six months, General Ne Win resigned, but resumed the prime ministership when Parliament amended the constitution to extend the period of the caretaker government, so as to allow the interim government adequate time to prepare for promised elections.[22]

At the time of the split and after the constitutional installation of General Ne Win's caretaker government, some felt that the military takeover was endangering democracy in Burma. The legitimacy of General Ne Win's government was seldom questioned. General Ne Win had earned his nationalist reputation as an early member of the 1930's "We Burmans" Association, and also as a trusted member of General Aung San's "Thirty Comrades," who were trained by the Japanese in 1941 to become leaders of the Burma Independence Army. But as *The New Republic* commented (November 10, 1958), "there is always the danger that younger officer elements whose horizons are not the democratic socialistic horizons of Ne Win may one day make illegitimate capital of the present crisis."

However, the younger officers did not act and General Ne Win proceeded to carry out the announced "national ideology" of the Defense Services. This rather unusual document had been in preparation since 1956 and was completed in October 1958. It embraced a threefold commitment to: "Freedom and the Restoration of Peace and the Rule of Law"; "Democracy"; and "the Establishment of a Socialist Economy." [23] General Ne Win as Prime Minister prepared the grounds for a new national and democratic

[22] For a more detailed discussion, see Maung Maung, "Burma at the Crossroads," *India Quarterly*, XIV (October-December. 1958) and Frank N. Trager, "The Political Split in Burma, " *Far Eastern Survey*, XXVII (October 1958), pp. 145-155. Also Frank N. Trager, "Political Divorce in Burma," *Foreign Affairs*, XXXVII (January 1959), pp. 317-327.

[23] For the full text see *Is Trust Vindicated*, *op. cit.*, pp. 534-541. This volume of 567 pages is the most complete record of General Ne Win's 1958-1960 regime. For a brief and competent survey, see John Seabury Thomson "The Ne Win Administration and After," Supplement, "A Second Chance for Burma: The Interim Government and the 1960 Elections," in J. S. Furnivall, *The Governance of Burma*, 2nd ed., enlarged (New York: Institute of Pacific Relations, 1960), pp. 133-154.

election which was held in February 1960. The major contestants were three parties: the Union party of U Nu, the Ba Swe-Kyaw Nyein AFPFL, and the crypto-Communists of the National United Front. The Union party and its allies won an overwhelming victory, capturing approximately 80 per cent of the 250 seats in the more powerful chamber of the bicameral Parliament. The NUF Communists failed to win a single seat.

U Nu, as expected, again became the Prime Minister—a post which until March 1962, he had held for all but approximately three years since Burma's independence. He delivered his first policy speech to the new Parliament on April 5, 1960, an able and eloquent exposition of democratic ideology and practice,[24] which embodied a call for a "crusade for democracy." "Burma," he said, "has just passed through a period in her history which is unique"; moreover her chosen "path of democracy is the most difficult that man has ever trodden in history"; "Burma's independence will be meaningless" without democracy which must be carefully nurtured until it takes "firm root . . . native to our soil." He recognized that a democratic government thrives on a constructive Opposition and that a democratic system requires—as Burma has had— free elections. He further pointed out that a democratic parliamentary system should respect the nonpartisan independence of the civil service administration and should abide by the constitutional rule of law in an orderly society which upholds "the freedom and equality of the individual against violation by the state." Though committed, as in the past, to planned economic activity in which various elements are retained in a socialized sector, he promised to set limits to the participation of the state so as to avoid the appearance and practice of "totalitarian" power.[25]

[24] *Burma Weekly Bulletin* (Rangoon: Government Printing Office, April 7, 1960). It is to be noted that U Nu's speeches in and out of Parliament since January 4, 1948 have been the major source of Burma's avowed policy. At considerable length he returned to this theme in his *Speech* to Parliament, Aug. 15, 1961. *Ibid.*, August 24, 1961, *et seq.*
[25] Burma has had a succession of "Plans" from the First or Two Year Plan in 1948 to the present. See Frank N. Trager, *Building a Welfare State in Burma* (New York: Institute of Pacific Relations, 1958). The most recent one is called *Second Four Year Plan for the Union of Burma* (1961-62 to

As in the past, he endorsed the philosophy of cultural pluralism as necessary and desirable in Burma's multi-ethnic society as it evolved into a national, unified, federalized entity.

It may be argued that this oratory has little reference to the daily business of democratic nation-building. It may also be argued that the act of the members of Parliament swearing to uphold the Union constitution and its laws (see footnote 25) is a *pro-forma* act having slight bearing on the actual state of affairs in Burma. But such arguments do not take into account the real characteristics of the ideological development of independent Burma. Nor do the occasional infringements of civil rights or freedom of the press mean that Burma is not committed to democracy.

For the new military coup in Burma and the dictatorship of seventeen leading officers established by the Union Revolutionary Council do not constitute denial of the Burmese commitment to democratic socialism. Rather, what has happened in Burma is an overwhelming indication that the institutional tasks of nation-building (retaining national unity and advancing the economic and social development of the country in terms of the ideology) were too much for the nationalist group who had brought independence to Burma. That the nationalists—faced with the tasks of rehabilitating their devastated country, of holding off ethnic and Communist rebellions, survived at all is a miracle. Initially a small group of radical patriots, sloppily imbibing a Marxist-Leninist view of history and society, the nationalists gradually rejected doctrinaire Marxism without losing faith in political and economic slogans, the mere reiteration of which they thought would change society.

Ever since its independence, Burma has lacked trained administrators, technologists, and others necessary for the business of government and the economy. A deep-seated suspicion has existed between the political leadership in power and the civilian bureaucracy, mitigated only somewhat by interdependence. The

---

1964-65) (Rangoon: Government Printing Office, 1961), 215 pp. This plan was subsequently approved by the Parliament. For an example of local explanation and criticism see *The Guardian* (Rangoon), Mar., 20-23, 1961.

factional political warfare which led to the split of the AFPFL in 1958 (after these groups had presumably agreed on ideology) was a major event in leading up to the present. For as this small group of nationalist leaders became constantly more differentiated, they failed to produce a coherent and competent group of leaders to succeed them.

In this turbulent ideological milieu, U Nu set about lining up his new Union party for the February 1960 elections. So tenuous was his majority in the 1958 Parliament that he organized a strenuous campaign, promising rewards to various sectors of the electorate. He promised more states (to the Arakanese and to the Mons) and more states' rights (to the Shans), which predicted the weakening of Burma's existing constitutional "federal" unity. He promised to make Buddhism the state religion, which naturally alarmed Burma's non-Buddhist minorities, and promised to nationalize sectors of Burma's economy at a time when Burma's economy showed declining vitality. U Nu, who was an honorable, religious-minded individual, and obviously Burma's outstanding political figure, began to fulfill his promises after an overwhelming victory at the polls. His faith in democracy and in Buddhism were never so eloquently and so frequently enunciated as during the post-election period of 1960.[26]

But U Nu did not wisely assess the costs of what he hoped to accomplish. Even if he had, he was handicapped by the further dissolution of whatever unity held together his own nationalist group, the Union party. For immediately following its victory his party began to exhibit irreparable splits. As in the fight which led up to the AFPFL division in 1958, there was again little or no

[26] There are a few Muslims and Christians among the Burmese leaders. But most are Buddhists. Burmese Buddhist culture patterns require of their adherents an individual, intentional morality (which, incidentally does not readily accommodate to the totalitarian potential of Marxism). That is, "the Buddhist Eightfold Path" is self-caused, self-walked, and self-directed. But Buddhism also embraces the social doctrine of *Metta*, or other-directedness. Hence, Burmese Buddhists have had little or no difficulty in reconciling social democracy with Buddhism. See Frank N. Trager, "Reflections on Buddhism and the Social Order in Southern Asia," *Burma Research Society Fiftieth Anniversary Publication*, 1 (Rangoon, 1961), pp. 529-543.

ideological issue between the factions, but instead charges of dishonesty, bribery, corruption, and ballot-box stuffing. At one stage, early in 1961, the bickering became so fierce that one wing of the armed forces, led by Brigadiers Maung Maung and Aung Shwe, proposed that the military take over the government. On the appeal of the Prime Minister, General Ne Win at that time decided against these officers and for U Nu. The officers were either assigned away from Burma as ambassadors or military attachés or allowed to resign. The threat of this military venture caused a temporary lull in the inner Union party fighting. But again in the second half of 1961 dissension broke out—and this time more fiercely, culminating in a party "primary" convention during the last week of January 1962. The winning faction was led by members of the dissident group whose roles in the AFPFL had precipitated the 1958 split.

And U Nu, despite his dedication to Burma's fate, seemed unable or unwilling to halt this deterioration. The country was moving toward political dissolution and economic stagnation. As I saw it when I was in Burma, in late March 1962; a military solution seemed to be the only possible one capable of arresting the decline. General Ne Win—a nationalist leader since the early 1930's—and his officers, including some who had been politically oriented by the Socialist party, made the final decision to take over the government early in the morning of March 2, 1962.

At this time, April 1962, one can only speculate about the future prospects of Burma. The military this time has abrogated the Constitution and dissolved executive and legislative functions. The Revolutionary Council rules. The military has reorganized the judiciary by combining the supreme and high courts into one court of appeal. Unlike the first military rule in October 1958, there has been no promise of early elections. Instead, there is study of political institutions in other countries in which the military have taken power. However, there is still much evidence to support the hope that General Ne Win will continue Burma's policy of "positive" and "strict" neutrality in foreign affairs while following a mixed enterprise system in the domestic economy—

what I have elsewhere called "a tropical variant of the Scandinavian pattern." The restoration of political democracy in Burma will be gradual. Until there emerges some sort of reliable and capable political alignment that represents a democratic socialist or social-democratic ideology most congenial to the Burmese, the restoration will be suspended. The major prerequisites for Burma's democratic future are not those relating to ideology, for on this score there is little argument in Burma except from the Communists and their allies. What is crucially needed is reliable and capable leadership.

COMMUNISM IN AFRICA

I. William Zartman

■ In Africa as elsewhere, Communism has presented itself as a fellow traveler and loyal ally of nationalism. The propaganda, aid programs, and diplomacy of the Soviet and Chinese governments emphasize the Communist-bloc countries' desire and intention to penetrate the African continent through identification of nationalism, Communism, and anticolonialism. This tactic is supplemented in Africa by a particularly strenuous effort to sell indigenous leaders, eager for industrial development, on the Soviet model of industrialization. These techniques, tested and proved in Asia, have so far enjoyed uneven and unreliable success on the African continent.

In the following essay, I. William Zartman, a Professor of International Studies at the University of South Carolina, describes and evaluates these efforts on the continent of Africa. His account includes the North African Arab states as well as the continent south of the Sahara. Professor Zartman, a specialist in the Afro-Arab field, is the author of two books: New Power: Decision Making in Moroccan Government Since Independence, and Government and Politics in Africa North of the Sahara, and of numerous articles for newspapers and journals. ■

Revolutionary Communism today is seeking to insert itself into the evolution of Africa. This paradox alone goes far to explain the complexities, uncertainties, and failure which are its three major characteristics. Experiences of two World Wars and a violent anti-imperialist revolution, which dominated twentieth-century history in Europe and Asia and led to Communist success in these regions, are largely absent from Africa. Even the northern part of the continent, which was a theater of war against the Axis and which attacked its colonial problem by use of violence, did not carry its experience in violence to the same conclusion as the countries of Eastern Europe or Communist Asia. Southern Africa, below the equator, where violence has broken out, may be more fertile in the future for Communist penetration, but to date its disorder has been more atavistic than progressive. In general, the postwar decades of change through which Africa has rushed have been peaceful and even orderly—revolutionary perhaps, with reference to the speed of change, but evolutionary in their nonviolent nature.

Faced with this new situation, the Communist approach to Africa has been profoundly influenced by the evolution of the continent itself. It has been complex in its nature and uncertain in its tactics. This analysis will focus on the fourfold nature of Communist penetration into Africa which reflects this complexity and uncertainty, and will attempt to bring out the balance of success and failure, both in past performance and in future prospects.

The influence of Africa on the nature of Communist penetration, however, suggests a preliminary review of salient and relevant characteristics of the African scene. Not the least or the narrowest of these is nationalism, accentuated pride in oneself. In this case, the "self" varies widely; it may be race (negritude), continent (Pan-Africanism), tribe (as in Katanga), or even state (as in a slowly increasing number of cases). Nowhere in this varying theoretical frame is there room for either the broad internationalism or the narrow class consciousness of Communism. Another broad characteristic is attachment to the elusive tenets of neutralism. On the one hand, this value distinctly refers to non-choice between two powers or ideologies in the cold war. It is the rationale of the power vacuum. On the other hand, it also includes under its tent such subsidiary ideas as compensation for dominant Western influence, freedom to choose the best of both systems, and fear of the more aggressive side. A third value which lies at the basis of both of these is anticolonialism, perhaps the broadest and deepest well of emotionalism in all Africa. Anticolonialism too has two sides; it has been used to justify attack on any action by a European—or even Western—power, but in growing degree it also creates awareness of danger from the neo-colonialism of the East.

A fourth characteristic of modern Africa is attachment to egalitarianism as a primary goal. There is thus a search for dignity in all types of relations with other countries, and a susceptibility to actions in international relations which bespeak solidarity or promise prestige. A fifth characteristic, and a goal of equal importance, is that of development. Africa is still an agricultural continent, living on an unorganized subsistence economy. The revolution of rising expectations has been most potent among its leaders—as opposed to its people—and it drives them to insistence on rapid economic modernization to make up for centuries of lost time. A sixth goal that is the partial result of these two characteristics is socialism, of a special "African" or "Arab" variety. Islamic notions of the welfare function and the Umma and African traditions of community solidarity give a historical background to the search for a modern ideology, accentuated by the training most African leaders have received in one brand or another of Marxism.

These six values and goals which characterize the modern African scene are ambiguous; they can be used as points of *entrée* by Communism, but they also contain facets which reduce susceptibility to Communist penetration. Manipulation of these goals and values to accentuate the first aspect at the expense of the second will, therefore, be one of the Communists' primary aims. There are, however, three additional characteristics which round out the relevant description of Africa, all of which have so far worked specifically against Communist penetration.

Although there is question whether some sort of class structure

—if only between traditional and modernist groups—can be discerned in African society, it is certain that there is only a very small proletariat, and that, furthermore, the chances of a labor-peasant front will have to await the time when modernization and the revolution of rising expectations touches agrarian society. The barrier here to the ready application of Communist doctrine is admittedly only temporary; urbanization is the primary phenomenon of changing African social patterns and will contribute in ever increasing measure to the proletarianization of a dislocated segment of society. With urbanization, too, comes organization, which has hitherto been lacking among workers, peasants, and intellectuals, and which has removed the possibility of Communist take-over of structured groups within society. As organization spreads, particularly among labor, opportunities open for "leaders of dissatisfaction," and the revolution of rising expectations will become a revolution of rising frustrations before the dislocated African societies attain a new balance of satisfaction between their means and desires.

In addition, there is no Communist party of importance in all Africa. Communist parties have been established in Egypt (1919), South Africa (1921), Morocco, Algeria and Tunisia (1936), Sudan and Somalia (1956), and Madagascar (1958), but they were small and frequently composed of Europeans from the metropolises. Today, in no African country except Tunisia is there a legally recognized Communist party,[1] and no country's estimated total of native Communists is greater than 2,000; the usual figure for most countries is less than 1,000. Furthermore, there is no place in the political system for a Communist party; the predominant single-party systems preclude Communist as well as other opposition parties, and true multiparty systems are rare. Where Communist parties have existed, they have found themselves forced to imitate the nationalist parties, running a very poor second. Decades of failure to organize indigenous groups deprive

[1] At the XXII Party Congress in Moscow in October 1961, Communist parties from Algeria, Morocco, Tunisia, Sudan, and South Africa were present, along with observers from the ruling (non-Communist) parties of Guinea, Ghana, and Mali. No other Africans were registered in attendance.

the Communists of a ready and obedient arm of Soviet policy and impose serious limitation on choice of action and application of doctrine.

Finally, Africa is a continent where religion is deeply ingrained in the social fabric. The animist gods are being exorcised from inanimate objects by the combined forces of both monotheistic Islam and Christianity, which give a truer insight into the nature of deity and its relation with man, and of modern technology, which gives a more realistic understanding of the nature of inanimate objects and their use for man. Communism, on the other hand, confuses the material and the spiritual as much as did animism. Whether Communism might enter into religious people's thinking through the back door of Christian and Muslim social philosophies is a moot, if important, question;[2] the fact is that today, important religious and lay spokesmen for both monotheistic religions in Africa make the point that religion is for their people an effective barrier to Communism. So declare Nasser, the late Mohammed V, Sékou Touré, and Haile Selassie, from four corners of the continent.

1

In this setting, the complexity and uncertainty of Communist tactics have been reflected both in concrete evidence from Africa and in reported disagreement within and between Moscow[3] and Peiping. As a result, the nature of Communism in Africa can be analyzed from four angles as take-over, imitation, cooperation, and disruption. These categories are admittedly schematic and sometimes even overlap, without destroying their analytical usefulness. At the same time, they display both diversity and contra-

[2] One of the most important and regrettable of visits to the bloc from Africa in recent years was the September 1961 visit of five 'ulama (religious elders) from Morocco, led by Istiqlal party President Allal al-Fassi. To many Moroccans this move in itself—and the visitors' "favorable impressions"—indicated the compatibility of Islam and Communism.

[3] An articles in The New York Times, April 16, 1961 ("Russians Called Split On Africa," by Drew Middleton) gives a suggestive discussion of internal Soviet uncertainty.

diction, elements of strength and weakness in the Communist approach.

Russian relations with Africa have long been an example of unsuccessful colonialism. Ever since the mid-fifteenth century, when Brother Varsonofii and his fellow traveler, the trader Vassili, visited Cairo, and the adventurer Nikitin stopped off in Somalia on the way back from India, the northeastern corner of Africa has been of interest to Russia. A Russian colony was briefly established in Eritrea in 1889 and two years later a Russian "military aid agreement" was concluded with the Negus. The 200-bed Soviet hospital now operating in Addis Ababa was first constructed in 1898, out of a Tsarist Red Cross mission during the Italo-Ethiopian War. The basis of African studies was also laid in Leningrad (St. Petersburg) University at this time. Tsarist Russia sent two medical detachments to the Boers, and in 1905, following the Boer War (and the Russian loss of prestige in the Russo-Japanese War), Russians schemed with Boer generals to foment a native uprising in South Africa. Any hopes Russia might have had to participate in the Great African Hunt were frustrated by its weak position in European politics. Yet Russia did take part in the Moroccan settlement in Madrid in 1880 and the Congo partition at Berlin in 1885.

The re-entry of Russia into the state system as a Great Power during World War II caused a revival of the pre-World War I approach. Soviet Russia was a party to the Tangier re-internationalization in Paris in 1945 and a candidate for trusteeship of Tripolitania at the United Nations, and has continued its historic interest in Ethiopia. Even more significant is the spirit of pride and vigor with which Russian scholars and statesmen recall their nineteenth-century penetration into Africa; it has reminded more than one observer of the same sort of spirit that was evident in European colonial writings of the Victorian Age. Haile Selassie may well have had some silent questions in addition to his voiced praise in 1959 when he was shown the Ethiopian exhibit in the U.S.S.R. Academy of Sciences' Institute of Ethnography, largely collected by Russians during the previous century.

The point here is not to suggest that Soviet Russia is only the direct descendant of Tsarist Russia, nor to imply that Russia is merely a colonialist state bent on recouping lost chances of a past century. The nature of Communist penetration is more complex than that. But comparison with nineteenth-century colonialism at least provides perspective to Communism's efforts at maximum penetration or take-over. Russian threats of "volunteers" for Suez, the Congo, or Algeria are essentially the same tactic as the German gunboat off Agadir.[4] Russian small arms have been passed to Egypt, Guinea, the National Liberation Front (FLN) in Algeria, and the Army of National Liberation-Kamerun (ALNK), just as other colonial nations "armed the natives" at the end of the last century. Ironically, Soviet aid to Congo, Algeria, and Morocco has taken the same form of "medical assistance" as Russia used at the end of the last century. Soviet Russian concentration on a limited number of African countries is merely an attempt to stake out a zone of influence, in repetition of the nineteenth-century with its congress of Berlin, Fashoda, and Moroccan crises. Finally, as the Sultan of Morocco before World War I asked for protection by France, so Bourguiba, ben Khedda, Lumumba, Touré, and Nasser have appealed for various kinds of Communist help in various crises since World War II. Other parallels could be drawn. More important than their historiographic value is the fact that they lead to the question: what are the chances of ultimate Soviet take-over of certain African countries as the ultimate stage in this colonial process?

Certainly, African attachment to national independence and anticolonialism makes Russian or Chinese colonization improbable in the present situation, and may even have forced a revision of Soviet goals in the African context. Nevertheless, the proposition bears examining, for there is nothing to guarantee that "the

---

[4] Russia is not unaware of the colonialist allure of its "volunteers." In Baghdad in April 1960, Mikoyan answered a correspondent's question about "volunteers" for Algeria by saying, "Do you understand what that could mean? If you think a bit, you will realize that such a question is useless. There are those who, hearing you, would rush to the conclusion that the Bolsheviks want to occupy Algeria with their volunteers and transform it into a colony."

present situation" is immutable within the changing context of current international relations.

A Communist take-over could be effected by Communist colonists or by indigenous Communists. At the present time, foreign Communist personnel are present only in very limited numbers in select African countries. Outside of bloc embassy staffs, there are about 2,500 Communist military and economic technicians in the African continent. Even with all other "private" categories, such as newspapermen, the total nondiplomatic personnel would scarcely exceed 3,000. Another group, which is even smaller but strategically placed in a few countries, comprises foreign Communist advisers from outside the bloc, such as French Communist technicians in the economics ministry in Morocco in 1959-1960 and possibly later. The total number of all foreign Communist personnel is conjectural, but it is certainly short of the number needed for a *coup d'état* in any country except possibly Guinea, where about half of the total is located. According to Conakry's claims in January 1962, this is exactly what the Russian embassy was meditating, and Russia was asked to replace the African expert, Daniel Solov, as Ambassador. Less clear charges of the same sort caused the arrest of the Communist Youth president in Liberia the preceding September. A take-over may also have been in the long-range Russian plans for the Congo during late 1960, although the Soviet approach seems to have undergone a number of changes.

Greater long-term possibilities are present through the development of indigenous Communist groups. Estimates of indigenous Communist recruitment in Africa have risen only very slowly over the past five years. Little specific information is available, but a few indications can be given. In Sudan, Malagasy, and Morocco, Communist proselytizing has had some success among student groups, although with no guarantee of permanence. In Nigeria, there has been some Communist activity among labor, resulting in the creation of a splinter Nigerian Trade Union Congress and a Nigerian People's party; labor infiltration has also taken place to a small extent in Gambia, Ghana, and Sudan. In Algeria and

Guinea, China is reported to have repatriated several thousand former members of the French army captured and indoctrinated in Vietnam. The Republic of South Africa is probably the only country in which the illegal party has remained well organized and intact, and has spread into African labor and other nonwhite political organizations of all types, capitalizing on resentment against apartheid.

In a number of areas, small "communistic" parties exist, or Communist sympathizers have formed the nucleus of a radical wing within the dominant political organization. In Malagasy, the Congress party for Malagasy Independence (AKFM) is Communist influenced and has strength in Tananarive and Diego-Suarez. The Union of Cameroon People (UPC) has had close ties with Communist China and also with the Soviet bloc, but the loss of its two leaders in 1958 and 1960 and the entrance of the moderate wing into legal political activity in 1958 have deeply cut into the strength and appeal of the radicals. The African Independence party in Senegal has drawn a handful of workers and intellectuals into a Communist-led party, but it was banned in 1960. In Mali, however, it merged voluntarily with the dominant Sudanese Union in 1959. The party of the African Rally-Senegal (PRA-Sénégal), the Revolutionary Socialist party of Benin (Togo and Dahomey), and the Gabonese Unity party are examples of the "communistic" groups. Other small parties of little direct significance use Communist slogans in other African countries, but their doctrinaire content—let alone understanding—is so slim that they probably inspire little confidence in Moscow.

Under changed circumstances these Communist or "communistic" groups might possibly attain sudden significance. Africa has shown frequent difficulty in keeping its domestic politics and its foreign connections separate; if in the future a local government or opposition party finds itself in need of allies, groups sympathetic with Russia or China may find a new role open to themselves in local politics. An example to keep in mind is Syria, where a build-up of Soviet personnel in 1957 brought the country dangerously close to Communist take-over with the sympathy of leftist but non-Communist political circles. It might also appear that, if aspirations toward modernization are frustrated by traditional leadership and rigid institutions, an extremist revolution along the lines of Cuba's could be considered by local modernists as the only way to attain their objectives. Yet in Africa, this alternative is improbable. Unlike the Middle East and Latin America, African countries are not likely to turn to Communism under the pressure of a fast evolving mass set against a traditional elite. The whole African society is being caught up in rapid social evolution; traditionalism lingers only in the bush, not in the palace. Even Morocco, Libya, and Ethiopia, the three "most traditional" societies, lack a Batista or a Castro, a Nuri es-Sa'id or a Qassem. In the last analysis, in Communist terms, African societies are not "ready" for take-over; the preconditions of a Communist society are not in place, and the instruments of take-over themselves are not available.

2

Since an analysis of Communist penetration as colonialism does not cover all the aspects of its nature in Africa, Communism can also be regarded as seeking to foster imitation, an approach that falls short of direct take-over but that is especially geared to the African scene. As early as the Second Comintern Congress in 1920, Lenin proclaimed that "the idea of soviet organization is a simple one and can be applied, not only to proletarian, but also to peasant, feudal, and semifeudal relations." Yet in reality this Communist model was never pushed very hard by Russia for use in Africa; instead, the colonial concept of the world was implicitly accepted as meager Communist attention to Africa was channeled almost exclusively through European Communist parties. Leninist doctrine on tactical cooperation with bourgeois democracy, Soviet anticolonial propaganda, European Communist success in contacting newly educated African elites, and finally Maoist theory and practice of peasant revolution prepared the way for a change in approach. But it was not until the death of Stalin and the beginnings of the sweep of independence across Africa —a movement which owed only very little to Communism—that Communist states turned to the newly opened field of action with a new approach.

Africa could be made over in the Communist image, according to peculiarly suitable Communist models for attaining the African's own goals. There is no indication that traditional doctrine on Communist take-over has been rejected; it has only been modified, loosened, softened. A dominant working class, supported by the peasantry and led by the Communist party, still remains the necessary condition for a Communist state. But until the time when these elements will have grown enough to fill their role in Africa, Communist states seek to foster a lesser goal of imitation. By advocating a Communist model for development, Russia, China, and the satellite can hasten the day when the elements necessary for a proletarian revolution will be in place. States that accept the Communist model for development, or parts of it, are not Communist states. But they imitate Communist ways and techniques and accept Communist aid and training, in emulation of the progress made in the U.S.S.R. over the past four decades and the forward leaps in China.

The Soviet model for development begins with pressure against colonial and neo-colonial domination by the West, until the attainment of political and economic liberation. African experience has shown that this pressure need not be violent, but it has also demonstrated that national bourgeois independence movements may stop in midstream with formal independence and still maintain economic cooperation with the West. According to Communist doctrine on independence, new states have a choice between a nationalist, capitalist future and a class-conscious, socialist future. The former, a more classic pattern, will end in the creation of a suppressed proletariat, leading to violent Communist revolution. In the latter, however, a pre-Communist stage can be attained through the combined efforts of the worker and peasant class, led by an active elite from their midst and now possible, thanks to the support of the "socialist" countries. Although close cooperation with the bloc is the most important condition of the noncapitalist form of development, there are also other characteristics such as nationalized industrialization, agrarian reform and cooperatives, elimination of feudal and colonial elements, centralized political and economic control.

Today, a variation on this model competes with the Soviet-sponsored image. The Maoist model allows no possibility for the capitalist stage—it equates it with continued colonialism, not with an indigenous option—nor even for a "noncapitalist" form of development. Instead, the Chinese model foresees direct access to "socialism" only through revolutionary violence by an active minority, against bourgeois nationalist governments if need be and with the support of the masses. National liberation movements are to be exploited, dominated and absorbed, rather than relied on. There is heavy accent on human capital, and an integral part of the model is the myth of success of the communes.

If the Africans have rejected both of these models as a whole, they have accepted pieces from them. Economic aid, technical assistance, trade, and student training are the three weapons used to implant the model in Africa.

The bloc has granted about $1 billion in credits to African countries through 1961. There has been an increasing tendency for Russia and its European satellites to standardize terms at 2½ per cent interest, with repayment scheduled over twelve years, usually beginning after some of the aid has time to work into the local economy. China's credits are interest-free and repayable over a ten-year period beginning at the end of the credit period. Russia concentrates increasingly on large prestige projects; China and the satellites cover more varied programs. The negotiations as well as the signature of the agreements are accompanied by much fanfare, and then each project undertaken within the credit terms is also heralded. Comparison of the credits and the expenditures, however, shows that specific allocations fall far short of the extended credits. The most notable example is Ethiopia, second largest (after Egypt) recipient of aid on the continent, 96 per cent of whose $114 million credit remains unallocated. On the other hand, Egypt's two-stage $325 million loan for the Aswan Dam has been fully programed for use by 1964.

An even closer application of the model comes through technical assistance. Communist countries have granted African states the benefit of techniques which are characterized as the unique products of the socialist system. In the continent of hydroelectric power par excellence, Russia specializes in big dams, as at Aswan, Konkouré, and Bui, and boasts of their importance in size and technology. Mali experiments with two Russian-named techniques for clearing sandbars from the sluggish Niger. Russians are planning port developments in Tema, Tangier, Conakry, and Alexandria. Even Mauritania considers Soviet processes for stabilizing sand under roadbeds. China advises tea-drinking Morocco on tea growing, and rice-eating Guinea on rice farming. Egypt has a Russian reactor, and Ghana is to get one. East Germany built Guinea's first printing office and also was joined by Russia and Czechoslovakia in setting up three radio stations. In Guinea, two hundred Communists from bloc countries teach school, and 135 more advisers work within various ministries, aiding the process of decolonialization as they progressively replace the remaining Frenchmen.[5] The three states of the UAS have each received seven civil planes from the U.S.S.R. to set up their national airlines; Russia then built Africa's longest airstrip at Accra, and Czechoslovakia extended air service from Prague through Zurich to Rabat, Conakry, Accra, and, recently, Bamako. Since the IL-14s and IL-18s—which some local observers call "Illusions" instead of Ilyushins—need unusually frequent servicing, Russia is installing a central maintenance base for West Africa at Bamako. In these and many other cases, the bloc has emphasized

---

[5] However, one aspect of Communist technical aid, usually overlooked by the "sinister little group of men" theories, is brought out in an interview of Philippe Decraene with an East German technician in Guinea, who said, "The only interest of my two-year stay here is that they have permitted me to improve my French and to discover good French wines and French cooking," "Guinee An IV: Voyage au bout du monde," Le Monde, December 30, 1961.

its unique and diverse capability in conquering the material problems of development with its exportable technological skills.

The logical extension of this activity is seen in the increasingly frequent exchanges of technical missions between bloc and African countries to discuss problems, needs, and solutions for the developing continent. In accordance with the model, Communist assistance plays to the desires of developing states, even more than to their needs, by emphasizing industrialization at the expense of agricultural development.

Although increased trade between Africa and Communist countries is only natural (and involves some very unsuspect countries such as Rhodesia and South Africa), it fits in with the model and with African wishes by being an instrument of decolonialization. Bloc trade takes up only 5 per cent of Africa's exports, but 90 per cent of this trade is carried on by the U.A.R., Morocco, Algeria, Sudan, Ghana, Guinea, Nigeria, and the Rhodesias. Egypt is the leader, for the U.S.S.R. is its largest customer and the U.A.R. takes up about two-thirds of Africa's imports and exports with the entire bloc. A certain amount of commercial activity may be counted off as normal; the danger point in relations occurs when the bloc dominates a nation's trade patterns, as in Egypt and to a fast-growing extent in Guinea. Russia offers a tempting market; it swallows without qualms the excess cotton of the Nile, the cocoa of Ghana, and the bananas of Guinea, to the surprise and enjoyment of the Russian consumer. The opportunity to pay off credits in kind increases this trade, to the relief of African governments lacking hard currency and burdened with single-crop economies. The prize for model economic relations was given in October 1961 by the Soviet delegate to the United Nations Assembly Economic Committee, who cited Egypt as one of the three non-bloc countries—and the only one in Africa—"who had attained economic independence." The price for such relations is shown by Guinea, whose fiat-backed currency is at the mercy of bloc trade.

The most effective long-term method of fostering imitation is through the direct training of Africans in Communist institutions. Sékou Touré is the only African President who is known to have had training behind the Iron Curtain in his youth, but most countries have sent official delegations, including the head of state of Sudan, Egypt, Guinea, Ghana, and Ethiopia, to Moscow (and in Touré's and Nkrumah's case, to Peiping) to look around. One of the most effective such trips was Nkrumah's in July 1961, when Russian hospitality was so overwhelming that the guest became the first non-Communist chief of state to endorse Soviet policy in Germany and also praised Soviet nationality policy as a model for his own Union of African States. More important in the long run are African students in bloc schools, labor institutes, and training programs. The most striking institution is the Peoples' Friendship University for 6,000 students from underdeveloped countries, founded in 1960, named after Patrice Lumumba in 1961, and processing 193 Africans in its first year (1960-1961) program. African students are also enrolled in other Russian schools in Moscow, Kiev, Odessa, and Leningrad, in satellite institutions in Warsaw, Prague, Budapest, Leipzig, and East Berlin, and to a small extent in China. Five hundred and seventy Guineans, 435 Ghanaians, over 100 Egyptians, 50 Somalis, 32 Malians, 40 Sudanis, and 20 Ethiopians are in bloc institutions on long-term training scholarships.

However, this approach has met some serious difficulties. Forced with the necessity of choosing between a free institution of learning capable of handling the inquisitive minds of African youth and a reversion to the political indoctrination of the University of the Toilers of the East during the 1920's, Moscow—predictably—leans more and more to the latter while claiming the former. The result has been a rash of defections and indignant letters from disillusioned African students. While national student groups exist in bloc schools and China encourages a Union of African Students as a propaganda agency, a similar union in Russia seems to have been disbanded in 1960 after showing too much independence. Technical training, however, appears to have met with greater pedagogical and political success.

Imitation is its own greatest reward. It is nevertheless instructive to look for a possible counterpart to this outpouring of aid and guidance. Little appears on the surface. Economic and technical aid is given "with no conditions or privileges attached," and there appears to be no direct commitment imposed on students whose education, room, board, and spending money is a Soviet gift. Many anticipated demands have not materialized; Egypt has not (yet) provided a Russian submarine base to replace Saseno, nor has the rumored base at Conakry been constructed; Guinea did not join the ruble bloc when it left the franc zone; and Ghana has not left the sterling zone nor Mali the franc zone. In fact, Africa tends to regard Communist aid as much its right and opportunity in the context of cold-war competition as Western aid, and to include nonintervention as a rigid corollary of both. In African countries—such as those of the Casablanca bloc— where the domestic government philosophy resembles Leninist, Stalinist, and Maoist ideas of centralized organization, there is a spirit of admiration and sympathy, among the governing elite, with Communist methods, at least in specific cases and at higher levels of abstraction. Imitation is limited, however; as Ambassador Stevenson has written, "When you think how eager the Soviets have been to act as grand marshal in the African freedom parade, it is no small thing that they have been denied such an opportunity in most of Africa."

Imitation will continue to provide a comfortable leg to stand on in the future. Economic and technical aid and trade is as normal a feature of the present world when it comes from the U.S.S.R., satellites, and even from China as when it comes from the West, and it is likely to continue its regular increase of past years. Applications to Friendship University fell from over 43,-000 to 6,000 between 1960 and 1961, and some countries, including the U.A.R., have been slow in using up their scholarships; but agreements for giving Africans technical training in bloc countries are still on the upswing. On the other hand, the credit system of aid does allow flexibility in response to changes in African politics. When Congo and Ethiopia indicated that they were less interested in following Soviet suggestions than in simply receiving its money, the aid program slowed down, indicating that Communist and Western attitudes toward the relationship between aid and politics are basically similar.

A projected evaluation of the use of the Communist model for development must include some productive and counterproductive possibilities. It has already been suggested that successful imitation of the model for development may lead to the growth of a dissatisfied proletariat, an awakened peasantry, and a Communist-trained intellectual group that could serve as the nucleus of a revolutionary organization. This does not, however, appear to be the most likely of possibilities. As trade, aid, and assistance programs strengthen African economies, increase technology, and train personnel, given the current African desire to "seek the African way," they tend to strengthen native response to native problems and make Africa stronger in its independence. To the extent that this possibility develops, it means that in Africa the piper will call his own tune and the payer will be poorer in the long run. A third possibility remains, however, that the "African way"—which, by Africans' own admission, must be found before it can be followed—may be so cluttered with wild outgrowths as to be a barrier rather than a path, thus opening the way to proponents of the Communist model by frustration rather than by persuasion.

Imitation has occurred most frequently in the radical countries of the Casablanca bloc, partly because of the natural affinities that some of their concepts of domestic government have with the Communist system. The proclamations of these countries are more ambitious and more political than those of the African moderates. There is greater emotional attention to sore spots such as Mauritania, Algeria, Israel, the Congo, and colonialism in general, often as an attempt to distract local attention from difficult domestic problems; at the same time, there are grandiose schemes for domestic panaceas—the Aswan High Dam that might only keep up with population increases, the Moroccan National Promotion Project that would cost three times the development budget, the Ghanaian plans for cocoa that evidence a greater statistical than agricultural expansion. Frustration in these projects may provide the Communist model with its biggest *entrée*.

3

A third way of understanding Communist penetration can be simply on the basis of cooperation in foreign relations. Most of the present benefits which Communist countries draw from their contact with Africa fall within this category. The speech with which Sékou Touré greeted President Brezhnev in Conakry in February 1961 illustrates the situation. The Guinean President, Africa's own winner of the 1961 Lenin Peace Prize, began by stating that "the sentiments of the Guineans . . . are not Communist and the Democratic party of Guinea is not a communist party," but he finished by proclaiming that "M. Nikita Khrushchev is identified, on the international scene, with the ardent and common will of all the people of the world who are still oppressed. We have chosen between the forces of exploitation and oppression characteristic of imperialism, colonialism and neo-colonialism, and the socialist forces." The purpose of Communist states in this situation is to maximize African support for their own foreign policy by capitalizing on the natural coincidence of policy aims with anticolonialist nations and by increasing the radical content of neutralism.

This retreat from take-over and imitation to simple cooperation is not without its benefits of consolidation, but it has led to a second change in Communist approach to Africa within less than a decade. When the U.S.S.R. rediscovered Africa in 1955, it considered the continent an open field for its activity; by 1960, it had bent with the trend of African events and had begun to concentrate its attention on the radical group of African states. Chinese policies took a similar turn, starting with broad identification with newly independent nations, and then shifting to a limited number of like-minded governments and revolutionary movements as its policies hardened in 1958, the year China began its interest in Africa. This development may not be doctrinaire, but it is quite natural in international relations; the expansion of relations and the intensification of activity tends to force a state to choose sides.

The 1960-1961 United Nations session gave the most notable examples of this tactical shift in Communist attention in Africa and of the use of foreign policy cooperation based on radical neutralism. At the time, of his famous shoe-pounding speech, Khrushchev attacked the Afro-Asian group, vetoed the moderate Tunisia-Ceylon resolution on the Congo, and increased his bitter campaign against the Secretary-General and the United Nations. He carried with him the radicals of Africa, who soon withdrew their troops from the Congo. In the same session, Russia rebuffed the African moderates—the majority of the continent—by vetoing the admission of Mauritania. Three months later the five African radicals who were willing to endorse Morocco's claims to Mauritania met to form the Casablanca group. They were soon joined by the "Provisional Government of the Republic of Algeria" (GPRA) which Russia belatedly followed China's lead in recognizing. Since this time, both Russia and China have sought active foreign policy cooperation with the Casablanca Six—Guinea, Ghana, Mali, Morocco, the U.A.R., and GPRA—and have opened diplomatic relations with all of them. It must not be thought that the bloc is indiscriminately supporting the desires of Africa's radicals; it is rather using them when it suits its own ends. In the 1961 session, the veto against Mauritania was dropped when its threatening use brought Western and moderate African agreement to admit Mongolia, much to the public disappointment of Morocco.

Foreign policy cooperation draws its basis from a well-cultivated field of propaganda, important to a continent so conscious of official pronouncements. Russia has always been an active member of the United Nations Trusteeship Council, using its debates for propaganda purposes, and it requested membership in the United Nations Economic Commission for Africa on its formation in 1958. Communist participants dominated the first Afro-Asian Peoples' Solidarity Conference held in Cairo in December 1957; its organization has no responsibility and no functions, but it provides a common propaganda platform for African, Asian, and Communist representatives. In October 1960, another conference by the same name was held in Stalinabad, and Russian, Asian, and African delegates joined in passing resolutions condemning colonialism, the "dirty war" in Algeria,[6] and "collective imperialist aggression" in the Congo. A Russian delegation from this Conference was at the All-African Peoples Conference in Tunis in January 1960—but it was absent in the next meeting in March 1961 in Cairo. Probably the most important recent example came out of the Belgrade Conference of Non-Aligned Nations in September 1961; the U.S.S.R. had approved Africa's earlier and nearly universal outcry against French atomic testing in the Sahara, but the well-timed threat of a 50-megaton explosion in Siberia stilled protests against Soviet testing. Where Russia cannot pass as a poor, nonwhite, ex-colonial, Asian nation, China can. As a prominent participant in the Bandung Conference in 1955, and as an even more active member of the Afro-Asian Peoples' Solidarity Organization since 1958, China has an important role to play in building on antipathy to colonialism and imperialism and in shaping neutralism in a radical direction.

The immediate foreign policy purposes of this propaganda are essentially three. In cooperation with other African states, Russia and China seek to increase the number of radical governments in Africa. Recognition of the Stanleyville Congo regime—whose dead leader, as it turned out, was neither capable of achieving reincarnation among the living nor of exerting influence from the spirit world—and immediate support for Guinea and Mali, whose desire to be ostracized from the French Community was readily accommodated by the other members, are examples of unsuccessful and successful application of this policy. Russia and China also seek to isolate the United States and the West in Africa and through the use of African issues. Certainly much of the current

[6] The use of "dirty war" is an interesting sidelight. It was used with such success applied to the war in Indochina that Communist propaganda took it over for use in Algeria. The effect has not been the same.

American dilemma over relations with Portugal, France, and South Africa stems largely from concrete problems with Angola, Algeria, and apartheid. But the exacerbation of these problems and their use to provoke ultimate splits within NATO, the United Nations, or among pro-Western African nations derives from Communist utilization in foreign policy. Communist states above all seek to make themselves into the leading spokesmen for anticolonialism, for this is by far the simplest way both of guiding common elements of African and Communist ideology and of increasing the radical content of neutralism. This aim is facilitated by the fact that, through adroit and insistent propaganda, Russia and China have created the impression that by definition they cannot be colonialist or imperialist. On the other hand, the aim is important to them, for this impression must be maintained, against growing African appreciation of the colonialist nature of Communist penetration. As Margery Perham has said in the 1961 Reith Lectures, "These two attacks, the Communist and the anticolonial, are simultaneous, and the Communist states are working hard to make them a fully combined operation. . . . This fusion has not yet happened."

In addition to increasing the number of radicals in Africa, the bloc also seeks to increase support for new Communist states; Guinea was the first non-Communist state to recognize East Germany, although it quickly reversed itself under pressure from West Germany. Less clear is the question of China on the United Nations. China works to exchange recognition with new African states. The extent to which Moscow actually wishes to see Peiping in New York, however, is as uncertain as the extent to which Russia wishes to see China in Africa. Certainly the opportunity of having a major Communist state outside of the United Nations, gathering sympathy for its isolation and unhindered by the necessity of taking a stand in a public vote, is valuable to the Communist bloc. As an outlaw from the society of nations, China is free to act as an outlaw. There are, however, differences between Chinese and Russian foreign policy. Chinese affinity for movements of revolutionary violence led to immediate recognition of the Algerian "Provisional Government" (GPRA) when it was founded in 1958, with Russia following only two years later; Russia had its relations with France to consider; China did not. As a result, the "China group" is a distinct entity within the GPRA and included Premier Benyoussef Ben Khedda—although Chinese advice against negotiations has not been heeded. China has sought to bring neutralist sentiment under its personal control, or, short of that, under the control of its own candidate for neutralist leadership, Sukarno of Indonesia. Toward this end, it sought to enroll Ghanaian and Sudanese support for a second Bandung Conference just at the moment when Tito was calling the Belgrade Non-Aligned Conference for which China was not eligible.

Many of these Communist foreign policy achievements are in the line of "sloganery," but slogan-wielding is more than mere verbiage. It is the fabric of ideology and the background of policy. Certainly this type of Communist activity will continue in Africa, for propaganda and diplomacy are normal ingredients of foreign relations. In the realm of particulars, there is no reason not to expect cooperation between Communist and African nations on specific issues, particularly since the new composition of the United Nations places the numerically important and substantially weak states of Africa and Asia in a mathematically deciding position—short of two-thirds but more than one-third of the General Assembly.

In a broader sense, however, there are weaknesses to the present Communist foreign policy approach, weaknesses which have already been reflected in narrowing the area of fruitful cooperation from the continent to the "core countries." Africa is not a bloc; it does not act as one except at the most general levels—such as symbolic declarations of "equality" and "anticolonialism"—and its unity even on these slogans has been more and more fragile as real national interests and ideologies develop. Cooperation with the United Nations can thus be expected on a bilateral basis or, at best, with small groups of friends. Communist propaganda has also tried to develop abstract, emotional slogans as a basis for foreign policy cooperation, and has been successful enough to have become identified with values such as "anticolonialism" and "independence." These slogans have been useful, but they are not eternal; the remaining colonial possessions in southern Africa (and the slivers and chips on the western African coast) will give reason to prolong their life for a while, but other matters of greater substance will gradually take precedence and the shibboleths of today will become simply tomorrow's headstones for yesterday's issues. The Communist world will certainly discover new slogans; yet none have the simplicity and effectiveness of these two, and none —not even "development"—can benefit from coincidence with such a dramatic revolution in human affairs as was the colonial liberation. The alliance between Communist propaganda and reality is being broken, and any cooperation between Communist and African countries can only suffer as well.

4

Neither a Communist take-over, nor imitation, nor even broad foreign policy cooperation with Russia or China is likely in the short run in many African states. The most profitable Communist attitude in these cases is the encouragement of disorder, both for disorder's sake and also for the purposes of preparing take-over, disturbing alternative plans for development, or making the country susceptible to threats in foreign policy. The use of anticolonial slogans, the Soviet attitude throughout the Congolese crises, military and propaganda efforts to keep the war in Algeria burning bright, the use of Angola and Algeria to split NATO, the use of the Mauritanian issue to split Africa, membership in the Trusteeship Council and application for membership on the Economic Commission for Africa, encouragement to Guinea to leave the franc zone, and arms supplies to Egypt and Somalia—all of these tactics are dual in purpose and one of the purposes is simply the creation of disorder. This is an aspect that has been too little emphasized. While there is no rigid rule that calm countries do not communize, it is generally true that a stable system of government dealing successfully with local issues is unlikely to fall into Communist hands unless directly conquered. It is unlikely that the Soviet Union is interested in taking over Africa's manifold and complex problems at the present time. But anything which weakens the new African states—particularly those cooperating with the West—is in the Communists' interest.

More than just a haphazard affair, disorder is fostered by the place of revolutionary violence within Communist ideology. Much has been made of the differences between Russia and China on this point. Differences between the two powers are real and some of the most important of them have already been discussed. But the differences over the use of revolutionary violence can be exaggerated. Nigerian students returning from Moscow tell of revolutionary training camps for Africans, just as do Cameroonian trainees from Peiping. Indonesian pilots and Algerian cadets were trained on Czech and Polish aircraft in Egypt in 1958, just as Algerians using Chinese material are now training Angolan partisans. Military and paramilitary training schools are reported in Rügen, Naumberg, Lusatia, and Moscow, as well as in Peiping. There is not a revolutionary movement in Africa which does not benefit from Russian as well as Chinese support, although in some cases, such as the ALNK, there is a marked sympathy for Peiping. The fact is that both Russia and China back the use of revolutionary violence, although their agents may be in conflict with each other within any given revolutionary movement. Neither of the protagonists of Communism has yet gone so far as to espouse the internal contradictions inherent in a doctrine of evolutionary Communism.

Communism does not lead national revolutionary movements in Africa; it follows them. The bigger—more "national"—such a movement grows, the less susceptible it is to Communist control; the history of the Algerian FLN's relations with Communist countries is a good example. Communist attempts to foster disorder through revolutionary movements, therefore, can be divided into small harassing groups which are Communist-dominated and national liberation movements which have relations with Communist countries. In the former category are the UPC; in the latter category are the FLN, and the Union of Angolan People and the Popular Movement for the Liberation of Angola. Here again the consummation of colonial independence has changed the African picture and reduced the examples of Communist penetration.

Independence, however, does open up another type of possibility for sowing disorder,[7] that of using radical governments as agents of violence in continental relations. When the signers of the 1950 Tripartite Declaration refused to arm Egypt, Czech arms were forthcoming, the first case of Communist aid of any kind to Africa (with the exception of the Ethiopian hospital founded by the Tsars). When France refused to give planes to Morocco, following a Moroccan take-over of French army installations, the Crown Prince in a pique went to the Russian Embassy and Russia obliged with twelve MIG-17s and two MIG-15 trainers. Military aid has been given to Ghana, Guinea, Mali, Congo, clandestinely to Somalia, and, in larger quantities, to Algeria. Although the day is long past when Nasser ran to Khrushchev as the Sixth Fleet approached Lebanon, as recently as December 1961 the U.S.S.R. and Czechoslovakia delivered matériel including submarines, destroyers, MIG-19s, and land armaments to the Egyptian military forces, already almost exclusively supplied by the bloc. There are about 235 bloc military technicians in Guinea, Ghana, Morocco, Mali, Sudan, and the U.A.R., and four hundred Ghanaian cadets are to receive training in Russia. All of these countries have border problems and extraterritorial claims—Mali, Algeria, and Morocco are in a three-cornered contest over part of the Sahara; Somalia covets part of Ethiopia; Ghana presses Togo and Ivory Coast; Guinea eyes Portuguese Guinea; and Egypt looks beyond Gaza. Communist encouragement of an arms race in Africa and support for radical territorial claims is an even more effective means of bringing disorder than more modest dealings with small insurrectionist groups. Khrushchev's feeding the hand that spites him by continu-

[7] The French Communist technicians in the economics ministries in Morocco may be another example of creating disorder, although there are many other reasons for Morocco's economic problems. The danger is present, however, and is even more serious in Guinea.

ing arms aid to Egypt portends continuing military assistance based on long-range hopes rather than short-term friendships.

5

Some over-all characteristics can be drawn from the Communist attempt to foster take-over, imitation, cooperation, and disorder in Africa:

1. An analysis of these four goals shows the great flexibility of the Communist approach. These goals are not mutually exclusive and in some cases may even be mutually supporting. They offer a range of alternatives from which to choose; when one fails, another may supply an effective channel for operations. Thus, Soviet attention toward Ethiopia has in the past been frequently colonial in nature; slow application of the large Soviet credit is a result of Ethiopian reluctance to imitate, and so, through Somalia, policy may turn in the future to disorder. Russian and Chinese attention to Guinea runs along the lines of imitation and cooperation, with either of the other two alternatives as distinct future possibilities. The rejection of these latter two alternatives by the GPRA in 1961 leaves imitation and cooperation as possible avenues of influence. The Congo has slipped from a colonial approach to disorder to a probable future attempt at a foreign policy basis for influence. The importance of this flexibility is that it allows Communist countries to take advantage of new situations. Past examples of such new situations which foreshadow similar changes in the future include the collapse of the Mali Federation in 1960, which caused a sudden radical turn of Sudanese (Mali) policies and a shift in diplomatic relations from Nationalist to Communist China, or increased Moroccan devotion to its irredentist claim over Mauritania, which became the immediate cause for the formation of the Casablanca bloc, or a renewed Somali drive to regain Ogaden, which may already have underlain Somalia's sudden decision late in 1960 to open relations with Communist China.

2. The other side of this complex coin, however, is the uncertainty that reigns within the Communist world over how to attack

the African problem. The remarkable opportunities offered by the rise of the African nationalist movement were missed by the Communist bloc. Future opportunities for penetration will be less widespread and less dramatic. It is to the Communists' credit that they have learned from their unprofitable policy of dealing with colonial Africa through European Communist parties,[8] although this lesson was forced on them by the turn of events. It is simply not true that Communist states gain great benefit from a genial "people-to-people" program under which masses of technicians "live with the natives." With the possible exception of Guinea, the relatively few foreign Communists in Africa are carefully cloistered under the watchful eye of the local government, and Europeans with a long history of acquaintance with the countries are still more numerous and more open in their contacts throughout the countries. Sympathy with Communists, to the extent it exists, is still more a result of local campaigns to spite European powers than an evidence of deep affinity with the East. Furthermore, there is nothing doctrinarily promising about the current African scene. In this situation, Communist approaches are hesitant, uneven, and often heavy-handed; nowhere have they led to any immediate lasting benefits for the world Communist movement. In some cases the fourfold approach may be flexible and interrelated, but in other cases it is internally contradictory. Disorder is not conducive to imitation, and cooperation is a temporary matter which admits that take-over is not presently possible.

3. A single black-or-white evaluation of Communist penetration is not possible. On one hand, Communist states have greater influence in independent Africa than they had in colonial Africa before 1956. This is only natural. On the other hand, with two exceptions—the economy of Guinea and the armaments and the trade of Egypt—Communist influence is nowhere dominant. In the rest of the continent, Communist pentration is well behind

[8] There is a Department of West Asian and African Affairs in the Chinese Foreign Ministry, and in February 1961 the African Affairs Section in the Soviet Foreign Ministry was divided into a First (northern African) Section and a Second (Black African) Section. Since late 1960, the Chinese Communist party also has a Special Committee for Africa in its Secretariat.

Western influence, and independence is a consciously guarded value. It will take a dispute or frustration of major proportions—of the type already discussed—to change this picture.

This fourfold analysis is particularly important because it offers an outline for Western policies within the same area. The guidelines of American policy have been the containment of Communism throughout the world and the encouragement of positive goals for the welfare of the populations throughout the Free World. In contrast to Communism, it is therefore important that the West (a) contribute to the elimination of violence and disorder through its influence in Africa, (b) emphasize the common values of the Free World and their application to the African situation in order to strengthen the basis for mutually advantageous foreign policies, (c) aid and support specifically African models for development in response to the deep-felt desires of leaders in this area, and (d) increase an awareness of the colonial nature of Russian, Chinese, and satellite penetration into new areas. Proper understanding and evaluation of the nature of Communism in Africa can thus be used to implement the one slogan which seems to have currency in both Eastern, Western and African discussions: Africa for the Africans.

3

The Case of the Recalcitrant
Working Classes

SPAIN: FIRST TEST OF A
PEOPLE'S DEMOCRACY

Julian Gorkin

■ The Spanish Civil War occupies a unique position in the moral and political history of the twentieth century and, perhaps one can say without exaggeration or sentimentality, in the history of the modern era. From the eighteenth-century Enlightenment to the Spanish Civil War, the "Western" mind was dominated by the "idea of progress," which looked, above all, to the progressive emancipation and moral improvement of man through reason. In the political sphere, there developed a rough—albeit oversimple—identification between "left" politics and working-class movements. This background made it possible, especially for those who observed it from a distance, to conceive the Bolshevik Revolution as a great leap forward and the Soviet Union as a somewhat mystical embodiment of dominant Western values. The Spanish Civil War was the climax of the drama in which Communism was cast as at once the hope and fulfillment of mankind: all else has been denouement.

The Spanish Civil War provided the world with operational definitions of the "popular front," of the Soviet "defense of democracy," of Soviet style "working class solidarity" and of "revolutionary morality." It also provided the world a number of articulate, impassioned anti-Communist writers and poets who journeyed to Spain filled with idealism and hope, and who, like the Ancient Mariner, must tell again and again the story of what they saw and experienced. This story still has the power to shock.

Julian Gorkin, one-time founder and secretary of the Federacion

Communista de Levante, and later editor of the POUM newspaper La Batalle, is the author of Canibales Politicos: Hitler y Stalin en España, and editor of the books of El Campesino. He is representative of a generation of Spanish working class and democratic leaders who have neither forgotten nor forgiven the Spanish betrayal of the Spanish Republic by its soi-disant ally.

The editor has declined to translate Señor Gorkin's account into the "value-free" language fashionable in contemporary social science, on grounds that it is no violation of objectivity to call perfidy by its own name. ■

The Popular Front program, adopted by the Seventh Congress of the Communist International (1935), was meant to be applied primarily in France to uphold the Stalin-Laval pact and to counteract the Anti-Comintern pact between Germany, Japan, and Italy; due to a twist of circumstances, however, it was Spain where it had its fullest and most disastrous application. It has been repeatedly said that the Spanish Civil War was a general rehearsal for the Second World War; what is not clearly understood is that it was also the first testing ground for "popular democracy," perfected forms of which we have been obliged to witness in a dozen countries during the postwar period. The men and methods used to convert these countries into Kremlin satellites were tested in Spain. For this reason, among many, the Spanish experience had and continues to have historical and universal significance.

Spanish Communism before the Popular Front

Spain remained neutral during the World War of 1914-1918. It was divided, however, into two clearly defined currents of opinion: the traditionally reactionary element sided with the Central Powers and the liberal republican and socialist element with the Allies, particularly with Republican France. The war profoundly accentuated the chasm between the two Spains. And while the belligerent countries shed their blood and wrought havoc upon one another, Spanish industrialists and businessmen—principally Catalonians and Basques—made handsome profits and enjoyed great economic-financial prosperity.

Another consequence of the war was increased radicalism of the Spanish proletariat and of workers' movements. The Union General de Trabajadores[1] (UGT), under the leadership of the Partido Socialista Obrero,[2] and the anarcho-syndicalist-inspired Confederación Nacional del Trabajo,[3] enjoyed extraordinary popularity. In August 1917, the first attempt at a general strike took place. After its failure the four Socialist leaders—later elected to Parliament— Largo Caballero, Besteiro, Saborit, and Anguiano were sentenced to life imprisonment. During 1920, Spain had 1,316 strikes and 230 terrorist attempts.

The triumph of the Russian Revolution produced extraordinary reverberations in Spanish peasant and industrial workers' circles. Not understanding the true nature of Bolshevism, the overwhelming majority of the Socialists and the anarcho-syndicalists gave it their moral support. As early as April 1920, the majority of the Executive Committee of the Federación de Juventudes Socialistas[4] (under the influence of two emissaries secretly sent by Moscow, the Russian Borodin and the Hindu Roy), resolved to found the first Communist party. A special convention of the Partido Socialista Obrero, which took place in June, voted to enter the Communist International; 8,260 supported affiliating, 5,016 opposed, and 1,615 abstained. Only the influence of Pablo Iglesias, the old founder and leader of Spanish socialism, prevented support from being near unanimous. The convention sent two emissaries to Moscow to gather information: Fernando de los Ríos and Daniel Anguiano. They were instructed to present three conditions: (1) that the Communist International recognize the political autonomy of the Partido Socialista Obrero; (2) that the latter have the

[1] General Union of Workers—the Socialist Trade Union.
[2] Worker Socialist Party.
[3] National Confederation of Labor; the anarcho-syndicalist trade union.
[4] Federation of Socialist Youth.

right to revise in its conventions any doctrine definitely adopted by the Communist International; and (3) that Moscow work toward unifying all Marxist parties.

In Berlin, De los Ríos and Anguiano met Angel Pestaña, the anarcho-syndicalist leader, who was returning from Moscow quite disillusioned. Bolshevism was not what he and his comrades had believed it to be. A dictatorship had been established in Russia and the jails were filled with anarchists, revolutionary socialists, and Mensheviks. The subsequent trip of other anarcho-syndicalist emissaries, among them Gaston Leval, was to place the powerful Confederación Nacional del Trabajo in opposition to Soviet Communism.

In July 1921, when the P.S.O.'s two emissaries returned to Madrid, the National Committee held a meeting. The thundering reply from Moscow was delivered: "Instead of the three conditions which you propose, we propose to you the adoption of the twenty-one conditions approved by the Second Congress of the Communist International." They agreed to call a special convention on April 9th. Iglesias, De los Ríos, Caballero, Besteiro, and Prieto, the Socialist leaders with the greatest prestige, declared themselves unequivocally opposed to the twenty-one conditions and to joining the Third International. The final vote was 8,808 votes opposed to the Communist International and 6,025 in favor. Out of the resulting schism came the Communist party of Spain. The small party founded a year before at the time of Roy and Borodin's trip united with it.

Fernando de los Ríos recorded his impressions on his trip to Russia in a widely read and discussed book. During an interview with Lenin, the Spanish professor had interrupted one of Lenin's statements to ask him: "And how about liberty?" And Lenin answered him with another question: "Liberty for what?" De los Ríos inferred that this reply was tantamount to a negation of liberty from the mouth of the Bolshevik chief. I, who was founder and Secretary of the Federación Comunista de Levante,[5] did not interpret Lenin's reply in the same manner. I believed that Lenin had

[5] Communist Federation of the Levant.

meant only that the dictatorship of the proletariat would not grant its enemies the liberty to destroy it. Exiled a year later for political reasons, and a Communist functionary for eight years, I began to realize as early as 1925, in Moscow, that I had been wrong, that Bolshevism meant, indeed, the negation of human liberty. Evidence for this led me to break with the Bolsheviks in 1929.

In a normal or relatively normal situation, thought control, bureaucratic centralization, and discipline from above—all characteristics of Communism before Stalin's victory—are intolerable to Spanish individualism. Consequently, the intellectuals who affiliated with the Spanish division of the Comintern soon left it. Bolshevism was never able to obtain a solid foundation in the trade-union movement and was soon reduced to an insignificant political force. Sectarian policies, and slogans of "Down with the bourgeois Republic!" and "Long live the Soviets!" prevented Spanish Communists from making a good showing in the elections held after the Republic was proclaimed in 1931. General Krivitsky was later to acknowledge that after five years of Republican government in Spain, despite costly propaganda, the P.C.E. [6] had succeeded in attracting only 3,000 members. In a Parliament of 500 deputies it held only one seat. During these five years the Republican government refused to recognize the U.S.S.R. and to maintain diplomatic relations with it. Subsequent to the Popular Front and Soviet intervention in Spain, this insignificant party, which had sixteen deputies and about 25,000 members, was to become the prime political force in the country with about a half million members. To the naïve or trustworthy of our Western world, who accept almost as a dogma the belief that Communism cannot win power in the West, I offer the Spanish experience. I know of no people more rebellious and individualistic than the Spaniards; yet this people was to surrender to the dual Nazi-Fascist and Communist experience.

[6] Partido Comunista Española (Spanish Communist party).

The Intervention of the Kremlin in Spain

Count Ciano's *Diary* and the secret documents found in Nazi archives indicate that if the democratic governments had adopted a relatively vigorous attitude during the Spanish war, Rome and Berlin would have abandoned Franco to his fate or else pressed for negotiated peace. Nonintervention had tragic consequences. It tied the hands of the democracies. It screened Hitler's and Mussolini's open intervention on Franco's behalf. It abandoned the Republican zone to Stalinism. For this disastrous policy the democracies were to pay a high price: the downfall of a friendly Republic following the triumph of an ally of Nazism and Fascism, public confirmation that the democracies could not be expected to retaliate against future aggressions, an opportunity for the totalitarian powers to test their arms and men; the Second World War; and, upon its conclusion, the conquests of Stalinist imperialism and the present dramatic cold war which threatens the destiny of humanity. From the long and the short point of view, the Spanish war was the first great battle for world domination.

But what interests us here are the motives and the methods of the Kremlin. In my capacity as international secretary of the POUM [7] and as member of the Central Militia Committee—the true government of Catalonia during the first months of the Civil War—I had occasion in September 1936 to hold a friendly conversation with Jules Moch, Undersecretary of State during the presidency of Leon Blum. Among other things, he told me:

> We are convinced that intervention in the Spanish conflict will drag us into war with Germany. And under what conditions? Exposing ourselves to remaining isolated. The French government has asked the English and the Russians what their attitude would be in the event that we should contribute actual aid to the Madrid government. London replied: "The British Government considers itself as much an enemy of the fascists as of the communists. Since

[7] Partido Obrero de Unificación Marxista (Unified Marxist Workers' party, a Trotskyite group).

there now exists a country in which both of these forces are waging war against one another, let us abandon them to their fate. We refuse to intervene." Moscow's reply is even more pontifical. In sum it is: "The Franco-Soviet Pact of 1935 obliges us to lend reciprocal aid in the event that one of our two countries finds itself attacked by a third power, but not so in the event of war which results from the intervention of one of our two countries in the affairs of a third."

France feared isolation and war and Leon Blum sincerely believed that the best way to help us was to establish nonintervention. I indicated to Jules Moch that Rome and Berlin, who had made previous commitments with Spanish reactionaries, had not and would not adhere to nonintervention even if they accepted the pact. I asked them to follow suit. But they did not. In fact, they did not even fulfill a commercial treaty, signed in December 1935, by which France agreed to sell arms to the legitimate Spanish government. On its side the Chamberlain government posed the problem in a false and hypocritical manner: at the outset, the Spanish war was between Fascist subversion and the legitimate democratic Republican government; if it later turned into a war between Fascists and Communists, that was because the default of the democracies created the conditions for the rise of Communism. And what about Stalin's attitude? It was, undoubtedly, the most hypocritical of all. Officially he did not wish to compromise himself in the least; he even subscribed to the nonintervention pact, unofficially he bade the French Communist party pressure the Blum government into intervening in the Spanish war, and he had his international organizations and agents pave the way for intervention inside and outside of Spain. It was not very difficult to understand his strategy—I believe I was one of the first to do so.[8]

Stalin wanted, more than anything, to remove the dangers of war from his frontiers to those of central and western Europe and, simultaneously, to emphasize the contradictions and grounds for conflict between the principal European powers: France and Eng-

[8] *Canibales Politicos* (*Hitler y Stalin en España*), by Julian Gorkin, Mexico, 1940.

land on one side, Italy and Germany on the other.[9] If France intervened in the Spanish war and dragged in England, while Italy and Germany intervened on the opposite side, so much the better. Lenin had always eulogized the transformation of an imperialist war into a revolutionary civil war; Stalin, in a base, unprincipled tactic, hoped to transform a revolutionary civil war into an eventual imperialist war . . . among all the opposing powers. The problem for him was to remain officially neutral up to that moment when it suited him to cease being so. (Let us add immediately that what he did not accomplish during the Spanish war he did obtain later, over the corpse of the Spanish Republic, by means of his pact with Hitler.)

But at the same time Stalin felt that it was necessary for him to emerge from political and diplomatic isolation; he would be able to utilize the Spanish war and even the Committee for Nonintervention for this purpose. If he could prolong the war and impose his influence on Spain—or on one of the zones of conflict—by means of the Spanish Communist party, the International Brigades, and his agents, he would not only reinforce the French-Soviet pact, but would be able to force England to enter the pact or to sign a similar one. And finally he would wield a powerful weapon for negotiating with Hitler. The blood and fate of the Spanish people did not concern him one whit; the only thing that interested him was his game of foreign politics. There exists today much evidence to support these facts.

Let us begin with Moscow's *sincerity* in praising the tactics of the Popular Front in Spain. In regard to this we possess, among others, the invaluable testimony of Jesús Hernández, ex-director of the central Communist organ, ex-deputy, ex-minister, ex-commissar of war, and ex-member of the Comintern Executive.[10] When the electoral results of February 1936 became known, he and the general secretary of the P.C.E., José Díaz, held an interesting meeting with Stepanov and Codovila, the two permanent delegates from Moscow before the arrival of Togliatti (Al-

---

[9] For further discussion of this strategy see Michel Collinet's essay on France.
[10] Jesús Hernández: *La Grande Trahison*, Paris, 1953.

fredo). These delegates were preoccupied with only one thing: to disrupt the leftist bloc with utmost speed and to discredit the socialists in favor of Communism. Hernández raised several arguments:

> In the early years of the Republic, in the name of the policy of class war, Moscow compelled us to fight against the socialists and the anarchists by accusing them of being "social fascists" and "anarcho-fascists," and we thereby played into the hands of the monarchial reaction. In the name of democracy against fascism and of the Popular Front, do you want us to do the same thing now? In the present situation, that policy can lead to disaster.

What was the exact situation? The coalition of the Right had won 4,446,000 votes and 164 seats in the Chamber of Deputies; the Popular Front, 4,840,000 votes and 277 seats. The electoral system and distribution of votes favored the Popular Front in the number of seats in the Chamber, although the number of votes was almost equal. Everyone feared that the rightists, who controlled the economic organizations, the army and the Church, would not accept the electoral results, but would intensify their conspiracies. Relying on sixteen deputies in the Chamber and a freshly won popular following, the Communists prepared to resort to their familiar tactic of increasing their strength by undermining parties of the left. Obviously, all segments of the Popular Front shared responsibility for unleashing the military-fascist reaction and the Civil War, but, as in France and Germany, a very large share of this responsibility must be assigned to the Communists. Pre-empting the Left is the principal device by which the Communists gain a mass following. For this reason democratic-socialistic forces have repeatedly been proved to be a principal target of Communist parties.

The military-fascist rebellion broke out on July 18, 1936. On the 21st, a meeting of the Comintern and the Profintern was held in Moscow for the sole purpose of examining the Spanish situation. It was decided to hold another meeting in Prague on the 26th of July; at this meeting the syndicalist-Communist French leader

Gastón Mommousseau, head of the European office of the Pro-fintern, presided. The principal agreements were as follows: the creation of a fund of one thousand million francs to aid the Spanish Popular Front; the administration of this fund by a committee composed of Thorez, Ercoli (Togliatti), "La Pasionaria," José Díaz, and, if possible, Largo Caballero; the formation of a brigade of five thousand men, recruited from foreign workers and having at its command a group of pilots and sufficient arms to fight as an independent unit.

At first glance these agreements seemed friendly enough, as if inspired by the purest revolutionary solidarity; as manipulated by Stalinism, they constituted a first draft of the Machiavellian tactics that Stalin proposed to apply. As we shall soon see, the creation of the fund of one thousand million was requested to conceal a veritable economic-financial piracy. By including on the administrative committee of that fund the most esteemed socialist leader and secretary general of the U.G.T., Largo Caballero, one to whom they gave the hypocritical tag of the "Spanish Lenin," the Communists initiated a skillful political operation: they would try to convert him into their pawn; then, thanks to his great prestige, they would penetrate Socialist and U.G.T. circles. And finally, the first "independent" international brigade—which was to be followed by others—was summoned in order to veil the penetration and the actions of its military and police agents.

But at the same time that the Kremlin accomplished this veiled intervention and penetration by means of international organizations under its control, it officially continued to proclaim its nonintervention. On Thursday, August 28, 1936, the Commissar of Foreign Relations signed a decree prohibiting "export, re-export, or movement toward Spain of all classes of arms, munitions, war material, airplanes, and warships." When made public this decree created the greatest confusion in workers' groups and, above all, in Communist groups. Moscow had asked for their active solidarity with the Spanish people, then she herself publicly refused it means of defense, just as the bourgeois democratic governments had done! The consternation was greatest in Spanish Communist circles. Togliatti and Duclos came to Madrid to explain the Kremlin's nonintervention. These two men and the permanent emissaries, Stepanov, Codovila (Medina) and "Pedro" or Gueré (Erno Geröe, the infamous provocateur of the Hungarian revolution and the victim of a recent purge, was then the agent of the Comintern and of the G.P.U. in Catalonia) held a meeting with the Politbureau. Togliatti summarized the order he brought as follows: "The U.S.S.R. must guard its security as its prize possession. A hasty attitude can cause a break in the balance and unleash war throughout the East." Everything must be subordinated—including the fate of the Spanish people—to the security of the U.S.S.R. The Spanish comrades were expected to understand this; but they had great difficulty in doing so. They nonetheless accepted it and submitted.

Jesús Hernández, who has described the meeting, adds: "If during the first weeks Stalin had sent us arms instead of 'advisers' and 'technicians,' the blows against the enemy would have been mortal." But it did not suit Stalin's purposes—this, Hernández was to realize later—for the enemy to receive mortal blows and for the war to end rapidly; what did suit him was its prolongation, until the desperate fall of the Republic under his dependency, and international complications. General Goriev, Soviet military attaché, told Hernández shortly afterward: "The essential thing would be to win the armaments race against the Francoists. They are now receiving airplanes and tanks from Italy." Goriev did not know how to justify the Kremlin's attitude; he tried to console Hernández by saying that the first shipments would come soon. (Let us immediately add that the military technicians of this early period, Goriev, Grissen, Stern, Chaponov—and later Ambassador Rosenberg, the consul-general of Barcelona, Antonov-Ovseenko, and many others—were shortly afterward recalled by Moscow, accused as "traitors," and liquidated. The fact is that they were unable to comprehend Stalin's real betrayal of the Spanish people.)

After mulling it over for about two months, Stalin decided to exploit the Spanish situation more thoroughly. A crisis of the government presided over by the republican José Giral arose and Largo Caballero set about forming an authentic Popular Front government, at the heart of which was to be the U.G.T. and the C.N.T. The Francoists, staunchly supported by Rome, Berlin, and Portugal, were rolling toward Madrid; against the abundant modern equipment at their disposal—airplanes, tanks, artillery—all that the Republican militiamen could present was courage and a few bad guns. At the same time Stalin recognized the dangers and possibilities of the new situation. The Politbureau of the P.C.E. turned down the proposal to enter the government formed by Largo Caballero. When Stalin was informed about this decision in Moscow, he ordered the P.C.E. to enter the government. And for the first time in history a non-communist government was able to boast two Communist ministers: Jesús Hernández in Public Education and Vicente Uribe in Agriculture. (In a country with Spain's characteristics, the two Cabinet positions were of much greater importance than appears at first glance.)

During the early days of September Stalin called a meeting of the Russian Politbureau in the Kremlin and decided on "definite aid" to the government just formed by Largo Caballero. Everything was mobilized around this decision. About the middle of the same month a propaganda and recruiting center for the International Brigades was established in Paris. This bureau consisted of Thorez, Gottwald, Togliatti, Longo, and the Soviet general of Polish origin, Karol Swierczewski (General Walter). Yagoda, at that time head of the G.P.U., simultaneously received orders from Stalin to establish a secret branch of the G.P.U. in Spain. With Yagoda presiding, a meeting was held in Lubianka on the 14th of September, attended by Uritsky, of the Red Army staff and chief of military forces of the G.P.U., and Slutsky, chief of the foreign department of the G.P.U. The nomination as head of the G.P.U. fell to Commander Orlov (also known as Nikilsky, Schewed, Lyova). It was determined that all the activities of the Comintern in Spain—beginning with those of the P.C.E.—were to be under the jurisdiction of the G.P.U. Yagoda himself was to superintend the operation from Lubianka; Slutsky and Krivitsky were to assume control abroad. There was to be absolute secrecy.

Concerning the motives of Stalin in Spain, Krivitsky said:

> Stalin, in contrast to Mussolini, wished to play his game in Spain without risking anything. Soviet intervention could have been decisive at particular moments if Stalin had risked on the government's side what Mussolini risked on Franco's side. But Stalin risked nothing. In fact he even made certain beforehand that there was enough gold in excess in the Bank of Spain to amply cover the cost of his material aid to Madrid. Stalin always tried in every way possible to avoid engaging the Soviet Union in a conflagration. His intervention was accompanied by the slogan: "Keep out of the line of artillery fire." This slogan marked our line of conduct during our entire intervention campaign.

The moment Stalin had his batteries strategically placed, he decided to make a public gesture which had extraordinary repercussions. As Secretary General of the Communist party (Bolshevik) of the U.S.S.R.—that is, acting as party leader, without directly compromising the Soviet government—he sent the following telegram on October 16th to José Díaz, Secretary General of the Spanish Communist party:

> By helping the revolutionary masses of Spain within our possible means, the workers of the Soviet Union are only fulfilling their duty. They realize that the liberation of Spain from the oppression of fascist reactionaries is not merely a private matter of the Spaniards, but the common cause of all advanced, progressive humanity. Fraternal Greetings.—Stalin.

This telegram was enthusiastically received by the workers of the whole world, who had embraced the Spanish cause but who felt the anxiety of impotence. It galvanized the popular masses of Spain. Unlike the capitalist democracies, who indirectly seemed to favor Franco's victory, the great Russian Revolution and its leader Stalin were hastening to the aid of the Spanish Revolution! For the handful of men who understood the dangers of this aid, the situation became extraordinarily difficult. In the bosom of our own party our arguments met with fierce resistance. Placing his faith in this telegram and in the promises of the Russians, Largo Caballero himself issued quite an optimistic proclamation on October 28, assuring the people that the government already had at its disposal tanks and a "powerful air force" and announcing "a victorious counteroffensive." This did not prevent the precipitous departure of the Madrid government and its installation in Valencia. The capital, gravely threatened by the Franco forces, was entrusted to the Junta of Defense, presided over by General Miaja, behind whom moved a collection of communist agents.

Had Socialist leader Largo Caballero, whose honesty was unquestionable, been deceived with respect to the amount of Russian arms—and their quality, or had he yielded to the felt necessity of infusing soldiers and masses with a little optimism? Perhaps both simultaneously. Jesús Hernández says:

> The first Soviet supplies arrived towards the end of October, four months after the beginning of the war. A truly ridiculous quantity was all that came; nevertheless, they were received with real joy. "They are the first," we thought, "more will come later—and then more—all that we need." Two ships crossed on the high seas: one coming from Russia headed for loyalist Spain, with its holds almost empty, and one from Cartagena bound for Odessa with 7,800 coffers of Spanish gold.

And he adds further on:

> And the great campaign of illusions began: six flat-nosed airplanes were supposed to turn into 600, a dozen light tanks into a division of heavy tanks and 50 machine guns were supposed to make enough noise for 5,000. Like the miracle of the wafer.

There is abundant testimony on the terrible quality of these arms; we shall limit ourselves to citing that of the anarcho-syndicalist leader Diego Abad de Santillán:

> One of our coastal barges intercepted a shipment of arms destined for the International Brigades. It was unloaded in Barcelona and checked and we saw that it contained old useless guns ante-

dating the war of 1914-18, paid for in advance and without argument by the central government.[11]

Krivitsky on his part makes three statements of utmost importance, all confirmed by Jesús Hernández: (1) All the foreign purchasing offices of arms for the Spanish government were under the direct control of the G.P.U. (2) These agents were under orders to supply only that equipment which was indispensable for sustaining the fronts. This made offensive operations and, of course, eventual defeat of the enemy impossible. (3) The supply of arms was to serve as a means of pressure and blackmail to subjugate the Republic and its men—especially Catalonia, where Stalinism found the greatest resistance.

All evidence agrees that the famous Soviet aid to Spain constituted a most scandalous business deal for the Kremlin. The latter did not actually begin sending arms until it had in its hands most of the Spanish treasury. One of the first to speak of "the lucrative aspects of the aid given by the U.S.S.R. and its subsidiary Communist parties" was the Socialist leader and ex-Minister of National Defense, Indalecio Prieto.[12] According to his statements, "On October 25, 1936, 7,800 coffers filled with gold, in coin and in bars, were shipped from Cartagena, gold which constituted the *greatest* part of the reserves of the Bank of Spain." Jesús Hernández and "El Campesino"[13] confirm this fact. The former very precisely: "Of 2,258 million pesetas (70 per cent sterling gold pounds) which represented the reserves of the Spanish state in 1936, they demanded a deposit of 510 tons of gold, or 1,581 million gold pesetas, more than half of our national treasury." And he adds: "On November 6, the Spanish gold reached Moscow. And on November 6, General Mola's cannons roared at the gates of Madrid and enemy planes shot at our militiamen, who lay flat on the ground, roaring with rage and shooting their guns

---

[11] Diego Abad de Santillán, *Como Perdimos La Guerra*, Buenos Aires, 1940.
[12] Indalecio Prieto, "Cómo y por qué salí del Ministerio de Defensa Nacional" (*Intrigas de los Rusos en España*, Paris and Mexican editions, 1940).
[13] Valentín González "El Campesino," *Life and Death in the U.S.S.R.*, published in fourteen countries.

against Hitler's and Mussolini's planes (which Franco got without paying a cent in advance)." And he adds a fact that coincides with Indalecio Prieto's observation: the Soviet banking elements who were in charge of Spanish gold in Moscow—Grinko, Margulin, Cagen, Ivanovsky, Martinson—were directly under Stalin's direction. Lastly, Krivitsky appraises the Bank of Spain's reserves at $700 million (in 1936) and speaks of this messy deal.

Was this all? Jesús Hernández' book, published after his departure from the U.S.S.R., describes another facet of the swindle. For on the Seventh of November celebration of 1936, the Communist emissary Murial, convalescing from a wound received at the front, accompanied a delegation of the Spanish Popular Front to Moscow. He had orders not to permit the delegates to discuss or ask questions about the problem of armament supplies. There was the usual military parade in Red Square, with a great display of artillery, cards, and aviation; the Spanish delegates could not conceal their bitterness, thinking that a small part of that equipment would be enough to win the war. Then during visits to factories, the workers smilingly and proudly asked them if they were satisfied with the supply of arms sent by the U.S.S.R. "Arms?" We are still waiting for them," the Spaniards answered in the midst of general surprise. "What? We have increased our production and work extra hours without pay and even donate a portion of our salaries to help you." Indeed, everywhere one read this motto: Speed up production to help the Spanish people. The Communist emissary Murial, wounded at the front, was embarrassed. Not only had the Spanish people been robbed, but under the pretext of the Spanish war the Russian people were robbed also.

Indalecio Prieto has told us of other robberies, this time carried out by the French Communist party. Negrín gave Thorez "2,500 million francs" in 1936 for the purchase of war material and for propaganda. "Hungry for money, the French Communist party incessantly tried to justify its unquestioned squandering of funds, continually demanded greater sums of Negrín and Mendez Aspe." (The latter was Negrín's Finance Minister.) The Communist newspaper *Ce Soir* was founded and supported by Spanish money. The French Communist party acquired twelve merchant ships from *France Navigation*, bought with Spanish funds. However, when one of these ships later transported Spanish exiles to Chile, Negrín paid a high sum for the transportation. Jesús Hernández adds another fact: the luxurious building of the Central Committee of the French Communist party converted into a fortress, was constructed with Spanish money. "El Campesino" has revealed that during the exodus from Catalonia, three trucks filled with gold left the Castillo de Figueras bound for the French Communist party. In short, Russian and Spanish Communist agents obtained, for unverified expenses, fabulous sums of money from the Spanish state. Strachevsky, the Soviet commercial delegate, once presented a letter to Prieto for his signature for "$1,400,000" without the least justification; Prieto refused to sign it, but Negrín hastened to comply. The full extent of Communist robbery of the Spanish government may never be discovered.

The First Test of "Popular Democracy"

The central nucleus of foreign Communist agents wound up in the International Brigades. They did not exceed five or six hundred soldiers. Very few of them were Russians, although a large number who came from countries dominated by fascist dictatorships had gone through Soviet schools and were fanatical Stalinists. The Russian military and technical experts who silently arrived in Spain did not exceed two thousand. Only officers and pilots were ever at the front; the others served in the rearguard. With this handful of men Moscow practically took possession of Spain and carried out the first test of "popular democracy." "The majority of these technicians," Krivitsky reports, "belonged to the Russian General Staff. They were military instructors, engineers, industrial specialists, technicians in chemical warfare, aviation mechanics, radio operators. . . . To the greatest possible extent, these members of the Red Army remained isolated from the civilian population and lived apart." Almost all of them used Spanish first and last names. "It was funny to see the efforts they made to pronounce them," Clara Campoamor, ex-Republican deputy, attests. General Ivan Bercim, of Lithuanian origin, exercised military control; and Arturo Stachevsky, of Polish origin, political as well as economic-financial control. Both had proved themselves for many years in the U.S.S.R.; Stalin chose them personally. Control of the G.P.U. was exercised by the so-called Commander Orlov. Representing the Comintern, in this order, were: Togliatti, Stepanov, and Codovila. In Catalonia, the famous "Pedro" (Erno Geröe) simultaneously represented the Comintern and the G.P.U. One of his police-terrorist collaborators was Lazlo Rajk, executed a few years ago in Budapest. Performing their roles as heads of the International Brigades were the Frenchman André Marty—the so-called "butcher of Albacete"—and the Italian Luigi Longo. They were the chiefs; it would be possible to make an extensive list of their military and police collaborators, the overwhelming majority of whom—who survived—occupy important positions in the Italian and German Communist movements and in the satellite countries.

The exact size of the International Brigades is still not known. When the war was over, General Franco's government declared that 125,000 men bound for the International Brigades had crossed the frontier. He himself states that not all of them served simultaneously. They generally served as shock troops and they suffered such casualties that it was necessary to send in replacements three or four times. As we shall see later, the terror imposed by Marty, Longo, and Commander Carlos J. Contreras (Vittorio Vidali, who participated in the plot to assassinate Trotsky and is today the head of the Communists in Trieste) produced innumerable victims and precipitated numerous desertions. In 1937, the year in which the Brigades were at the height of their activity, there was a total of five brigades in the firing lines, which, taking into account the instruction corps and auxiliary personnel, amounts to a total of 35,000 men. The other 90,000 were the reinforcements who came to replace casualties. These figures are confirmed by Louis Fischer in his book *Why Spain Fights On*, the English edition of which bears a preface by Clement Attlee. And Fischer was in a position to know the truth.

How is one objectively to characterize the International Brigades? I am referring to those controlled by the Communists, since the C.N.T. and the POUM also had fighting units, though much smaller ones, made up of foreign volunteers. Communist agencies, directed by agents of the G.P.U., conducted intense recruiting in almost all countries; other agents situated at frontier villages tried to direct the volunteers toward Albacete, where the general staff of the Brigades acted with complete independence—without the slightest Spanish control. The Brigades comprised all types of men: authentic, heroic idealists who came to Spain to fight for human liberty against dictatorships that were oppressing their countries, exiled Communist fighters politically unemployed, adventurers of every stripe (these were in a minority) who had nothing to lose, simple mercenaries of the sort who proliferate in all wars. Those who fought, fought well—bravely, heroically, suffering enormous casualties. They contributed to saving Madrid in its moments of greatest peril. Spaniards owe enormous gratitude to those sincere fighters, both those who died and those who survived. Moscow used the International Brigades, however, to gain control of the government, and to commit and conceal the worst outrages. Many members of International Brigades—and not a few Communist fighters—were killed from behind; I met many others in prisons living out the most terrible dramas, examples of which I shall cite later.

In the name of creating a superior moral dialectic—the so-called proletarian morality—Lenin advocated duplicity and falsehood as tactical political weapons. Stalin and his followers turned duplicity and falsehood into the basic everyday instruments of their policies. Spanish Communists, always ready to betray their nation in the name of the Soviet fatherland, appeared to be the most sincere and loyal patriots around. They and their "advisers" vociferously defended antifascist unity and the Popular Front; meanwhile, in practice, they fomented envy and rivalry, promoted dissension absorbed those whom they could use—even if only for the moment —and eliminated those who were obstacles. In the name of unity, they began absorbing the Juventudes Socialistas; [14] (thereafter called Juventudes Socialistas Unificadas[15]) which became a docile instrument of the Communists. (Santiago Carrillo, their secretary general, was a follower of Caballero, but had no compunctions about renouncing his father, the honest old Caballerista soldier Wenceslao Carrillo.) In the name of unity, they absorbed the independent workers' parties of Catalonia—with the single exception of the POUM, which they eliminated by terror—and they formed the so-called Partido Socialista Unificado de Cataluña (PSUC), [16] creating for themselves the base which they had lacked in this important industrial region. It did not take them long similarly to dominate the U.G.T. of Catalonia and, in the name of unified action with the C.N.T., to divide and undermine the latter. Under express orders from Stalin, Ambassador Rosenberg confronted Largo Caballero almost daily with the necessity of forming, by means of a fusion of Socialists and Communists, the Partido Unico del Proletariado; [17] the opposition of the old Socialist leader was one of the causes of his downfall. During the entire war, and always in the name of unity—and victory—they exploited to the hilt the rival tendencies between Caballero and Prieto socialists: first they utilized Largo Caballero's "leftism" to infiltrate the Partido Socialista and the U.G.T., then they utilized Prieto's "moderatism" to liquidate Largo Caballero and to protect Negrín; finally they utilized the ambitions of the latter who was now their tool, to liquidate Prieto and to impose their dictatorship. The Communists invoke "coexistence" to conceal the suppression of all their adversaries and "unity" to bring about unity through *their* dictatorship. Obviously when all other forces and movements are suppressed or neutralized, unity—totalitarian unity—is a fact. This was the experience of Spain—later of several other countries.

The strength of non-Communist socialist and leftist forces was

[14] Socialist Youth.
[15] United Socialist Youth.
[16] United Socialist Party of Catalonia.
[17] United Proletariat party.

further undermined by a policy in which Stalinist agents cooperated with Spanish rightists. Under the pretext of not frightening the bourgeois and petty-bourgeois forces and of consolidating the militia into the regular army under a single command (all of which seemed at first glance necessary and logical), the P.C.E. and the P.S.U.C., as well as their peripheral organizations, were attracting rightist elements who were happy about this fortuitous protection and no less happy about the suppression of workers' councils and of agrarian reform. With every means within their reach this alliance of Communists and rightists began to send authentic revolutionaries to jail or to their death. During the year and a half that I spent in the jails of Madrid, Valencia, and Barcelona—from my arrest in June 1937 until the collapse and exodus from Catalonia, in January-February of 1939—I rubbed elbows with several thousand leftist socialists, anarcho-syndicalists of the C.N.T. and the F.A.I. (Federación Anarquista Ibérica),[18] POUMists, ex-militiamen, and members of the International Brigades. That is, with antifascists and anti-Stalinists. In the jails I was able to verify—better than in the street—the cold-blooded betrayal of the Spanish revolution. It was there that I understood that Stalinism represented a permanent form of the counterrevolution. If most people did not recognize this truth, it was because they believed that only Nazi-Fascism-Falangism stood for counterrevolution. One *seemed* to exclude the other; later it was seen, by the Hitler-Stalin pact and by successive Communist state actions, that in this respect as in many others the Spanish experience was prophetic and universal.

To gain control over the army, political commissars were used. This institution, invented by Carnot and perfected by Trotsky in the Red Army, was thoroughly utilized by Stalinists in Spain. Circumstances were wonderfully on their side. The bulk of the officers—traditionally reactionary-monarchist and imbued with a strong caste spirit—were on the rebel side; of those who remained behind in the Republican zone those on the enemy side were shot, and the majority of the others felt that they were victims of

[18] Iberian Anarchist Federation.

popular distrust. (Unjust distrust in the majority of cases, but understandable enough in the circumstances in which the civil war broke out.)

In the militia period, each party and each organization had its own political commissars. Was it not an eminently socio-political war? The commissars seemed to answer a dual need: surveillance over the career soldiers and maintenance of socio-political morale in the fighting units. By means of unbridled propaganda, a skillful distribution of arms and supplies in general, all sorts of pressures —alternating between favoritism and terror—the Communists, and particularly the political commissars, wound up dominating the forces of the Republican Army, especially after the dissolution of the militias and their incorporation into the centralized army under orders from a single command.

The "Socialist" Julio Alvarez del Vayo, a fellow traveler of Bolshevism even before October 1917, an admirer of Lenin from the Switzerland period, of Trotsky until his deportation to Prinkipo, and of Stalin afterwards—was not only Minister of State (Foreign Affairs) but General Commissar of the Army in the Largo Caballero government. In the first post he obeyed Litvinov to a much greater extent than the President of the Spanish Cabinet, and in the second post, Moscow agents. "El Campesino" relates that "La Pasionaria," in the name of the Politbureau, ordered him to go from Madrid to Valencia for the purpose of holding an interview with "Comrade Alvarez del Vayo." Present at the interview was Ercoli (Togliatti). Del Vayo made a speech telling him that the Red Army's obedience to Bolshevik discipline depended on the political commissars; the moment had arrived for liquidating the socialist, anarcho-syndicalist, and POUMist commissars and replacing them with Communist commissars. Aware that "El Campesino" might be concerned with the reaction of the aforementioned movements, Togliatti invoked discipline and told him: "Follow Comrade Alvarez del Vayo's orders." And "El Campesino" followed them. In the *Epistolario Prieto-Negrin*, he states, among other significant things:

The first meeting of the High Council of War was held at my request in Valencia, a few days after its reorganization and the object of the meeting was to deal with the problem of the Commissariat. I read to you the figures that were painstakingly gathered in regard to the political affiliations of the Army commissars. These figures revealed that the communist *officers* represented an infinitely greater percentage in proportion to the number of members of said Party; but, in addition to the communist *officers* there were many others of the Juventudes Socialistas Unificadas, who were under Communist control, and of the Partido Socialista Unificado de Cataluña, also under Soviet control, and many others who disguised their membership under the simple syndicate name of U.G.T. Added together these diverse groups gave the communists an overwhelming majority in the Commissariat.

Regarding the principal sources of power, Prieto supplies the following information in the same document:

Undersecretary of the Land Army: Cordón, communist; Undersecretary of Aviation: Núñez Maza, communist; Chief of the Air Forces: Hidalgo de Cisneros, communist; Chief of Naval Officers: Prados, communist; Commissary of the Armies of the Central-Southern Zone: Hernández, communist; General Director of Security: Cuevas, communist; General Director of Carbineers: Marcial Fernández, of the Partido Socialista Unificado de Cataluña, controlled by the communists and affiliated with the Third International.

Others could be added to this list. In another document Prieto affirms that in conjunction with every important or relatively important post—military, air, naval, police, or merely technical—there was either a Russian adviser or one obeying Russian orders. They all obeyed Kremlin agents instead of the respective ministers. Since the Communist party had few fighters of long standing, it seized upon the assortment of adventurers and undesirables that it had recently enrolled. All who submitted to the Communists felt protected, elevated, exalted nationally and internationally; but those who put up resistance were slandered, persecuted, assassinated. Even in the military hospitals, one had to show his

Communist card or at least be a sympathizer to have food and enjoy decent care.

The consequences of this Communist domination were catastrophic. The Republican troops had assured the heroic defense of Madrid by pushing back the Germans at Jarama and defeating the Italian legions on the plateaus of Guadalajara. Then a sort of truce was established which, if prolonged a few months longer, would have inevitably damaged the Republican cause. It was necessary to recover the initiative in the war. Largo Caballero and his immediate assistant, General Asensio, planned an important large-scale offensive on the Estramadura front, to accomplish the following: the occupation of Mérida and Badajoz, the cutting off of the rebel troops of the north from those of the south, a similar cutting off between the Portuguese frontier and Moroccan communications, that is, the Mediterranean routes from which the enemy received supplies and mercenary troops and the ultimate occupation of Sevilla. If this offensive had succeeded, it would have been possible perhaps to end the war. In fact, parallel with these military plans, Largo Caballero had initiated secret negotiations among the powers—excluding the U.S.S.R.—for the reestablishment of peace; the four powers—England, France, Germany, and Italy—seemed well disposed to expediting these negotiations.

Stalin wanted none of this. He did not favor the possible success of this sort of negotiation nor the fact that it would increase the popularity and prestige of the old Socialist leader, who was beginning to constitute a serious obstacle to Stalin's policy. Stalin was not interested in the outcome of the Spanish war and even less in an understanding between the European powers. Consequently he decided to sabotage the operations, and in the process liquidate Largo Caballero and General Asensio.

I spent several months in the State Prison of Barcelona with the latter—and with other generals of the military staff who were arrested for Communist purposes. We struck up a close friendship and I learned many things. (The first person to relate all this, in a series of sensational articles published at the end of the war, was my good friend Luis Araquistain, ex-counselor of Largo Caballero and ex-ambassador in Paris.) But the most substantial testimony to date is that of Jesús Hernández. He and Uribe, the two Communist ministers, one day received an invitation from General Kulik, the only one of the Russian generals who arrived at the beginning of the civil war and who had not been summoned to Moscow and shot. Togliatti and Codovila likewise were present at this interview. Kulik, in his post as general commander, had fixed up a table of caviar, vodka, and other choice Russian products. Since they spent an hour discussing things in general, Hernández asked him what the purpose of the meeting was.

"I am waiting for an important piece of news from the Ambassador of Valencia," Kulik limited himself to saying. Finally a coded communication was brought to him. When it was decoded, he passed the paper to Togliatti and said in a tone which did not allow for a reply: "Affair closed."

The Caballero-Asensio plan was not to be realized; the Communist ministers, the Soviet apparatus, and the Communist party must avoid it at all costs. In its stead there was to be an offensive by Brunete and Navalcarnero, an offensive demanded by the Soviet command which the Spanish fighters thought senseless. (This offensive, which took place at the beginning of July 1937, proved to be a veritable disaster.) The downfall of Largo Caballero, despite his enormous popularity and backing from all political and military Spanish forces, was decided upon at a meeting of the Politbureau at which were present Togliatti, Stepanov, Codivila, Gueré (Erno Geröe), Marty, Orlov, and Gaikis (the Russian chargé). Hernández and Diaz resisted the dismissal of Largo Caballero on grounds that it would expose the dissension within the Republican forces and might precipitate a series of disasters.[19]

[19] Hugh Thomas, the British historian, has described this extraordinary meeting as follows in his definitive work on the Spanish Civil War:

An astonishing meeting of the Spanish Communist Party executives was shortly held, attended by Marty, Togliatti, Codovila, Stepanov, Gero, Gaikis, the Russian Chare, and Orlov himself. Togliatti bluntly announced that he wanted Largo Caballero removed from the Premiership. Diaz and Hernandez protested. Diaz added that Spanish Communists ought not al-

Hernández himself was finally forced into making a violent denunciation of Largo Caballero, a denunciation which precipitated a governmental crisis. At this meeting it was decided that Largo Caballero should be replaced by Dr. Negrín; Hernández himself was to negotiate terms with Negrín. In the first days of May, Erno Geröe and the police services under his orders forcefully occupied the Central Telephone Exchange of Barcelona and invoked the famous "acts of May," which cost the lives of a thousand people; the streets of the Catalonian capital were covered with barricades, and the masses—as well as the fighters of Aragon—asked for the formation of a CNT-POUM General Council. The CNT did not accept, turning what might have been a severe Communist defeat into a Communist victory. The assassination of the CNT and POUM militants began. In Valencia the two Communist ministers demanded the dissolution of the POUM and the arrest of its leaders; since Largo Caballero emphatically refused, the Communists provoked the gravest gubernatorial crisis of the entire war. The revolution was lost and, with it, after a series of bloody catastrophes, the war.

Negrín, under the influence of Moscow agents, formed the so-called "Victory Government." Indalecio Prieto occupied National

ways to have to follow the lead of Moscow. Fear or ambition kept the other Spaniards from speaking. Stepanov said that it was not Moscow, but "history" condemned the Prime Minister, both for his defeatism and for his defeats. Marty agreed with him. Diaz called Marty a bureaucrat, and Marty growled that he was a revolutionary. "So are we all," said Diaz. "That remains to be seen," answered Marty. Diaz told Marty that he was a guest at meetings of the Spanish Communist Party. "If our proceedings do not please you," said Diaz deliberately, "there is the door." Uproar followed. Everyone stood up. La Pasionaria shrieked "Comrades! Comrades!" The Hungarian Gero sat open-mouthed in astonishment. Orlov appeared imperturbable. Togliatti looked serene. Codovila tried to calm Marty. Such scenes were unheard of at meetings of Communist parties, especially when the potentates of the Comintern were present. Eventually, Diaz was brought to accept Togliatti's proposal if the majority voted for it. Needless to say Diaz and Hernandez were alone in voting against it. Togliatti next said that the campaign to destroy Largo Caballero should begin at a meeting in Valencia. He blandly suggested that Hernandez should make the keynote speech. As for the next premier, Juan Negrin, the Finance Minister, would be the best choice. He was less obviously pro-communist than Alvarez del Vayo, and less actually anti-communist than Prieto. (*The Spanish Civil War*, Harper and Row, New York, 1961, pp. 404-405.)

Defense—War, Navy, and Air. As his later writings show—he went through the most bitter experiences of his life—he had to consent to the arrest and the trial of the leaders of POUM, the kidnapping and assassination of Andrés Nin (of which I shall speak more later), the arrest of the generals who had collaborated with Largo Caballero—Asensio, Martínez Monge, Martínez Cabrera—and an infamous campaign aimed at the destruction of Caballero and his Socialist party and of the U.G.T. supporters. He also helped preside over the loss of the entire north. Prieto had numerous occasions to observe proof that the principal agencies officially dependent upon him did not obey him but rather the Russians. During the collapse of Asturias, when he believed that the destroyer *Ciscar* had been placed in safety (in accordance with his instructions), the ship was destroyed by the Francoists because, obeying the orders of the Soviet naval technical expert and of the Chief of the Naval Staff (the Communist, Prados), it had not evacuated the port where it was anchored. For the purpose of demoralizing the enemy rearguard, he gave orders to bomb Zaragoza, Pamplona, Vitoria, etc.: the Russians issued a counterorder and they were not bombed. He gave orders not to bomb Valladolid; Valladolid was bombed. Negrín made him give the Russians two enemy planes shot down behind Republican lines: a Messerschmidt, which the French technicians were extremely interested in examining, and a Heinkel which was needed for Spanish bombardments. But the most disloyal and horrible maneuver was that of Teruel.

Toward the end of 1937, the morale of the Republican troops and of the rearguard was quite low; the victory at Teruel, planned by Prieto and by General Saravia, changed that. It constituted a truly heroic feat. Two months later, in February 1938, Teruel again fell into Francoist hands, to the great surprise of the Minister of Defense and his military staff. "It is a Russian maneuver against you," some of his co-workers told him. He refused to believe it.

"El Campesino," after his sensational escape from the U.S.S.R. (1948), shed light on the treacherous Soviet maneuver which indeed was directed against Prieto. The maneuver was entrusted to the Soviet generals Gregovitch and Barthe, and participated in by Spanish Communist commanders Modesto and Lister. First General Saravia was dismissed from office and replaced by Modesto. The artillery was then taken from the anarcho-syndicalist troops which protected Teruel. "El Campesino" was commanded to allow himself to be encircled with his division in the plaza; Lister and Modesto would subsequently come to his rescue.

"Are you trying to liquidate the Popular Front?" "El Campesino" asked Gregorovitch. "Do you think that we Communists are ready to handle the situation by ourselves?"

"It's not a question of liquidating it, but rather of making it submit to our will," the Soviet general explained to him. "The Socialists and the anarcho-syndicalists must be discredited and public opinion must be shown how the Communist divisions are the only ones capable of resisting until the very last. The loss of Teruel will be blamed on the others; we, by resisting until the end, will come out of the whole thing with greater prestige."

"El Campesino" obeyed. While he remained encircled in Teruel for several days, nobody came to his aid. Franco, who personally directed the enemy operation, announced his death. Prieto believed it completely and sent condolences to his "widow." But "El Campesino" recklessly broke the Francoist blockade, saved the bulk of his division and his own life. They had wanted him to die in order to cast his body at the feet of the Minister of Defense and discredit him. Jesús Hernández has revealed that Orlov plotted an attempt on Prieto's life: a machine placed in his official automobile was meant to make him leap from the car while it was in motion and kill him and his guard. Hernández threatened a scandal and saved Prieto's life. But under the pseudonym of "Juan Ventura" and with Negrín's knowledge, Hernández began a slander campaign against Prieto, accusing him of being a "pessimist" and a "defeatist" and of wanting to "negotiate with the enemy." Under Russian pressure, Negrín finally sacrificed him and, in addition to the Presidency of the Cabinet, got for himself—that is, for the Communists—the post of National Defense.

But the most important weapon used by Soviet agents and the Spanish communists was terrorism. The Bolsheviks had relied heavily on terror to consolidate their power in the U.S.S.R. Stalin relied on terror to win and maintain control. Krivitsky affirms that his immediate superior, Slutsky, who had received orders to organize the G.P.U. in Spain on the pattern of the organization in the U.S.S.R., achieved an enormous success: in December 1936, almost everything was already under his control and "even the ministers trembled under Soviet authority." On the seventeenth of the same month, *Pravda* announced that repression would be carried forward in Catalonia as energetically as it had been in the Soviet Union. The Kremlin mouthpiece was referring to the ghastly trials held in Moscow, followed by the shooting of Zinoviev, Kamenev, Bukharin, and all of Lenin's guard, and the bloody purges held in the entire Soviet territory. POUM was the only voice in Spain with the courage to protest these crimes. Moreover, we in POUM were the only ones to realize that Stalin would not hesitate about the lives of Spanish revolutionaries who protested when he had all the old Russian revolutionaries killed. But nobody or almost nobody paid any attention to us at the beginning, in the belief that we were letting ourselves be carried away by our inveterate anti-Stalinism; when they began to realize it for themselves, it was already too late.

According to Krivitsky, in March 1937, General Berzin himself sent a secret report to Voroshilov, then Commissar of War, telling him that everywhere there were complaints against the terrorist abuses of the G.P.U. in Spain. This report fell into the hands of the terrible Yejov, Yagoda's successor in the Lubianka. Krivitsky concludes:

> Yejov, as grand marshal of the immense purge which was then taking place in Russia, regarded Spain as if it were merely a Russian province.

Directly or through intermediaries, the G.P.U. controlled all that nominally controlled by Spanish Republican forces. Prieto states that the creation of the S.I.M. (Servicio de Investigación Militar[20]) was due to the initiative of "certain Russian technicians" (G.P.U.). He resisted at first, but finally gave in, believing that he would be able to control the appointments and their duties. But it did not work out that way: the S.I.M. inevitably fell into the hands of the G.P.U. Prieto states:

> I fell into disgrace because, by dismissing Commander Durán, I attempted to prevent the Office of Military Investigation from falling into the hands of the Russians, as did the General Board of Security when Lieutenant Colonel Ortega was at the head of it.

Who was this Commander Durán? An ex-actor, apparently without political affiliation, who had risen with extraordinary rapidity not at the front, but by serving as interpreter for Russian soldiers; he must have been primed for some time to fill a police office, for unbeknown to other Spanish Communist soldiers, he enjoyed Orlov's and Stachevsky's greatest confidence. Because Prieto dismissed him from control of the S.I.M., Stachevsky broke political and personal relations with him and resolved to get rid of him. And we now know from Jesús Hernández that Orlov plotted his "accidental" death. By means of the S.I.M., the G.P.U. succeeded in terrorizing everybody and dominating everything. They arrested, tried, and assassinated in their own fashion. Neither ministers, judges, lawyers, nor anyone else dared to do anything against the S.I.M.-G.P.U. Four days before my arrest in Barcelona, I had a dramatic interview with my old friend, the Socialist Julián Zugazagoitia, Minister of Government. The latter told me with profound bitterness: "I have ordered the liberty of two of your comrades four times and the constable has disobeyed my orders. The constable obeyed a secret authority who is higher than the minister, higher than all the ministers. I don't know what to do."

I felt that I was irrevocably lost, but I pitied that man.[21] The total number of murders committed by the Communists during

[20] Office of Military Investigation.
[21] Later, handed over to Franco by the Gestapo and Vichy, Zugazagoitia was shot in Madrid.

the Spanish Civil War will never be known exactly. In Madrid, Barcelona, Valencia, and Albacete the Communists had their own "camps" and the torture used in these was frightful. I was familiar with some of these "camps" and spoke with hundreds of prisoners who had been in them; many of these prisoners were shot, others committed suicide, and still others emerged with broken health. (In my book *Canibales Politicos* I have given numerous examples of the torture used; besides my own, there exist many hair-raising testimonies.) Not only were anti-Communist Spaniards killed, but no small number of lukewarm foreign Communists and numerous members of the International Brigades. André Marty, for example, had to defend himself against an accusation raised against him before the Politbureau of the French Communist party. In a written report he stated that the Valencia police, not daring to try numerous "undesirables and Franco agents," sent them to Albacete to be incorporated into the Brigades.

> Very few of them ransomed themselves by fighting courageously; the majority proved incorrigible and committed new crimes. They even killed the guards in the concentration camps where we had them enclosed. In view of these facts, I had to work quickly and apply the death penalty. At any rate, the number of those executed does not exceed five hundred, all genuine criminals. The Spanish situation is serious, but not grave. From now on, all of Red Spain will be governed by the communists. The police as well as the battalions of the Republican Guard and the brigade of agents instructed by Russian specialists, behave admirably and are performing veritable miracles.

The most appalling case—and the one which produced the greatest scandal in Spain and in the entire world—concerned my friend and colleague Andrés Nin. Ex-Secretary of the Profintern in Moscow, he was expelled from the U.S.S.R. in 1928. From the beginning of the war he held the post of political secretary of the POUM. He was the Counselor of Justice of the Provisional Government of Catalonia. Arrested at the order of Orlov at the same time as I, he was transferred to Madrid and then to Alcalá de Henares, where a kidnapping was simulated and an attempt made to attribute it to the Gestapo. Jesús Hernández has recounted the frightful torture which they subjected him to. They wanted to make him sign a "confession" admitting that we were agents of Franco, Hitler, and Mussolini, as defendants of Moscow had admitted. If he had succumbed to torture, we would have been condemned to death and executed immediately afterward. But Nin refused. And he had to be killed. Palmiro Togliatti himself was in charge of communicating the news of his death to the Kremlin. Nin's sacrifice—and a violent international campaign—saved the lives of the rest of us.

The Communists' conduct completely demoralized the Republican zone. Was it worth fighting in the name of means and ends as despicable as those of the Nazi-Fascists? In November 1938, the Soviet ordered the crossing of the Ebro—an apparently heroic feat. Of 90,000 soldiers who crossed the Ebro, 70,000 perished. The army that was to defend Catalonia was decapitated. Shortly afterward Stalin withdrew the International Brigades from Spain. The Francoists were able to occupy all of Catalonia without encountering the least resistance. Some months afterward—March of 1939—Togliatti and Stepanov forced Negrín, in the Central Zone, to stage a *coup d'état* with the sole purpose of instigating a counter *coup d'état*—that of Colonel Casado and General Miaja—which would precipitate a general collapse. They wanted to place the responsibility of this disaster on the other antifascist parties and organizations and to salvage the prestige of Spanish and international Communism. There were, among others, two outstanding witnesses to this plan: one by the Socialist leader Trifón Gómez and another by Jesús Hernández. The latter states that Stalin and Manuilsky approved of all that had been done by their agents in Spain. The Kremlin hangman could fling the cadaver of the heroic Spanish people upon the negotiating table in his pact with Hitler. Out of this came World War II.

CZECHOSLOVAKIA: THE CLASSIC MANEUVER

Ivo Duchacek

■ In Czechoslovakia, the "revolution" was not conducted by Soviet occupation armies as in the other Eastern European Soviet satellites, but it deviated no less from the stereotyped, utterly mistaken idea of a Communist revolution. Communism came to Czechoslovakia by way of coup d'état, executed in the classic manner. The revolution came after, imposed from above on workers, peasants, middle classes and aristocracy alike, by a minority government which gained power by stealth and exercised it in the protective shadow of the Red Army.

Curzio Malaparte has pointed out—and others have demonstrated in practice—that the modern state, with its centralized administrative, military, police and communications structures, is particularly vulnerable to the coup d'état. The coup d'état is the swiftest, neatest way to seize power illegally. It requires minimal bloodshed, few actors, funds or weapons. Once it has been executed the conspirators possess the arsenals, the treasury, and the communications monopoly which the modern state can turn against any mass uprising.

The example of Czechoslovakia is important to students of Communism because the "peaceful take-over" provides an instructive lesson in the methods by which an advanced country may succumb to Communism without electoral success or violent revolution. In the following article, Ivo Duchacek recounts how and why it happened that the most industrially advanced, democratic nation in Eastern Europe fell under Communist control in

February 1948. His account reveals the ingredients of Communist success. The most important of these was failure on the part of democratic political leaders to comprehend fully the character of the force which challenged them and Czech democracy. ■

Despite its location bordering Communist nations, Czechoslovakia was the one Eastern European country whose future as a democracy in the postwar period seemed reasonably secure. Industrially, agriculturally, and politically, the differences between it and its Eastern European neighbors were great.

Czechoslovakia's standard of living was the highest of any country in Eastern Europe, comparing favorably with the countries of Western Europe. In the interwar period after achieving national independence, Czechoslovakia developed its industrial plants and became one of the worlds major producers and exporters of heavy industrial products, shoes, and textiles. Spared physical devastation by the Second World War, Czech industry, working for the Nazi war effort, developed further. After 1945, the mines and power plants, the armament, machine tool, and automobile factories were nationalized with the consent of the five principal political parties. Land problems which historically have caused so much unrest and discontent in Eastern Europe did not exist in Czechoslovakia, for Czech and Slovak peasants, aided by reforms after the First and Second World Wars, largely owned the land they tilled.

Internally all political parties agreed on the need for reforms in the Czechoslovak administrative structure which emphasized regional decentralization and autonomy. Externally the Communist party and the non-Communist parties were equally disturbed by the possibility of some future revival of a German *Dranq nach Osten*. They were unanimous in desiring a close and friendly alliance with the Soviet Union; but while the Communists regarded the tie to Moscow as the cornerstone of the nation's foreign policy, the other parties wished to complement this link by close friendship with Britain and France.

The hope that Czechoslovakia might escape the fate of Poland or Rumania and succeed in remaining friendly with the Soviet Union without becoming a Communist satellite rested on a long tradition of parliamentary democracy, industrial and agrarian progress, democratic socialism and trade unionism, and respect for civil liberties. Geography offered the possibility that Czechoslovakia might serve as a bridge between East and West and that it might achieve a unique synthesis of the individualism and humanism of Western democracy and the collectivism and communalism of socialism. Given such background and favorable circumstances, there seemed good warrant for the optimism with which Czechs viewed their future.

The Communist seizure of power in the February 1948 coup blasted these hopes. The impact of the coup has become all the greater in subsequent years as a democratic and socially progressive nation has been replaced by a totalitarian satellite, exemplifying docility and subservience to the Soviet Union.

For Communists, Czechoslovakia has been important not only because it was the first industrial country to go Communist, but because the "peacefulness" of the Communist take-over provided an object lesson in the methods by which Communism may be introduced into an advanced country by nonviolent, albeit extraparliamentary methods. As A. I. Mikoyan declared at the 20th Congress of the Soviet Communist party:

> . . . a different way was that of the revolution in Czechoslovakia. As a consequence of a favorable condition which had been created in Czechoslovakia after the war, the socialist revolution developed peacefully.
> Power was obtained by the Communists who had concluded an alliance not only with the political parties which, politically, were close to them but even with those bourgeois parties which supported the common National Front. The Czechoslovak people won by way of peaceful evolution of the revolution.

"Different" indeed, as Mikoyan affirmed, was the revolution in Czechoslovakia which brought the Communists to power. But the significant differences of tradition, history, and economic, political and social development which distinguished Czechoslovakia from the countries of Eastern Europe were precisely those which should have prevented the Communists from taking power. Nonetheless, Czech democracy yielded to Communism, to those fundamentally similar factors which determined the triumph of Communism elsewhere in Eastern Europe. Today, above all, when Communists in many Asian countries are attempting to usher in Communism by way of "peaceful evolution of the revolution," an analysis of the Czechoslovak experience is relevant.

The Legacy of the Second World War

In war, the values of a free society are inevitably subjected to enormous pressure. A democracy in war must abandon some of its most cherished rights to maximize values necessary for national survival. When freedom and diversity are sacrificed to national unity, a climate is psychologically prepared which is ideally suited to the growth of authoritarianism.

The economic and social fabric of a nation is deeply affected by modern war which involves the entire population. Economic disruption may range from mild economic hardships, like food rationing, to complete devastation. There is an uprooting of broad sectors of the population either as a consequence of wartime labor and military mobilization or as a result of enemy action. It is therefore no exaggeration to say that were it not for the disruptive effects of the First World War on Russian society, the October Revolution would have never taken place, and Lenin would have died in his Swiss exile.

In 1945, after six years of Nazi occupation, when Czechoslovakia emerged a free and reunited country (with the exception of Ruthenia, which the Soviet Union had annexed in February 1945), its economy was in a difficult situation. For six years Czechoslovak resources and skills had been geared to the economic needs of Nazi Germany. Added to the problem of reorganization required by the return to more "normal" conditions were the difficulties caused by the expulsion of three million Sudetens. There was also chaos, financial and managerial, complicated by the incredibly tangled situation of property rights, resulting from wartime Nazi confiscation of Jewish and Czech property and postwar Czech confiscations of Nazi and Sudeten property. Nationalization, or at least strong centralization, was therefore almost a necessity rather than a matter of socialist dogma or principle.

The structural changes in the government effected by Nazi rule were also valuable to the Communists, for the Nazi totalitarian pattern of life and political organization had corrupted the pluralistic free society which existed in prewar Czechoslovakia. The previous multi-party system had been replaced by the Nazi one-party system. Democratic trade unions had been dissolved; labor and management were forcibly drafted into the Nazi Labor Front. Czech universities had been closed, and primary and secondary education reshaped to fit the need to Nazi ideology. Moreover, the war waged by Nazi ideology and military power against the peoples of Czechoslovakia had aroused attitudes of resistance which favored nationalistic values to the detriment of democratic values. Debates, disagreement, and political diversity were bound to appear harmful in the period of struggle for national survival. The Communists took advantage of this situation in the underground resistance movements to denigrate the previous forms of parliamentary democracy, especially the concept of a parliamentary opposition and of the free political parties. They argued that political democracy had been one of the causes of the nation's defeat at the hands of Nazi Germany. People's democracy, with its emphasis on national unity and coalition government as an expression of such unity, was prescribed as the system required to lead Czechoslovakia through its postwar difficulties. In the pursuit of their totalitarian aims, the Communists exploited the existing situation to prevent a resurgence of democratic institutions.

The new institutions, as a result, were democratic in name only: there was a Parliament, but its decisions were reached without meaningful debate and always unanimously; there was a coalition

Cabinet, but it had no opposition; and all mass organizations, including the trade unions, were subservient to the unified political authority.

Hopes Versus Realities

The democratic leaders of Czechoslovakia were not always aware that postwar realities ran counter to their hopes and purposes. Quite understandably, the democratic leaders relied on the democratic impulses of their people in the struggle against Communism. They knew that the majority favored democracy (after all, even in the free parliamentary elections of 1946, 62 per cent of the people had voted against the Communists). The law, the constitution, the democratic traditions of the country favored the emergence of a democratic Czechoslovakia. There also seemed good warrant for the hope that the majority could live with its Communists, since they did not take complete control of the country in 1945, although they had the power to do so. The leaders of the country also trusted the Soviet noninterference pledge, contained in the 1943 Treaty of Alliance, hoping the Soviet Union would prefer their freely offered friendship to coerced support of a nation oppressed and ruled by a pro-Soviet minority. Hence even those who were not particularly pro-Soviet abstained from anti-Soviet criticism, believing it possible to isolate the domestic issue of Communism versus democracy from the problem of Czech-Soviet relations.

Also, the democratic leaders considered Communist participation in the government a safeguard against the transfer of contentious issues from the floor of the Parliament to the streets. The democrats felt sufficiently strong to oppose the Communists by constitutional means; they knew how difficult it would be to try to combat them by extralegal means. They expected difficulties but hoped that after twenty years of constant opposition the Communists would be fair in Parliament and act as democrats. Given this context of hopes and expectations, it is clear why the democratic parties regarded the National Front as just another form of democratic coalition government. As a result, instead of uniting to oppose the Communists, they quarreled among themselves and encouraged Communist divide-and-rule tactics.

Finally, the democratic leaders and their parties were taken in by what appeared to be the new face of the Soviet Union, and then fatally miscalculated the realities.

A New Soviet Image

In East Central Europe (with the exception of Poland and the Baltic states), Czarist Russia and the Soviet Union had always appeared less conspicuously expansionist than Germany. There was, moreover, at the end of the war, a deep-felt and genuine gratitude for the Soviet victory over the brutal imperialism of Nazi Germany. Many political attitudes of the East Central Europeans have been and still are colored by a fear and mistrust of Germany, and these attitudes were shared by the people of Czechoslovakia. There were also two other important factors which caused the Czechoslovaks to look toward victorious Moscow with considerable expectation; first, historically, when the Czechs and Slovaks suffered foreign rule (the Hapsburg empire, 1618-1918), they often looked to Russia for their salvation; second, memories of Munich produced elements of anti-Westernism unknown to the country prior to the Second World War and stimulated the hope that the Soviet Union might assume the role of protector against any renewed Germany aggression. Given these factors, as well as gratitude to the Red Army, and sentimental pro-Slavism, it is not surprising that the widespread pro-Soviet atmosphere affected not only foreign policy but also domestic policy. The Communists skillfully exploited the prevalent sentiments, identifying themselves with the U.S.S.R. and trying to persuade many voters that a vote for a local Communist candidate was, in fact, a vote for Soviet protection against the possibility of renewed German aggression.

In short, in 1945 the Soviet Union seemed to many Czechs to be the only great power left on the continent of Europe, and realistically, their country had to be prepared to live under the shadow of the Soviet giant.

However frightening this prospect was to some, many were reassured by what seemed a profound change in the image of Soviet power. During the war the Comintern disbanded; Moscow fought the war with slogans appealing to patriotic nationalism, not proletarian internationalism; the Orthodox Church was revived and re-established; a newly established All-Slav Congress preached the racial unity of Slavs instead of the class struggle; Stalin's amended constitution of 1936 gave the component republics of the U.S.S.R. the right to conduct their own foreign policies and have their own armed forces. And in the backdrop was that image of comradeship-in-war which linked Josef Stalin with Franklin Roosevelt and that old crusader against Bolshevism, Winston Churchill.

The non-Marxist image of a new nationalistic Russia was strengthened by Soviet support for the expulsion of three million German Sudetens (whose existence gave Hitler his pretext to dismember and occupy Czechoslovakia in 1939), a move which satisfied growing Czech nationalism. In addition, this brutal expulsion, without any compensation for confiscated property, increased the gulf of hostility between Czechoslovakia and Germany, intensifying Czech dependence on Russia for protection.

As early as 1946 some Czech leaders began to revise their optimistic views of the future role of the Soviet Union, trying in vain to counterbalance the weight of Soviet influence in Czechoslovakia by treaty arrangements with the West. These attempts to build a "bridge between the East and the West" were vehemently opposed by the Communists. The "neutral Bridge" lacked the necessary foundations since agreement among the great Western powers was lacking. There was only the Soviet shore on which to pose one end of the bridge; the other end was suspended in the air —the thin air of Western Europe prior to the establishment of NATO. Instead of serving as a bridge between two worlds, Czechoslovakia became a Soviet bridgehead.

The classic texts of Lenin and Stalin pose the following conditions as necessary for a Communist revolution: the oppressed masses and the ruling classes must feel it is impossible for the *ancien regime* to carry on; the intelligentsia must have undermined allegiance to the *ancien regime* and prepared the way for revolutionary change; the peasants must be ready and willing to use violence to crush the old order and should be disposed to join the revolutionary proletariat; and finally, there should be a favorable distribution of forces on the outside, with the supporters of the reigning order isolated internationally and the Communist minority confident of direct or indirect support from the proletarian state already in existence.

In the case of Czechoslovakia, the last condition proved the decisive factor. In the final analysis, there can be no question that the fall of Czech democracy was due to the pressure of Soviet power, which encouraged and emboldened the Communist minority and paralyzed the democratic majority. Klement Gottwald, the Communist leader of Czechoslovakia, frankly admitted as much in a speech to the Central Committee of the party on November 17, 1947. Said Gottwald: "There is a basic difference between 1920 and 1948. In 1918 . . . the Soviet Union was engaged in a war for its own survival . . . it had to fight foreign intervention . . . and could not be a visible support for us. In 1945 it was just the opposite. Our liberation [from the German occupation] came clearly from the East. In spite of capitalist hopes, the U.S.S.R. did not come out of the war weakened. The international distribution of respective strength was totally different in February 1948 from that of 1920."

Two Faces and Two Phases

In a non-Communist authoritarian society the Communist movement rarely has any choice but to operate as a conspiratorial, underground organization. In a free society the Communist party resembles the Roman deity Janus: it has two faces, one seemingly peaceful and speaking of coexistence; the other, masked and hidden from public view, is conspiratorial and subversive.

When the Communist party cannot reasonably expect to seize

power, it devotes itself to weakening the fabric of society in order to prepare the ground for a future *coup d'état* or to serve the interests of Soviet foreign policy. In this phase it wears the mask of peaceful coexistence. It vies for favor in the political arena, claiming its belief in unrestrained freedom of expression and demanding for the movement freedom of assembly. It competes in free elections and participates in the legislative assemblies. Sometimes the Communists may enter a coalition cabinet, even if they cannot dominate it. They enthusiastically exploit all the opportunities for proselytization which a free, pluralistic society offers: the party organizes, supports or penetrates different mass organizations (trade unions, social-reform movements, cooperatives) in the effort to influence, dominate, or destroy them; and it leads or supports movements of mass agitation which further its immediate or long-range goals.

In the case of Czechoslovakia, except for a relatively short period during the Second World War when the Communists were forced underground, the party has always operated as both a respectable party among others and as a conspiratorial movement. From the founding of the democratic republic in 1930 until 1938; the Communist party was always a legally recognized party. In the free elections of 1935, the last to be held before the war, the party obtained 10.3 per cent of the popular vote. The Communists went underground, subsequent to the Nazi occupation of the country in 1939, as did the other principal political parties. Its best known leaders—Klement Gottwald, Rudolf Slansky, Vaclav Kpecky— went to Moscow; some went to London; and some, like Antonin Zapotocky, spent their war years in a Nazi concentration camp. At the end of the war, upon their return to Prague, they publicly proclaimed their determination to achieve a Communist Czechoslovakia through democratic means.

Perhaps Moscow and the Czech Communist leadership really believed—certainly the rank and file and many intellectuals did— that Czechoslovakia might become the first country in the world freely to vote itself into Communism. In 1946, Klement Gottwald stated that the party would obtain a majority in the elections scheduled for the spring of 1948. It is an open question whether he believed this or was attempting to create an impression of victory so inevitable to intimidate those who might try to oppose it.

In the free elections of May 1946, the Communist party won more than 38 per cent of the popular vote. This was an impressive success, but a year later by the spring of 1947, the atmosphere in the country had begun to change. In Parliament, real debates began to take place for the first time in the postwar period. The non-Communist press began to criticize the Communists, cautiously avoiding the delicate issue of Czechoslovakia's respective relations with her ally, the Soviet Union, and her friends in the West. Although the country was still led by a Communist coalition government without true parliamentary opposition, Czech politics began to assume its more normal prewar guise. People began to feel that they had emerged from the worst and—barring direct Soviet intervention—would be able freely to shape their national destiny.

A year before the parliamentary elections scheduled for May 1948, significant signs of the developing anti-Communist trend appeared. Elections held at the universities and technical colleges of Prague and Brno were fought partly over political issues. The National Socialists and Christian Democrats gained a crushing majority of 75 per cent of the students' vote; the combined Communist and Socialist vote was reduced to 25 per cent. These elections took place in the fall of 1947. In December of that year there was an even more significant confirmation of the changing mood of the country: the Communist Ministry of Information organized a secret public-opinion poll, with results indicating that the party would decline 10 to 15 per cent in the 1948 elections.

If abstractly these losses did not appear crushing, they were more serious when projected against the actual distribution of political power within the National Front coalition. On the basis of the elections of May 1946, the Communists combined with the Social Democrats had a majority in Parliament (114 Communists and 39 Social Democrats as against 147 National Socialists, Christian Democrats, and Slovak Democrats). It was a slim majority, but as a Soviet embassy official noted, it sufficed to govern the country democratically against the other parties. However, the opportunity to blackmail the non-Marxists into submission within the framework of the National Front was theatened by this expected decrease in the Communist vote (it was thought that many disillusioned Communists would vote for the Social Democrats and thus restore the traditional balance on the Left).

There was also the threat of a change which had begun to develop in the mood and orientation of the Social Democratic party itself. At the National Congress of the Social Democrats in Brno late in 1947, the party leadership changed hands. The openly pro-Soviet and pro-Communist chairman Zdenek Fierlinger was replaced by the left-wing but less pro-Communist Bohumil Lausman. Under Fierlinger, the Social Democratic party had become a docile satellite of the Communists. Under Lausman it was expected that the Social Democrats, while seeing eye to eye with the Communists on such matters as collectivization of the economy, would oppose them on all issues touching upon civil rights and liberties, and would work with the other three non-Marxist parties.

More than anything else, perhaps, this change in the orientation of the Social Democratic party convinced the Communists that the tide was beginning to run against them and that their hope of coming into power through elections was a vain one. In 1948 after the coup, Klement Gottwald testified that the shift in Social Democratic attitudes had an important effect on Communist thinking: ". . . the reaction attempted to prepare a shift in the existing distribution of power before the elections in 1948 took place . . . they attempted to isolate the Communists. There was mainly the well-known campaign against the left wing of the SDP, against Comrade Fierlinger. The reaction thought they would succeed . . . [in] isolating the Communists and confronting them with a unified phalanx of all other parties, and (they thought) that the Communists would capitulate!"

The Communist party decided not to "capitulate," that is, to permit the will of the people to express itself and to accept it. It is safe to assume that some time in the latter part of 1947—perhaps in the period either preceding or immediately subsequent to the establishment of the Cominform (September 28, 1947)—the Kremlin and the leaders of the Czech Communist party decided to abandon legal, parliamentary methods and proceed along conspiratorial lines.

It was at this time, too, that the Kremlin resorted to open pressure against the Prague government, making it unmistakably clear that it regarded Czechoslovakia as part of its orbit in Eastern Europe. Thus, in the summer of 1947, when the Czechoslovak government unanimously decided to accept Marshall Plan aid (all the members of the Cabinet, including the Communists, voted for it), the U.S.S.R. presented an ultimatum on July 9, 1947, calling upon Prague to reverse its decision or face the loss of Soviet "friendship." Czechoslovakia reluctantly complied. The democrats assumed the West would understand their difficult position and accept the fact that when forced to choose between the Soviet Union and the West, they had no alternative but to accept Moscow's dictate. At the same time they hoped the Soviet Union would be reassured by their choice. In fact, the Cabinet's original acceptance of Marshall aid must have confirmed Moscow's view that the National Front government, infiltrated as it was by the Communists, was nonetheless far from being 100 per cent reliable.

Soviet pressure reached its climax as the Communists staged their coup. One day before the coup occurred, Soviet deputy foreign minister V. A. Zorin suddenly arrived in Prague. Meanwhile, the Soviet press on February 22 carried stories declaring two hundred million Soviet citizens were allied with the Czech Communists. The implications of these press reports were obvious. Whatever Soviet intentions really were, they produced exactly what Moscow desired: paralysis. The open intervention of a high Soviet official in the midst of what should have been a domestic crisis made it clear that the crisis would not be solved on its own merits and within the context of domestic issues. V. A. Zorin's presence was worth two Soviet tank divisions.

The Strategy of Infiltration

The Communists easily staged their coup in Czechoslovakia because they never abandoned their conspiratorial level of operations while acting as a legal parliamentary party. Never sure of their victory through ballots, they had provided their most trusted members with bullets; and when political issues were transferred from the floor of the Parliament to the streets and public squares, armed force spoke louder than passionate quotations from the Czechoslovak constitutions or the writings of Tomás Masaryk. This had been the principal weapon on which the democratic leaders relied in February 1948, and it had little effect.

Nonetheless, in examining the reasons for the Communists' successful seizure of power in Czechoslovakia, it would be a grave mistake to view the coup as an event which sprang full-blown on a day in February 1948. Success was made possible by the depth and breadth of conspiratorial infiltration of the key positions in local and central government and in the mass organizations. The process, begun during the war, was accelerated during the postwar period. How the Communists seized power is best understood by surveying their strategy of infiltration during these years.

Local government in prewar Czechoslovakia paralleled the French rather than the English or American systems. It was a mixed form of government whose officials were partly elected and partly appointed. On the district and provincial levels, a governor appointed by the Central Government (Ministry of Interior) ruled with the assistance of locally elected councils. The parallel with the French prefectorial system is obvious.

Even before the war, Czechoslavaks recognized the necessity of decentralizing local government. Centralized Nazi control during the war further underscored the virtues of decentralization. This especially appealed in Slovakia which traditionally favored local initiative and autonomy. Particularly during the war, Slovakia developed strong national consciousness, and some Slovaks called for full independence and separation from the Czechs. The minimum demand, a large degree of autonomy within the Czechoslovak state, was partially satisfied by administrative decentralization, promised by the exiled leaders during the war and put into effect soon afterward.

The nuclei of local government were to be formed, in principle, by the active resistance leaders either during the occupation or shortly thereafter. Before the liberation took place, secret National Committees together with partisan units served as centers of national resistance and aided the advancing armies of liberation. The Soviet high command naturally established early contact with the National Committee through parachutists and other agents. Inevitably the Soviet espionage and saboteur network in the German rear tended to overlap the local Communist party organization. Local Communist agents served as spies for the high command; Soviet spies became local leaders. Thus the plan for greater local autonomy, although democratic in principle, facilitated Communist infiltration at a time when military operations had split the country into a number of isolated areas. With the assistance of the local commander of the Red Army, Communists were able to capture most of the key positions in local governments.

After the war, the National Committees constituted the basic units of government on the local, district, and provincial levels. The governor or prefect, appointed by the central government in prewar days, was eliminated. In principle, as a given piece of territory was liberated by the Red Army, the National Committee in the area was supposed to be elected. In fact, the prevailing chaotic conditions made this impossible and National Committees were self-appointed, with elections postponed until later. The Communists succeeded in postponing them until after the *coup d'état*; and even longer.

Local governments normally can influence the voting preferences of the local population. In postwar Czechoslovakia, the local governments had an enormous influence. The National Committees were in charge of the prosecution of all pro-fascists and Nazi collaborators. They also supervised the distribution of the landed properties of the expelled Sudeten Germans. The Communists, who were usually at the head of the police or agricultural sections of the local and district national committees, used their power to label their opponents "fascists" or "collaborators," to punish the hesitant and anti-Communists, and to remunerate the faithful. The relatively high percentage of votes which the Communists obtained in the free parliamentary elections of 1946 is in part due to the power and corrupting influence they had in the key positions of local government.

By the end of September 1945, Communists had local control throughout the country with the exception of certain areas in Slovakia and Moravia. In fact, the ratio of local areas under Communist control to those free of control was more favorable in Czechoslovakia than in any other country where the Communist march to power seemed originally to have begun from below. It is not altogether clear, in view of this, why the Communists did not take over the country in 1945 when the Red Army was still on Czechoslovak soil. Perhaps Moscow did not want to antagonize the United States, which was then still present in Europe with its armed forces. Perhaps the Czech and Slovak Communists felt it would be too risky to seize power in a country whose central government they did not yet control. Even the Communists themselves felt this called for explanation, for on November 17, 1948, Klement Gottwald, speaking to the Central Committee of the Communist party declared: "From May 1945 until February 1948, our way was complicated. There were not always and everywhere clear and definite results . . . here and there in our ranks some impatience was shown . . . and not only impatience but doubt that we had chosen the right way in May 1945. . . . When February was a success, some comrades voiced the opinion that we had unnecessarily lost all the time between 1945 and 1948. Some said: What we did in February 1948 we could have done in May 1945, and everything would be fine by now. . . . But our party and our people inevitably had to go through this school of three years in order to make what happened in February possible. . . . The period from May 1945 to February 1948 was absolutely necessary."

So long as local autonomy and decentralization could weaken

its adversaries and help to undermine the power of the coalition central government, the Communist party strongly advocated strengthening the powers of the National Committees and encouraged nationalism in Slovakia. The party even adapted its organizational structure to meet the needs of its nationalist line. The Czechoslovak Communist party, while representing the entire country in name, limited itself to proposing candidates for elections in the Czech districts of Bohemia and Moravia. The Slovak Communist party with a undefined relation to the more inclusive party had its own secretary general, executive committee, and press. After the seizure of power, local autonomy was minimized; indeed, support of Slovak nationalism, especially after the emergence of Titoism, was condemned as a bourgeois deviation. The prominent Slovak Communist and post-February foreign minister of Czechoslovakia, Vlado Clementis, was executed for this alleged crime in Prague in 1952.

Communist infiltration of the Central government proceeded simultaneously with penetration of the local levels, but the Communists never won full control of the central government until the 1948 coup. However, Communists effectively employed the technique of coalition government to maximize their influence in the Benes government. Before the Second World War, the Czechoslovak Communist party had never participated in a Czech government; it had always been in the opposition. At the end of the war, when the Communists decided to enter a coalition with parties which it had called reactionary, bourgeois, and capitalistic before the war, the prevailing conditions and political atmosphere enabled them to secure important posts in the Cabinet to which they were not entitled by their electoral strength.

During the war the main exile centers of political activities were first Paris until 1941 and then London. In 1945 the military situation made it mandatory for President Benes to begin his return home via Moscow. In Moscow, anticipating victory, confident Czech and Slovak Communist leaders identified themselves with the power and prestige of their hosts. The climate did not favor a strong stand by the democratic Czechoslovak leaders, separated as they were from their homeland which was being liberated by the Red Army. In the negotiations for the distribution of Cabinet posts, the Communists outmaneuvered their democratic opponents.

The Communists got a stranglehold on those Cabinet posts which were of strategic importance to their conquest of power. These positions included the ministries of the interior, agriculture, information, national defense, and the office of premier. The leaders of the democratic parties vied for positions of glamor and prestige: presidency (Edward Benes), foreign ministry (Jan Masaryk), ministry of foreign and internal trade. Under normal conditions, these posts would have been important; they were much less so in a country living under the shadow of the Soviet colossus. It should also be remembered that the presidency, under the Czechoslovak constitutions, was a symbolic and ceremonial office, much like that of the presidency in the Fourth French Republic, a fact obscured by the exceptional personal prestige of the first Czechoslovak president-liberator, Tomás Masaryk.

The ministry of the interior controlled the national police, directed criminal investigations and supervised local government. The control of this ministry gave the Communists a vital weapon; without it, the February coup would have been difficult if not impossible. Communist exploitation of this ministry was facilitiated by the confusion of the war and postwar situation. Some reform of the Czechoslovak police was universally regarded as necessary, since there had been considerable cooperation during the war between the Nazis and local police. The Communist minister of the interior and his aides took full advantage of the reform opportunities presented to integrate the key positions in the national police with those in the Communist Party. Moreover, the Ministry's authority to open or close wartime collaboration cases gave the Communists a formidable means of silencing opponents who feared persecution, justified or not. Thus, the Communists were able to project into the period of peace the wartime atmosphere of personal insecurity.

The expulsion of the Sudetens also helped strengthen the power of the Interior Ministry, in charge of the technical aspects of the transfer. The expulsion was carried out with unnecessary brutality. In part this was a reflection of a chauvinistic reaction to Nazi behavior during the war, but it was also a display of toughness on the part of the Communist-controlled state apparatus. The purpose was to terrorize not only the expelled Germans but also the Czechs who witnessed the expulsion.

Communist control of the Ministry of Agriculture was designed to give the party easy access to the countryside which, before the war, was under the influence of the right-wing Agrarian party, the middle-of-the-road Christian Democratic People's party, and to a lesser extent, the National Socialist and Social Democratic parties. (The latter had considerable support among agricultural, landless peasants.) The Communist party's negligible influence before the war changed radically in the postwar period. Despite the anti-collectivist traditions of the Czech and Slovak farmers and the many warnings of the non-Communist parties as to the ultimate collectivist aims of the Communists, their control over the Ministry of Agriculture gave them the means of infiltrating the countryside. The Ministry (and the Communists) gained credit for distributing much needed fertilizers and farm machinery (ironically, these came from the U.S.A. through the mechanism of the U.N.R.R.A. program) and for distributing to the peasants a considerable amount of land. Some of this land came from the farms owned by the expelled Sudetens; the rest was made available as a result of a land reform directed against the few remaining large landowners and the Catholic Church which had remained largely untouched by the prewar land reform.

The Ministry of Information, which the Communists controlled, was of less immediate importance to them in the period before the coup. It proved vital during the coup since the Ministry controlled the physical facilities for broadcasting, news distribution, film production, and the allotment of newsprint. However, until the seizure of power, the non-Communist press was relatively free. The author, for example, edited a political weekly in Czechoslovakia, and, until the coup, managed his paper with relative freedom despite protests by the Soviet government requesting the

Czechoslovak government to suspend publication because of criticisms of Soviet policies and hostility to Communism.

During the period of the coup, Communist control of the Information Ministry and the distribution of news proved decisively important. When the machinery of the coup was set in motion, the people of Czechoslovakia were able to read, hear, and see only the Communist version of events. If President Benes had not been a sick and broken man, and if, as Chief of State, he had wanted to speak to the people of Czechoslovakia or summon the army for help in crushing the coup, he would have found it almost impossible to do so. Between his voice and the microphone of the Prague Broadcasting System stood a leading member of the Communist party politburo, the Minister of Information Vaclav Kopecky.

General Ludvik Svoboda was the Minister of National Defense in the first postwar Czech Cabinet. A professional soldier, Svoboda had been commander of the Czechoslovak corps, formed by Czechoslovak refugees on Soviet soil and within the framework of the Soviet army. Svoboda, although not a Communist, was pro-Soviet, and many of his assistants, in particular the Chief of Military Intelligence, were Communists. Nevertheless, at the time of the coup the Czechoslovak army was not fully under Communist control. One can only conjecture how the regimental commanders would have responded if Benes had ordered the army to oppose the workers' militia. Indubitably a number of commanders would have obeyed the orders of the President, who was the constitutional commander-in-chief and whose popularity among many officers and the majority of the rank and file was high. In all likelihood civil war would have erupted.

Today, in the light of the unopposed Soviet intervention in Hungary, many Czechs and Slovaks in exile maintain that Benes' fear of Soviet intervention and his skepticism as to Western support led him to make the right decision. As one Czech leader in exile commenting on the Hungarian uprising has written: "When fully armed great nations hesitate to use their arms in defense of freedom, who would dare to ask an unarmed small nation to commit suicide?" Yet it may be maintained that the form of suicide is important. Had Benes ordered the army into action, Czechoslovak democracy would doubtless have perished, but its fate would have alerted free men to the nature of the Soviet threat and Czechoslovakia would have written an inspiring page in history.

The dominant position of the Communist party within the National Front coalition did not rest only on the party's control of the key ministries. To explain it adequately, one must also take into account the role played by the Czechoslovak Social Democratic party, led by Zdenek Fierlinger.

Before the war the Communist party was the weakest of the socialist parties. The leading Marxist party was the Socialist party which traditionally was democratic and anti-authoritarian. During the war, profound changes took place within the ranks and leadership of the Social Democratic party. The prewar leaders had been liquidated by the Nazis, and the labor unions were partly terrorized and partly corrupted by Nazi Labor Front tactics. A new Social Democratic party leadership emerged, composed of personalities as compared to the prewar leadership. Fierlinger, who was the Czechoslovak ambassador to Moscow, had been a member of the Social Democratic party but had never counted as one of its leaders. Under him as its spokesman and finally its chairman, the party took on a pro-Soviet orientation.

In the maneuvers which preceded the formation of the first coalition government for liberated Czechoslovakia, the Communists deliberately did not claim the premier's office. Instead they backed Social Democrat Fierlinger for the job. They maintained—doubtless with tongue in cheek—that the Western democracies might take it amiss if a Communist became premier; and they rejected the proposal made by the non-Communists that a Communist take the premiership in return for non-Communist control of the Ministry of Interior. In supporting Fierlinger for premier, they disarmed possible suspicion of their intentions among the Social Democrats and won their backing in the coalition government.

Communist capture of key positions in government was complemented by infiltration of the important mass organizations, rendered easier by the broad agreement among the major parties on the need to purge these organizations of those who had proved traitors or unreliable during the Nazi occupation. The party vigorously carried out these purges, and under the slogan "unity, reform and purge" took over dominant positions in the "transmission belts" which mediated between the party and the masses.

The first target for infiltration was the labor unions. Before the war, they represented a vigorous movement, well organized according to ideological trends and controlled by the political parties that sponsored them. In the interwar period there were almost as many ideologically oriented trade unions as there were major political parties: for example, there was a Communist Trade Union Congress, a Social Democratic Trade Union Congress, and similar organizations organized under National Socialist, Catholic, and even Agrarian auspices. During the war the Nazis merged all the Czecholsovak trade unions into one Labor Front. In the postwar period, the Communists changed the name but altered little else, keeping the totalitarian structure of the Nazi Labor Front in force. Antonin Zapotocky, a well-known Communist enjoying some genuine popularity among the workers, became chairman of the unified labor movement. The Communist-controlled Central Council of Labor enrolled in its ranks all the wage earners and salaried personnel of Czechoslovakia, including white-collar civil servants. It was an easy matter to purge the unions, including civil service workers, to remove potential opposition, and to convert the unions into an instrument that would make easier the ultimate conquest of power.

Other mass organizations suffered a similar fate. The agricultural cooperatives and associations, the youth movement, the Sokols, the Boy Scouts, were all unified, reformed, purified, in a word, *gleichshaltet*; and in the process Communist-infiltrated and-dominated.

Zapotocky's Central Council of Labor was so powerful that it could effectively block or nullify policies of the coalition government that ran athwart Communist aims. Indeed, whenever the government decided upon a measure which affected the national economy, implementation of the measure required the consent of the Communist party acting through the Labor Union Congress. Hence between 1945-1948 the labor unions were frequently referred to as a "state within a state" or as a "second government."

Action Committees

Communist penetration of the local and national government and its domination of the important mass organizations might seem enough to have given the party the essential levers of control for the ultimate conquest. But the party possessed one other vital form of institutional support when it finally staged the *coup d'état*: the Action Committees.

Superficially the Action Committees resembled the councils of workers, soldiers, and sailors which first made their appearance in Russia in the 1905 upheaval under the name of soviets and which then played a crucial role in the October Revolution. But there were significant differences between the Russian Soviets of 1917 and Czechoslovak Action Committees of 1948. The Action Committees, not meant to provide an alternative to Central government, did not combine the workers, soldiers, and peasants into one unit under the direction of the Communist party. They were not organized on a territorial and all-inclusive basis but along functional, institutional lines. Prior to the coup, the most trusted members of Communist cells in every branch of Czechoslovak government, in all major nongovernmental institutions, i.e., industry, were instructed to prepare the formation of Action Committees. For example, in the Ministry of Health, which was headed by a Christian Democratic political leader, the most reliable Communist members of the agency formed an action committee whose composition reflected all categories of personnel, both higher and lower. When the coup got under way, this Action Committee appeared at the office of the Ministry of Health and ordered the Minister and his non-Communist assistants out of the office. The take-over was as simple as that. What could the Minister do but obey when his erstwhile subordinates, waving submachine guns, asked him to surrender his power and leave his office at once?

The Action Committees quickly replaced the legally elected or legally appointed directors of all important institutions and agencies in the nation. An Action Committee took over the direction of the State Opera and immediately proceeded to purge performers and technical and custodial staff. Other Action Committees took over the Central Offices of Fire Brigades, the Conservatory of Music, Charles University, the Association of Writers and Journalists, and all the Ministries whose chiefs were not Communists. They took control of Parliament, the local district and provincial National Committees, the railroads, the Boy Scouts, all publishing houses, the media of communication. In effect, the Communists had held a large measure of control over organizations and institutions before the coup; now by purging non-Communists of those known to be hostile, they made their control complete.

Action Committees also infiltrated the non-Communist parties. Here it was the Communist fellow travelers who were given the task of purging these parties. They proceeded by excluding from the parties in question their principal leaders, in particular the Ministers who had precipitated the government crisis by resigning from the Cabinet, most members of Parliament, and many who occupied the leading party staff positions.

Thus the National Front, ostensibly a coalition of Communist and non-Communist parties, became in reality an empty shell. The Communists called it the "regenerated" National Front. True, it was still a coalition; but the representatives of the non-Communist parties were chosen by the Secretariat of the Communist party and not by the executive bodies of the respective parties. This kind of National Front, of course, typifies the pattern which prevails in all the "people's democracies," including Communist China.

The Technique of the Coup

The summer of 1947 marked the turning point in Czechoslovakia's struggle to survive as a democracy. With the rejection of Marshall Plan aid and the creation of the Cominform, the tragic denouement of democratic Czechoslovakia began to unfold as

Communist preparation for the *coup d'état* gathered momentum on a variety of fronts.

The process of "mobilizing the political climate" got under way. This tactic involved vehement attacks on the adversaries of Communism in the effort to charge the political climate with the highest possible voltage and provide the pretext for the coup. The first and most natural target was the Slovak Democratic Party which had won in the elections of May 1946 a 62 per cent majority against the Communists in the province of Slovakia. The Communists publicly charged it with high treason, espionage, and a separatist conspiracy. The purpose of this campaign was to heat the political atmosphere, create fear among the opportunists in other parties, and isolate the Slovak Democratic party from their non-Communist Czech partners.

Popular leaders among other Czech non-Communist parties also fell prey to Communist ire. Chief target here was the leader of the National Socialist party, Vice-Premier Peter Zenkl. His outspoken criticism of Communism and his public advocacy of a Czech alliance with the West to balance the Soviet alliance made him a prime Communist target.

Another National Socialist under constant attack was the Minister of Justice Prokop Drtina. Drtina had operated the Ministry of Justice fairly and incorruptibly; he had repeatedly frustrated efforts of the Communist Ministry of Interior to conduct politically motivated investigations.

In the summer of 1947, time bombs were sent to Drtina, Zenkl, and Jan Masryk. They were intercepted in time. Investigation by the Ministry of Interior established irrefutably that the bombs had been prepared and sent from the Communist party headquarters in the town of Olomuc, Moravia. Several Communists were arrested. One Communist member of Parliament lost his parliamentary immunity and was arrested after it was proven that he had participated in organizing secret arsenals for the Communist party in Olomuc. In retaliation the Communist Ministry of the Interior accused the National Socialist party of having organized an espionage service for Western powers.

In the increasingly tense climate of worsening relations between the Communist and non-Communist members of the National Front, the Communist Minister of Interior ignited the spark to produce the explosion which destroyed Czech democracy. The ostensible occasion was Communist reform of the police in the Prague district. The Minister of the Interior nominated eight new police inspectors, all Communists. The majority of the police inspectors previously had been Socialists. The provocative nature of this "reform" produced a quick reaction from the non-Communist parties, including the Social Democrats. First they called upon the Communist Minister of Interior to suspend his reform. He refused. The coalition at once faced a critical impasse. Obviously the Cabinet could not continue to operate if one Minister successfully opposed the collective will of the majority.

Twelve ministers belonging to the National Socialists, Christian Democratic People's, and Slovak Democratic parties handed their resignations to President Benes. They expected the President would refuse to accept them and would call for immdiate elections. The three Social Democratic ministers who had sided with the other non-Communists in demanding that the Minister of Interior obey the will of the Cabinet majority had a fateful moment of hesitation. Instead of resigning from the government, they placed their portfolios at the disposal of their party Executive Committee. President Benes thus had to choose his course of action amidst what appeared to be a relatively even split in the Cabinet.

Even today, with the benefit of hindsight, it is difficult to say whether or not it was a mistake for the twelve ministers to resign. Had they accepted the Communist thesis that the Minister of Interior could take any action without deferring to the collective will of the majority in the Cabinet, obviously they would have paved the way for the piecemeal conversion of Czechoslovakia into a police state behind the façade of a parliamentary democracy. On the other hand, had the resignations succeeded in forcing elections, the democratic parties confidently believed that they would crush the Communists at the ballot box. But this assumed that the Communists and Moscow would permit the realities of the situation to be altered by the mathematics of the polling booth. The assumption was doubtlessly naive, for democratic faith in constitutional methods stood in stark contrast to the Communist reliance on extraparliamentary and anticonstitutional methods of action.

The Communists were now ready to take to the streets. The plans for the conquest of power had been laid out in advance. At the end of 1947 it was already common knowledge that arms had been widely distributed among Communist workers. It was only a matter of time before the workers went out into the streets. The Central Council of Labor and the Peasant Union, both controlled by the Communists, announced they would hold mass conventions in Prague on February 22 and 29, respectively. These conventions would bring great numbers of Communist workers and peasants into Prague. The climax of the crisis was set for the last week of February 1948.

A hint of the impending events was given on February 15 by A. Jungmann, one of the Communist trade-union leaders: "If the democrats do not like the slow road to socialism, we can take the quick one . . . the labor meeting next Sunday will decide which road to socialism we shall take . . ." On the same day, Antonin Zapotocky declared bluntly: "Away with the Parliament if it does not fulfill the program of the labor unions."

The governmental crisis broke on February 20 with the resignation of the twelve non-Communist Cabinet Ministers. With Prague thronged by workers and peasants preparing for the conventions of their organizations, the machinery of the coup was set in motion. The conspiratorial cadres within the trade unions emerged into the open. Communist workers armed with rifles and machine guns paraded down the streets of Prague and other large cities to cow those who might be tempted to resist. Mass demonstrations and public meetings were quickly organized to create an impression in Prague and elsewhere of overwhelming popular support for the Communist cause. Only the university students dared contest Communist control of the streets. They paraded to Prague Castle, the residence of President Benes; but their march had little but symbolic effect. On February 24, the Communists called a general strike; strong-arm tactics sufficed to keep from their jobs those workers who refused to heed the appeal for solidarity with the Communists. The strike was a success.

Meanwhile, the Communist-controlled strategic Ministry of Interior was taking precautionary moves. It ordered several additional police regiments to Prague after the police had taken an oath of allegiance to Communist Prime Minister Klement Gottwald. Their presence in Prague strengthened the public impression of Communist invincibility; even the police were on their side. The Ministry of Information manipulated its control over the media of information to fill the Czech people with revolutionary slogans, threats to Communist opponents, descriptions of Communist mass meetings, announcements of political arrests of democratic leaders. The Action Committees of the nationalized paper mills announced that no newsprint deliveries would be made to anti-Communist newspapers; the Action Committees of the National Railroads embargoed the delivery of all newspapers that did not support the program of the regenerated Communist-controlled National Front. Within a few days, the Action Committees within the non-Communist parties, helped by the police and workers' militia, took over non-Communist press. The day after, these papers appeared again with no noticeable change on the surface—the same make-up, same name, but the line followed by each paper was straight Communist.

Thus the Communist tide flowed on. Action Committees formed for the climactic event in the months and years before the coup now came into the open. Within a week they had seized the strategic levers of control. The overwhelming majority of the Czechoslovak people was anti-Communist; a great percentage of the workers was non-Communist, but opposition to the coup was virtually nonexistent. Dreading Communism, most of the people of Czechoslovakia dreaded violence and civil war with its possibility of Soviet intervention even more. In consenting to the formation of a Communist-nominated and-dominated Cabinet, President Benes was yielding to the strategy of infiltration and subversion that seemed irresistible. Another country had gone behind the Iron Curtain, and a new chapter had been added to the Communist technique of *coup d'état*.

FRANCE: THE PARTY OF THE EAST

Michel Collinet

■ The French Communist party is the largest, the most thoroughly organized, and the best financed of all French political parties. A rarity among Communist parties, it is supported by a large section of the industrial workers of a highly industrialized nation. After World War II, it made substantial inroads in some rural areas. It enjoys the support of a large portion of French teachers and intellectuals, and the sympathy of more. In successive elections of the Fourth Republic, it secured more votes in national elections and controlled more seats in the Chamber of Deputies than any other party. It publishes more newspapers and journals and books than any other party, has more dues-paying members, and more paid functionaries dependent upon the party for their livelihood. Certainly its membership is more disciplined than that of any other French political party. Of all major French parties it is the least likely ever to come to power.

The P.C.F. (Parti Communist Français) is a near model Bolshevik party in other respects. No Communist party in the world is more starkly obedient to the U.S.S.R. than the French party. Again and again it has made sudden, extreme, and dramatic shifts of policy when the needs of Soviet foreign policy required it. No Communist party suffered greater popular opprobrium from the Nazi-Soviet Pact and none more quickly reoriented its activities to support the Pact. The indifference of the P.C.F. to national aspirations; its illegal activities, its readiness to exploit democratic liberty in order to destroy it, have all been revealed repeatedly.

In the following essay, Michel Collinet, a distinguished historian of the French labor movement, reviews the history of the Communist party with special emphasis on its relations to the trade unions. Agrégé of the University of Paris and former Attaché of the Centre National de la Recherche Scientifique, M. Collinet has been active in French trade unions since 1929. He has written widely on the labor movement and politics. His books include La Tragedie du Marxisme (1948), La Condition Ouvriere (1951), Esprit du Syndicalisme (1952), Du Bolshevisme (1957). He has been a frequent contributor to a number of professional and political journals in France and elsewhere. ∎

A BRIEF SURVEY OF FRENCH COMMUNISM

Although the standard of living and general working conditions are much the same throughout Western Europe, the strength of the Communist movement varies considerably from country to country. In spite of some successes immediately after World War II, Communism became once again a minority party, much less important except in France or Italy than the Socialist or free trade union movements. In most European countries, Communism was reduced to a conspiratorial sect of more interest to counterintelligence organizations than agencies of social policy. But in France and Italy its influence on the working class and a portion of the intelligentsia remains very important. The discrepancy between Communist success in these countries and elsewhere in Europe cannot be explained by the condition of wage earners in these countries, because French workers enjoy as great, or greater, material advantages than those of the Benelux countries and the German Federal Republic. The strength of the Communist movement in France can be explained only by reference to France's unique democratic and socialist traditions which antedated the establishment of the Communist party, and which have been successfully exploited by the Communists. The following brief survey of the history of the Communist movement in France will enable the reader to study the movement in the light of the social and political circumstances which have alternately fostered and hindered its development during the past forty years.

ORIGINS OF COMMUNIST INFLUENCE

During the latter part of the nineteenth century, the French labor movement was composed largely of mutually hostile factions, which were the legacy of the various socialist doctrines circulating in France during that century, and of the conflicts which followed the repeated uprisings and repressions of the working-class groups. The Socialist party was established in France only in 1905, long after its establishment in neighboring countries—although French socialism actually antedates them all. It was not the outgrowth of one particular doctrine such as Marxism, which exercised complete control over its followers, but rather an amalgam of various currents of thought ranging from antiparliamentary anarchism all the way to a form of progressivism similar to traditional bourgeois radicalism. The French labor movement developed during a century in which civil wars, riots, *coups d'état*, massacres, and deportations followed one another in rapid succession.

Democratic republics were twice forced—in 1848 and 1871—to adopt repressive measures against the rebellious workers of Paris. The army was, as usual, assigned the disagreeable task of quelling these demonstrations. In consequence, there developed within the labor movement strong feelings of antiparliamentarianism and antimilitarism together with deep scorn for universal suffrage. These traditional attitudes contributed importantly to the strength of Communism in contemporary France. Communism was originally hailed by some revolutionary groups as the victorious standard-bearer of the romantic traditions of the nineteenth century and the vehicle for revenge against the bourgeois republic which had destroyed the Paris commune.

Antiparliamentary and even antigovernment feelings were very widespread among the unions. Whereas in Germany, Belgium, and England labor unions and labor parties were closely allied, in France they were rivals. The most striking example of this is found in the absolute independence which the CGT maintained vis-à-vis the Socialist party. This independence was formally proclaimed in 1906, in the "Charte d'Amiens," a document replete with hostility toward all political parties. From the time of its establishment in 1895, the CGT was controlled by revolutionary syndicalists whose ideas were closely akin to those of anarchists and contrary to the parliamentary and democratic views of the socialists.

The CGT was quite outspoken about its desire to destroy the central government and to replace it by a federation of worker communes and autonomous unions. Its preferred method was "direct action" and the "general strike," rather than any effort to secure legislation favorable to workers. This orientation precluded the development of mutual aid and cooperation of the type which had enabled unions in Germany and Belgium to recruit numerous members and to become economic and financial forces to be reckoned with.

French unions did not engage in large-scale recruitment programs; they did not have substantial sums of money at their disposal; they were jealous of their independence; and they were not well disciplined except during strikes. Until 1914, only convinced revolutionaries belonged to unions (approximately 5 per cent of the working-class total). United by only the loosest ties, their administrative and structural weaknesses rendered them extremely susceptible to successive revolutionary doctrines. This is the reason that Communism, following on the heels of anarchism, was able to attract such a large following within the trade unions. Although well-organized and better disciplined, the Socialist party also reflects the erratic nature of its early years. Many differing philosophies were to be found among its members, and its regional subgroups enjoyed a great deal of autonomy.

The outbreak of World War I provoked a profound moral breach in the CGT and in the Socialist party between members who responded to their country's call to arms and those to whom the very idea of patriotism was anathema. The latter remained obdurate and demanded an end of hostilities and the overthrow of the government. Some of the Socialists who held this latter view met with Lenin and Zinoviev at Zimmerwald and Kienthal. In Paris, Leon Trotsky allied himself with the pacifist minority groups of the CGT—Pierre Monatte, Alfred Rosmer, Merrheim, and others—and Trotsky's influence proved a decisive factor in their conversion to what later became Russian Bolshevism. Referring to this period, Trotsky later wrote:

> Revolutionary syndicalism which was in many ways the precursor of contemporary Communism in France, developed the theory of the "militant minority"; that is to say, the theory of a Party, but never transformed itself into a Party.[1]

Syndicalists and anarchists who comprised only a very small percentage of the working class, made their numerical weakness a doctrinal virtue and adopted the theory that only an elite group, a "militant minority," was capable of leading the way to revolution. But this theory was not any better developed than the CGT itself. Bolshevism, by building a permanent dynamic organization, was to replace this vague, ill-defined idea with a theory of a centralized bureaucratic organization staffed by professional revolutionaries.

From the point of view of pacifists and revolutionaries, the prolongation of World War I was grist for the revolutionary mill. The outbreak of the Russian Revolution in 1917 further encouraged them. Strikes became commonplace and large numbers of soldiers mutinied. Bolshevism immediately gained a great deal of prestige, because it appeared as the most adamant of all parties in demanding an immediate end to the war. The revolutionary minority saw in this an opportunity to compensate for its inability to prevent the outbreak of war in 1914. When revolution spread in Central Europe in 1918, it stirred up in France a

[1] *Bulletin Communiste*, 12 April 1923, p. 145.

violent desire for political and social change which could not be satisfied by the Clemenceau government's law guaranteeing an eight-hour day. Widespread strikes disrupted the country in 1919 and 1920. Anarchists and Communists, both of whom were pro-Soviet, thought they detected in this confused situation omens foretelling the establishment of a French Soviet republic. Those who did not look to Moscow (Jouhaux, Merrheim) considered these strikes essential in counteracting the reactionary government which had been voted into office in November 1919. Bolshevik influence and sympathy for the Third International increased in the ranks of Socialists who had previously broken away from the First International. This led to the break which took place in 1920 and 1921, within the Socialist party and subsequently among the unions themselves.

THE BIRTH OF COMMUNISM IN FRANCE

When World War I came to an end, two overriding ideas captured the attention of Europe and the world. One was the plan of President Wilson to establish the League of Nations and its affiliate the International Labor Organization. The other was concerned with the Russian Revolution, which was brought about by workers' committees within Russia and which later spread to Central Europe. Anarchists and syndicalists saw in this system of autonomous federated soviets the realization of their dream of a stateless Utopia. They applauded with antiparliamentary glee the abrogation of the Russian constitution but failed to understand the true nature of the Communist party with its bureaucratic discipline and its highly centralized dictatorship.

This nature was first revealed in 1920 when the French Socialists were presented with the twenty-one conditions for membership at the Second Congress of the Communist International. These conditions entailed the transformation of a democratic party into a totalitarian organization of professional revolutionaries owing complete allegiance to the International, that is, to the Russian government. Without these antidemocratic conditions of membership, French Socialism would have retained its unity in spite of temporary differences of opinion. The split in French Socialism did not occur between former minority members who supported the Russian Revolution and the former majority which supported a policy of national union. The split, rather, was between those Socialists committed to democratic ideas and those who were ready to establish a soviet system in France at any cost. For example, Jean Longuet, pacifist and member of the minority during the war, remained a Socialist, whereas Marcel Cachin, intermediary between the French government and the belligerent "socialist" Mussolini, became a Communist. Almost 110,000 members of the party out of a total membership of 180,000 supported Communism, but, of these 110,000, three-fourths later withdrew from the party or were expelled by it.

The predictable result of this rupture, planned and executed by Moscow, was to eliminate from the French political arena the influence of both Socialists and Communists who were much too involved in fighting each other to exercise any influence in the country. The field was thus left open to the conservative and nationalistic wave, whose successive leaders were Alexandre Millerand and Raymond Poincaré. Their policy of isolation, together with their hostility to the newly created German republic, contributed to the creation of an antidemocratic and anti-Semitic atmosphere which assisted the rise of Adolf Hitler. At this point France was considered the leading country of Europe and was in a position to determine the political future of the continent. Moscow used to its own advantage the revolutionary ideas current among the French to neutralize their activity through dogmatic isolation and finally to divert them from constructive undertakings which ought to have been the aim of a democratic party opposed to the followers of an outdated nationalism.

The split on the political party level also existed within the trade unions. There also was a left wing, consisting of pacifists and anarchists who sought to identify their libertarian ideal with the Soviet regime. Commenting on this, Lozovski, secretary of the Communist International Federation of Trade Unions (himself a future victim of Stalin's madness), wrote: "In all truthfulness, the trade unions of Russia not only aided the revolution, they made it." [2]

In order to gain the support of French revolutionaries, Moscow carefully disguised the real dictatorial character of the Bolshevik party, which is the very negation of the revolutionary ideals of the French CGT that had been laid down in 1906 in the famous Charte d'Amiens. A regrouping within the unions took place in 1919. The war was no longer a cause of basic conflict. The conflicts now concerned the aims of unionism in general. Against the Soviet ideal, Jouhaux, to whom certain minority members such as Merrheim allied themselves, advocated the development of a nationalized economy and a program of evolutionary reform within the existing democracy. In 1921, the reformists and the revolutionaries split the CGT, although Lenin preferred to see the Communists remain in the CGT in order to infiltrate it effectively.

The creation of a new revolutionary apparatus, the CGTU,[3] did not at first signify a Communist victory, since the new organization was controlled by anarchists who would not tolerate being subordinated to the Communist party and to the Comintern. The Communist minority organized to drive out anarchists who quickly recognized the dictatorial nature of Bolshevism after the uprising at Kronstadt and the liquidation of the Ukrainian supporters of Makhno (1921). The Communists were forced to resort to trickery in order to remain within the CGTU. With Moscow's approval, the Communists swore allegiance to the Charte d'Amiens and pretended to support the independence of trade unions even against their own party. In 1923, the CGTU

[2] *Bulletin Communiste*, 7 October 1920.
[3] Confédération Générale du Travail Unitaire. [It is typical of the Communist semantics that a schismatic trade-union movement which ruptured the unity of the labor movement should have been called the *United* Confederation of Labor.—Ed.]

supported the Communist international organization of trade unions without, however, recognizing the leadership of the Communist party.

Similar opposition became apparent within the ranks of the French Communist party. The militants were opposed to the subordination of unions as well as to the over-all tactics and methods of the Comintern. As in the Socialist party, they formed factions, and in a democratic vote a majority declared against the policies laid down by the Kremlin. The French Communists of this period retained their democratic habits and proceeded to debate at length the policies they thought ought to be followed in the future. Moscow reacted violently. All those members who resisted the dictates of Moscow, in particular the free masons, were expelled from the Communist party in November 1922, at the time of the Fourth Congress. From that point on, the French Communist party was subjected to the directives of Moscow and the policy of the United Front which the majority of its members rejected.

THE COMINTERN IMPOSES ITS SYSTEM UPON THE FRENCH COMMUNISTS

Two years after the birth of Communism in France, the Comintern took complete control and rigorously enforced the twenty-one conditions of membership. Thus perished the hope shared by numerous French Socialists in the period immediately following the end of the war that it would be possible to create a distinctly French brand of Communism not organically subordinated to Moscow. The year 1922 witnessed the disappearance of the last vestige of democratic procedure in the party. Its leaders were henceforth to be named by Moscow; the party was to be completely subordinate to the demands of the Soviet Union which badly needed a breathing spell in which to reshape its economy and consolidate its position vis-à-vis the outside world. This was sought through a rapprochement with capitalist groups so influential with the government of Central Europe.

The military type discipline demanded of militants corresponded to the development of a new organizational structure, adapted to the operation of fractions (*noyautage*) and espionage, and designed to safeguard the party in case it was forced underground. This was all part of the program of "bolshevization" of the party, carried out under the direction of the ruthless Zinoviev, then chief of the Comintern. At the same time, the PCF liquidated as dangerous to monolithic thought and action the sections of several dozen to several hundred members which provided an opportunity for discussion and the exchange of opinions. They were replaced by cells organized on the basis of streets or places of work. These were small, isolated one from the other, and devoted only to executing decisions reached elsewhere. In practice, only the party bureaucrats—professional representatives of its permanent organization—maintained contact with these cells within which the slightest breath of criticism was immediately stifled. The PCF thus became more bureaucratized and compartmentalized than business, more hierarchical and disciplined than any army.

By coordinating the activities of the factory cells with those of the fractions within unions, the party was able to gain control of the CGTU. Many of the former syndicalist cadres left it, and those who remained found themselves completely powerless. The CGTU lose half of its membership in the course of a very few years, but it became, nevertheless, an organ of the Communist party, whose dominant role was officially acknowledged in the union's by-laws adopted in 1929. Marcel Cachin himself came before the Federal Congress to announce "the death of anarchosyndicalism." Thus, after having exploited the strength of the anarchists and the former revolutionary syndicalists to destroy the reformists, the Communist party rid itself of its erstwhile allies who had served as willing pawns. Revolutionary syndicalism, previously so powerful in France, remained a force only among very few groups and small, widely dispersed unions completely without influence.

The control of unions was, and still remains, the principal objective of Communist parties in industrial countries. Experience has shown that in all instances where the Communist party has not succeeded in accomplishing this objective, it remains ineffective. Such is the case, for example, in Belgium where the Socialist unions, thanks to a strong organization, were able to resist infiltration and pressure from the Communists. In France, the revolutionary syndicalist tradition rejected the idea of a strong organization in the name of freedom for unions and members. This insistence upon freedom facilitated the Communist efforts at infiltration through their cells which remained well-disciplined and ready to assume control whenever the opportunity arose. However, until 1936, the Communist party was unable to penetrate the old CGT, which was ever on the alert. The PCF had to be content with defeating its revolutionary rivals in the CGTU. The Comintern had decreed in 1930 that 75 per cent of the party's activities be devoted to union matters. This was, in its opinion, the best method for breaking the isolation of Communism in the industrial countries.

Encouraged by their success within unions, the Communists have since used the techniques of front organizations and infiltration to gain access to the most diverse social groups.

The "bolshevization" created a new kind of party, alien to all French political traditions. Its bureaucratic and authoritarian structure required new cadres who were also alien to the political traditions of the country. The Leninist schools concentrated on the recruitment of young people with no knowledge of the prewar and wartime working-class movements. Many young people were enrolled in 1920 in *Jeunesses Communistes* and were destined to form, in later years, the cadres of the Communist apparatus. Completely imbued with Leninism (of Lenin's later period), their orientation had nothing in common with that of the prewar Socialist or union leaders; their primary aim was to help the Comintern rid the party of old-line members who were considered too independent. This new generation of militants was charged in July 1928, by Manuilsky and the Comintern, with the task of gaining control of the French Communist party. It was referred to as the *Groupe Barbe-Celor* and included Maurice Thorez, Franchon,[4] Semard, and Monmousseau. The majority of the founders of French Communism—Boris Souvarine, Alfred Rosmer, etc.— had been expelled in 1924.

Thus, the methods of the Comintern were first to exploit the good will built up during and after the war among the principal minority leaders favorable to the Bolshevik Revolution and then to replace these leaders with younger men trained by, and subservient to, Moscow. Its program was laid down by Moscow which, from time to time, changed it without consulting or giving prior warning to the French party.

After several unsuccessful efforts, Moscow finally found its ideal errand boy in Maurice Thorez, who, as Secretary General of the PCF since 1936, became the true monarch of French Communism and the symbol if its subservience to Soviet policy. An unofficial agent of the Soviet government, Thorez has weathered all crises faced by the PCF and eliminated any challenge to his sovereignty. He survived the Nazi-Soviet Pact, which shook the party to its foundation, and, more recently, the profound disturbances precipitated by the Hungarian Revolution and the campaign against the "cult of personality." The duration of Thorez' reign has given the French party the reputation, among the most orthodox European Communists, of being the least "de-Stanlinized" and the most subservient to the Soviet bureaucracy.

There is no reliable correlation between changes in leadership and changes in political strategy. Once the original Communists were eliminated, the leaders of the PCF were sublimely unconcerned about implementing policies contrary to those they had advocated a few weeks earlier. The twists and turns of the line were never determined by French conditions but by the domestic or foreign policy requirements of the U.S.S.R. Like other Com-

[4] At present Secretary General of the CGT.

munist parties, the French party remains a Russian pawn in an international chess game. This is the conclusion which even a rapid examination of Communist policies will demonstrate irrefutably.

Communist policies vary all the way from a frontal attack on all of its enemies—socialists, democrats, and reactionaries—to alliances with any one of them directed toward that enemy whom Moscow deems for the moment most threatening to its plans for expansion. Depending upon the circumstances, that enemy may be democratic socialism, fascism, or Nazism. The history of the French party during the years 1920-1961 (as well as the history of other Communist parties) is the story of a succession of contradictory policies and slogans, policies without any necessary relation to fluctuations in the political and economic situations of the country.

The initial period ended in the early part of 1922. This was the period of direct assault upon European nations and upon the Socialist parties and unions considered by Lenin as the last rampart protecting capitalism and parliamentary democracy. When the French Communist party was established on February 1, 1921, this attack was already in full swing. The idea of world revolution which spread after the war caused great concern among the nations of Europe. The Red Army was defeated in Poland. Fascism was spreading in Italy. In France itself, the general strikes of 1920 were broken and dissatisfaction spread rapidly through the working class. The French party gave every appearance of being a latecomer on the political scene. The French Communist party was the offspring of numerous defeats and the disintegration of the revolutionary forces rather than the guiding force or the catalyst of this force.

Also, hardly one year after its difficult birth and its brutal break with democratic socialism, the party was forced by the Comintern to extend the olive branch to the same men it had denounced as traitors. Moscow found it necessary to reverse its course. The Soviet Union was ravaged by famine and its economy ruined. These conditions forced the Kremlin to appeal to the democracies for help and to sign a treaty with the Weimar Republic for which it had nothing but scorn. The tactics of this second period can be summarized in the concept of the United Front. The overriding concern of the Communists was to avoid being isolated in the midst of a hostile Europe. Those who did not understand these shifts at first protested but finished by bowing to the inevitable and renouncing their old democratic habits of protest. Since the "United Front" was to be accompanied by insults and actual accusations characteristic of Leninism, it remained purely verbal, and totally ineffective. In spite of its efforts, in 1923 the Communist party found itself along in its antimilitarist campaign against the occupation of the Ruhr by French troops. It was alone, too, in the 1924 elections and thoroughly defeated by a coalition of the socialists and radicals. In 1925, it was alone once again, this time in its advocacy of "fraternization" between French troops and Moroccan insurgents.

These defeats had very little, if any, effect on international events such as the diplomatic recognition of the U. S. S. R. by the French government, or the signing of a commercial agreement in connection with the Soviet Union's New Economic Policy, initiated in 1921. The trips of English trade-union leaders through the U. S. S. R. did not bring about a reconciliation between the CGTU and the CGT. Nevertheless, it was reasonable to hope that a movement toward a more liberal regime in Russia might have fostered unity of action, but at the same time the Communists were advocating a so-called solidarity of socialist and European trade unions; under the growing influence of Stalin, repressions were accelerated against Socialists and opposition Communists within Russia.

THE TACTIC OF CLASS AGAINST CLASS

The Soviet regime has a certain internal logic. The abandonment of the NEP, the collectivization of farms, the liquidation or deportation of millions of peasants and opponents of all types, were accompanied in Europe and particularly in France by a violent offensive against the democrats and the parties of the Left. Stalin offered his terrorized and starving subjects an explanation of his policies by postulating a so-called conspiracy against the Soviet Union on the part of capitalists and socialists from all over the world. French and English working-class socialist parties were denounced as fomenting war against the U.S.S.R. The advent of Stalinist despotism marked the beginning of the period which the Communists consider as the third period. It lasted from 1928 to 1934 and was characterized by the myth of capitalist encirclement and of an alleged war being prepared by the democracies against the Soviet Union. Such was the ideological counterpart of a regime enforcing the construction of "socialism in a single country."

In France, this period witnessed the introduction of a tactic termed the struggle of class against class. Instead of considering reactionary forces as its main enemy, it vented its spleen on the democrats and Socialists, branding them "social fascists" or the "left wing of fascism." This tactic, used in the elections of 1928 and 1932, contributed to the election of rightist parliamentary majorities and governments. At the same time, the idea of a United Front was superseded by a new slogan, "United Front from below." All those who were not followers of Stalin were expected to combine in a "reactionary" or "fascist" bloc. The party sought no further collaboration with the Socialists and union members, but concentrated its efforts on those in sympathy with opposing movements, seducing the sympathizers of these movements of inciting members against their leaders who were denounced as "fascists." Strikes were fomented, not against owners, but against free unions and the law establishing social security (i.e., the 1930 strike of textile workers in northern France). By these machinations, the Communist party began to alienate its members. At the same time, membership in the CGTU over which it had had official control since 1929, declined from 500,000 to less than 200,000.

The result of this was that the truly reactionary Right, supported by genuinely fascist organizations, grew more rapidly than had the Nazi movement in Germany. Hitler, who had also profited by Communist policies, had shown them the way to power. On February 6, 1934, fascists and Communists together mounted the attack on the Chambre des Deputés, the former shouting "down with the Republic," the latter crying "down with social fascism." Their slogans differed, but they were united in the struggle against parliamentary democracy. A purely spontaneous demonstration by the workers was required to secure Communist participation in the general strike of February 12, called by the CGT and the Socialist party. Even then, they attempted to transform it from a demonstration in defense of democracy to one in favor of Soviet dictatorship. However, a growing number of Communists, fearful of seeing a repetition in France of recent events in Germany, became extremely uneasy about the insane pro-fascist policies of the party leaders and the Comintern. They called for a popular front which they described as the political alliance destined to defend democratic liberties and promote reforms to diminish the unemployment which was then widespread.

THE STRATEGY OF THE POPULAR FRONT

It was 1934 when Hitler consolidated his power by liquidating his nationalist allies and establishing dictatorial power over the Reichswehr. He hid neither his aggressive intentions nor his will to resume the historical German drive for expansion to the east; Stalin therefore found himself facing the need for allies in the West who could also be pitted against the Third Reich. Bit by bit, he abandoned the tactic of "class against class" and sought a rapprochement with the democratic forces. In July 1934, he ordered the French Communist party to sign the pact providing unity of action which the Socialists had been seeking for several months. From this agreement dates the beginning of the fourth period, called the period of the "Popular Front," which lasted until the signing of the Nazi-Soviet Pact in August 1939. It was a period of great progress for the Communist movement in France.

The explanation of this progress is found in the misery of economic depression and the anxiety provoked by the agitation of French fascists who did not hide their desire to imitate Mussolini or Hitler. The Communists were successful in their effort to make it appear that they were no longer an agency of the Soviet Union but were merely the most militant and active of the parties of the Left in defending democratic liberties. But the PCF in fact looked beyond this defense of democracy. In the Stalinists' strategy, the PCF's role was to prevent, at any price, the negotiation of a pact of nonaggression between France and Nazi Germany. To this end, the PCF worked incessantly to enlarge the Popular Front and extend it as far as possible, past the Radical party, to the democratic parties of the Right who shared anxiety about Hitler's intentions. They dropped from the program of the Popular Front any advocacy of limiting or reforming capitalism; they ignored workers' grievances, and opposed a plan devised by the CGT to combat unemployment by increased economic controls. The PCF sold out support of any antidepression measure and concentrated exclusively on the struggle against Hitler. They were quite ready to buy success in that struggle through an alliance with the nationalist parties of the Right.

This attitude implied abandoning the traditional pacifist and antimilitarist slogans which always antagonized an important portion of the population. On May 15, 1935, Stalin announced that the PCF should support the policy of active national defense, including enlargement of the French army. After having signed the Franco-Soviet Pact with Pierre Laval, head of a rightist government, Stalin declared that he "understood and fully approved the policy of national defense undertaken by France in order to maintain its armed forces at a safe level." Twenty-four hours later, the PCF abandoned its traditional antimilitarism and, with the announcement that "Stalin is right," became the militant supporters of the French army. To the revolutionaries who criticized its reversal of policy, Thorez gave the now famous response, "We have listened to Stalin, as we shall listen to him always," [5] a promise which Thorez *never* betrayed.

This purely tactical return to a nationalist and democratic posture was sufficient to secure the party a great success in the municipal elections of 1935. In the Paris region alone, they triumphed in twenty-seven suburban communities. Since then, control of these municipalities has always played an important part in the strength of the PCF. [6] Their official automobiles and gasoline have been available for transporting militants. Their cultural budgets have been used to finance books, brochures, and magazines for the party. Their assembly halls have been available as free meeting places. Their welfare programs have been administered so as to make useful propaganda for the Communists and to gain adherents among the politically apathetic. Finally, municipal governments served as useful vehicles for establishing factories in the localities where Communist cells had until then existed only on paper.

Similarly, it significantly assisted the Communist unions and auxiliary groups (cultural, sports, and women's organizations, etc.) through which the party extended its domination over the inhabitants of the areas. Having sufficiently consolidated their position within the factories through the development of new cells, the Communists could now look forward to the reunification of the trade unions. They renounced—on paper—any intention to maintain the fractions with which they planned to infiltrate the unions and they obtained from the Socialist leaders of the CGT, who

[5] *Humanité* (principal newspaper of the PCF), May 24, 1935.
[6] Of a total of 35,000 communes, the party triumphed in 2,700. Before this election, it had controlled only a few.

were singularly blind to the realities of the situation, equal representation (one Communist for every one free trade unionist) in the industrial and departmental federations. The reunification of unions took place in March 1936. At the outset, Communists and fellow travelers comprised less than a third of the membership, and in some unions less than 15 per cent. But the principle of equal representation, supported by the existence of their own cells within factories, assured them considerable maneuverability.

THE POPULAR FRONT IN THE SERVICE OF STALIN

Nonetheless, it would be false to believe that the Communist hold on workers' organizations had for its end the promotion of social revolution. Stalin saw in France a means by which he could divert Hitler's attention from his drive toward the East. It was necessary that France become sufficiently strong and unified to disturb Hitler and that the French Communists do their best to exacerbate and foment conflicts between France and Germany. "France must be free, strong, and happy," the PCF proclaimed at a celebration of 100,000 members. For this reason, it adopted the policy of "the outstretched hand to Catholics" and advocated union of all Frenchmen, including the nationalists, provided they were anti-German and relatively pro-war.

The fact that this policy was directed solely to the relations between Stalin and Hitler accounts for the failure of the Communist party to exploit for revolutionary ends the enormous strike of June 1936. The leaders of the PCF did not have their minds on revolution and were as surprised as everyone else at the scope and success of the workers' occupation of factories. The Communist leadership was suddenly faced with the fact that, while the popular front had international purposes from the point of view of the Kremlin, it had an almost exclusively domestic and social meaning for its working-class sympathizers. The strike of June 1936 developed, not on orders from above, but from the rank and file. Its novel and widespread character aroused the concern of bourgeoisie and peasantry, whose participation was required in various front organizations. The leaders of the PCF therefore maneuvered to stop the strike as quickly as possible and to prevent its turning into a political strike. They left to the non-Communist majority of the CGT the job of negotiating a collective agreement with the industrialists, while they, the PCF leadership, utilized their factory cells to take charge of the new unions which developed after the strike.

Aided by the inexperience of the mass of the new unionists, the PCF prudently and patiently eliminated non-Communists from the leadership of the new unions. By the end of 1938, it was obvious that the Communists controlled the majority of the CGT, but they were smart enough to leave the top positions to non-Communists like Jouhaux who agreed with them on international questions. Unity with Jouhaux and other non-Communist anti-Fascist trade-union leaders was shattered the day after the Nazi-Soviet Pact: The Communists were expelled from the CGT before they had time to utilize the majorities they had acquired in numerous unions. Even before this, however, the trade unions had already lost a large portion of their members who had been demoralized as much by the Communists' maneuvers as by the incapacity of the CGT to conserve the advantages they had obtained in 1936. In the three years following 1936, the membership of the CGT fell from five million members to one million.

The period of the Popular Front in France provided an instructive proving ground for tactics which would be carried out in most of the countries of Europe after World War II. In Spain, the Comintern experimented with the establishment of a "people's democracy" when it gained sufficient power to expel from the Republican government—then under attack by Franco—all the authentically independent democratic groups. In France, it formally supported a Socialist government at the same time that it attacked it in working-class organizations. However, the PFC failure to participate in the government prevented it from obtaining solid positions in the high and middle echelons of the national administration. The lesson learned from this failure was not forgotten in the following years.

The fifth period of the PCF began in August 1939, with the stunning announcement of the signing of the Nazi-Soviet Pact, and ended when German troops marched into the U.S.S.R. The Pact provoked an immense stupefaction, following on the heels of four years of "patriotic" agitation by the Communists, who had missed no opportunity to add fuel to the fire in questions of Franco-German relations. The signing of the Pact revealed— suddenly and definitively—that the Stalin smiles at the democracies had been nothing but a form of blackmail designed to force Hitler to deal with the Soviet Union. Negotiations between the Nazi and Soviet governments had been under way since March 1939. Throughout the time they were in progress, the French Communists viciously abused the French government at the slightest sign of any intention to negotiate with Hitler. This duplicity led to the collapse of the French Communist party in September 1939, a fact which was partly obscured by its having gone underground after the Pact.

One month after the Pact, the Comintern ordered the underground party to sabotage the national defense effort and to propagate defeatist attitudes. The Secretary General of the PCF, Maurice Thorez, deserted and took refuge in Moscow. With the signing of the Pact, the war of the democracies against fascism became an "imperialist war" to crush a peaceable Germany. And suddenly the Communists regained Leninist fervor in combating "imperialism." In the years since the Pact, the Communists have attempted to hide and to falsify their policies during 1940, but the truth is a matter of public record. Rossi's books, and later, the testimony of former Communists, document the efforts of the

French Communist party to obtain power under the aegis of the Third Reich. Through approaches to the Nazi authorities and attempts at fraternization with militant Nazis, the PCF sought to gain recognition as a reliable friend of the Nazis. The Nazis' rejection of these overtures and the continued antifascist sympathies of some Communist militants led to the defeat of Stalin's pro-Nazi policy in France. In the unoccupied zone, François Billoux, still a member of the Politbureau, volunteered to serve as a witness for the prosecution in the trial against the "warmongers" Leon Blum and Daladier. If Hitler's declaration of war against Russia was a surprise for Stalin and Molotov, it was a still greater surprise to their agents in the French Communist party.

THE COMMUNIST PARTY IN THE CAMP OF THE DEMOCRACIES

In June 1941, the sixth period in the history of the French Communist party began, when, in spite of itself, the Soviet Union found itself thrown back into the camp of the Western democracies. Overnight, the French Communists again became superpatriots. They began immediately the task of implementing the directives of Stalin: "Partisan units must be created in the regions occupied by the enemy . . . bridges and roads must be destroyed, supply depots must be burned. . . ."[7] etc. The new policy also included individual terroristic attacks on Nazi soldiers, carried out without regard to the dreadful reprisals by occupation authorities against the civilian population. The PCF formed its own underground army: the Francs Tireurs Partisans (FTP). Although the PCF collaborated with General de Gaulle and sent two representatives to the provisional government in Algeria at the time of its formation, it refused to integrate its troops into the national underground army—Forces Françaises de l'Interieur (FFI). On occasion, the FTP resorted to force against the FFI in disputes over arms sent in by parachute, and to executions of its fellow

[7] Speech of July 3, 1941.

resistants when it recognized them as former adversaries from the Trotskyite, syndicalist, or anarchist groups. The FTP concentrated on recruiting from workers who were evading forced labor for the Nazis and in some regions conducted a terrorist dictatorship which attacked innocent peasants as well as Nazi troops and their French collaborators. The Communists unleashed an uprising in Paris in August 1944, hoping to seize power before the Allied armies reached the city. Thanks to the almost accidental arrival of the Leclerc division, this scheme failed. Nevertheless, out of the FTP the party created a new army of the interior, the *milice patriotique*, and made no effort whatsoever to hide its intention of gaining power as soon as possible.

The tactic now employed by the Communists was basically the same as that which prepared the way for the Communist victory in Prague in 1948. On the one hand, the party cooperated "loyally" with all the agencies of the new regime: the government of General de Gaulle, the National Council of the Resistance, the Consultative Assembly, the local and departmental committees of liberation. On the other hand, it used its partisan troops to win and exercise paragovernmental power in various parts of France. France was saved from civil war by the presence of Allied troops and the withdrawal of Stalin who, being more preoccupied with the military situation than with revolution in the West (which was a violation of the Teheran agreement), suddenly ordered an end to the Communist offensive in Western Europe and the dissolution of the movement's private armies. This did not prevent the French Communist party from conserving important positions which had been gained in the civil and police administrations. In the unions, which were reorganized after the liberation, the Communists played the same double game as they did in politics; at the lower level they used violence to drive out democratic leaders of local unions, even those who had actively resisted Vichy. On the highest official level, they cooperated in the reconstruction of the CGT. At first the minority group in the central bureau of the Confederation, they became the majority when Louis Saillant joined their ranks, a favor which Moscow repaid later by naming

Saillant Secretary General of the Communist controlled International Federation of Trade Unions (Federation Syndicale Mondiale).

Having renounced armed insurrection against the provisional government following the decision of Stalin, the French Communist party ostensibly accepted the regime, participated in governments, and placed its agents in positions of authority. Master of the CGT, the Communist party monopolized the trade-union movement. The laws of 1945 and 1946 established in the factories committees elected by the factory workers. These laws became invaluable instruments for transforming factories into bastions of the Communist party. For a year, the CGT maintained a monopoly of these *comités d'entreprise*. Its rival, the Confederation Française des Travailleurs Chretien (CFTC), was not even permitted to submit a slate of candidates for the elections until much later. The great majority of these committees fell easily into the hands of the Communists. With the considerable funds supplied by the entrepreneurs at their disposal, the committees directed the mutual aid and welfare enterprises and exercised unqualified domination over the personnel of factories, a control which was not contested until several years later after the CGT had been split and the Communists again thrown into opposition. The French Communist party proposed to the Socialists the creation of a united working-class party. This tactic which had succeeded in the occupied countries of Eastern Europe, was defeated in France largely by the energetic opposition of Leon Blum. Nevertheless, the PCF became the largest of the French political parties with more than one million members, gained 28 per cent of the votes in the election, and a half a dozen posts in the government. It appeared in 1946 that nothing could prevent the legal victory of Communism in France. Thanks to the support of four-fifths of the Socialists, the Communist candidate for president of the Council, Maurice Thorez, obtained 259 votes out of 579.

Each time there was a conflict between the Soviet Union and the French government, the Communists openly defended the position of Moscow against that of the government in which it participated. In Algeria, they advocated political integration and demanded repression of the Nationalist movement of Messali Hadj. Their plan was to lead France, *and its overseas possessions*, into the Soviet orbit; to this end, they abandoned their traditional policy and opposed all indigenous nationalist movements or separatist tendencies in the colonies.

On the domestic social front, they broke up spontaneous strikes declaring that "strikes are an arm of the trust." Nevertheless, strikes broke out in 1947 in the automobile industry, the postal services, and the printing trade. These strikes were directed as much against the Communists as for higher wages.

During the first six months of the Ramadier government in 1947 in which the Communists held the portfolio of national defense, the Communists did not dare attempt to complete their constitutional accession to power by revolutionary action. Moscow needed a government with a non-Communist façade which would oppose Anglo-American policy on the question of a peace treaty with Germany. The Communists found themselves in conflict: they did not dare resign from the government much less overthrow it by a *coup d'état*, because they could not disrupt the Allied conference held in Moscow in April 1947. Stalin was counting on the support of France at this conference to insure Soviet participation in the occupation of the Ruhr. Much to his surprise, however, the French delegate Georges Bidault supported the point of view of the Western allies. After this the PCF openly opposed the government and was expelled from its ministerial posts on May 5, 1947.

For the moment the PCF became even more dangerous having regained its freedom of action, but for several months it followed an uncertain course. It first accepted the Marshall Plan, then, following the suit of Molotov, rejected it. Its dilemma was the same as that of Stalin in 1947: It vacillated between alliance with the West, which would be temporarily profitable, and launching the cold war.

THE FRENCH COMMUNIST PARTY AND THE COLD WAR

At the September 1947 meeting of the Cominform, the die was cast and the seventh period of the Communist party's history opened with the declaration of a new war. The French Communist party made a pathetic self-criticism. It confessed to having failed to profit from its legal power and to having not properly understood the "historic" antagonism between Moscow and Washington. It swore to attempt belatedly to recapture the power it had lost when it quit the government. To this end, it undertook the political strikes of October and November 1947, called in France "Molotov's strikes." These were not directed by the CGT but by a clandestine committee of Communists presided over by André Marty, a man whom Moscow had great confidence. These were strikes which were supported by the "contributions" of the "unions" of the Communist countries. The French government lacked the strength to put down these strikes successfully, and the Communist party would have been successful had the strikes had the support of the working class. But the workers quickly lost interest when they understood the political purpose of the strikes. The CGT lost many members and was split. A large number of trade unionists formed a new non-Communist union—the Confederation Force Ouvriere (CGT-FO). Other unionists joined similar autonomous organizations. This resounding defeat suffered by the Communist party at the beginning of the cold war had serious repercussions on the trade-union movement. For several years the PCF looked for reasons to incite new political strikes: the miners' strike of 1948; the strike against the Indochinese war in 1950; the strike against the "bacteriological germ warfare" in Korea in 1951; the strike against the presence of General Ridgway in 1952. Each time they suffered a greater defeat and it appeared by 1952 that the Communist-controlled CGT had become incapable of mobilizing a thousand workers for *political* action. Simultaneously the strikes of white-collar workers and professionals lost their intensity following the stabilization of prices after 1952 and the continued increase in their real wages. Since this time, the CGT has not dared to stage a mass protest, even for strictly economic reasons, for fear the two other trade unions (F.O. and C.F.T.C.) will not support it. The 1953 strike of postal and railway employees was begun by the free trade unions. The CGT followed their initiative and did not have the strength to continue the strike alone after the other two federations decided to withdraw. The CGT supported the Christian trade unions and Force Ouvriere in strikes in Nantes and Saint-Nazaire in 1956 and 1957. In general, the CGT has avoided any prominent role in strikes for fear of the humiliation which follows each defeat. It has proceeded with caution. Communist cells in factories have continued to agitate and incite "spontaneous" demonstrations among unorganized workers. In response to the "demands of the masses" the CGT proposes that the free trade unions take the lead or join in united action. If these latter refuse, the CGT is rarely able to pursue the "spontaneous demonstration." Above all, the PCF has attempted to conserve its organization and cadres.

The history of the CGT has repeated that of the CGTU. The reason is the same! the Communist leadership's determined effort to use the unions to gain Moscow's ends rather than working-class objectives. The membership of the CGT dropped from approximately six and one-half million members in 1946 to not more than a million to a million and a half members in 1961; the CGT has also lost half of its affiliated unions. It retains solid strength in the public services, but in industry its power has literally vanished into thin air. It was estimated that of 45,000 salaried workers at the Renault factory at Billancourt, only 3,000 were still members of the CGT. In spite of its relatively small number of members, the CGT still wins shop elections easily. It has disproportionate electoral strength compared with the free trade unions because of its disciplined cadres and its continued domination of the majority of the *comités d'entreprises.*

If one analyzes Communist policy since the beginning of the

Cold War, one must distinguish two phases, the second of which begins with the death of Stalin. Until 1953, the U. S. S. R. conducted a frontal attack against the free world, and the PCF engaged in open war against all other French political parties, this war being most intense against the Socialist party which was denounced as an agent of American imperialism and a warmongering party. At the same time the Communists concentrated their effort on attacks against NATO and attempted to sabotage military transports destined for Indochina. The pinnacle of this aggressive policy was reached in 1951 and 1952 in the campaign against so-called germ warfare and the demonstrations against General Ridgway when he arrived to take command of NATO in Paris. At the same time, in the name of national independence which was said to be menaced by the "avengers" in Bonn, the party directed blows against European integration and the establishment of the European Defense Community. For these campaigns the party created the *combattants de la paix et de la liberté* after 1951 called the *mouvement de la paix* in which was assembled what one might call leftist nationalists, of whom there are rather many among the Paris intelligentsia, and whose principal characteristic is its hostility to European unity and to NATO and its sympathy for Chinese Communism and the so-called neutralist countries. The *mouvement de la paix* has one foot in the neutralist camp and the other in the Soviet. Its role is to separate France from the American "warmongers."

After 1953, the Communist objectives did not change. These objectives remained the disruption of NATO and the prevention of European unity. But the aggressive tactic had suffered total defeat and the PCF substituted for it a more subtle strategy. The cornerstone of this plan was an alliance with the Right against European unity. In 1954, the PCF supported Mendes-France who they believed would not oppose the claims of Viet Minh and would prevent the establishment of the European Defense Community. In October 1953, Jacques Duclos announced that he was ready to form an alliance with any Frenchman who opposed the EDC. He was even ready to extend his hand to Daladier, considered until then his worst enemy. On August 30, the combined votes of the Communists and nationalists of all tendencies, defeated the EDC with the discreet aid of Mendes-France. This was the first true success of the French Communist party in the cold war.

THE STRENGTH OF THE FRENCH COMMUNIST PARTY

What has been said about the CGT could equally well be said of the Communist party. Unified from 1936 to 1945, the CGT increased its membership and avoided schisms. During the period of the Popular Front (1935-1938) and of its participation in the government (1944-1947), the Communist party saw its membership increase from 80,000 to 340,000, and again from 300,000 to 900,000. After the rupture of 1947 its isolation from democratic forces precipitated an important loss of membership. The best estimate is that the membership of the PCF had fallen to 300,000 in 1954 and to fewer than 250,000 by 1959. [8] In 1959 the party had only 225,985 members of which 49,490 were women. Furthermore, investigations by the party leadership revealed that it was no longer successfully recruiting French youth. In 1954, 11 per cent of its members were under twenty-five; in 1959 only 5.6 per cent. Between 1954 and 1959 its losses were roughly the same in all socio-professional categories, so much so that its social composition has been scarcely modified in five years. As of 1959 the composition of its membership was approximately as follows: 40 per cent—workers in privately owned industry; 5 per cent—agricultural workers; 15 per cent—workers for publicly owned enterprises, or petty bureaucrats; 8 per cent—peasants; 6 per cent—small merchants and artisans; and, the remaining 26 per cent comprised housewives, retired people, intellectuals (2 to 3 per cent) and persons without definite professions.

[8] These estimates can be verified by a report of Madame Jennette Vermeers to the Central Committee, November 26-27, 1961.

The party's loss of members had important repercussions on its organization and its press. In 1947 the party included 36,283 local and factory cells. The number of cells had dropped to 19,219 in 1953 and to approximately 18,000 in 1958. The decline of the Communist press is even more drastic. In 1947, the party published 31 dailies, 18 national weeklies, 107 local weeklies. In 1959, there remained only four dailies, three national weeklies, and 18 local weeklies. One might believe that since the Communist press has lost the great majority of its readers and the party half of its cells, its influence would have been seriously reduced from 1947 to 1958. The electoral figures prove the contrary and demonstrate that the party's influence has scarcely varied during the Fourth Republic. Its votes fluctuated between four and a half and five and a half million, approximately 25 to 28 per cent of the total vote cast. Depending on the mode of election, the number of Communist deputies has varied from 160 to 100. We have already seen that many nonmembers vote for the CGT within factories at elections of factory representatives. So do many non-Communist party members support the party in political elections. The suffocating atmosphere of the party and the ritual humiliation of self-criticism repels the mass of Communist sympathizers who still possess a liking for freedom and independence which the party denies to its members. To this fluctuating group, whose importance it is difficult to evaluate, must be added a large protest vote which systematically registers protest against the parties in power. The considerable gap between the party's electoral influence and its disciplined membership explains why it has had no inclination for the last ten years to organize street demonstrations and even less to promote revolutionary action. Its prudence is reinforced by the fear of increasing its isolation from the democratic parties and the free trade unions and, for the last three years, by its desire to avoid determined government repression.

THE CRISIS OF 1956

The *de facto* alliance with the anti-European Right was broken by the outbreak of war in Algeria. The PCF supported the FLN not only against the French government, but also in its conflict with the M. N. A. and Messali Hadj. In the beginning it organized manifestations in favor of peace among the recalled conscripts, but it did not advocate the various attempts at mass desertion advocated by certain anarchist groups. When the Socialist government of Guy Mollet was installed, the Communist party supported the special powers demanded by the government for continuing the struggle against the FLN. That is to say, in spite of certain opposition in its own ranks, the PCF preferred a *rapprochement* with the Socialist party in power to maintaining an intransigent pro-FLN policy on Algeria. The year 1956 was critical for the PCF. The revelations of Khrushchev at the Twentieth Party Congress, the uprisings in Poznan and Warsaw, and above all the Hungarian revolution shook the party as it had never been shaken before. Khrushchev's speech detached a large number of intellectuals from the party, even those who had closed their eyes to the most spectacular crimes of Stalin. This speech was made more significant to Communist intellectuals by Maurice Thorez' efforts to imitate Stalin by establishing his own "cult of personality." The "intellectuals" in the party had been encouraged to dedicate essays and dithyrambic poems to him. But the Fourteenth Congress of the PCF, held in July 1956, was a triumph for Thorez. The anguish of the intellectuals would have been quieted if the Hungarian revolution had not occurred to rekindle their pangs of conscience. In university, literary, and artistic circles, expulsions and resignations occurred in rapid succession. Most of those who left the party at this time rallied around the new Parti Socialiste Unifié (P.S.U.). There were some resignations among leaders of the CGT, none among leaders of the party. Within the working class itself, a circle of hostility isolated Communist militants and detached from them a substantial number of sympathizers. In the partial elections of 1957, the party lost up to 48 per cent of its votes in some localities, and an average of 20 to 30 per cent. The CGT lost between 10 and 30 per cent of its votes in elections in which it participated. Socialist participation in the government and in the Suez fiasco prevented the Socialists from benefiting by the Communist losses. Nevertheless, five years later, the PCF is still weakened by a sort of permanent crisis, although superficially the Hungarian tragedy appears to have receded from the public eye.

THE PCF AND THE FIFTH REPUBLIC

The presence of 150 Communist deputies in the Chamber, to whom may be added 50 extreme right Poujadiste deputies was a decisive factor in the crisis of the Fourth Republic. To oppose this divided but virulent opposition group, there was only a majority itself internally divided among Socialists and extreme Rightists. Within the parties themselves, there was agreement on almost nothing particularly on the war in Algeria. Five million Communist voters who in other countries would have supported democratic parties and a liberal reform policy, wasted their vote by supporting a party controlled by a foreign power.

"*It is neither of the Right nor the Left,*" said Guy Mollet in speaking of the PFC, "*it is of the East!*"

When the rebellion in Algeria of May 13, 1958, placed the very existence of the regime in question, the democratic parties rejected the embarrassing encumbrance of Communist support. The CGT alone attempted a general strike May 19th and May 27th, both of which attempts ended in total failure. The man in the street preferred General de Gaulle to a "Communist democracy," the character of which had been spelled out in the ruins of Budapest and the assassinations of Imre Nagy and Pol Maleter.

The Communist electoral campaign during the referendum

was also defeated, but it suffered its greatest blow in the legislative elections of November 1938. In these, the PCF lost 1,650,427 votes, or 26.4 per cent of those it had received in 1956. This mass of voters who were detached from the PCF did not support the Socialist or traditional democratic parties, but instead, voted for the UNR; that is, for de Gaulle, who they believed could resolve the Algerian problem and end the war. But this mass, not integrated into other independent democratic organizations or the free trade unions, remains unpredictable, subject to the fluctuations of the political and economic situations. One can say three months later, that under the policy of financial austerity and the menace of unemployment, one part has already returned to supporting the PCF in the municipal elections; but while this electoral success permitted the party to hold on to its municipalities, it was not accompanied by any serious increase of supporters. At the moment, the leadership of the party admits that "each month, thousands of anti-Communist leaflets are distributed to all members of the party and to workers sympathetic to the party." (Central Committee Report of January 22, 1959.)

These leaflets are evidence that the internal crisis of the party is not yet at an end. They originate with opposition Communists who in previous years were satisfied to protest against the lack of internal democracy in the party, the dictatorship of the Secretariat, and its unconditional allegiance to the Soviet Union. But in 1949, Maurice Thorez, in his speech before the Fifteenth Party Congress, denounced the appearance of a "new revisionism" in the ranks of the party which rejects Marxist-Leninist doctrines, particularly the doctrine of the progressive pauperization of the working class. Thorez' reply to the revisionists was that the Gaullist regime was the tool of the monopolies and that the principal objective of the party was its overthrow "by peaceful means, including utilization of parliamentary democracy." For this task he advocated an alliance with all Republicans, that is, he proposed the creation of a popular and anti-Gaullist popular front.

Because of its systematic hostility to the Gaullist regime, the PCF condemned the de Gaulle speech of September 16, 1959, and denounced the principal of self-determination for the Algerian people as a simple maneuver designed to gain time, "an effort to obtain by trickery, confusion and corruption that which could not be imposed by force." [9] One month later de Gaulle invited Khrushchev to visit France and while there the Soviet chief approved the principal of self-determination for Algeria. Predictably, the Central Committee of the French Communist party proclaimed its change of opinion: it too approved the Algerian policy of General de Gaulle, denounced one month before as a "corrupt effort." At the same time, however, it accused de Gaulle of having made an alliance with the "avengers" in Bonn and of refusing to "normalize" the Berlin problem. In other words, after the Summit Conference the French Communist party downgraded its struggle against the Gaullist regime to focus its attention on the Berlin problem and the East German treaty, the issues which were of true interest to the Soviet government.

The defeat of the Summit Conference and the renewed tension surrounding Khrushchev's aggressive actions in Berlin led to a renewal of hostility toward the Fifth Republic. At the Sixteenth Congress of the PCF held in May 1961, several leaders who supported a more opportunistic policy were expelled from the Politburo and the Secretariat—not, however, without arousing serious trouble among the "progressiste" sympathizers. The isolation of the party would have been inevitable if the rebellion of the generals in Algeria and the terrorist campaign of the OAS (the Organization of the Secret Army) had not occurred, disturbing public opinion and reviving among Democrats and Socialists an orientation favorable to a common action with the Communists. The ineffective efforts of the government to repress fascist activity furnished the Communists with an unexpected argument for reviving an antifascist popular front from which it had so profited in 1936. There was reason to fear that this isolation, begun in 1947, and accentuated by the Hungarian tragedy, would be broken by the end of 1962 because of the uncertainty of the domestic situation and the real weakness of a government which wanted to be

[9] Declaration of Jacques Duclos in L'Humanité, September 17th.

strong but could not be. "Peace in Algeria" and "Down with the OAS" were the watchwords around which Democrats were ready to rally. It is possible that part of them will be disposed to make an alliance with the Communists to achieve them. Thus, the repercussions of the Algerian affair attenuated the internal crisis within the French Communist party, provoked by the XXII Congress and the breakdown of international Communist unity. [10]

IN THE WAKE OF THE XXII CONGRESS OF THE COMMUNIST
PARTY OF THE SOVIET UNION

After the XX Congress of the Communist party of the Soviet Union, the leaders of the French Communist party did as much as possible to soften the de-Stalinization campaign. Thorez, who for twenty years had called himself the "first Stalinist of France," was content to describe as "errors" what Khrushchev had denounced as the crimes of Stalin. After the XXII Congress, Thorez was forced to go further; he too denounced Stalinism, the absence of "collective leadership" and of "democratic control" inside the Party. He aligned himself with the leaders of the Kremlin against the Albanians and, with more caution, against the Chinese, but he found a new scapegoat in the Italian Communist leaders who posed indiscreet questions concerning the social and political causes of the Stalinist despotism. As early as June 1956, Thorez had asked Moscow to censure the imprudent comments of Togliatti.

In 1961, Thorez launched a veritable polemic against the Italian Communist who, in addition to denouncing the crimes of Stalin, raised questions about the regime which permitted or encouraged

[10] The Algerian crisis was resolved without the development of a "popular front." However, the emergence of an informal electoral alliance among Socialists, Communists, and Radicals during the elections of November 1962 suggests that de Gaulle himself may prove an issue on which the Communists can break out of the political isolation in which they have languished since 1947.—Ed.

these crimes and asked for a more complete explanation. In addition, numerous Italian Communists challenged the principal of *unanimity* within the party and declined to see the Russian party as a model for the international Communist movement. Against this heresy, Thorez and the leaders of the French party directed all their energy, asserting that, despite the errors of Stalin, they were no less faithful to the Soviet government and adding that the idea of a Communist policy independent of that of Moscow appeared to them scandalous.[11] For reasons of their own political security, Thorez and his associates stifled anti-Stalinist reactions which spread among the rank and file of the French Communist party.[12] They were aided by France's internal situation which claimed the lion's share of the rank and file members' attention, making it easier for the party to postpone the examination of embarrassing questions. For this reason it is doubtful that the revelations of the XXII Congress of the Communist party of the Soviet Union would have in France the same repercussions as in Italy.

CONCLUSION

In the foregoing historical review of French Communism, we have seen that the strength of the party *is in all circumstances* a result neither of the grandeur of the Communist "ideal" nor of its tactical genius. It is the result of the French government's incapacity to resolve its problems. An absurd economic situation precipitated the 1935 Popular Front. The defeat of 1940 and the collaborationist Vichy government led to the participation of Communists in the government in 1944. The aftermath of the Algerian war and the consequences of "decolonization" could conceivably re-

[11] Thorez asserted, "When we think of the great accomplishments of Stalin to which we continue to pay homage, we are deeply moved. We feel bitter at the idea that he found it necessary to resort to such methods." *L'Humanité*, November 22, 1961.

[12] The Communist leaders of the *Mouvement de la Paix* were forced to accept a protest from the movement against the resumption of nuclear tests by Khrushchev.

store the party despite the disillusionment of thousands of former Communists who are not convinced of the fraudulent character of Communist regimes. Isolated, the party is incapable of corroding public opinion. As the militant left wing of a reform movement, it would again gain an attentive audience. In other words, it has influence only to the extent that it can obscure its ends and adopt those of democracy which are in fact opposed everywhere by Communist regimes. The perspicacity and determination of parties and governments which claim to oppose totalitarianism will be measured by their refusal of such an alliance.

ITALY: THE POLITICS OF UNCERTAINTY

Pio Uliassi

■ Like the French Communist party, the Italian party has a mass following a big professional bureaucracy, a powerful press, and a large bloc of seats in the Parliament. Unlike the French party, the Italian Communist party has avoided political isolation until recently by a generalized alliance with the Left, "Nenni" Socialists. This alliance contributed to the polarization of Italian politics and strengthened the conservatives' voice within successive Italian governments by forcing center parties to look always to the Right for coalition partners and parliamentary support. It also inhibited competition between Socialist and Communist parties and thereby safeguarded Communist strength against a vigorous challenge from the Left. The breakdown of the alliance threatens at last to isolate the PCI, and, as always, isolation portends debilitation for the Communists and reinforcement for the parliamentary regime.

In the following essay, Mr. Pio Uliassi, a specialist on the Italian political scene, suggests that the threat of isolation and the decline of organizational vigor have strengthened the revisionist tendencies and pressures within the PCI.

Mr. Uliassi is a long-time student of Italian politics. Formerly associated with the Human Resources Research Office and the Institute for Defense Analysis, Mr. Uliassi is currently a Senior Fellow at Columbia University's Research Institute on Communist Affairs where he is completing a book on the Sociology of the Italian Communist movement. ■

In Western Europe, where most Communist parties are political sects of little significance, Italy presents a striking contrast: the Italian Communist party (PCI) is a major force whose influence is manifest, not only in the political arena but in nearly all spheres of activity. Only in France have the Communists been able to operate on a comparable scale. But while the French Communist party (PCF) was quickly isolated after World War II, the PCI banded with the left-wing Socialists (PSI) in an alliance that could never be ignored, and was often feared, by the moderate political parties striving to place parliamentary democracy on a firm basis in Italy. Until very recently Italian politics was polarized into a bitter struggle between Red and Black—between an extreme left-wing opposition dominated by the Communists and a center coalition dominated by the (Catholic) Christian Democrats (DC).

The strength of Italian Communism after the collapse of the Fascist regime was somewhat surprising; before 1926, when Mussolini finally outlawed the political opposition he had already reduced to impotence, the PCI had been a rather small party. In a sense, the postwar PCI was a heritage of Fascism. After 1943 the party's backers came largely from social classes that had once supported the Socialists but for one reason or another were disillusioned with the PSI—with its futile revolutionary postures, its incessant factional squabbles, above all with its utter collapse before the Fascist onslaught in the 1920's. The PCI was the most obvious alternative to the PSI. A considerable number of Italians who despised the oppressive and sorry Fascist regime came to view the Soviet Union as the ideal land of "socialism" and "freedom." The PCI of course shared this prestige by association; it won its own laurels during the years of the anti-Fascist resistance; and, after the war, it consolidated its hold over more than one fifth of the electorate.

With such strength, it is obvious that the PCI remains a force to be reckoned with in Italy. But the emphasis in this essay is not on the strengths but on the weaknesses of Italian Communism. The thesis, in fact, is that the PCI has passed its apogee, and that unless a major political crisis reverses the trend of Italian politics the party will be forced to undertake a radical doctrinal revision or face almost certain isolation and decline.

RED VERSUS BLACK

When Benito Mussolini was finally overthrown by a *coup d'état* and arrested in the summer of 1943, a number of anti-Fascist parties, including the Communists, immediately resumed full-scale operations, but under extremely difficult and hazardous conditions. The southern provinces of Italy were occupied by the Allies and nominally ruled by a royal government, while the central and northern provinces were occupied by the Germans and nominally ruled by a puppet Fascist regime headed by Mussolini, whose rescue by the Germans soon after his arrest was one of the more improbable episodes of the war.

The Communists faced a fundamental problem: whether to make a direct and violent bid for power or adopt a more subtle or moderate strategy. At first the PCI and five other anti-Fascist parties, which had banded together in a Committee of National Liberation (CLN) and considered themselves the legitimate representatives of the Italian people, refused to collaborate with the royal government headed by Marshal Pietro Badoglio and recognized by the Allies. Some Communist leaders and others on the extreme Left advocated revolutionary action, arguing that the time was ripe for such action: the country was in utter confusion, its traditional political and economic institutions were destroyed; the conservative ruling groups were discredited and disorganized, while the left-wing parties enjoyed growing prestige and power. The more impulsive Communist revolutionaries, however, were restrained by PCI Secretary Palmiro Togliatti, who returned to Italy from the Soviet Union in the spring of 1944. He rebuked the local Communist leaders for their "sectarian tactics" and offered to support the royal government and to collaborate with all groups willing to join in what he called the imperative task of the moment

—"to drive the Germans from Italy and destroy every remnant of Fascism."

Togliatti's decision helped to precipitate a reversal of CLN policy and all six CLN parties quickly joined a new Badoglio Cabinet. The Communists themselves remained in all subsequent wartime government coalitions, although they never succeeded in obtaining such key Cabinet posts as the Ministries of Foreign Affairs, Defense, and Interior. During the same period, Communist partisans took a leading part in the armed resistance in the German-occupied provinces. By participating within the legal framework in areas under Allied control, and carrying on guerrilla warfare in areas under German control, the Communists were able to establish a foothold in some of the key areas of Italian society—the national and local government administrations, labor unions, cooperatives, and numerous other organizations and institutions.

After the war the PCI, in part because it was constrained by the presence of Allied occupation forces, continued to operate along the general lines laid down by Togliatti in 1944. The Communists remained in government coalitions, but their "legalism" and "parliamentarism" (for which they, together with the French Communists, were rebuked at the first Cominform meeting in 1947) could not disguise the fact that their objective was to push the country, sooner or later, toward a totalitarian regime similar to those emerging in Eastern Europe.

In the 1946 elections for the Constituent Assembly (the country voted to make itself a republic at the same time), the Communist and Socialist parties, which were allies, together received almost 40 per cent of the votes cast, and the extreme Left seemed well on its way toward capturing a dominant position in the government. But domestic and foreign developments soon reversed the trend. Once the war had ended, the Communists were unable to prevent a rapid disintegration of the anti-Fascist coalition. In January 1947, the Socialists split over the issue of collaboration with the Communists, leaving the PCI allied with a badly shaken, seriously truncated Socialist party. At the same time, tensions between the extreme left-wing parties and the Christian Democrats brought them to the breaking point; and in May 1947 the Christian Democratic Premier, Alcide de Gasperi, provoked a cabinet crisis that left the Communists and Socialists stranded in the opposition. The domestic events paralleled, and in fact partly reflected, the international cold war, and by the time of the 1948 parliamentary elections, the first to be held under the country's new republican constitution, Italian politics as polarized into a pro-Western bloc of center parties, dominated by the Christian Democrats, and a Communist-Socialist opposition organized as a Popular Democratic Front (FDP). The Front was decisively defeated (it drew 31 per cent of the valid vote) and the Communists lost any hope of immediate acquisition of power.

The next five years were perhaps as turbulent as any in the peacetime history of modern Italy. In July 1948 an attempted assassination of Togliatti touched off a brief, abortive uprising, apparently without the approval of the national Communist leaders. The uprising showed that the Communists still had a strong and efficient revolutionary apparatus, but this was the first and last effort of its kind. However, strikes, riots, and mass demonstrations continued to be a normal part of Communist political action for some years and were directed against both the domestic and the foreign policies of the center governments of the period; these disturbances had some value, at least for propaganda purposes. In the 1953 parliamentary elections the Communists and Socialists (who ran on separate tickets this time) made something of a comeback by winning 35 per cent of the total vote, while all four of the center parties lost votes and the Christian Democrats, in particular, lost the absolute majority in Parliament that they had won in 1948.

At the time, the Communists' vigor, their electoral success, and their apparently secure alliance with the Socialists seemed to augur a continued growth in strength; Italy appeared to be the one country in Western Europe in which a Communist-dominated Left might actually come to power through the ballot box. In retrospect, however, the year 1953 can be seen as a turning point in the PCI's fortunes and the beginning of a slow, usually undramatic but nonetheless profound crisis that persists to the present.

THE ELEMENTS OF CRISIS

As the foregoing review suggests, the Italian Communists have relied mainly on legal, electoral techniques in their struggle for power. Since the twentieth CPSU Congress in 1956, this approach, which was largely empirical at first and often smacked of pure opportunism, has been given a more explicit theoretical formulation as "the Italian road to socialism." Considerable controversy exists within the party as to the exact meaning of this and how it can be reconciled with the Leninist orthodoxies to which the Communists pay lip service. Still, most Communists have always agreed on the immediate tasks before them: to build up the party's electoral and parliamentary strength; and—since they could not realistically expect the PCI to win an absolute majority on its own—to cultivate alliances with other political groups and above all with the Socialists. These two objectives suggest a convenient framework for describing the external manifestations of the Communist crisis.

Organizational decline. Between 1926 and 1943 the PCI was a small and select cadre organization operating in exile and underground. A few years after the Fascist regime was toppled, the party was so swollen that some of its older militants complained that two million members were "too many to make a revolution and too few to win an election." But the party leaders knew what they were doing. They certainly were not ready to make a revolution and believed that they could not attract and hold a large electorate unless they could convert the newly aroused enthusiasm for the PCI into firm allegiance. This they did quite successfully by creating a mass organization held together by an intricate network of social relations. In recent years, however, the party and its numerous satellite organizations have shown unmistakable signs of having passed their period of maximum effectiveness.

Fluctuations in party membership are one limited but important measure of Communist successes and failures. Unlike some other Communist parties, the PCI publishes a great deal of information on the size, geographic distribution, and social composition of its membership. All that need be noted here is size. With the possible exception of the Indonesian Communist party, the PCI remains the largest Communist movement outside the Soviet orbit in terms of membership, and by all odds the largest Communist party in Western Europe: for years its membership hovered about the two million mark. The achievements of recent years have been less impressive, however. The net loss of 416,000 between 1954, when claimed membership reached a peak of 2,145,-000, and 1961, when it fell to 1,729,000, represents about 20 per cent of the top figure. In the same period, membership in the Communist Youth Federation (FGCI) fell from 431,000 to about 200,000—a precipitous loss of young people which eventually will almost certainly be reflected in a more rapid contraction of the PCI itself. The Communist-dominated Italian General Confederation of Labor (CGIL) has also been slipping steadily: membership figures for labor organizations are notoriously unreliable, but the returns for shop-steward elections show that the CGIL's vote dropped from about 65 per cent of the total in 1954 to about 48 per cent in the last few years. As significant as the numerical decline of the PCI and its affiliates is the fact that participation in most party-sponsored activities has become more and more casual and sporadic.

Both trends—declining numbers and decreasing participation— are worrisome omens for Communist leaders. The party organization and its specialized agencies were designed to help create political loyalty or to enforce conformity, but to do these things well they must be pervasive influences in daily life—and in most parts of the country, the PCI organizations are hardly that any more, certainly not by the standards of the early postwar years. For a great many reasons, most Communist sympathizers are not so

deeply involved in party affairs as they once were, nor so dependent on the party's cultural and propaganda media for their view of
the world and on the party itself for such elementary satisfactions
as friendship, jobs, and help in emergencies.

A restriction of party influence is also apparent if the PCI is
viewed in terms of its "external" functions—that is, as an instrument for acting on the larger political environment. Today neither
the militants nor the rank-and-file Communists can normally be
counted on to support the kind of mass actions that were common
in the early postwar years. The plain facts are that time and circumstances have drained the party of much of its organizational
strength and revolutionary vigor and that, to a greater degree than
Communist leaders are willing to admit, the PCI has been transformed into an electoral machine, still capable of attracting as
many votes as in the past (many of them are by now traditional)
but otherwise a pale reflection of what it was in more heroic days.

Paradoxical as it may seem, most Communist leaders find the
party's continuing electoral strength far from reassuring. Of course,
it enables them to retain positions of power in local governments
and to make the PCI a parliamentary force that cannot be ignored.
Still, for psychological and doctrinal reasons that need not be examined here, even the most revisionist Italian Communists do not
want to see their party transformed into a "purely" or "primarily"
electoral machine. Furthermore, they fear that sooner or later organizational weakness will be reflected in electoral instability or
decline. For the moment, at least, they would seem to have little
cause for worry on this score. The Communist vote in the last two
parliamentary elections shifted only one tenth of one per cent,
and shifted *upward*—from 22.6 per cent of the total vote in 1953
to 22.7 per cent in 1958. However, detailed analyses of these and
subsequent local elections suggest that the PCI's hold on the electorate is somewhat uncertain in areas where the party organization
is weak—where, for example, the ratio of party members to voters
is rather low (as it is in most of the south).

Although there is no definite indication that the Communists'
share of the vote will be cut back seriously in the immediate future,

neither is there any evidence that it will increase significantly, barring a political miracle. For a party committed to a legal, parliamentary strategy of power and obviously dissatisfied with the prospect of perpetual opposition, the only hope of success lies in alliances. This is the simple fact behind the Communists' desperate efforts to maintain close ties with the Socialists.

The Socialists: friendly enemies. When the hybrid coalition thrown together under wartime conditions fell to pieces in early 1947, the Italian Communists would have been as isolated as their French comrades if they had not been protected, in a sense, by Pietro Nenni's Socialists. Just as they had found the Communists invaluable allies during the later years of the anti-Fascist resistance, most Socialists considered the Communists indispensable partners in their postwar battles against the moderate defenders of the "capitalist" democratic state. Because of this the Communists for years were able to enlist massive Socialist support for their policies and—a necessary corollary—to discourage the rise of an independent Socialist movement that might in time become a competitor and perhaps an opponent of the PCI. The Communists and Socialists were closely linked through "unity of action" agreements that, in various forms, remained in force from 1934 to 1956, except during the period of the Nazi-Soviet pact. The PCI-PSI alliance, and its gradual dissolution through Socialist initiative in recent years, are facts of tremendous importance in Italian politics.

In the immediate postwar years, the Communists and many Socialists advocated a rapid fusion of their two parties. Early in 1946, PCI Vice-Secretary Luigi Longo boasted that in some localities collaboration between the two parties had already taken "the form and consistency of a true and proper organization unity." But the proposed fusion was never carried out, mainly because most Socialists found it unpalatable or at least premature. The Communists themselves eventually decided that the separate existence of an allied Socialist party was preferable to outright absorption of the PSI: the Socialist organization attracted members and voters who would hesitate to support the PCI directly, served as a link to progressive forces further to the Right, and in general gave the Communists an aura of respectability that they could not have retained in full political isolation. Even after the fusion issue was dropped, however, the Socialists fought bitterly among themselves over the scope and nature of collaboration with the Communists, and in January 1947 Giuseppe Saragat led the first of a series of fateful secessions from the PSI. The Social Democratic groups that emerged from these schisms were never able to match either the numerical strength or the working-class appeal of the parent body and soon became minor auxilliaries of the Christian Democrats. At the same time, Socialist divisions— and the discredit into which the Social Democrats soon fell with the left-wing electorate—helped the PCI to establish its hegemony over the PSI. For some years there was considerable justice on the side of those who dismissed Nenni and his party as subservient tools of the Communists.

All this began to change about 1953. A growing number of Socialists, led by the same Nenni who once dismissed democratic critics of the PCI as "bourgeois philistines," grew restive in a sterile opposition from which they saw no exit so long as they remained allied to, and practically indistinguishable from, the Communists. Furthermore, the Socialists became uncomfortably aware that, for all their common immediate interests, the ultimate objectives of the two left-wing parties differed far more radically than they had once assumed. The result was a slow and often ambiguous process of Socialist disengagement carried out over a number of years when Nenni, as one observer put it, symbolized his party as a man "perpetually wrestling with his conscience in public." The Communists had formidable means for restraining the autonomist impulses of their allies and used them effectively. But relations between the two parties took a dramatic turn after the 20th CPSU Congress and the Hungarian rebellion of 1956, when the Socialists bitterly criticized the Soviet Union, reaffirmed their democratic values, and denounced their unity-of-action pact with the PCI.

The two parties drifted farther apart after 1956 and today most Socialists are no longer inclined to see a providential harmony of interest between their party and the PCI, although enough of them to make a difference in Italian politics still view Communism as a tainted but legitimate variant of the Socialist tradition and the PCI itself as a party with which the PSI shares considerable political ground. For reasons too complex to review in these pages, Socialists still collaborate with Communists in labor unions, cooperatives, and most local administrations. However, Nenni's "Autonomist" faction, which has a slim but probably secure majority in the party, refuses to conclude a general political alliance with the PCI at the national level and is rapidly moving toward close cooperation with the moderate democratic parties. In 1962 a Center-Left government headed by Christian Democrat Amintore Fanfani was formed with the indirect parliamentary support of the Socialists (who helped to elaborate its program, although they remained out of the cabinet itself and even abstained on the vote of investiture). For the Communists, this was a shocking if not unexpected development and one that placed them in a difficult position: unable to insert themselves in the governing coalition and uncertain about the profitability of all-out opposition.

RESPONSES: WHAT NEXT?

It is difficult these days to read PCI publications without sensing a change in the party: the arrogance so characteristic of Communists can still be found in much of what they write, but there is also a tone of uncertainty. They have reason to be concerned. Unable or unwilling to make a violent attack on the country's institutions, increasingly skeptical about an eventual collapse of the Western capitalist system under its own "contradictions" or under Soviet pressures, Italian Communist leaders have staked everything on a strategy that now seems inadequate as a formula for winning power. The PCI has failed to win an electoral majority and it has failed to build lasting alliances with political groups that share most of its immediate programmatic objectives but reject its ultimate aims. The party seems condemned to isolation and probably hopeless opposition unless it can find a way out of its present difficulties.

Tactical maneuvers. Like any political movement, and far more than most because of its ties to the Soviet Union, the PCI is the prisoner of its own past and resists any real change in its basic doctrines and practices. Its leaders almost invariably try to meet new situations with tactical responses—sometimes subtle, sometimes cynically crude. The history of the past few years provides numerous examples to illustrate this point.

As the Socialists have loosened their ties to the PCI, the Communists have tried to hold their allies in check by every means at their disposal—by attempting to blur ideological distinctions between the two parties; by evoking memories of their common past struggles; by emphasizing their current common interests in labor unions, cooperatives, local governments and their shared views on many national issues; by intimidating Socialists who for one reason or another are personally dependent on Communist favor; by accusing the PSI Autonomists of drifting toward a "betrayal" of the working classes; and so on. They have also made some concessions to their allies: for example, the Italian General Confederation of Labor has introduced a refreshing amount of controversy at meetings of the World Federation of Trade Unions; and the PCI itself takes a noticeably less hostile view of the European Common Market than the Soviet Union—or, for that matter, than the French Communists. However, neither the attacks on the PSI nor the concessions to it have removed the causes of the Socialists' discontent with their old allies, although they have undoubtedly made the PSI's disengagement more difficult and slower.

For a time some Communists apparently believed that the Socialists' independence, if kept within limits, might even be useful to the PCI: at least it helped to bring a partial thaw in the domestic cold war. As already noted, the counterpart of the Communist-Socialist alliance for some years after 1947 was the fairly stable alliance of the four center parties—a combination of progressive and conservative forces having little in common except their attachment to parliamentary democracy and their opposition to Communism. After 1953, and more seriously after 1956, the more progressive groups within the center parties sought agreement with the Socialists while the more conservative groups, opposing the Socialists and finding it increasingly difficult to maintain stable center coalitions, tended to look to the rightist parties for support. These conflicting pressures created a confused and uncertain political situation which the Communists occasionally exploited to make their aid seem indispensable to the democratic Left. The most notable episode of this sort occurred in the summer of 1960 when the Communists, with some justification, claimed a large part of the credit for overthrowing Christian Democratic Premier Fernando Tambroni, who had attempted to remain in power with neo-Fascist support after he had failed to recruit a majority for his Cabinet among the center parties.

With the formation of a center-left government in early 1962, a new political equilibrium seemed to be in the making and the Communists faced a serious problem: What attitude were they to take toward a government supported by the Socialists and committed to a program of basic reforms, many of which the Communists themselves had long advocated? At first they wavered, but the official party position that finally emerged, not without considerable resistance from some of the more radical and dogmatic party members, was one of "constructive" opposition: the Communists had reservations about the government "formula" and suspected the motives of the moderate conservatives who suddenly were willing to collaborate with the formerly ostracized Socialists; but the PCI would support the major parts of the center-left program.

Such tactical flexibility helps the Communists to keep in touch with the democratic Left, but more than a few influential party leaders apparently wonder whether the PCI can really avoid political isolation if the present quasi alliance between Socialists and Christian Democrats proves lasting and fruitful. And even if it does not, the Communists have no reason to believe that the democratic Left will find a popular front more appealing than it does now, unless Italian politics reaches a dangerously polarized stage. These are some of the prudential concerns that create discontent among Italian Communists and strengthen their already marked tendency toward doctrinal revision.

The temptations of revisionism. For a variety of reasons—the experiences of the party in exile and in the armed resistance against Fascism, the preponderance of intellectuals in the party elite, the intimate contacts of Communists with non-Communists in all fields—the PCI has retained a political vitality that makes it something of a unique phenomenon among the Communist parties of Western Europe. In comparison to the French party, for example, it is an "open" party, far less crudely dogmatic, far more sensitive to the realities of its immediate situation. In fact, heresy has been endemic for years within the PCI. It has, of course, been kept in check by a number of forces—among them the resistance of an entrenched party apparatus and the widespread reluctance to risk a serious, and probably divisive and debilitating, controversy with Moscow. At times, however, Italian Communists have not hesitated to attack some of the hoary dogmas of the movement: in 1961, for example, the XXII CPSU Congress, and Khrushchev's renewed denigrations of Stalin, set off one of the most acrimonious PCI debates since the late 1920's. And even the bowdlerized columns of the party's official daily carried uncommonly blunt criticisms of the Soviet Union and its rulers. Heresy is perhaps too strong a word to use at a time when the international movement is seriously shaken by a crisis of authority. The Italian Communists have, however, shown a tendency to strike out on their own on matters that are quite sensitive—for example, questions such as the nature of modern capitalism and the meaning of freedom.

A more independent PCI analysis of modern capitalism was perhaps inevitable once the party took seriously the idea of a "national" road to socialism. In any case, the vigorous economic expansion of Western Europe has prompted the Communists to undertake the "creative research . . . on the economic development of the capitalist world" for which Secretariat member Giorgio Amendola called in late 1961 and which he claimed had been discouraged in the past by the "need" to preserve formal unity within the international movement. The threat, and then the actual formation, of the center-left government provided another incentive for the Communists to take a fresh look at some of their assumptions as they pondered, in what they considered the proper Marxist manner, what economic forces underlay the new political situation and what their implications were for PCI policy. Although it is not feasible to discuss here the intraparty controversy on such economic-political issues, two of its aspects are worth noting. First, the currently dominant faction in the party rejects "catastrophic" projections of capitalist development and advocates a reformist economic program in terms that are difficult to dismiss as purely tactical expedients. Second, the relatively free and often public debate of problems so central to Communist theory marks a significant departure from the usual past practice; it can be explained, at least partly, by the almost inescapable need to give the party's tactics, and indeed its whole strategy, a refurbished doctrinal basis at a time when some conventional Communist views seem at odds with economic reality and when the party, for a variety of reasons, is in no mood to accept passively whatever guidance comes from Moscow.

The Socialists and other left-wing democrats in Italy have welcomed these signs of independence in the PCI, but they insist that what really puts the party beyond the democratic pale is not its economic theory but its view of what constitutes a democratic party in a free society. These are issues that most Communists are normally inclined to evade, but they have not been willing or able to ignore them completely in recent years. Quite a few party leaders have at one time or another openly criticized the hierarchical structure of the party and its stifling of internal debate; some of them have gone so far as to ask for the creation of organized factions, at least during the periods when party congresses are held. The PCI as a whole is of course a notorious advocate of "polycentrism" within the international movement; furthermore, in obvious reaction to the customary secrecy of Communist international meetings and the veiled terms of the Sino-Soviet dispute, many

PCI leaders have asked that differences between Communist parties be clearly defined and publicly aired. What is far more important, Italian Communists are increasingly dissatisfied with abstractions about the "essentially democratic" nature of any "truly socialist" society that once did service in the party and are addressing themselves to the problems of "socialism and freedom" in somewhat more concrete and responsible terms. This is evident, for example, in their denunciations of Stalinism (that "monstrous degenerative process," as one old party maverick put it); in their almost anguished search for a more serious analysis of the causes of Stalinism than has come from the Soviet Union or from others in the international movement; and in their tendency to emphasize the need for the diffusion of power and for institutional guarantees of freedom "even" in a "classless" Communist society.

As these brief observations suggest, the revisionism of the PCI (if it can be called that at this early stage) is moving in two directions: first, Italian Communists are quite openly reassessing the economic and political characteristics of the society in which they find themselves. Second, they are moving (far more cautiously, to be sure) toward a reassessment of the Communist experience itself—partly, no doubt, as a matter of expediency but partly also in response to their growing awareness of the tragic contrast between professed ideal and reality in countries where Communists have come to power.

To summarize, the domestic and international developments of recent years have convinced a growing number of Italian Communists at all levels of the party that the traditional doctrines and practices of the movement are either undesirable in themselves or incompatible with political success in the Italian context, or both. In other words, the PCI is faced with two intricately related crises —a crisis of ideology and a crisis of power. The situation is inherently unstable and almost certainly will bring important changes in party strength and perhaps orientation in the coming years. It is of course impossible to predict whether such changes will reduce the party to a narrow sect alienated from the rest of Italian political society or—what now seems barely conceivable—whether they will slowly bring the PCI, or a substantial part of it (perhaps as the result of a schism if internal pressures reach the bursting point) closer to the democratic traditions of the West.

GREAT BRITAIN: THE COMMUNIST PARTY AND THE TRADE UNIONS

Henry Pelling

■ The failure of the world's most advanced industrial nation—Great Britain—to produce the world's most revolutionary working class prompted Lenin to write the essay on imperialism, in which he introduced into Communist theory several extremely useful, but nonetheless profoundly revisionist, doctrines. To account for the failure of English workers to fulfill their "inevitable" historic role, Lenin found it necessary to project the class struggle from the national to the international arena, to redefine class roles in terms of relative concepts such as standard of living, and to introduce the notion that a whole class could be seduced into abandoning its historic mission.

The following chapter demonstrates that the stubborn constitutionalism of the British working class has proved even more difficult to deal with on the practical than on the theoretical level. The history of the Communist party of Great Britain is the history of an effort to achieve through political action what presumably inexorable laws of history failed to produce: the transformation of the British working class into an instrument of proletarian revolution.

Henry Pelling was born in Cheshire, England, in 1920, and took his undergraduate and doctoral degrees at Cambridge University. He served in the British Army for four years during the war. Since 1949, he has been a Fellow and Tutor of The Queen's College, Oxford. He is the author of several books on the British Labor and Socialist movements, including: A Short History of the Labour Party

(1961); Origins of the Labour Party, 1880-1900 (1954); and British Communist Party (1959). Mr. Pelling has also studied and traveled widely in the United States, and has written a volume entitled American Labour, published by the University of Chicago. ■

When the Communist International was founded, shortly after the Russian Revolution, there seemed little possibility of creating a strong Communist party in Great Britain. The Labour party had been in existence since 1900, and had been recognized by the Second International as an organization "adopting the basis of the class struggle." But the party constitution did not commit the membership in any way to a belief in Socialism: the Labour party was, in fact, a federation of trade unions and Socialist societies, with the trade unions dominant. Thus in 1917, the affiliated Socialist societies could muster no more than 50,000 adherents among them, while the trade union membership amounted to almost two and a half million. It is true, of course, that Socialist principles had begun to influence the union leaders and their following, and in 1918 the party formally committed itself to a Socialist constitution. But as R. H. Tawney has suggested, this baptism of the trade unionists as "Socialists" had little reality.

Even the small band of 50,000 members of Socialist societies provided indifferent material for a Communist party. The largest group was the Independent Labour party (I.L.P.), which claimed 35,000 of the total; but Lenin himself had described this group, not without some justice, as being "independent only of Socialism, and very dependent indeed on Liberalism." It was the leaders of the I.L.P. who had agitated among the unionists for the formation of a Labour party: their Socialism was of an undogmatic, opportunistic type which saw nothing wrong in an electoral alliance with the Liberal party. The other Socialist groups affiliated to the Labour party were the Fabian Society (2,140 members), a body of essentially eclectic middle-class opinion; and the British Socialist party (B.S.P.) which claimed a membership of 10,000, and which alone of all the societies mentioned expressed a faithful adherence to the doctrines of Marxism. Yet even the B.S.P. had been bitterly divided on the question of whether to oppose the war and had only done so at the cost of the resignation of its founder, H. M. Hyndman, and many of its best known members, who went off to foster their own variant of Marxism in support of the British war effort—"Anglo-Marxism," as it has been described.

The great strength of moderate constitutionalism in the British working-class movement was naturally a disappointment for those dogmatic Marxists who had assumed that this most advanced capitalist country would produce the most revolutionary working class. Lenin explained the apparent contradiction by arguing that Britain's position as an imperial power, enabled the British workers to benefit from the exploitation of the Empire: they thus became a "labour aristocracy" whose leaders "constantly deserted to the side of the bourgeoisie."

Whatever the explanation, there could be no doubt of the very moderate character of the British Left. As a consequence, the British Communist party, which was formed after complicated negotiations in 1920 and 1921, consisted not so much of a substantial slice of the main bulk of the Left—as for instance the French Communist party did—but rather of a conglomeration of tiny fragments on the extreme wing of, or altogether outside, the main party of the Left. The largest political element was the British Socialist party, already mentioned, but weakened by dissension and much smaller than its claimed total of 10,000 members. But many of the most prominent leaders of the new party were industrial radicals, usually former members of the Socialist Labour party, a small British version of the American De Leonites. Men like Arthur MacManus, J. T. Murphy, Willie Gallacher, and Tom Bell were better known for their activity as leaders of the Shop Stewards movement in the factories than for their association with political organizations; and some of them tended to be as bitterly hostile to the Labour party as they were to the leaders of official trade unionism.

Thus at the very outset the two most marked features of Communism in Britain were the numerical weakness of its supporters and their remoteness from the main current of left-wing politics. It is true that the B.S.P. was affiliated to the Labour party, but this was a link of only two years' duration, and the tradition of the group was one of isolation from the broader movement; and, in any case, the new recruits from the S.L.P. could have easily made up for any lack of bitterness that their new allies lacked in attacking the leaders of the Labour party and the trade unions— the "labour fakirs" as they called them in imitation of De Leonite phraseology. It should be added that there was a certain geographical or ethnic sectionalism about the bitterness of the S.L.P. toward the national leadership of the unions and the Labour party, for it was significant that this tiny group found the great bulk of its support in the "Celtic fringe" areas of South Wales and Clydeside. There, and there alone, were to be found elements sympathetic to "dual unionism," which in the generally homogeneous working class of Britain was for the most part much less acceptable than it was in the United States.

The hostility of the nascent Communist party to the "Hendersons and Snowdens"—a hostility that was readily reciprocated— was indicated most clearly by the controversy which almost prevented its formation. The controversy was about whether the party should seek representation in Parliament or not, and if so, whether it should seek affiliation to the Labour party as the B.S.P. had so recently done. One of the opponents of parliamentary action, Sylvia Pankhurst, who belonged to the well-known suffragette family, appealed to the authority of Lenin himself, and Lenin took the trouble to express his views, not only in letters of reply to Sylvia Pankhurst, but also in his work *Left-Wing Communism, an Infantile Disorder*, which was published in 1920. In this work the willingness of Lenin, the critic of right-wing opportunism, himself to advocate highly opportunistic tactics is very evident, Lenin said:

> The British Communists should participate in Parliament, should from within Parliament help the masses to see the results of a Henderson and Snowden government, should help the Hendersons and Snowdens to defeat the combined Lloyd Georges and Churchills.

And later:

> I shall be able to explain that I wanted to support Henderson with my vote in the same way as a rope supports the hanged—that the establishment of a Henderson government will prove that I am right and will accelerate the political death of the Hendersons and Snowdens as was the case with their friends in Russia and Germany.

More explicitly, Lenin pointed out at the second Comintern Congress:

> The British Labour Party . . . is a very peculiar party, or more correctly, it is not a party in the ordinary sense of the word. . . . A party affiliated to the Labour Party is not only able to criticize sharply, but is able openly and definitely to name the old leaders and to call them social-traitors.

It was opportunistic statements of this type, which did not conceal an abiding hostility to the Labour party leadership, that encouraged Willie Gallacher, the leading opponent of political action by Communists, to come round to the view that affiliation was a desirable stratagem.

Unfortunately for the Communists, however, their debate on the tactical advantages of affiliation had been going on in public: the "Hendersons and Snowdens" had had plenty of opportunity to find out why the Communists proposed to seek affiliation. Consequently, when the newly elected Communist party officers applied to the Labour party for affiliation, they were met with a dusty answer. Arthur Henderson in reply quoted from a report of the Communist conference that "The antagonism to the Labour Party was general, but those for affiliation held the opinion that such antagonism would be best waged within their own camp." On this he commented:

If this statement means anything, it surely means that the Communist Party is less concerned with "the broad principle of independent working class political action" than with disrupting the Labour Party and conducting an intensified campaign within its ranks against its policy and methods.

The decision of the Labour party executive to reject Communist affiliation was debated at the following Labour party conference (1921), and Arthur Henderson sought confirmation for the executive's view. The principal point that he made in his speech was of the incompatibility between loyalty to the Labour party and obedience to the Moscow leadership of the Third International. The conference supported him by an overwhelming majority on a card vote—by over four million to less than a quarter of a million.

Such was, for the Communists, the disappointing pattern of their early contacts with the Labour party. It was a pattern that was to be repeated over and over again in somewhat similar form. There was always a small minority of Labour party members—represented in 1921 by the quarter-million card votes—who wanted to see the Communist party affiliated in order to preserve the "unity" of working-class politics: but the majority, led by the national executive, was always opposed to concessions to the Communists, even at times when opinion in the movement strongly favored a friendly policy toward the Soviet Union. Some observers, indeed, have been puzzled by the contrast between the generally cordial attitude of British Labour party and trade-union leaders toward the new Russia, and their adamant hostility to Communism at home. The explanation is to be found in large measure in the leaders' natural fear of the emergence of a rival focus of leadership in Britain, such as was threatened by the Shop Stewards movement in the First World War, or by the later Communist-directed "minority movement." The secretary of a British trade union might well find the solidarity of his union, and therefore his own livelihood, to be jeopardized by Communist activity in Britain; it was not likely that his position could be similarly threatened, at any rate in the short run, by the consolidation of the Bolshevik regime in Russia.

The Labour party was indeed, as Lenin said, "a very peculiar party," and it took time for its relationship with the Communists to be cleared up. As we have seen, the Labour party was a federal body—as it still is today—consisting of trade unions and Socialist societies which had affiliated on behalf of their membership. But from 1918 onward it was decided to provide a place in the federation for constituency Labour parties with individual members. Although the affiliation of the Communist party as a body was rejected in 1921, and again on each succeeding occasion when the issue was raised, it was still possible for individual Communists to become members of the Labour party, not only through their union affiliation if they were trade unionists, but also as individual members of constituency Labour parties. They were also able to attend party conferences as delegates, and were eligible to be adopted as official Labour party candidates for Parliament. Consequently, when late in 1921 the Comintern formally adopted the policy of the United Front, it was possible for the Communists to secure notable successes by identifying themselves for electoral purposes as closely as they could with the Labour party. In 1922, two Communists were elected to Parliament—one of them, Walton Newbold, having stood as a Communist, though without Labour opposition, at Motherwell in Scotland, and the other, an Indian Parsee named Saklatvala, having secured adoption as the official Labour candidate for a London constituency.

These problems of Labour-Communist relations had not been solved when in 1924 a Labour government was formed; and the very existence of the Communist party, tiny though it was, turned out to be a grave embarrassment on its flank. One of the major features of the policy of the Labour Prime Minister, Ramsay MacDonald, was his attempt to secure a resumption of diplomatic and commercial relations with Russia; the tactics of the Conservative Opposition, on the other hand, were devised to suggest to the country—and also to the Liberal Party on which this minority government relied for parliamentary support—that Labour was not sufficiently firm in its dealings with Communists either at home or abroad. When the Labour Attorney-General withdrew a prosecution against J. R. Campbell, the editor of a Communist paper, who had published an article of a *prima facie* seditious character, the Conservatives seized the opportunity to launch a violent attack on the government, and, as a result, the Liberal M.P.s began to waver. A vote of censure was moved and carried in the House of Commons, and MacDonald decided to dissolve and fight a fresh General Election.

Thus the issue of domestic Communism brought about the downfall of the government; but more was to follow, for just four days before the polling the national newspapers published the so-called "Zinoviev Letter," which purported to contain sensational revolutionary instructions for the British Communists from their masters in Moscow. Even today the authenticity of the Zinoviev Letter is still in doubt; but at the time it provided fresh embarrass-ment for a party which was defending itself before the electorate on a charge of being "soft" on Communism: for it was at first accepted as genuine both by Ramsay MacDonald and by the Foreign Office. The election turned out badly for the Labour party, which had now to go back into opposition; and the Commu-nists were naturally blamed for the outcome.

It was in the midst of this turmoil—in fact, just before the General Election—that the Labour party at its annual conference resolved to close some of the loopholes in its constitution which allowed Communists to pose as Labour party supporters. It was decided, in the first place, that Communists should no longer be eligible for endorsement as candidates. A further resolution went so far as to ban Communists from being members of the Labour party in any capacity, but this decision could not be implemented owing to the federal structure of the organization, and reformula-tion of the resolution's intention had to await the Conference of the following year.

It was then decided, on executive recommendation, that Com-munists should be barred from individual membership of the local Labour parties. Communists were still free to join the party as trade unionists and even to represent their trade unions as delegates at the conference; but at least one avenue of influence was now closed to them. The decision led to the secession of several local Labour parties, which were sufficiently under Communist control or sufficiently sympathetic to Communism to refuse to accept the new discipline. These rebel parties continued a shadowy existence for a few years under the aegis of the National Left Wing Movement, a body theoretically independent of direct Communist control but in fact heavily financed from Comintern sources.

The Communist party still remained tiny, with only 4,000 members in 1924, and its setback in the Labour party seemed likely to circumscribe its activities. But there was another area in which it could still exert influence—that of trade unionism. The direction of Communist activity in the unions, in Britain as elsewhere, was under the control of the Moscow headquarters of the Red International of Labour Unions, or "Profintern." The British subsidiary of this body was originally known as the British Bureau of the R.I.L.U., but in 1923 it took the title of National Minority Movement. It was the purpose of the Minority Movement to coordinate the activities of Communists and sympathizers in each industry. The support of non-Communist sympathizers was naturally an important part of Communist strategy at a time when there was widespread and militant unrest; but the National Minority Movement was to be firmly under Communist control, however many non-Communists joined it. The instructions for Britain, as laid down by Lozovsky at the Fourth Comintern Congress, referred to the need for the establishment of

> . . . a relationship between the Party organisation and the [industrial] opposition, which by its very nature is heterogeneous—in such a manner that the Communists could not be charged with striving to mechanically dominate the entire opposition movement. This goal—i.e. the goal of winning the working masses for Communism—we must work for under these circumstances with the utmost care, definiteness and staying power.

To strengthen the work of the British Communists large sums of money were sent from Russia, for the Moscow secretariat attached

great importance to securing a grip upon the British labor movement. Various publications were financed, catering to different
industries, and as far as possible committees and offices for each
industry were set up. But it was only among the miners, dissatisfied as they were at this time with their wages and working conditions, that a really warm response to the propaganda of the
Minority Movement was found. In 1924 the Movement secured
its greatest success with the election of its nominee, A. J. Cook, to
succeed the conservative and anti-Communist Frank Hodges as
secretary of the Miners Federation of Great Britain. At the end of
the same year the "Anglo-Russian Committee," a joint consultative committee of the General Council of the T.U.C. (Trade
Union Congress) and of the Russian trade unions, came into
existence—a remarkable indication of the good will existing in
Britain toward the Bolshevik regime in Russia. In 1925, just at the
time when the Labour party was excluding Communists from
individual membership, the T.U.C. authorized its general council to pursue a policy fully in accordance with Communist aims: a
policy of militant activity on behalf of the miners.

The Communists were in fact not numerous enough to play a
major role in the General Strike of 1926; moreover, many of their
leaders had been put in prison through the foresight of the Conservative government, which had staged a special trial of twelve
leading members of the party. Thus, although there was much
hesitancy on the T.U.C. general council during the nine days of
the General Strike, there was never any question of an alternative leadership asserting itself in favor of a more vigorous policy.
On the whole, the labor movement had no feeling for unconstitu-
tional action; and the strike itself only helped to dissipate once
and for all the vague syndicalist tendencies which had prevailed
since the war. After the collapse of the strike nearly all sections of
the working class lost their taste for militancy; only the miners,
who had been fighting their own battle since long before the
other unions came in to help them, continued a bitter but hopeless struggle for several more months. They were supported by
the Communist party, and for the period of the struggle the

Communists recruited many miners as members, only to lose them when the strike was at length broken, the futility of its continuance at last apparent. By the end of 1927 the membership of the Communist party, which had risen to about 12,000 shortly after the General Strike, was down again to 7,000 and still in decline.

At the end of 1927 the picture presented by the British Communist party was of an insignificant group of extremists clinging to the edges of the labor movement and trying desperately to extend its influence by a number of ingenious expedients such as the National Left Wing Movement and the Minority Movement. These expedients corresponded very closely to what was now an international pattern: in 1926 Kuusinen had spoken his famous words about the need for each party to build up a "solar system" of dependent bodies to recruit sympathizers of particular causes for the wider purposes of extending the influence of the Comintern. Such bodies were intended in Lenin's terminology to act as "transmission belts," by which the driving force of Communism would make itself felt throughout the labor movement. Among such bodies in Britain, besides those already mentioned, were the International Class War Prisoners Aid, which was used to raise funds for strikers or other "victims of class warfare," and the League Against Imperialism, the central organization of which was set up in Berlin in 1927. The League had a special importance in Britain owing to the extent of the British Empire and the responsibilities which the Comintern had given the British party for developing Communism within its bounds, and especially in India. There was also the National Unemployed Workers' Movement, which was perhaps the most successful of the British "satellite" bodies; it had been under Communist control ever since its foundation in 1921 and seemed to be the only organization of any importance acting directly as a political pressure group on behalf of the unemployed. Through all these bodies the influence of the party extended far beyond the bounds which the limited total membership would suggest: for these organizations, although actually under party control, appeared independent and contained many people who were only sympathetic with the organization's stated aims. Many of these people, of course, became alienated when they realized how the party was using these bodies for its own ends; but others were persuaded to join the party after a short initial membership in a "satellite" organization, and in this way each such body played a certain part in strengthening the hold of Communism.

In 1928, however, this whole system of "transmission belts," or "bridges to the masses" as they were sometimes called, was seriously damaged by a drastic change in the Comintern line. Partly for reasons of domestic consolidation, and partly to remedy the disastrous situation in China, the Russian leadership under Stalin now put forward a thoroughly sectarian policy: the social-democratic parties, whose alliance had up till now been actively pursued, were to be denounced as "social-fascist," and the trade-union leadership in Britain and other Western countries was to be attacked as serving only to betray the working class. This policy, "Class Against Class" as it was somewhat inappropriately called, was at first resisted by the Central Committee of the British party, which gave only lip service to the Comintern instructions and sought to salve what it could of the good relations that had been built up with the left wing of the labor movement. It seemed quite unnecessary, for instance, to have to brand as "social-fascists" such militant leaders as A. J. Cook, the miners' secretary, who though not a Communist had worked closely with the Minority Movement, or James Maxton of the I.L.P., who had become chairman of the British section of the League Against Imperialism. Unfortunately, however, the slightest hint of opposition was enough to set in motion the harsh discipline of the Comintern, whose leaders were in any case looking for scapegoats to atone for the failure of the British party. In 1929, both the British and American parties had to undergo the humiliating experience of Moscow intervention in the composition of their leaderships. In Britain the changes brought to the top positions in the party three faithful Stalinists—R. Palme Dutt, the half-Indian intellectual who after an Oxford education had become the theoretician of the British party; Harry Pollitt, a boilermaker who had acted as secretary of the Minority Movement; and William Rust, a younger man who had been secretary of the Young Communist League. Although Rust died suddenly in 1949, this Stalinist control of the party has remained otherwise intact until after the death of Stalin, rendering loyal service to Moscow in governing the British Communists and in "advising" those of other countries. Pollitt, for instance, acted as the agent of Moscow at the Indian party congress in 1953-1954 just as he had done, rather more brusquely, for the U. S. Communist party in New York in 1929; and Dutt was constantly on hand to transmit instructions for the parties "within the sphere of British imperialism."

Yet although these new leaders, using the stern discipline of "democratic centralism," were able to consolidate their power within the British party, they could not prevent the party from losing influence as a result of the sectarian policy of "Class Against Class." The four years that followed—1929 to 1932—were years of acute industrial depression, of exceptionally widespread unemployment, and of political crisis. The Labour government which took office, again with Liberal support, in 1929 was quite unable to deal with the situation, and after two years it broke up with Cabinet dissensions which resulted in the secession of the Prime Minister and several of his closest colleagues. These circumstances seemed almost ideal for the development of the Communist party as an effective alternative to the moderate Left. But the Communists, isolated as they were from the labor movement as a whole by their own policy, could obtain no hearing for their views.

In the trade unions the Minority Movement, which was now under orders to establish an "independent leadership of the working class," had virtually abdicated its footholds; and the National Left Wing Movement, whose original purpose of winning the Labour party rank and file might now have been accomplished, had been closed down at the end of 1928 in accordance with Comintern policy. The National Unemployed Workers' Movement remained and doubled its membership, reaching a total of almost 40,000 toward the end of 1931, but this was an absurdly small proportion of an unemployed army which now numbered about three million. Communist control of the League Against Imperialism had been revealed in all its nakedness by the expulsion of its unoffending chairman, Maxton; and Cook had also been denounced as, in effect, a traitor to the working class. Finally, the antagonism of the Communists to both the T.U.C. and the Labour party had prompted both bodies to retort with bitter denunciation. In 1928 the T.U.C. had instructed its secretary Walter Citrine, to prepare a report on "methods of disruptive elements within the trade-union movement," and Citrine had presented a most scathing exposure to the 1929 Congress. On the basis of the same evidence, early in 1930 the Labour party executive published a list of satellite organizations of the Communists party and forbade its rank and file to belong to any of them on pain of expulsion.

Such was the heavy political toll of a policy dictated from Moscow without reference to British conditions. Comintern and Profintern headquarters, which sent out innumerable directives for the conduct of even the most trivial affairs in Britain, seemed to have no conception of the strength of opposition in the British labor movement to any suggestion of "dual unionism" such as was implied in the slogan of the "independent leadership of the working class." It is true that two Communist unions were successfully formed—the United Mineworkers of Scotland and the United Clothing Workers—but these two bodies, small as they were, were poor compensation for the loss of Communist influence in the existing unions and the virtual disintegration of the Minority Movement. The United Mineworkers of Scotland was based on Fifeshire and was fairly strong there, but it completely failed to displace the existing union, the National Union of Scottish Mineworkers. The United Clothing Workers, which was confined to the East End of London, secured an initial success, but its progress was vitiated by the party's constant attempts to use it for political rather than industrial purposes. Both unions owed their successful foundation to deep-seated hostilities among workers in the industries concerned, but for that very reason they could not make themselves sufficiently comprehensive to eliminate their older competitors in the same industries.

Taken as a whole, therefore, the policy which was forced upon the British party in the so-called "third period"—1928 to 1933—can only be described as very damaging to its prospects of emerging as a mass organization. Although the period was uniquely favorable from many points of view, the party secured no lasting successes in these years. At the end of 1932 the total membership was only 5,600, as against 7,400 in the autumn of 1927; and since 1929 there had not been a single Communist member of the House of Commons.

It is true that, under the influence of the failure of the "Class Against Class" policy, the directives from Moscow had as early as 1931 begun to swing away from the completely sectarian attitude first expressed in 1928. By 1932, for instance, a good deal of attention was again being directed to work in the trade unions, at any rate at the lower levels, and there was some discussion of the concept of the "United Front from below." But the subtleties of this adaptation of the policy were at first difficult to comprehend and to adopt, and it had little effect in preventing the final collapse of the Minority Movement which took place in 1932—a year which also saw the disastrous failure of an attempt to found a revolutionary seamen's union. It was only in 1933 that events took a new turn, not so much perhaps because of the introduction of new Communist policies, although there were important changes in this respect, as because of the impact of world affairs on the Left in general, which now became more sympathetic to attempts to secure the unity of all "progressive" forces. It was of course Hitler's coming to power that led at once to the Comintern instruction that an approach should be made to the social-democratic bodies for some program of concerted action and that while such negotiations were going on the Communist parties should stay their criticisms of these bodies. But this was only the first move: the Soviet government itself still remained very cautious in its attitude to Nazism, and evidently hoped for the continuation of the friendly German-Soviet relationship of Weimar days; and in Britain at least it took some time for the Communist party to work back to the policy of the United Front as it had operated before 1928. The leadership of the Labour party and the T.U.C. lost no time in rejecting the Communist overtures of 1933; and the General Council of the T.U.C., fearing fresh attempts at Communist infiltration, in 1934 introduced the "Black Circular" which barred Communists from acting as delegates of trades councils. The legacy of "Class Against Class" was thus proving difficult to shake off.

There was, however, one group of Socialists who were prepared to toy with the Communist offer. This was the Independent Labour party, a rapidly declining group which had seceded from the Labour party shortly after the breakup of the Labour government in the crisis of 1931. The I.L.P. had a great name in British Socialist politics—it was the party of Keir Hardie—but there was now very little left of its earlier strength, and it was hardly larger than the Communist party itself. But it was worth "capturing," and the Communists were very pleased when it agreed to a program of joint action on major questions. Its experienced leaders, however, had never approved of collaboration with the Communists, and they managed to wrest the group free from the association after only a year. This was done after an elaborate and instructive open correspondence with Moscow on the subject of the proposed I.L.P. affiliation to the Comintern: the I.L.P. leaders asked for guarantees to ensure the genuinely international character of decisions binding on themselves; and they used the evasive replies which they received to justify the severance of their existing ties with the British Communists. The break between the I.L.P. and the Communists was facilitated, ironically, by the increasing readiness of the Soviet government to ally itself with the Western powers. The I.L.P. was quite as much a pacifist as a Socialist body, and it had long regarded the League of Nations, which the Soviet government entered in 1934, as an association of cynical property-owners quite unworthy of support. Communist opportunism as displayed in these years thus shocked the older leadership of the I.L.P. and its rank-and-file idealists; and so it was for the most part only the younger members who carried on with the "unity" idea, some of them going so far as to secede and join the Communist party when the collaboration of the two parties was broken off.

In other sections of the working-class movement, and indeed among the British public as a whole, the threat of fascism gradually began to be appreciated: and this had its effect not only in a widening of Communist influence but in a gradually but continually growing willingness of trade unionist and Labour party members to take up with the United Front campaign. The Communist party sought to encourage this sentiment by proposing an electoral pact with the Labour party for the 1935 General Election, and when the proposal was rejected by the Labour party executive, it still insisted on withdrawing all its candidates except two, one of whom—Willie Gallacher at West Fife—was elected. As soon as the election was over, the demand for affiliation, which had last been made in 1925 was renewed with fresh vigor. The Communist party, wrote Harry Pollitt,

> and its leadership is prepared to work honestly and sincerely for the strengthening of the working-class movement and the winning of a majority of working-class representatives on all local bodies and in Parliament. It is prepared to do this, not as a manœuvre or for any concealed aims, but because it believes that this would unite the working class and make it better able to face the immediate fight against the National Government, against Fascism and against imperialist war.

This appeal, effective though it was with the younger and less experienced members of the labor movement, cut little ice with the Labour party Executive. It was absurd to expect an enormous body like the Labour party to damage its electoral prospects for the sake of alliance with a revolutionary group still numbering only about ten thousand members. The National Council of

Labour (a joint organization of the leadership of the T.U.C. and the Labour party) issued a special manifesto, *British Labour and Communism*, which emphasized this point:

> After years of intense and expensive propaganda, the Communist Party represents no substantial part of British public opinion. It has completely failed to win the people to the cause of dictatorship. What reason is there to believe that its affiliation with the Labour Party, or its unity with the Labour Movement, would strengthen the ranks of Labour? Experience shows that it would create confusion of thought, dissension, and disruption. Its principles, rooted in violent revolution and dictatorship, are diametrically opposed to the basis upon which has been established the strongest Labour Movement in the world.

These arguments sufficed to secure approval for the executive's attitude at the 1936 conference of the Labour party by a majority of about three to one. But with the establishment of a "Popular Front" government in France with Communist support, and more especially with the outbreak of the Spanish Civil War, the campaign for the "unity" of the Left continued to grow in strength. Much enthusiasm prevailed in Britain for the International Brigade, which contained a British battalion recruited from all sections of the labor movement but controlled, like all other units of the Brigade, by Comintern representatives. There was considerable impatience with the policy of "nonintervention" in Spain, which was initially accepted by the Labour party and the T.U.C., but which turned out to be something of a farce in view of the extensive commitment of Italian forces and German armaments on the side of General Franco. Consequently, "popular front" feeling found expression in public opinion in Britain, if not in the official policy of the Labour party. The Left Book Club, with its mammoth editions of books encouraging this course, was one symptom; the formation within the Labour party of the "Socialist League," a body of supporters of the "popular front" policy, was another. Early in 1937 the Labour party executive ordered the dissolution of the Socialist League on pain of expulsion from the party, and its leaders complied with the threat; but the dissent lingered on, and early in 1939 Sir Stafford Cripps, who had been the League's principal spokesman, and a number of other prominent rebels including Aneurin Bevan, were expelled from the party.

Meanwhile, the membership and influence of the Communist partly continued to grow, and its newspaper, the *Daily Worker*, which had led a highly precarious existence since its foundation in 1930, was able to establish itself without the need of further subsidies from Russia. The Seventh Congress of the Comintern in 1935 had given the national Communist parties a much larger measure of autonomy than they had previously had and had left them to manage almost entirely on their own financial resources; the Profintern had been wound up in order to promote the *rapprochement* with the Western powers; and communications between the Comintern secretariat and its affiliated bodies were supposed to be limited to major issues of policy. One of the results of the campaign for the "unity" of the Left was the decision to close down the struggling Communist unions in Britain, the United Mineworkers of Scotland, and the United Clothing Workers. Gradually the British Communists regained a certain position for themselves in the trade-union bureaucracy which previously they had spurned. Arthur Horner became president of the South Wales Miners Federation, and progress was made among the discontented London busmen's section of the Transport and General Workers Union. Yet in the last year before the outbreak of the Second World War, this Communist advance seemed to have found its limit. The party's membership advance slowed down; it was 16,000 at the end of 1938 and 18,000 nine months later. Such figures hardly suggest a very rapid tempo of expansion: and there were certain features of the international scene which gave potential recruits some reason for caution in joining the party. The Russian treason trials, and the dissension between Communist and non-Communist forces on the Republican side in Spain, troubled many consciences on the British Left; and the "popular front" movement clearly began to falter at this time, permitting the Labour party executive led by Herbert Morrison to win an easy victory for its policy at the Whitsun conference of

1939. Thus one more phase of British history closed without any major success for the Communists in penetrating the ranks of organized labor.

The tortuous changes of policy effected by the Comintern in the early stages of the Second World War are well known. Britain went to war on September 3rd with the approval of the entire Left except for the out-and-out pacifists. The change of line by the Comintern in the course of September was therefore particularly damaging to the British party and resulted in a considerable loss of members and even greater loss of influence, and there was serious trouble even in the highest leadership of the party. Harry Pollitt and J. R. Campbell both opposed the new line and had to be temporarily removed from the offices of general secretary and editor, respectively, which they were occupying. The absorption of Polish territory by Soviet troops and the invasion of Finland naturally only made things worse. The party membership dropped by about a third, in spite of the adhesion of certain crypto-Communists from inside the Labour party who found their existing positions no longer tenable. The Student Labour Federation, which was supposed to be the representative body of all students supporting the Labour party, turned out to be a body under Communist control, and it had to be disaffiliated from the Labour party; and the Left Book Club rapidly fell to pieces. As in 1928, but more suddenly, the new Comintern policy thus resulted in heavy setbacks to the British Communists both in their relations with the Labour party and in their position in the trade-union movement. It rapidly became apparent that the temper of the nation had little use for the "peace" policy which they had brought forward to replace their "antifascist" line.

As usual, however, the remaining Communists settled down to make the best of the situation, and they soon framed a new pattern of propaganda. Capitalizing on the misfortunes of the time, they agitated on questions of housing and of air-raid precautions, and in January 1941 they organized in London a "People's Convention" attended by some two thousand "delegates," supposedly representing over a million workers. The convention demanded "a people's peace" which was somehow to be secured by negotiation with both Germany and Russia. It was this activity which led to the banning of the *Daily Worker* by the Home Secretary a few days later—just five months before the invasion of Russia began. It was not without significance that the Home Secretary at this time was Herbert Morrison who, as a leader of the Labour party, had done much to limit Communist infiltration into the organized labor movement.

After all this, the amazing transformation in the popularity and prestige of the British Communists that took place after the beginning of the invasion of Russia in June 1941 seems in retrospect a little difficult to explain. It must be remembered that Britain at the time was in sore need of a fighting ally, and the Russians fought very much better than most people had expected them to do in the face of the full weight of the German army. Before the end of 1941 the Communist party membership was up beyond its 1939 highest, and after a further twelve months it reached 56,000 —the apogee of its strength. Both inside the labor movement and outside it, the party was bathed in the reflected glory of Russian military successes. In the factories, its policy up to June 1941 had been one of maintaining labor standards at the expense if necessary of increased production: but now it was prepared to make almost any sacrifice in order to turn out the arms for the "antifascist" war. The importance of such a change of attitude for the war effort must not be exaggerated: it has been shown that there were far fewer strikes in 1940 than there were in 1942 or 1943. But still, there were other factors which helped to account for this, and the party's attitude must have made some difference. Certainly after the invasion of Russia the Communists became sufficiently popular with the workers to secure easy and rapid promotion in the union hierarchies, so that in 1943 the T.U.C. general council was obliged to withdraw the "Black Circular" of 1934, and by the end of the war the Fire Brigades Union, the Electrical Trades Union, and the Welsh and Scottish Miners—

to mention only the larger unions—were almost entirely under party control; and even the mammoth Transport and General Workers Union, which had Ernest Bevin as its secretary, had appointed a Communist as one of its two representatives of the T.U.C. general council.

In May 1943, Stalin made a shrewd move in order to allay the suspicions of the Western powers: he abolished the Comintern. It would be possible to argue that this measure was largely effected with an eye to the situation in Britain, for the Soviet leader, sorely in need of supplies for his armies, must have been interested primarily in getting more liberal help from Britain and America, and, as it happened, the formal link between the American Communist party and the Comintern had already been severed. The British party had just recently renewed its application to affiliate to the Labour party, with better prospects than ever before, and the matter was to be voted on at the Labour party conference in June. The fact that the British Communists owed a special loyalty to the Comintern had always been the final, clinching argument used by the Labour party executive to defeat the plea for affiliation; and, indeed, the Comintern constitution had been republished by the executive as an appendix to their annual report. But if this was Stalin's motive, it had no immediate success: the proposal for affiliation was again defeated, although there was a sizable minority vote of 712,000 which must have included several large unions. As the war drew to its close, the Communists made the tactical error of supporting the maintenance of the Churchill Coalition at a time when the leaders of the Labour party had become convinced that they had a good chance of winning a General Election. The latter were triumphantly justified by events, for the Labour party won a substantial clear majority in the Commons in the election of 1945. What was more, the refusal of the Labour party leadership to permit any electoral collaboration with the Communists confined them to a gain of only one seat: Phil Piratin won the predominantly Jewish constituency of Mile End in London, and Gallacher was re-elected for East Fife. Two or three crypto-Communists were elected as Labour M.P.s, but in the nature of things they were quite unable for the time being to come out in their true colors.

Their electoral failures were a severe shock to the Communists. Their leaders had had their eyes too closely fixed on the situation in other countries—for instance, on the success of their sister party in France where Communist participation in the de Gaulle government had secured considerable advantages. After the dissolution of the Comintern they had altered the appearance of their party so as to assimilate it to the customary forms of the British labor movement: they had renamed their controlling committees, so that the Politburo became the "Political Committee," the Central Committee became the "Executive Committee" and the Control Commission became the "Appeals Committee." They also decided, in social-democratic fashion, to have an annual conference; and, more important, they abandoned their attempts to organize on a factory basis so as to secure as large a concentration of their power as possible for electoral purposes. All this, however, achieved so little at the 1945 General Election, and the party's influence in the parliamentary sphere was as nothing compared to its grip on the trade unions where it was within range of control of some of the largest unions in the country.

How was it that so small a party as the Communists could win a position of dominance in so many unions and could threaten to win control of the whole movement? To understand this we must bear in mind that only a tiny proportion of members are ever prepared to devote their time to exercising their democratic rights within the unions. Elections of officers and major decisions of policy are likely to be determined on votes rarely exceeding 5 per cent. Under these circumstances, a small, determined minority can rapidly obtain a foothold, and if its opponents do not mobilize in any way, it can carry a high proportion of its views into the official policy of the union. It can be shown mathematically that quite a small minority can dominate any democratic group if the unorganized majority continues to vote at random. And because the short-term political objectives of the

Communists did not appear to differ seriously from those of the Labour party in the period between 1941 and 1947, there seemed to be no reason for the non-Communists to form an anti-Communist bloc. Until 1947, the Communists were supporting the Labour government, and were continuing to urge the increase of productivity. There was some sniping at the Labour foreign policy: at first its shortcomings from the Communist point of view were blamed on the permanent officials of the Foreign Office and then on the Foreign Secretary, Ernest Bevin. It was only at the end of 1947, with the decision of the Soviet government to oppose the Marshall Plan, and with the creation of the Cominform and its adoption of the "two camps" policy, that the change in British Communist policy back to sectarianism occurred, and the party's gains inside the labor movement were once more jeopardized for the sake of loyalty to the international centre.

The new phase of relations between the Communist party and the British labor movement that began in 1947 may be said to have continued with comparatively little basic change ever since. By early 1948 vituperative attacks were being made on the Labour government, and at the 1950 election no less than a hundred Communist candidates were put up, all of them against Labour opposition. Possibly such an extended offensive would have had a measure of success if the Labour government had had a poor legislative record, or had failed to ensure a generous development of social services during its term of office. But as it turned out there was plenty to show for the five years of Labour rule, and the morale of the Labour party rank and file was accordingly high. The Communist political offensive thus gained little support from discontent inside the Labour party, and it turned out to be a disastrous failure: it led to the defeat of both sitting Communist M.P.s, and in the case of all but three of the hundred candidates, to the loss of the £150 deposit which by the British electoral law is forfeited to the Treasury if the candidate fails to obtain at least one-eighth of the total vote. As the crypto-Communist M.P.s had already been expelled from the Labour party, and, standing as independents, had also lost their seats, there was absolutely no representation of the Communist point of view remaining in the House of Commons. Another General Election took place in the following year, 1951, but this time the result was even worse for the Communists, for although they limited their total number of candidates to ten, not one of them saved his deposit. This was due in part to the fact that the Korean War had now broken out and had given the party a degree of unpopularity unparalleled since 1941.

In the trade unions, however, where the party had such a strong established position, the conflict was both more sustained and less decisive. The new Cominform policy was so much at odds with that of the Labour government that inevitably the latter's loyal supporters in the movement were roused to the problem presented by Communist infiltration in their midst. At the end of 1947, the secretary of the Transport and General Workers Union, Arthur Deakin, issued a warning to his colleagues; and shortly afterward a series of international events—especially the Communist coup in Czechoslovakia and the Berlin air lift—reinforced this warning. Late in 1948 the National Union of Mineworkers, whose policy was one of strict loyalty to the Labour government, was embarrassed by the behavior of its Communist secretary, Arthur Horner, who promised the union's support for the French miners' political strike against the Marshall Plan. Vigorous action by the loyal officials of the union, led by Will Lawther, was necessary in order to put the secretary in his place as the agent of the national executive. The initiative was now taken by the General Council of the T.U.C. which had only one Communist member: it issued a statement, *Defend Democracy*, which was reminiscent of its criticisms of Communist methods in the 1920's and which condemned the technique of coordinated intervention in union affairs by a body whose control lay outside the movement. The statement urged the unions to take action where necessary against these tactics of infiltration.

In the British trade-union movement the national organization has even less control over its affiliated bodies than the A.F.L.-

C.I.O. has over its chartered components. Action had now to be taken by the individual unions if they so desired, and their willingness to do so varied considerably. There were some unions, such as the Electrical Trades Union, where Communist control seemed to be too complete for any change to be possible; there were others, such as the General and Municipal Workers Union, where Communists had been barred from holding certain key offices since the 1920's and where consequently no serious threat now existed. It was in the marginal cases, where Communist influence was strong but not overwhelming, that action was possible: and it is true that among these were to be counted some of the largest and most influential unions in the country, such as Ernest Bevin's and Arthur Deakin's own union, the Transport and General Workers, and also the Amalgamated Engineering Union. Deakin was much concerned by the fact that in his own union the Communist party had by 1946 nine open members in a general executive council of thirty-four, and three members out of eight on the key finance-and-general-purposes committee. He resolved on a vigorous attack on them at the Biennial Delegate Conference in July 1949, and succeeded in persuading the conference to endorse the T.U.C. statement and to carry a resolution to prevent Communists from holding office in the union. The result was that in January 1950 nine full-time officers were dismissed for sympathy with Communism—among them being Bert Papworth, who had represented the union on the T.U.C. general council.

The same rapid purge could not be accomplished in the Amalgamated Engineering Union. For one thing, owing to its elaborate constitution, it was impossible for the secretary to dominate the union as Deakin did the T. & G.W.U. The Communists were well established, not so much on the executive council as on some of the district committees which had considerable powers. This was especially true in the London area. Consequently, any move to introduce a ban on Communist office-holding would have been unlikely to succeed, and apparently none was made. In the A.E.U., as in certain other unions, the battle against Communism was transferred to the union ballots; and it was significant that it was about this time that the opponents of Communism began to organize themselves—sometimes merely for the reform of a single union, as for instance in the case of the highly successful conference campaign committee in the Clerical and Administrative Workers Union; sometimes on a regional basis, as in the case of some Catholic groups; sometimes on a general and national basis, as in the group called "Common Cause" and in the more recent "Industrial Research and Information Service" which publishes a monthly circular, *Iris News*, to provide detailed information for the movement on the activities and strategy of Communist infiltration. Naturally, the period of the Korean War led to some setbacks for union Communists, and the shock of events in Hungary at the end of 1956 caused the leaders of the Fire Brigades Union to throw off their overt Communist allegiance. But the party remains entrenched in some small unions and in some sections of the Amalgamated Engineering Union; and the new secretary of the National Union of Mineworkers, Will Paynter, like his predecessor, Arthur Horner, is a loyal adherent of the party. Furthermore, the Electrical Trades Union was actually disaffiliated from both the T.U.C. and the Labour party in 1961 after a High Court action had disclosed election frauds by its Communist officials. The future of this strategically important union remains, at the time of writing, in the balance.

Thus, while the party's membership has declined from its peak of 56,000 in 1944 to just half that figure in 1961, and while its general political influence has slumped much more than this (owing to the prevalence of "passive membership" which the party in its early days would never have tolerated), it retains a certain grip upon important posts in the trade unions and, theoretically, at least would be in a position to do serious industrial damage in an emergency. In practice, however, the danger is not as great as it seems. The period of the Marshall Plan, when Communist unions were expected to do their utmost to sabotage recovery, passed in Britain without anything more serious than a few minor dock strikes. The existence of Communist strength in some of the union leaderships is more an indication of the difficulty of changing any leadership, once established, than a sign of widespread radical extremism among the rank and file. It is probably truer in 1961 than at any time in the last twenty years that the Communist threat in the industrial sphere is both recognized and held in check by the majority of non-Communists.

The observer may sometimes obtain the impression that British Communism is protected and even fostered by the existence of a strong political and industrial labor movement. These large and influential bodies appear to contain many fellow-travelers and sympathizers with Communism who put up an effective resistance to any attempts to discipline or outlaw the genuinely subversive elements. Such an impression would not be entirely false: it is certainly true that Conservative governments have taken stronger measures against the Communist party than Labour governments have done, and the only large-scale prosecution of Communist leaders—that of 1925—took place under Conservative rule. But if we examine the larger question of whether the Communist party's influence is enlarged or diminished by the existence of the Labour party, it is clear that other factors must be taken into account. In so far as the Labour party is successful in introducing measures of social betterment, it may be concluded that its effect is likely to reduce the residual social discontent on which Communism usually flourishes.

At the same time, the Labour party would obviously be serving Communist ends if it allowed its own ranks to be permeated, secretly or openly, by members of the revolutionary organization. In this respect, much must depend on the political experience and vigilance of the leaders of the Labour party, as well as upon the loyalty and common sense of the rank and file. We have seen that in 1924 Communists were rendered ineligible for endorsement as Labour candidates, that in 1925 they were excluded from membership of the local Labour parties, and that in 1928 they were prevented from being delegated to the party conference. All these measures were necessary to safeguard the peculiar federal structure of the Labour party from penetration, and they obliged the Communists to devise more devious methods of securing influence in the Labour party—none of them particularly effective in the long run. One of them was secret infiltration; and this tactic resulted in the temporary "capture" of some local organizations and in 1945 secured the election of a few crypto-Communists as Labour M.P.s. In general, however, the alertness of the Labour party executive and its disciplinary activities confined the damage to a minimum: constituency organization were if necessary disbanded and reformed; and even Labour M.P.s whose voting records seemed peculiar were readily expelled from the party.

The Labour party executive has also kept a close watch on the "satellite" organizations of the Communist party. It was in 1930, at a time when the sectarianism of "Class Against Class" was at its height, that the executive first instituted the system of declaring membership of certain listed organizations improper for members of the Labour party. At that time the list was fairly short, but it included the League Against Imperialism, the Left Wing Movement, the Minority Movement, and the National Unemployed Workers' Movement. Also listed were the Friends of the Soviet Union and the Workers' International Relief. In later years, the Communists created fresh bodies, especially at any time when a United Front policy was in favor: in 1934, for instance, various "antifascist" bodies made their appearance and were added to the Labour party's list; and in the years after 1945 a whole range of "peace" and "friendship" societies which had proliferated in response to the demands of international Communist propaganda had to be catalogued in turn.

On the whole, these measures of discipline inside the Labour party prevented the Communists from securing any great propaganda successes at its expense. At times, however, and particularly in the 1930's when the Spanish Civil War was raging, it was difficult for the executive to persuade the rank and file of the party that the measures were desirable. But the executive was never disavowed by the party conference, and a few years of political experience usually sufficed to convince individual critics that the Transport House policy was justified. It sometimes seemed a pity that the Labour party leadership never encouraged its supporters to stay inside the "satellite" bodies and "capture" or "recapture" them from the Communists. But the opportunities for success in this way were few, owing to the speedy consolidation effected by the Communists of any hold that they had once been able to assert. Usually, the only alternatives for such a body were continued Communist control or disintegration, as has been shown by the history of, for instance, the Labour Research Department (originally an offshoot of the Fabian Society, but "captured" by Communists in the early 1920's) and the National Left Wing Movement (extinguished by Communist orders in 1929).

All these threats to the position of the Labour party—whether by secret membership, or by enticing its loyal supporters into satellite organizations—have been of little importance, however, compared with the threat posed by the Communist bid for control of the industrial movement. For it remains true today as it was when the Labour party was formed in 1900 that the representatives of the trade unions have by far the biggest say in determinating Labour party policy, whether at the annual conference or on the executive. The fact that Communists are not allowed at the conference does not prevent a Communist union from finding members willing to represent it and its political attitude on the conference floor. For the most part, the Communist influence is strongest in unions with a strong Celtic membership—for instance, the Scottish and Welsh areas of the National Union of Mineworkers. But there has also been a certain amount of sympathy among the large factory population of the London area where the shop stewards movement secured a grip before and during the Second World War. It is this latter element, as much as anything, which accounts for the strength of Communism in the Amalgamated Engineering Union and in the Electrical Trades Union—a strength which as recently as 1960 could be an important factor in swinging the Labour party conference into support of unilateral nuclear disarmament. But, as we have seen, the general industrial threat appears to have been checked, especially since the whole issue of ballot-rigging has been publicized by the High Court case involving the E.T.U. in 1961.

Of the procedural tactics constantly used by British Communists to secure their ends in the democratic organizations of the Left—the "fraction" and the "nucleus" as they used to be called—it is hardly necessary to speak, for they do not differ from the pattern laid down by Lenin for the use of Communist parties everywhere. As early as 1925 the "fraction of ten" which was in action at the Scarborough meeting of the T.U.C. acquired a certain notoriety, owing to the publication of letters concerning its operation at the Communist trial of that year. It was not uncommon for the local organs of the trade-union movement, the trades councils, to fall under Communist control, and here the T.U.C. general council could often exercise plenary powers of discipline, as happened in the case of the London Trades Council, which was entirely reconstituted in 1952.

All in all, it may be said that in the past the Labour party and the T.U.C. have succeeded in preserving their structure fairly effectively against the influence of the tiny but energetic minority that assailed them. They were, of course, assisted by the sudden switches of Communist policy which took place as a result of external decisions having little or no reference to the special problems of the British situation. These switches were, in fact, very damaging to the British Communist party when they meant a move in the direction of sectarianism as was the case in 1928, in 1939, and in 1947. But the strength of the labor movement's resistance to Communism was due also to positive merits of its own leaders and members: to the vigilance of such officials as Arthur Henderson, Walter Citrine, Herbert Morrison, and Arthur Deakin; and to the homogeneity of the rank and file with their sense of loyalty to their officials and their abhorrence of "dual unionism." There was, indeed, a quality of morale and a sense of mutual confidence between officer and following in the movement which must in part have been due to the success of the Labour party and the T.U.C. in pursuing their own constructive policies—of advancing the social welfare by a program of reform through constitutional channels. Whether such morale and confidence can be maintained in the future is a larger question beyond the scope of this essay.

4

Old Tactics in the New World

COMMUNISTS IN THE C.I.O.

Max M. Kampleman

■ The history of the Communist Party of the United States of America (C.P.U.S.A.) provides another example of Communist efforts to achieve by political activism goals which should have been accomplished by the laws of capitalist development. Communist ideologies depict the U.S. as the prototype and bastion of capitalism—the principal antagonist in a two-sided struggle between "capitalist" and "socialist" systems. And, in fact, the U.S. has many of the defining characteristics of a highly developed capitalist state. It is highly industrialized; its industry is privately owned; it possesses a large industrial working class which "sells" its labor to owners of the means of production; profit is not only permitted but heavily relied upon to provide efficiency, initiative, and energy in the economic sphere; a free market is the principal mechanism for regulating the production and exchange of goods and services; it has demonstrated tendency to alternating cycles of prosperity and depression. As Marx and many predecessors predicted, the inequity of competition between individual workers with nothing to sell but their labor, and industrialists who could control the terms and conditions of employment, spurred the workers to unite and organize. From the outset, however, American workers have declined to believe they had nothing to lose but their chains. With the stubborn reformism which Lenin believed typical of trade unions, the American industrial proletariat has preferred to fight within the system rather than against it.

The consequences are well known: the American labor movement has helped reshape the capitalist system in the United States, it has achieved a uniquely high standard of living for American workers, and it has become a political force of capital importance. Its political power has been wielded to reinforce the American political system rather than attack it. Why? Why has the capitalist system in America failed to polarize owners and workers in class warfare? Why have American workers respected the "rules of the game" rather than demanding a new deck? Why have American workers proved impervious to the appeals of revolutionary ideologies in general and to Communism in particular? Why, in short, have American workers remained attached to the American social system rather than become alienated from it? The answer to these questions goes far toward explaining the failure of the Communist party in the U.S. and provides important insight into the dynamics of alienation.

Marx assumed that the psycho-social alienation which he observed among continental workers was a function of capitalism. Marx believed that the worker, having lost control over the conditions and product of his labor, came to regard his labor as alien to himself. The perception of his labor as a commodity to be sold on the market, in turn, distorted his relations with others and with himself. From regarding his labor as a commodity, the worker moved quickly to regarding himself as a commodity and his relations to others as functional, economic relations, determined by a "cash nexus." Sensing that the morality and religion of the established order were instruments of his repression, he trusted and honored no aspect of the system. He would disdain the rules of the democratic system, because he would have understood they were rules designed to secure and maintain his slavery; he would eschew constitutional limits because he would have understood they were rigged to limit only his freedom. Depersonalized, dehumanized by the processes of production, he would feel an intense if inchoate rage against the society which deprived him of himself. His rage was his honor; it was also, Marx asserted, the energy which would propel the revolutionary movement.

History has confirmed Marx's insights concerning the signifi-

cance of alienation in the modern world and the relationship between alienation and revolution. History has refuted his assertion
that alienation is a function of capitalist modes of production and
a specific attribute of industrial workers in a capitalist system.
Again and again in this book we have seen that alienation and
susceptibility to revolutionary ideologies are not invariably associated with any specific economic class or role. We have seen also
that Communist parties outside the Soviet Union—themselves
made up of persons alienated from the established order—achieve
their greatest successes when they appeal to other groups who,
for whatever reasons, share alienation from the existing social
order. In the underdeveloped areas, Communist parties normally
seek support among groups alienated from traditional culture without regard to economic factors. In the highly industrialized nations, Communists not only attempt to identify and recruit all
groups who are dissatisfied or depressed, but they assume that the
industrial working class will be dissatisfied with and alienated from
the existing system. This assumption leads them to concentrate
a large portion of their time on the trade unions and labor movements. Their success in recruiting members and workers among
industrial workers depends on the extent to which workers (a)
are satisfied with their share of available goods within the society,
and (b) are convinced that machinery exists within the existing
system for correcting inequities.

But if Communist success in forging union members into a
mass base for the Communist party depends largely on the extent
of workers' alienation from or attachment to the existing social
order, their success in converting unions—and other democratic
organizations—into useful and relatively docile instruments of the
Communist party depends on other factors. The experience of the
British and American labor movements with Communism demonstrates that control of a mass membership organization can be
gained where conversion cannot.

The middle-class leadership of the Communist party of the
United States early decided to make American workers and the
American Negroes the special targets of its efforts. Neither group

proved a happy hunting ground for large-scale recruitment. Both groups confounded the hopes and expectations of Communist leaders, because both demonstrated an indifference to revolutionary appeals and a determination to work out their problems by legal processes. Both preferred to settle their grievances within the system. The governing machinery of the trade unions, however, proved more vulnerable to Communist tactics than did the membership to Communist appeals. By boring from within key unions of the C.I.O., a minuscule minority of Communists was able to gain control over a substantial portion of the labor movement. The American experience, however, not only demonstrates the vulnerability of democratic organizations to infiltration and colonization by a disciplined minority, but it also demonstrates the capacity of a democratic majority—operating within the context of a free society—to reclaim control of its affairs.

In the following essay, Max M. Kampelman, a political scientist, attorney, and long-time student of the American labor movement, traces the rise and decline of Communist influence within the C.I.O.; Mr. Kampelman is the author of The Communist Party vs. the C.I.O., and has contributed articles to a number of scholarly and political journals. ∎

The organized labor movement in the United States is probably the largest and most active nongovernmental economic or political body in America. Primarily dedicated to improving the working conditions and raising the living standards of its members, its political, social, and economic influence reached far beyond its fifteen million members and their families.

The American labor movement has always had an attachment to the spiritual and material roots of the existing order, having been infused early with middle-class aspiration for self-employment. The mainstream of labor has not been "working-class conscious," and has rejected the concept of class war. Unions have in the main been "protectionist," reluctant to interfere with the existing economic and political system, anxious instead to share in the material fruits of capitalism. Beginning earlier than Marxism, American labor has always existed independently of the Marxist movement.

There have, however, been constant efforts from within and without to radicalize American labor. These influences and the response to them have helped shape both labor and the American society and are important for a full understanding of labor's role in the society. They help explain why trade unions have occasionally produced politically militant leadership and why the American labor movement was labeled "red" and "dangerous" by irresponsibles ever since the first group of Philadelphia shoemakers organized themselves into a union in 1787. The most recent important effort to convert the organized labor movement into an instrument for political revolution was made by the Communists.

The Communists have never been a significant numerical factor in American life or within American trade unions. The largest number of members which the Communist party has had in recent years is probably 70,000. Assuming that of this number one-half belonged to unions—and that would probably be an exaggeration—they would have had a maximum numerical strength of .0024 of the fifteen million labor union members. Yet at the height of their power, they dominated twelve to fifteen of the forty international C.I.O. unions.

For many years any charge, no matter how justified, that a trade-union officer was a Communist was likely to be dismissed as red-baiting. But there can be no doubt that the American labor movement and the C.I.O. specifically did have a serious Communist problem. The Communist problem began with the end of the First World War, was insignificant at first but grew in importance during the depression of the early 1930's, and reached its zenith with the formation and growth of the C.I.O. in the late thirties and forties. In the United States as in Europe and elsewhere, Communists were most active in the fields of transportation, shipping, fuel, metal trades, and other industries vital to the nation's economy. The strength they eventually gained in these areas gave them an importance in American society which was entirely disproportionate to their numbers.

World War I had strengthened the conservative leadership of the American labor movement partly of course because of war time prosecutions by the government. Critical groups, such as the I.W.W., the Socialist Labor party, and the Socialist party found themselves with little influence in the A.F.L. It was at this moment that the American Communist movement was born. Influenced by Leninism and the success of the Bolshevik Revolution of 1917 in Russia, a small, dedicated band of militant radicals attempted to gain control of the Socialist party and began preparing the country for rebellion. The deep inconsistencies between democratic socialism as expressed by the gradualist Socialist party majority, and Leninist elitism, was early apparent, and the Communists were expelled from the party.

In September 1919, the Communist party of America came into being, espousing a policy of "revolutionary unionism." Hostile to the American Federation of Labor and sympathetic to the Industrial Workers of the World, the Communists looked upon unions as "schools of communism." At ordinary strikes, leaflets urging the worker to overthrow the government and establish soviets were distributed. The revolution, however, did not come as quickly as expected and different tactics had to be used. With a more moderate appeal, unions established and run by Communists gained some following, particularly among foreign-born workers in the needle trades, food, and metals and among laborers. These unions duplicated and competed with existing AFL unions.

In May 1920, Lenin, for reasons that had nothing to do with America, published his pamphlet, *Left Wing Communism: An Infantile Disorder,* in which he urged Communists to go into existing unions and criticized the German Communists for not doing so. Benjamin Gitlow, writing of this period, said: "The publication of Lenin's pamphlet turned the trade-union policy of our Party upside down." Gitlow, at the time an important functionary of the movement, described the new approach toward major Communist activity in labor as follows:

The Bolsheviks from the time of Lenin to the present have never given up hope of capturing the trade union movement of the United States. Our Party received more assistance, more advice, more decisions on the trade union question than on almost any other question. Lenin was particularly anxious to win over the American trade unions. It was Lenin who conceived the idea that it would be possible for the Communists in the United States, by hiding their identity, to form an opposition bloc in the trade unions, which would enable them to dislodge the reactionary forces in control of the American Federation of Labor.

In December 1921, the Workers party was formed at a New York convention. Four years had passed since the October Revolution, and there was no indication that the mass of American workers would accept Communist leadership. Led by William Z. Foster, a prominent labor organizer in steel and meatpacking, the Communists began a policy of penetrating the AFL. Foster, a former Socialist and member of the syndicalist IWW, had a reputation as a successful labor organizer, having led the great Steel Strike of 1919. The Communists dropped the policy of overtly promoting revolution and adopted the strategy of obtaining a place for themselves in ordinary trade-union activity. In 1922 they formed the Trade Union Educational League (T.U.E.L.) intended as a rallying center for all progressive groups and individuals within the existing trade union movement. Foster became the head of the T.U.E.L., and the managing editor of its first publication, *The Labor Herald*, was Earl Browder.

The T.U.E.L. hoped to act as a revolutionary wing of the AFL and remain within it, but this strategy was difficult to maintain. The Communist (Third) International continued to proclaim the Lenin thesis of "permanent revolution" and the impossibility of establishing lasting socialism in one country within a capitalist world. The League and its leaders were thus from the outset obliged to subordinate trade-union policies to political objectives. The Workers party, becoming increasingly aggressive as a left-wing opposition, began to attempt to gain control of unions through active participation in union elections, and nominated its own opposition candidates. This policy lost the party the support of non-Communist progressives and left the T.U.E.L. and its leader, Foster, in 1923, exposed as Communists and nothing more. This, in turn, led to a great many expulsions from the AFL on the ground of dual unionism.

The T.U.E.L. now spearheaded an attack upon the AFL. The League's program called for a reorganization of the labor movement through a program of amalgamation under which craft unions were to be merged into industrial groupings. AFL reaction to the new policy was immediate. Drastic punitive measures against T.U.E.L. adherents were undertaken. Many unions insisted on loyalty pledges. T.U.E.L. members were removed from union offices and others were expelled. To meet these attacks, Foster advised his followers to sign membership pledges against the T.U.E.L. so as to avoid expulsion. The Communists remained a conspiratorial minority group and a policy of "boring from within" began. This program lasted until 1928 when the Communists appeared with another dual labor organization, the Trade Union Unity League, designed to follow a more independent policy.

The T.U.U.L. began what came to be known as the "Third Period" of the Communist party, which lasted until 1935. It was a "revolutionary period," characterized in the United States by a few spectacular T.U.U.L.-led strikes, but otherwise made scant impression upon the labor scene. In following this pattern, the American Communist movement was in harmony with Communist practice all over the world. Social Democrats were called "social-fascists," and new "red" trade unions were formed to compete with existing organizations. Among the new unions so formed were the National Miners Union, the Building Trades Industrial League, the National Textile Workers Union, and the Needle Trades Workers Industrial Union.

With the rise of the Nazis in Germany and the growing realization that the Hitler regime was not an interregnum before the Communist revolution but rather a real threat to the Soviet Union as well as to a free Europe, the Communist line wavered. The 1933-1935 period saw the first steps toward the creation of a

United Front. In March 1933, for example, the Executive Committee of the Communist (Third) International addressed a manifesto to all labor organizations and Social-Democratic parties asking them to unite. On March 30, the Communist party in the United States followed suit and addressed a call for united action to the AFL Executive Council, to the National Executive Committee of the Socialist party, and to other labor organizations. Some joint activity with the Socialist party began in late 1934 with the Joint Committee to Aid the Herndon Defense. Full acceptance and support of liberal capitalism as expressed by the New Deal, however, was slower to come and in fact did not arrive until 1935 and the Laval-Stalin Pact in May of that year. In the meantime, vilification of the New Deal and the AFL continued.

In 1934, the New Deal was still a "fascist conspiracy" against the workers and for war. Sidney Hillman, who was to become an apparent hero of the Communists during World War II was now repeatedly called an "NRA strikebreaker." A resolution passed by the Eighth Convention of the Communist party of the USA in April 1934 declared:

> The workers are rapidly learning the lessons of the strikebreaking role of the NRA and the betrayals of the AF of L leadership. The NRA, which promised without struggle better wages, shorter hours, and the right to organize, is more and more being exposed as the instrument of the capitalists for the greater, more intensive exploitation and oppression of labor. . . .

This was a far cry from statements in the same publication two years later in favor of "progressive New Dealers" and the plea to "help re-elect President Roosevelt" because of his support of collective bargaining, wages and hours, relief, social security, and other measures vital to labor.

The change in the international scene, which now dictated closer cooperation with "reformist" elements, led to the dissolution of the T.U.U.L. on March 16, 1935. Once again the Communists resorted to "boring from within."

The most dramatic evidence of the change was provided at the

Seventh World Congress of the Communist International in August 1935, in Moscow, by Georgi Dimitrov, general secretary and "hero of the Reichstag fire trial," who defined "the immediate and central task of the international proletarian movement: the establishment of unity of action amongst all sections of the working class in the struggle against fascism."

Anticipating this new policy which had been developing over two years, the Central Committee of the American Communist party in January 1935 declared itself against dual unionism. The futility of "building an independent Federation of Labor" was admitted by the 1935 "plenum" of the Central Committee. The April 1934 Convention of the party had resolved:

> . . . The whole Party must be mobilized for work in the AF of L, and a decisive turn towards winning the millions of workers organized in the AF of L unions and the Railroad Brotherhoods and isolating the bureaucrats. . . .
> Every Communist to carry on bolshevik work must establish and maintain contact with the non-Party workers. The Eighth Congress obliges every eligible Party member to become organized in a trade union and imposes upon the C.C. (Central Committee) the task of checking up on the fulfillment of this decision within three months.

Now in January 1935, the party Central Committee demanded concentrated work by its members in the AFL ". . . in view of the changing conditions of trade union work." Communists within the independent unions were urged to "carry out . . . tactics of struggle for trade union unity and affiliation to the American Federation of Labor." The Communist press was also ordered to change its tone with regard to the AFL.

Earl Browder, who had seen in the New Deal "the clearest example of the tendencies toward fascism" and who had said that Roosevelt's labor policies were the "American brother to Mussolini's Corporate state with state-controlled labor unions closely tied up and under the direction of the employers," now led his party members into the American Labor party in New York and demanded support of FDR. Many "fellow travelers" were freely recruited. A growing number of "front" organizations were created—principally by infiltration—including the Scottsboro Defense Committee, the National Negro Congress, the American Student Union, the Workers Alliance of America, and the American League against War and Fascism. It was Communists following this "line" who in 1937 moved on the CIO *en masse.*

Earlier in the new United Front period the Communist party directed all of its attention to the AFL. This drive continued during and after the CIO was breaking away from the AFL and becoming independent. For almost two years the Communists ignored, chided, and opposed the efforts of the young CIO. In spite of the fact that the CIO's program for industiral unionism agreed with the traditional Communist trade union policy. Unity within the AFL had been the declared slogan of the CP Convention and its Central Committee in 1935, and unity within the AFL it would be, said the Communist trade-union leaders, regardless of the CIO. This lasted until May 1937, by which time the CIO had also become attractive bait.

Chanting "CIO" like three notes in a new litany, the Communists found a home in 1937. And even though they were frequently to emphasize collective security rather than collective bargaining, John L. Lewis, parading Henry of Navarre's proverb, "In a battle I make arrows from any wood," asserted: "I'll work with anyone who'll work with me."

With Lewis willing to accept them, it was not too difficult for the Communists to become an integral part of the CIO organization, particularly since most of them disguised themselves as liberals or as American radicals in the democratic tradition. The Communist party itself encouraged disguise in the interests of building a "democratic front." In this effort, however, they never lost their cohesiveness or their sense of internal organization. From the beginning, they met as a caucus. Michael Quill, head of the Transport Workers Union and a member of that caucus, stated that as early as 1937 he and his associates met with a Communist party representative who was "assigned to dish out the instructions."

By 1938, Communists had obtained positions of trust, responsibility and authority, giving them complete or partial control in at least 40 per cent of the CIO unions, including the United Automobile Workers; the American Communication Association; the Newspaper Guild; the United Electrical Workers; the Federation of Architects, Engineers, and Technicians; the State, County and Municipal Workers; the National Maritime Union; the Office and Professional Workers, the Woodworkers of America; and the Cannery, Agricultural, Packing and Allied Workers.

Communist influence within the CIO might have continued to grow were it not for the apparent requirement that a Communist leader or trade union serve the immediate ends of the Soviet Union no matter how strange, obvious, or contradictory they might appear. The international developments surrounding the Second World War made that servitude particularly apparent as Communist leadership painfully and dutifully followed the tortuous relationship between the Soviet Union and Nazi Germany. Thus, in 1934, Communists looked upon the New Deal as a "fascist conspiracy," as "the American brother to Mussolini's Corporate State." In 1936, the Communists characterized the Roosevelt victory as that of "the majority . . . against monopoly capital." In August 1939, Earl Browder said that Roosevelt and the New Deal "capitulated to reactionaries."

Prior to the invasion of Poland in September 1939 and the Nazi-Soviet pact, the Communist party was calling for concerted action against "the fascist war makers." Simultaneously, the Nation Maritime Union adopted a resolution urging support "in the fight against fascist aggression," calling for legislation in the Congress. In February 1941, during the period of the Nazi-Soviet Pact, Joe Curran, the Union's International President, led the fight before the Senate Foreign Relations Committee against the lend-lease bill, saying: It "would help drive us into war." In June 1941, a few days after the Nazi invasion of Soviet Russia, the union issued a statement of policy for "full support" of "the present struggle of Great Britain and the Soviet Union against the forces of fascism."

These rapid changes in policy placed an added strain on the

relationship between the Communist and non-Communist forces within the CIO. In a measure, even though each position of the line attracted sympathizers and allies who agreed with the particular policy of the Communist group at the particular time, the constant changes tended to label Communist those who swerved with the Communists at every turn of the road, and also tended to remove doubts as to the primary loyalty of the Communist group to the U. S. S. R. The intensity of the Communists, their eagerness to conform to the Nazi-Soviet pact pattern, led them to undertake an intensive vilification of Roosevelt, who was fashioning American foreign policy in an anti-Nazi direction. This served to heighten tension within the CIO. It in turn stimulated the organization of an anti-Communist revolt.

During the 1940 presidential campaign, an intensive campaign against President Roosevelt was undertaken by the Communists. The Four Horsemen of the Apocalypse threatening the world were identified as "Hitler, Churchill, Roosevelt, and Mussolini." This anti-Roosevelt campaign suited the objectives of John L. Lewis, CIO head, who was involved in a personal vendetta against Roosevelt. Lewis supported the Republican candidate, Wendell Willkie. The Communist line within the CIO was to encourage and support Lewis. At the 1940 CIO convention, following Willkie's defeat when Lewis publicly announced that he would leave his post as CIO president, the Communists attempting to draft him chanted "Lewis is our leader," although a year later, following Russia's entry into the war, Lewis was called "a reactionary" and "an appeaser." The departure of Lewis and the selection of Philip Murray, his close friend and ally, as the new CIO President was to prove to be of great significance in the years to follow. Murray was a strong Democrat, a devout Catholic, a pragmatist—less interested in prophetic pronouncements and more concerned with the practicalities of trade unionism. It is this sensitivity to the practicalities of collective bargaining which early led to tension between Murray and the Communist faction.

To carry out their "isolationist" political objectives during the period from the Nazi-Soviet Pact in 1939 until the invasion of

Russia in June 1941, Communist-led trade unions began a series of strikes designed to hamper and embarrass America's defense efforts. One of the earliest and most famous took place in November 1940, at Vultee Aircraft, a plant of 4,000 workers at Downey, California. Active in the strike was Wyndham Mortimer, who has been termed "a man who has played a large role as a Stalinist agent in American labor for many years." Mortimer, then an international representative of the UAW, was placed in charge of organizing West Coast aircraft workers in 1938. The original dispute between the company and the union was over wages and that was speedily settled. Mortimer, however, broke off negotiations over grievance procedure and a no-strike clause. A twelve-day strike ensued which was finally settled on substantially the same basis offered earlier by the company. It was settled only after pressure had been brought to bear by the War and Justice Departments and a hurried flight had been made by UAW President R. J. Thomas to California. U. S. Attorney General Robert H. Jackson charged Communist inspiration of the strike.

The same Wyndham Mortimer was also prominent in a second West Coast aircraft dispute on June 6, 1941, when 12,000 workers went out at North American Aircraft. Richard Frankensteen, head of the UAW Aircraft division, labeled the strike as Communist-inspired, "an infamous agitation, the vicious maneuverings of the Communist Party is apparent." The strike was finally ended when President Roosevelt ordered the army to take over the plant on June 9, 1941.

A strike of 12,000 International Woodworkers Association members in logging camps and sawmills in the Puget Sound area broke out on May 9, 1941. This strike illustrated very clearly the split within the CIO during this period. The National Defense Mediation Board, of which Philip Murray was a member, attempted to settle the dispute. O. M. Orton, head of the union, walked out of the hearing, calling the Board an "all-out labor-busting and strike-breaking device." Murray immediately excoriated him publicly.

Probably the most serious Communist-inspired defense strike was one of seventy-six days duration at Allis-Chalmers in Milwaukee, February to April 1941. It was sponsored by Local 248 of the UAW, headed by Harold Christoffel. The strike began after eight months of wrangling during which seventeen work stoppages were called. No issue of wages, hours, or conditions was at stake.

Immediately after the invasion of Russia by the Nazis in June 1941, the Communist foreign policy in the United States drastically reversed itself, and this in turn had its equally drastic effect on their trade-union policies. A new "patriotic" policy came into being. From June until Pearl Harbor in December, the Communist position urged American intervention in support if the U.S.S.R. and Great Britain. After Pearl Harbor, the policy was one of all-out effort toward victory. Even with this new policy of patriotism, however, the extremes to which the Communists went served to bring them into occasional conflict with Murray and the rest of the CIO.

Prior to Pearl Harbor, for example, the official CIO positions was one of opposition to peacetime conscription, stemming from a widespread "liberal" reluctance to advance the power of government over the individual, and also from a pacifist orientation within the CIO's "intellectual" ranks. The Communists, on the other hand, fully embraced conscription and enthusiastically endorsed the principle of permanent selective service. This issue remained a troublesome one even after Pearl Harbor. In spite of President Roosevelt's urgings during the war in favor of a national service act, the CIO remained opposed to a labor-conscription program. In spite of that official CIO position, however, legislative representatives from pro-Communist unions continued to support labor conscription in the halls of Congress. This resulted in a great deal of friction within the CIO itself.

There were other evidences of strain between the Communists and anti-Communists during the wartime period. Some CIO leaders were convinced that even though the exigencies of war might call for international unity on the war front, democratic principles and democratic trade unionism were incompatible with the totalitarian nature of the Soviet Union. One of these leaders was CIO secretary-treasurer James B. Carey, who had been ousted as president of the pro-Communist United Electrical Workers after he supported Roosevelt in 1940 and in so doing broke with his mentor John L. Lewis. Carey and other CIO leaders featured in a significant conflict with Communists at this time.

Victor Alter and Henryk Ehrlich, internationally known Socialist leaders in Poland, were arrested in 1939 by the invading Soviet armies on the charge that they had collaborated with fascists. These charges were considered absurd by democratic leaders in the United States because the men were leaders of anti-Nazi opinion in Poland. After first being condemned to death and then having the sentence reduced to ten years at forced labor, they were suddenly released after a general agreement with Poland calling for amnesty of Polish prisoners. Just as suddenly, however, in 1941, they mysteriously disappeared. Inquiries brought only the information that they had been arrested again. Early in 1942, the Russian NKVD ominously declared that the two men were Soviet citizens. In February 1943, Molotov ordered Ambassador Litvinov to inform William Green, president of the AFL, that Alter and Ehrlich had been rearrested after manifesting hostility to the Soviet regime by making "appeals to the Soviet troops to stop bloodshed and immediately to conclude peace with Germany." He said they had been sentenced to death, and concluded, "The sentence has been carried out in regard to both of them." Later, it was learned that they had been killed as early as December 1941, soon after their arrest, so that they were dead even during the time the Soviet was apparently considering protests against their arrest.

In the course of these developments, liberals and labor leaders all over the world intervened. In the United States, distinguished persons, led by Albert Einstein and Eleanor Roosevelt, protested to the Russian government. In New York, a mass protest rally was organized to express America's indignation; after the announcement of the deaths, a memorial meeting was arranged. Mayor La Guardia, William Green, Senator Mead, and other distinguished leaders lent their names as sponsors and were asked to speak. James Carey accepted an invitation and spoke for the CIO.

The Greater New York Council, through Joseph Curran, its head, and Saul Mills, its secretary-treasurer, issued a statement declaring the Alter-Ehrlich meeting motivated "only by a deliberate effort of disruption" against the war effort.

A controversy on this issue also took place within the American Newspaper Guild. The strong New York Guild chapter accused Carey and those associated with him in the Alter-Ehrlich protests of destroying Allied unity. They were then chastised by the International American Newspaper Guild which itself protested the Russian action as a "cruel and unnecessary execution." In fact, the official newspaper, the *Guild Reporter*, carried a cartoon in which a man, labeled "OGPU," is holding a smoking revolver with which he has just murdered Alter and Ehrlich. He is looking in a mirror and his reflection is labeled "Communist Party of America."

All ties of "wartime unity" within the CIO strained and eventually broke as the war came to an end and as tension developed between the United States and the Soviet Union. In 1946, the New York CIO Council, for example, began to protest more actively against American foreign policy, and it picketed Winston Churchill during his visit to New York early that year. The National Maritime Union also stopped work on all ships for twenty-four hours in a political strike aimed at urging the return home of American troops overseas. At the end of the war the Communists' shift in foreign policy gave the anti-Communists within the CIO the cue actively to organize for the internal struggle. The struggle between the factions was to revolve around issues of foreign policy.

The CIO head, Philip Murray, felt unprepared for the struggle that was forming and feared that the division would weaken his organization. He was determined to preserve organic unity. His role was a strange and difficult one in spite of his unequivocal anti-Communism. His objective was to avoid a split within the CIO, and he determined to move slowly. At the 1946 convention of the CIO, at his direction and leadership, it adopted a noncontroversial reaffirmation of democratic faith as an essential part of its policy, including a final paragraph criticizing "the efforts of the Communist Party" and "other political parties and their adherents" to "intervene in the affairs of the CIO." The Communists swallowed hard as they accepted it.

The CIO convention statement on foreign policy that year also avoided a sharp break and attempted to reconcile the differences. A call for an end to the stockpiling of atomic bombs brought forth some criticism from anti-Communists who felt that the Soviet Union should be condemned for refusing to join in the U. S. plan for atomic control. Beginning with 1947, however, the "right wing" began to assert itself and to press for resolutions within the CIO unions and councils endorsing the Marshall Plan, calling for the abolition of veto power within the United Nations, and condemning all forms of totalitarianism.

It was clear that the Communists had been able to carry out a great many of their activities through the Industrial Union Councils that existed in many cities and states. These were organizations of various CIO locals in the same area which joined together to sponsor legislation and other forms of mutual aid. This form of union activity was in the main secondary to the bread-and-butter activity running the day-to-day work of a local union. A great many local unions merely went through the form of belonging to the Industrial Union Council without putting too much time into the activity. This made the councils easily subject to manipulation by Communists. In one geographical area, for example, the Middle West, Communists were in control of the following city and state industrial union councils: Detroit, Des Moines, Omaha, Milwaukee, St. Louis, Minneapolis, St. Paul, Chicago, Cincinnati, Columbus, Kansas City; Indiana, Wisconsin, Missouri, Iowa, Nebraska, Minnesota, and North Dakota.

Beginning with the 1946 convention of the CIO, it was significant that Philip Murray adopted an internal organizational requirement that local and state industrial union councils must confine their activities and statements to issues of local and state concern and could take no positions which conflicted with national CIO policy. They were also prohibited from sending delegates or making contributions to national organizations not recognized by the CIO. It was explained that this policy was essential because "oftentimes strangers have gotten into their midst and offered destructive propaganda."

The year 1947 proved to be a significant one in the CIO struggle against Communist influence. A number of the anti-Communist CIO leaders began openly to identify themselves with the National Conference of Anti-Communist Liberals, which was to become Americans for Democratic Action, and by 1948, the CIO and the ADA were working closely together in American politics. In 1947 too, Communists and "fellow travelers" within the CIO staff in Washington began to resign. Communist support of the CIO Southern Campaign was sharply repudiated. The die seemed to be cast, and by July 1947 Philip Murray was quoted as saying to the members of his executive board, "If Communism is an issue at any of your unions, throw it to hell out . . . and throw its advocates along with it. When a man accepts office . . . the office in a union . . . to render service to workers, and then delivers service to outside interests, that man is nothing but a damned traitor."

Murray invited General George Marshall to address the 1947 convention of the CIO, and the convention formally and enthusiastically supported the Marshall Plan and the Administration's foreign policy. The National Office of the CIO urged its officials and some of its staff members to work with anti-Communist slates within other unions and within industrial union councils. A number of these councils now began to adopt constitutional amendments barring Communists from holding office, declaring, "Communism is alien to the philosophy and desires of the American people."

The creation of the Progressive party in 1948 served once and for all to dramatize the split between the Communists and anti-Communists within the CIO. Michael Quill, head of the Transport Workers Union, later reported that a special Communist caucus took place during the evening prior to the January 1948 meeting of the CIO Executive Board, called by John Williamson, labor secretary of the Communist party. The apparent purpose of the meeting was to prepare for the expected anti-Communist activity at the executive committee board meeting. At the same time, they made plans to fight for resolutions supporting Henry Wallace. At the meeting the following morning, Philip Murray and Harry Bridges, head of the International Longshoremen and Warehousemen's Union, got into a serious dispute with regard to the Marshall Plan. The foreign policy argument that ensued led Murray to charge the existence of Soviet atrocities in Europe with specific reference to Hungary. Communism influence in the Wallace movement became more and more evident to the CIO leaders. The campaign was used as the issue to distinguish the anti-Communists from the pro-Communists and their fellow travelers. During this crisis, Joseph Curran and Michael J. Quill, key trade-union leaders within the CIO Communist caucus, split and joined Murray. Quill told Philip Murray that in 1947 at a meeting of some CIO leaders called by the Communist party, Eugene Dennis, general secretary of the Communist party, and John Williamson, the party's labor secretary, informed the group to disregard everything that happened at the CIO convention in Boston and that "the national leaders . . . of the Communist Party have decided to form a third party led by Henry Wallace." During the 1948 presidential campaign, the CIO spent as much energy attacking Wallace and his candidacy as they did Dewey and the Republican party. It became clear that Murray considered the support of Henry Wallace irreconcilable with loyalty to the CIO.

Quill and Curran's break with the Communist faction was highly significant. They had both been active spokesmen for their group and now set out to destroy Communist influence within their unions and in the CIO. They were fully familiar with their new enemies' technique and objectives. In fact, neither had ever taken great pains to deny their association. On September 23, 1937, speaking to the Rubber Workers Convention, Quill said, "I would rather be called a Red by the rats than a rat by the Reds." In that connection, an interesting colloquy took place at a private CIO hearing between M. Hedley Stone of the National Maritime Union, former member of the Communist party, and Harry Bridges. Stone sought to identify Quill as a former Communist and

Bridges as a Communist. When asked what additional proof he had besides testimony as to meetings that they had attended, Stone said:

> I couldn't prove a duck was a duck, except it looks like a duck and the whole world says "That is a duck," and it quacks like a duck, and that is what I was taught, that it was a duck, and I was raised that way, so until my dying day, until they change a duck to another name, I am going to answer when people point at it that that is a duck.

The House Un-American Activities Committee heard testimony to the effect that Quill had become TWU president after the Communists had instructed his opponent to withdraw so as to make the election unanimous. Former members of the Communist party testified that they had sat in Communist meetings with him, unit 19-S, and had collected his party dues. There was also evidence that he had solicited others to join the party.

There was no doubt that Quill had contributed to Communist publications; that he had supported Communist-front organizations; and that his foreign policy position had followed the Communists through collective security and the American League for Peace and Democracy, on the isolationist American Peace Mobilization, and then on the transformation of the imperialist struggle into a "peoples' war for freedom."

In 1948 at the national CIO convention in Portland, Oregon, the drive against the Communists continued to gain momentum. A number of industrial union council charters were revoked. Additional resignations within the CIO staff and more open anti-Communist activity by responsible CIO leaders took place.

In the two years since Murray had begun associating himself with the move against Communists in the CIO, the unions in which Communist influence was strong had decreased to about 15 per cent of the CIO membership, as compared to the earlier 25 per cent. The only large union still in pro-Communist hands was the United Electrical Workers with its 500,000 members.

The Portland convention turned out to be a costly one for the Communists. "We either have a policy in this movement or we do not have a policy," Murray asserted as he criticized the "ideological dive-bombers," "pouting people," "small cliques," "degraded thinkers," "dry-rot leaders," "afflictions on mankind." Walter Reuther, just as explicit but milder, put it this way: ". . . either get clear in the CIO or get clear out." Summarizing the year, A. H. Raskin, skilled labor reporter for *The New York Times*, said: "Eliminating Communist influence is an essential preliminary to building a sound labor movement, in the opinion of Mr. Murray and the rest of the CIO high command."

The following year, 1949, was spent establishing a basis for the final elimination of Communist influence within the CIO. By the time the national CIO convention met in November, the leaders were ready to deal with the Communist problem directly. A resolution was passed expelling the UE as "the Communist Party masquerading as a labor union" and chartering a successor union in its jurisdiction. This union was strong, ideologically committed, and militant. Its founding president, James B. Carey, secretary-treasurer of the national CIO, had been ousted from office in 1941, charged with "red-baiting." He began an effort to oust the Communists from control and, although without a union base, became a highly irritating thorn in the side of the Communists. The UE was in a very strategic position affecting national defense before and during the war. About three-fourths of its membership was employed in defense industries, manufacturing aircraft and marine equipment, gauges, aerial cameras, motors, and cartridges. On August 1, 1948, the *Daily Worker* declared: ". . . the main industrial base of our party is in electrical. That base which is weak and shaky must be guaranteed and strengthened." Carey, with the help of Murray, Reuther, and other CIO leaders, was now prepared to take the membership of the union away from Communist control.

The 1949 convention also voted to expel the Farm Equipment Workers Union. Charges were also brought against ten other international unions on the ground that they were "consistently directed toward the achievement of a program or the purposes of the Communist party rather than the objectives and policies set forth in the constitution of the CIO."

Mr. Murray named a committee to hear the charges, evidence, and testimony against the accused unions and to decide whether their charters should be revoked by the CIO executive board. Hearings began in December 1949. As a result, in 1950, four unions with fewer than 100,000 members were expelled from the CIO. They were the United Office and Professional Workers; the United Public Workers; the Food, Tobacco and Agricultural Workers; and the Mine, Mill and Smelter Workers. The cause of the expulsions was clearly stated:

. . . the Communist movement, from its inception, purported to be a movement of working people. Its basic thesis was that a new order of society must be created by revolution of the working classes and that the "dictatorship of the proletariat" must be established. Because of this basic thesis, Communist philosophy has always been predicated upon the use of trade unions as an instrument of Communist policy and as a weapon by which the Party would emerge. . . . The Communist movement has thus always sought to operate through trade unions, to speak in the language of labor and as a spokesman and leader of labor, and thus, by trickery and stratagem, to direct labor toward the goals of Communism.

Communist activity, the report added:

. . . is based upon one fundamental objective—the support of the Soviet Union, the country in which the Communist Party first achieved its goal of dictatorship. . . . The policies which the Party adopts are stated to be policies for the achievements of the goals of American labor—not for the advancement of the cause of the Soviet Union. But over a period of years, it is clear that the goals of American labor, as stated by the Party, are always found to be those policies which will aid the Soviet Union. As the tactical position of the Soviet Union in the world has changed, the program of the American Communist Party "for American labor" has accommodated itself. And, when it seemed in the interests of the Soviet Union for American labor to forsake its heritage and to adopt policies contradictory to the whole fabric of the labor movement, the Communist Party adopted such policies.

Shortly thereafter, following additional hearings, the American Communications Association, the International Longshoremen and Warehousemen Union, the National Union of Marine Cooks and Stewards, and the International Fur and Leather Workers Union—the remaining Communist-led unions within the CIO— were expelled.

A most interesting by-product of the trials is found in a description of the activities of two former union officials. Their lives reveal something of the operations of the Communist party within the union and the impact of those operations on the individuals caught in the net.

First is Homer Wilson, who lived in Strawberry Plains, Tennessee. He became a member of the Mine, Mill and Smelter Workers Union in October 1934, when that union was affiliated with the AFL. His fellow members and mine workers elected him to serve first as union committeeman and then as local union president. As a local president, he became acquainted with staff members of the union. They told him that they belonged to the Communist party and discussed party activities in his presence. They were men of superior education who impressed him. In 1941, they invited him to become an international organizer. In 1942, he was elected to represent the Southern District as a member of the international executive board. He assumed office in January 1943, working out of the Alabama office.

> As quick as I got down there, Mrs. Franz and Alton Laurence invited me to lunch with them along with Mr. Rob Hall, who was an organizer for the Communist Party. I had lunch with them, and we discussed problems then facing the Mine, Mill and Smelter Workers in that area, and they also pointed out to me their contacts throughout the International Union.

Wilson was impressed with the fact that the party had a great deal of influence within the union and that "it would be to my advantage to join the Party." He apparently did not formally join, but "I give it a lot of consideration." The Communist party at this time strongly supported the war and was thoroughly patriotic.

There was, therefore, no reason for Wilson to see any conflict between his American loyalties and his friendship for the Communist party.

One other factor impressed him. "This Mr. Hall that was the party organizer was a very highly educated man, and I liked to associate with him at that time. In fact, I got him to help me with a report I had to draw up for a district conference, and he did a very good job on it." Mr. Hall seemed accustomed to these chores for the unions as part of his party activities: "He said he done that for all of the Mine-Mill organizers, and some other CIO unions in that area."

When Mr. Wilson became a member of the union's executive board in January 1943, he joined the pro-Communist caucus, since it seemed to be the pattern which brought him prestige, influence, and the satisfaction of associating with better-educated people. Nor did belonging begin to embarrass him before 1946, for his union's policies were strongly in support of his government's policies.

The life of our second man, Kenneth Eckert, tells a more sophisticated and interesting story. Eckert was born and raised in Toledo, Ohio. He worked on a railroad until 1930 but during the Depression was laid off along with thousands of others. He joined an organization called the Unemployment Councils in Toledo which he later found was organized by the Communist party to promote the interests of the unemployed. Its announced aims seemed worthy. The councils wanted to obtain unemployment relief, and sought to find homes for the evicted.

> I found out later, however, when I came to learn more about these things, that the misery and grief of the unemployed, and the organizations created to capitalize on that, that the intention was merely to use those organizations as a transmission belt, as has often been said, and said originally by Lenin, in order to carry out the policies of the Communist Party, and extend them to a broader mass of people who could be brought into such an organization but would not be ready to accept the program of the Communist Party as such.

Eckert soon became head of the organization and led many of its demonstrations. He organized a camp of unemployed on the Toledo courthouse lawn at the time of an American Legion convention. Later, in his own township of Washington, where relief had been cut off, he helped organize about a thousand people who walked into the largest store of a food market chain in Toledo "and cleaned it out."

Following these activities, early in 1932, Eckert accepted an invitation to join the Communist party, although he had "very little or no knowledge of what it stood for, its principles, or [knew] very much about it." He had, however, some knowledge "of the broad concept of socialism, my former father-in-law having been a member of the Socialist party during the first World War and after that for some time." Within a few months, he was approached by the district organizer of the Communist party in Toledo who informed him that he had been selected by the party to attend a party school. Eckert welcomed the opportunity, although he did not know the school's location. It developed that the school was the International Lenin School at Moscow, "located on Vorofskaya Street, the former palace of one of the favorites of Catherine the Great who had had it built for one of her lovers, Pushkin." Eckert spent fourteen months at the Lenin School. When he returned, Communist leader John Williamson told him to resume his activities in the unemployment movement. In Toledo, however, he was assigned to become an organizer for the Trade Union Unity League in the automobile industry. He also organized a local in Toledo and participated in other labor disputes. In 1934, the *Literary Digest* accused Eckert and Louis Budenz of leading the violent Electric Auto Lite strike.

His next assignment was as secretary of the Communist party in Toledo. He stayed there until the Trotskyite trials in Russia, when he was removed from his post for alleged Trotskyite tendencies. He then went to the West Coast and to sea. Later he returned to Michigan where he became an organizer for the National Association of Die Casting Workers and then Chicago regional director for that union.

Eckert then entered the army and spent a year overseas. His services brought him in contact with a large number of Russian displaced persons. This contact he said, helped him to break intellectually with the Communist party, even though the organizational break didn't come until later. He queried, with his "smattering of Russian and a few words in German," all Russians he could meet "to find out pretty much just what things were like since he had been in Russia in 1933."

Following the war, the Communist party again made overtures to Eckert, who was reinstated to membership and became active. The reconciliation proved temporary.

Eckert's final summary to the CIO investigating committee is worth quoting for a further understanding of the operations of Communist control within labor unions:

To summarize what I have said here, gentlemen of the Committee, I have tried to show here insofar as I have personal knowledge of these events, and insofar as I have been personally involved in them, that the allegations made against the union are correct, are absolutely true. The Communist Party, through having counseled the leadership, through its influence in the leadership of this union, first of all through the top leadership, and secondly, this leadership, who hired the staff members—these staff members, who are in almost every instance members of the Communist Party, are the people who negotiate the contracts for the rank and file, for the local unions, who are the people who are able to influence the people in the local unions. It is this machine set up, top leaders of the organization down through the staff members, who are able to transmit the decisions from these people outside the union to the union itself, and to make it the policy of this Mine, Mill and Smelter Workers. It is by that method, followed over a considerable number of years in Mine-Mill, that builds the record, as I stated in my opening remarks, for anyone to see where the policy of the Mine, Mill and Smelter Workers deviates not one iota from the position of the Communist Party, although as I said previously, many people sincerely believe that they are following the correct policy.

The decisiveness of the CIO victory over the Communist party is in a measure illustrated by the fact that Communist-led unions in 1949 claimed a membership of more than two million and are today estimated to represent no more than a few tens of thousand workers. The real measure and significance of the outcome, however, must be spelled out in broader terms. Equally important are the lessons learned from the experience.

The trade union is an important seat of power in a democracy. How does a union leadership in our society continue to maintain its hold on the membership while carrying the union through contortions which lead ultimately to a thoroughly unpatriotic political position? The power of nationalism and patriotism is great, and their hold on American citizens has been a potent fact in our history. Yet many thousands of American citizens have supported Communists as their union leaders, and even today some continue to vote for these leaders in secret elections under government supervision in the face of a barrage of hostile editorial comment, speeches, and Congressional investigations which expose their leaders as Communists. Various explanations suggest themselves.

To begin with, we must note the climate which permitted the Communists to gain their initial power and influence. The period beginning with 1933 was characterized by increasing acceptance of the Soviet Union in public opinion and intellectual circles. It was also a period of extraordinary fluidity in the labor movement, since new organizational vistas were opening and there was a dearth of competent union leadership to explore them. It is also clear in retrospect that where established unions had firm leadership, as in the garment and clothing trades, the Communists made little headway, but where that leadership was not strong, as in the electrical and automobile industries, or was corrupt and ineffective, the Communists were able to fill the vacuum and establish control.

Second, Communist success in gaining and keeping influence and control is partially explained by their mastery of the techniques of group organization and manipulation. Decision-making within a Communist-dominated union is always, as we saw demonstrated with the Mine, Mill and Smelter Workers, the seamen's unions, and the Transport Workers Union, controlled by the party faction. On occasion, the party faction will utilize "front" leadership; thus Albert Fitzgerald, a Catholic, became president of the Electrical Workers. Even where "front" leadership exists, however, key members of the Communist party are placed in strategic positions within the union; the office of secretary-treasurer is one such post, the editorship of the union newspaper is another.

The manipulation of democratic procedures so as to yield results beneficial to the Communist minority is an established technique of Communist control. One of the important and significant characteristics of American trade unions, as of voters generally, is a tendency toward apathy. The typical union member frequently has little desire to attend a meeting after his day's work is done. He would far rather go to a movie, watch television, or seek other forms of personal pleasure. He is quite content to leave all business matters of his union in the hands of his officers and a few active members. This is true so long as these officers and leaders are able to win economic gains. Union leaders interested in developing membership participation have had to resort to such devices as door prizes and fines to stimulate participation. Union leaders interested in maintaining minority control merely take advantage of this apathy. Communists usually come to union meetings well organized and well caucused. Many of them will be fully instructed with resolutions all prepared in their pockets. The evidence is likewise clear that the caucus is usually trained and disciplined and prepared to stall all night at a meeting in order to exhaust the non-Communist members present. Another well calculated technique used by the Communists is that of undermining and discrediting the opposition. This is usually accomplished by slogans, violent denunciations, and disciplinary action against opponents who are labeled "racists," "labor saboteurs," and "scabs," among other things.

An additional refinement of this technique is the occasional use of violence and intimidation. The National Union of Marine Cooks and Stewards affords a good case in point. A thorough study of that union's control mechanism was undertaken in 1952 by the Senate Subcommittee on Labor and Labor-Management

Relations with the cooperation of the National Labor Relations Board. Senator Hubert H. Humphrey in his introduction to the study pointed out that the leaders of the union were able to remain in control "by terrorizing the real and imagined dissidents within the union, by depriving critics of their jobs, by slander, vilification; by intimidating government witnesses to its illegal activities, by perverting the union's judicial machinery into an instrument of reprisal, by intimidating the employers into becoming parties to their totalitarian methods. In brief, this Communist-dominated union has remained in power by corrupting the basic democracy of a union to create a little totalitarian system of its own."

The intimidation was both physical and economic. In one case, the wife of a member of the opposition group was beaten in her home. Anti-Communists risked being beaten or threatened by officers of the union or by hangers-on around the union hall when they came in the vicinity. Attempts by anti-Communists to obtain jobs also met with great difficulty because of the union hiring-hall provision which had been entered into between the union and the management. The hiring hall, normally a useful mechanism for stabilizing the hiring policies in the maritime industry, was perverted into an instrument of attrition against opposition elements within the union. Employers, to avoid trouble, permitted themselves to become agents through which the union leadership imposed its rule of terrorism and discrimination against all who dared to oppose its Communist policies.

A third possible explanation for Communist power within the American labor movement is the fact that union members have frequently demonstrated their ability to compartmentalize their loyalties. The members of the United Mine Workers had proved their trade union loyalty to John L. Lewis on many occasions, but then voted for Roosevelt and not for Willkie in 1940. The labor movement in Ohio is a strong one with a loyal membership which has gained many concessions from employers, but union members did not follow the leadership of their trade-union officers in 1950 when these leaders urged support of Mr. Ferguson

COMMUNISTS IN THE C.I.O. : 373

against Mr. Taft for United States Senator. In the same way, it is clear that members of Communist-led unions continue to support their trade union in collective bargaining arrangements while they often silently ignore the political recommendations of the unions' leadership.

There is a fourth possible explanation. Some of the Communist-led unions had achieved maturity, stability, and harmonious relations with management. A union such as the Fur and Leather Workers, for example, has been able to realize high wages, reasonable hours, and good working conditions within the industry. One labor historian evaluated these factors in the following manner:

> Like the rank and file workers in other industries, members of the Fur Union are concerned with immediate improvements and pay little heed to the ultimate goals and objectives of the union leadership. The fact that Communists dominate the union has not frightened members, especially since many of the members have radical inclinations. Nor are they deeply interested in the part that the union plays in the larger labor movement, as long as wages go up, hours go down, and working conditions improve.

In the fur industry, the union's position has been so strong as to establish a feeling among many of the smaller fur manufacturers that the union could force them out of business if it should be so inclined. The great economic strength of the union—which has meant great economic gains for the members—has kept many members loyal to it in spite of the political views of its leaders. This is equally true in many other Communist-led unions.

Fifth, the cry "Communist" has been used so often by antilabor employers and editorial writers to besmirch the legitimate aspirations of trade unionism that many workers have become suspicious of such charges. This, no doubt, explains in part why Harry Bridges is able to continue his control over the West Coast longshoremen and the Communist leadership of the International Union of Mine, Mill and Smelter Workers maintains its power.

Finally, we must understand that the revolutionary political philosophy of Communist trade unionism is most frequently not discernible in the collective bargaining policy of the unions. Collective bargaining has not been used by the Communists to achieve Communism in America nor to achieve the economic revolution they advocate. It would be difficult to distinguish between the CIO International Union of Electrical Workers and the independent Communist-led United Electrical Workers on the basis of the minimum contract standards of these two unions. The economic demands of Communist-led unions have on the whole been orthodox trade-union demands. In fact, no innovation in collective bargaining techniques or demands can be attributed to the Communists or to their unions. The innovations resulted from the leadership of the non-Communist Unions. Product royalties for welfare funds, for example, were pioneered by the miners and by the musicians; unemployment assistance by the International Ladies' Garment Workers Union and the Amalgamated Clothing Workers Union; pensions by the miners, steelworkers, and auto workers; the guaranteed annual wage by the UAW and UE and Steelworkers; health benefits by the Amalgamated Streetcar Employees and the ILGWU.

The differences arise where the interests of the Soviet Union are involved. Prior to World War II, during the Communist "isolationist" period, there were Communist-led strikes in plants doing defense work, such as North American, Vultee Aircraft, and Allis Chalmers. During the war, Harry Bridges led his union into an active policy of collaboration with employers and no-strike pledges on the waterfront. During the war, too, the UE and other Communist-led unions actively supported wage-incentive plans as their contribution to a "win the war program," a line which ran counter to the traditional opposition of American unions to "speed-up" in industry.

There is very little evidence to show that the Communists seek to achieve economic revolution or the overthrow of capitalism through the trade-union movement. There is, however, overwhelming evidence that the goal of Communists in the trade-union movement is support of Soviet strategy in foreign affairs, regardless of what that strategy happens to be at any particular moment. Communist unionism, therefore, does not so much represent a trade-union philosophy in any meaningful sense of the term as a system of power.

The traditions of the American labor movement are quite hostile to the philosophy of Communism. The philosophy of the American labor movement, insofar as it is possible to speak of its philosophy, is one of humanism. This humanistic approach explains why it is that the American labor movement has not considered itself as representative of narrow class or sectional interests, but rather of the broad mass of the population.

The tradition of humanism within the American labor movement helps explain why the Communists, in spite of their skill, zeal, and dedication, were unable to make even greater headway than they did. A study of labor history shows that there have never been any AFL international unions under Communist control. There are today no unions under Communist control in the merged AFL-CIO. And even at the height of their influence within the CIO, Communist-controlled unions accounted for more than 25 per cent of the total CIO membership.

The Communist party could not successfully adjust to the prevailing philosophy of humanism within the American labor movement. Its inflexible loyalty to the immediate interests of the Soviet Union made it impossible for the Communist party, and for Communist-led unions, to adapt to the shifting attitudes of Americans toward the Soviet Union. The Communist could demonstrate his loyalty only by absolute conformity to the party. He could not, dared not, and did not criticize the Soviet Union.

It is this characteristic of inflexibility and rigidity on behalf of the Soviet Union which has made it possible to identify Communist trade-union leaders and thus strengthen those who would negate their influence. Here, indeed, is the Achilles' heel of Communist trade unionism in America.

COMMUNISM AND INDIGENOUS SOCIAL REFORM PARTIES IN LATIN AMERICA

Robert J. Alexander

■ *In the following essay Professor Robert J. Alexander discusses the efforts of Communists and indigenous reform parties to capture the leadership of the social revolution which is underway in Latin America. Professor Alexander's treatment of this subject not only reflects his broad knowledge of Latin American society and politics, but also demonstrates the importance of avoiding historicism in the analysis of social change.*

Understanding the character and direction of social change in progress in Latin American society, Professor Alexander understands too that the ultimate course and consequences of this change depend on who is able to organize it. Genuinely spontaneous mass action is not only exceedingly rare, but it cannot be sustained. To affect the structures of power, mass demands and expectations must be organized. They may be either represented or manipulated by the organizations which serve as spokesmen of them. Demagogues and/or Communists typically seek power by tactical identification with the demands of discontented persons. Here lies the basic difference between Communist and indigenous social reform parties in Latin America. The reform parties are the outgrowth of indigenous protests and aspirations. They share indigenous reform values as well as express them. Communist parties in Latin America, as elsewhere, seek power in the name of reformist hopes and expectations, in order to accomplish ends unrelated to them. They advocate distribution of land to peasants in order to achieve collectivization. Again in Latin America, we see that Communist parties grow by concealing their own values.

Robert Alexander, a Professor of Latin American history at Rutgers University, carefully leads the reader through the diverse patterns of social and political development which characterize the Latin American scene and analyzes factors working for and against the emergence of Communist regimes in these countries. Professor Alexander is the author of Communism in Latin America, Prophets of Revolution, and other books on the area. His articles on Latin American society and politics have appeared in a wide range of journals. ▪

Latin America is in the midst of a profound social revolution. The future of the Western Hemisphere depends largely on whether the leadership of that revolution remains in the hands of indigenous political groups or is seized by Communist parties. The Communists, though they try to confuse the issue as much as possible, are well aware of what is at stake. If their opponents in Latin America are to see the situation clearly, they must carefully distinguish between the indigenous forces working for social change and those under the control of Moscow and Peiping.

The Communists of Latin America have followed the general pattern of Communism throughout the world. As a result their attitude toward rival parties, and particularly toward indigenous social reform parties, has varied widely from time to time. The purpose of this chapter will be to trace the approach of Latin American Communists to these indigenous groups, which represent the most important obstacle to Communist success, and to draw certain conclusions from this. First, however, we shall note certain general characteristics of the Communist movement in Latin America and briefly describe the indigenous social reform parties.

General Characteristics of Latin American Communists

One fundamental fact must be stressed in discussing Latin American Communist parties: they are an integral part of the world Communist movement. Latin American Communists have benefited from time to time from the kind of wishful thinking which for a number of years obscured the real nature of the Chinese Communist party. For example, it has been argued that they are "merely agrarian reformers," or that they are "more Latin American than Communist." All such statements are completely unfounded. Although the Latin American Communists have with some difficulty adapted themselves to the milieu in which they operate, nonetheless they have been as genuinely servants of Lenin, Stalin and Khrushchev as have their confreres in every other part of the world.

From the earliest days, the international Communist apparatus has been at work in the Latin American countries. In 1919 and the following years, a delegation of the Comintern which included the Russian Borodin, the Japanese Sen Katayama, and the Indian M. N. Roy, operated in Mexico in order to organize affiliates of the Comintern in the Latin American countries. During the 1920's and 1930's, a Latin American bureau of the Comintern had its headquarters in Montevideo and actively intervened in the internal affairs of the various national Communist parties. Throughout this period, various Latin Americans served on the Executive Committee of the Comintern, and the Latin American parties were represented at Congresses of the Communist International.

During the existence of the Comintern, the International did not hesitate to interfere openly in the day-to-day activities of the various Latin American Communist parties. During one of several conflicts within the Argentine party, the Comintern threw its support to Victorio Codovilla, thus giving him control of the party—which he has maintained ever since. In the 1920's the Montevideo bureau of the Comintern ousted the leadership of the Chilean party at a time when that group was fighting bitterly against the dictatorship of General Carlos Ibáñez. In 1929 the Comintern rejected a plan of the Peruvian Communists to launch a legal "Socialist party" as a front for their activities. And as late as 1940, a Comintern representative ousted the whole top leadership of the Mexican Communist party.

Since the dissolution of the Comintern, the relationships between the Latin American parties and Moscow have been less obvious but just as real. Leaders of the various parties frequently visit Moscow either for political directions or for training. There is good evidence that some of the parties receive financial help from the international Communist apparatus. The activities of the Latin American parties were carefully recorded and commented upon by the Cominform's pamphlet *For a Lasting Peace, for a People's Democracy*. Latin American Communist leaders have manned the staffs of collateral Communist organizations such as the World Federation of Trade Unions.

The Latin American Communists have followed all the twists and turns of the international apparatuses political line. During the period from the founding of the Comintern until Lenin's death, the Latin American parties, like those elsewhere, were consolidated into organizations "of a new type," and anarcho-syndicalists, left-wing Socialists and other non-Bolsheviks, who had at first been attracted to the movement were weeded out. During the late 1920's, concurrent with the struggle for power in the Soviet Union, there were bitter factional fights in the Latin American parties which in one way or another were assimilated into the Soviet struggle. Since the victory of Stalin in the Soviet Union and the Comintern, the Latin American parties have been as monolithic and subject to the "cult of leadership" as any in the world.

During the Third Period, the Latin American Communists played their part by being as sectarian and superrevolutionary as anyone in Moscow could have desired. In the succeeding Popular Front period of the Comintern, the Latin Americans completely reversed their position, becoming the friends of everybody, including a number of Latin American dictators. Once again they shared the general Communist isolation during the Nazi-Soviet

Pact days, and then with the attack on the Soviet Union by Hitler, they joined once more in a super-Popular Front.

Since the end of the Second World War, too, the Latin American Communists have followed the general line of the international Communist movement. They have stressed anti-United States agitation at the expense of everything else and they have attempted to picture themselves as the most extreme of nationalists—at least wherever their countries' relations with the United States were concerned. Like Communists everywhere they have followed a more flexible and opportunistic policy in the affairs of their own countries.

Throughout the existence of the various Latin American Communist parties, there has been one thread running through all their changes of policy—namely, support for and subordination to the Soviet Union. In 1929 the Communist parties of Latin America declared that their principal duty was "defense of the Soviet Union." In 1945 each Latin American party in turn followed the lead of Brazilian Communist leader Luiz Carlos Prestes in proclaiming that in the event of a conflict between their country and the Soviet Union they would automatically side with the U.S.S.R. At the present time, a good part of the propaganda of the Latin American Communist parties is devoted to praising the accomplishments of the Soviet Union and other members of the Communist bloc and in stressing the Soviet Union's alleged role as leader of the "forces of peace."

No deviation relative of the Soviet Union is permitted within the ranks of the Latin American Communist parties. It is significant that no Latin American Communist party has suffered the kind of crisis experienced by the British and American Communist parties as the result of the Khrushchev speech and Hungary. Only a few second-rank leaders here and there in Latin America faltered as a result of these events.

Whereas loyalty to the Soviet Union has been one of the lodestars of Communist behavior in Latin America, persistence on the path toward dictatorial power within their own respective countries has been the other. They have used any means to get added influence for their parties: working with dictators; democrats; social reform parties; or even with extreme conservatives. Whatever has seemed useful at the moment has become policy. During the late 1940's and early 1950's, the tactic of "dual Communism" was adopted in a number of countries in which there were dictatorships. The parties split, one faction supporting the dictatorship and "helping" it run the labor movement, the other opposing the dictatorship and trying to inveigle the opposition into a united front.

Usually the Communists have been far from achieving their goal of dictatorial domination of the country in which they were operating. However, in two instances they came close, and in one they succeeded. In 1946-1947 three Communists served in the first Cabinet of President Gabriel González Videla of Chile, and during this period—which this writer witnessed on the spot—they behaved toward other political groups, particularly in the labor movement, as if they already had power in their hands. They used terror against their rivals on the Left and in the trade unions, terror which included the murder of some second-rank opposition leaders. They did not gain through this terrorism, however. Power was not yet really theirs, and President González Videla used the first available opportunity to get rid of the Communists in his Cabinet, later becoming their most bitter enemy.

In Guatemala in the early 1950's, the Communists had their second chance. There they used their close personal relationship with President Jacobo Arbenz and their control of the labor movement and key governmental institutions, to try to force all other government parties into a "United Democratic Front" to which these other parties would have been subordinated and of which they would have been the masters. The overthrow of President Arbenz in July 1954 short-circuited these plans.

The Communist finally achieved power in Cuba following the overthrow of the military dictatorship of Fulgencio Batista in 1959. This was their first success in the Americas. Although the movement led by Fidel Castro was not Communist, pro-Communist elements had a leading role in it. By the end of 1959 this pro-Communist element had seized control of the movement and the government. Final victory of the Communists was sealed in July 1961, when the remnants of the Fidelista movement merged with the Communist party of Cuba, with the Communist party members holding all key positions in the merged group.

The power and influence of the Latin American Communists has varied from time to time and from country to country. In general, they were strongest during the Popular Front period of the late 1930's, during and immediately after World War II and after the victory of Fidel Castro in 1959. They were weakest in their periods of sectarian isolation. Their influence, except in Guatemala, declined a great deal in the years after World War II. However, there are now Communist parties in every Latin American country; they remain potentially a force to be reckoned with throughout the hemisphere, and they are actually in power in one of the twenty republics.

The Communists have met varying attitudes on the part of government of the Latin American countries; one cannot describe a consistent pattern in their reception. Some democratic governments like those of González Videla in Chile in 1946-1947, Lázaro Cárdenas in Mexico in the late 1930's, or Arevalo in Gatemala in the late 1940's have been friendly toward the Communists. Other democratic regimes have been hostile to the point of outlawing the local Communist party. On the other hand during the same periods dictatorial regimes such as that of Batista in the late 1930's and early 1940's, of Trujillo in the Dominican Republic in 1946-1947, of Pérez Jiménez in Venezuela in the early 1950's, and of Odría in Peru, have been very friendly to the Communists. Other dictators have suppressed the Communists as they have suppressed every opposition or potential opposition group.

Three things are clear, however. First, dictators generally have no principled reason for opposing the Communists and will work with them while posing as "anti-Communists" if that seems expedient. Second, the Communists have no principled reason for opposing the dictators and will work closely with them if there is something to be gained for their party or if the dictator is anti-United States.

Third, local dictatorships provide, in any case, no real protection against the spread of Communist influence. This is true not only because the Communists may work with the dictators and spread their own influence at a time when democratic opposition groups cannot function adequately, but also because when the Communists are persecuted along with other parties by the dictatorships, they know more than most democratic groups about how to conduct underground activities. The Communists' sharing of persecution by a hated tyrant tends to obscure the differences between them and the other groups which oppose the dictator.

That the dictatorships are no brake on the development of the Communists is demonstrated by the examples of Peru and Venezuela. From 1948 to 1956 in the first case and from 1948 to 1958 in the latter, these nations were submitted to the rigid dictatorships of Generals Manuel Odría and Marcos Pérez Jiménez, respectively. The Communists in both countries split, one faction backing the tyrant, the other opposing him. When the regimes were ousted, it was obvious that the Communists had an influence, prestige and power such as they had never enjoyed in the period before the dictatorial regimes seized control.

Nature of the Latin American Social Revolution

The only groups in Latin America which can really effectively fight the Communists for any long period of time are the indigenous groups seeking social change. These groups appeal to the same elements in the population as do the Communists; they present programs which meet the widespread popular demand for social, economic, and political reform. They have the advantage over the Communists in that they have some real possibility of carrying out their promises and can do so without subordinating their countries to totalitarianism and control from abroad.

Before we can adequately understand the nature and role of the indigenous social reform parties, we must examine the nature of the transformation which Latin America is undergoing. This movement of change has been fundamentally altering the pattern of life which has existed in most Latin American countries virtually since they achieved their independence a century and a quarter ago.

Before the First World War, most Latin American countries were dominated by a land-holding aristocracy, which was small in number, but controlled most of the wealth-producing resources of the country. Allied with them were small mercantile groups in the cities and the equally small professional classes, usually recruited from the other two groups. The great mass of the people lived on the land in a state of semiservitude. In the Indian countries (Mexico, Guatemala, Peru, Ecuador, Bolivia) and in some others, the peasants were semiserfs, cultivating the landlord's acres and rendering him personal service in return for the right to farm a very small portion of land to provide their families with a miserable existence. In other countries the social and economic institutions of a slave plantation economy persisted although the legal institution of slavery had disappeared in America by the end of the nineteenth century.

The nations' political and cultural life was monopolized by the small oligarchy as was their economy. Politics was a game played by the ruling classes and the top military men, although the elite would sometimes recruit members of the lower classes into their contending armies in the frequent civil wars. Generally, the illiterate population, an overwhelming majority of the people, was barred from voting, and even where it was given the franchise, it was usually forced to vote as the landlords and employers dictated.

This system was an inheritance of colonial days. The wars of independence had had little practical result in terms of the great masses of the people, they did little more than substitute native landlords and merchants for the former appointees of the "mother country" in the offices of government, and give the local armies a large say in the management of public affairs.

Undoubtedly the first influence which began to undermine this ancient social, economic, and political system was the demand from Europe and the United States for the agricultural and mineral products these Latin countries were capable of producing. In Argentina, Britain's demand for grains and meats resulted in the development of commercial agriculture throughout the Pampas, in the construction of a large railway network to get these products to the ports, and in the conversion of Buenos Aires into a large modern city. In Chile the demand for nitrates and later for copper had a profound effect. In Mexico the development of mining and petroleum, in several countries the growth of coffee production, in still others the growing demand for sugar, all had a deep impact on the established way of life.

These export industries, which generally grew up on the margin of the traditional agricultural economy (though they sometimes influenced the whole of agriculture), had a number of effects. They developed large groups of wage workers for the first time, gave a general impulse to the expansion of the Latin American nations' economies, and strengthened the cities politically. They also made the economies of these countries dependent upon world trade in a way which they never had been before. The export products came to represent a large proportion of the total national income, and in return for these products the Latin American countries bought increasing amounts of manufactured goods from abroad. The slightest alteration in demand or price of the goods which these countries were exporting could profoundly effect the lives of many thousands of people dependent directly or indirectly on the export-import trade.

At the same time that this change was occurring in the economies of the Latin American countries, these nations were being influenced by political developments in other parts of the world. The upper classes, particularly the intellectuals, had always tended to copy the ideas which were in fashion in Europe and to a lesser degree in the United States. Hence, the extension of political democracy in Europe had already begun to have its impact on Latin America before World War I. The democratic slogans of that war, the resurgence of nationalism in many countries as a result of it, and most particularly the Bolshevik Revolution in Russia, had profound effects on the thinking of the Latin American intellectuals, through whom they were transmitted to other elements in the society.

Meanwhile, almost by accident, the first contemporary Latin American social upheaval had gotten under way in Mexico with the outbreak of the Mexican revolution in 1910. Although this began as a mere attempt to keep Porfirio Diaz, who had been dictator for thirty-five years, from re-electing himself again, it soon took a different path. Many of those recruited into the revolutionary armies sought to give another content to the movement, to use it to right the wrongs of the peasants, the urban workers, and the Indians and mestizos who made up the great majority of the population. Their point of view won out, and the Mexican revolution became a movement for agrarian reform, extensive labor and social legislation, trade unionism, the expression of Mexican nationalism, and for the development of the nation's economy and the raising of the standards of living of its people. It is important to note that the Mexican revolution antedated that of Russia by eight years, and that the revolutionary constitution of 1917 was promulgated two months before the abdication of the Czar.

The First World War had another effect. It stimulated the industrialization of Latin America. These countries were cut off for a time from the nations to which they had sold their export products, and throughout the war they were unable to get the manufactured goods which they needed in sufficient quantity. The upshot of this was that they began to produce many of these products for themselves on a considerable scale. Although the rhythm of industrialization subsided after the war, it was revived again during the Great Depression when the failure of the great industrial powers to buy Latin American agricultural and mineral products meant that the Latin American countries did not have sufficient foreign exchange to buy the manufactured goods they needed. Again forced to provide for themselves, most Latin Americans became convinced that their government should give support to and actively encourage the growth of manufacturing. This belief was reinforced during World War II when the experience of the previous war was repeated.

The Latin American social revolution can be said to have begun during World War I. Today it is a movement which seeks four kinds of change. First, it seeks an alteration in class relationships. With the growth of industry and the cities, power has been passing from the rural and commercial oligarchies to the middle and lower classes of the cities. This has stimulated demands for agrarian reform, trade unionism, social and labor legislation, and universal education.

Second, the Latin American social revolution has sought to assert the national sovereignty of the particular countries. Although politically independent republics, there was a widespread feeling that the Latin American states were economically "semicolonial," since many of their principal resources were being exploited by foreign firms. In addition, their economies depended on international markets for their chief exports, markets which were controlled in the great industrial countries not in the Latin American nations. Therefore, there has been a demand for transfer of key industries—public utilities, sometimes mining and petroleum, to the hands of nationals or governments of the Latin American countries, and for control by these governments of the whole process of foreign investment within their frontiers.

Third, there has been an extensive demand for economic development, which has sought to provide the Latin American countries with more balanced economies. In this way countries would be less subject to the vagaries of international markets which, in the opinion of most Latin Americans, would increase the peoples' standard of living considerably.

Finally, the Latin American social revolution has often incorporated a demand for the extension of political democracy. This has meant not only the transfer of effective political power to the masses, but also the guarantee of the individual rights of freedom of speech, press, assembly, and belief.

It is in this last area that the Latin American social revolution is threatened. There are those—among whom the Communists are a major group—who argue that political democracy can and should be sacrificed if necessary in order to achieve the other objectives of the Latin American social revolution (as we shall see, some of the indigenous social reform parties take this point of view). Certainly, if the Latin Americans become widely convinced that economic development, the expression of national sovereignty and the achievement of class realignments cannot be achieved by democratic means, or will be seriously delayed by democratic methods, totalitarians of both Communist and indigenous types will have their way made much easier. It is obviously important that believers in democracy in both parts of the hemisphere do all they can to prevent such convictions becoming prevalent among the masses of Latin America.

Nature of the Indigenous Social Reform Parties

The indigenous parties working for social reform are of many varieties. Some of them are based more or less on European models, while others are of a uniquely national origin.

The traditional parties of Latin America prior to the First World War were the Conservatives and Liberals. The former were the principal supporters of the Catholic Church, defending the Church's right to extensive property, control over education, marriage, and allied matters. The Liberals, on the other hand, were anticlericals and sought to have the state expropriate Church property and assume control over educational affairs of general concern.

In many of the Latin American countries, the Conservative and Liberal parties have disappeared. In others—Chile, for instance—their importance now comes from their role as defenders of the status quo. Much of their voting strength comes from those rural areas where the landlord can still get his workers to vote as he tells them to. However, in a few countries the Liberal parties have taken the leadership in carrying out a program of social and economic transformation. The four principal cases in which this is true to some degree are Uruguay, Colombia, Honduras, and Argentina.

The Uruguayan equivalent of the Liberal party is the Partido Colorado. Under the leadership of a president belonging to the Colorado party, José Batlle y Ordõnez, Uruguay became one of the first countries to embark on the Latin American social revolution just before and during the First World War. Batlle's government nationalized the central bank, part of the insurance business, the port works of Montevideo, part of the packing industry, the oil distribution business, electric power, and other facets of the economy, some of which had been foreign-owned. He started a program of protection for Uruguayan industry and established one of Latin America's most extensive social security systems. His regime also enacted a law providing for the eight-hour day and other labor legislation. Finally, although he did not undertake an agrarian reform, he did support a program which assured the eventual death of the traditional land-holding pattern and the extension of primary education to the rural population.

In Colombia, the Liberal party came to power in 1930 after a long period of Conservative rule. During the following sixteen years of Liberal rule, particularly during the four-year administration of President Alfonso Lopez from 1934 to 1938, the government carried out an extensive reform program. This included protection of industry, enactment of labor legislation, encouragement of trade unionism, and the establishment of a progressive income tax. Subsequently, the Liberal party moved to the Right, and a movement arose within its ranks under the leadership of Jorge Eliecer Gaitan, which sought to carry out more extensive reforms. The assassination of Gaitan on April 9, 1948, brought this movement to a halt, provoking a civil war and a series of dictatorships which came to an end only with the overthrow of President Rojas Pinilla in May 1957. Unfortunately, after that the Liberal party leadership was unable to understand the need for further reform, particularly in land-holding patterns, and as a result the totalitarian elements in the country gained wide support.

From 1932 to 1948 during the dictatorship of Nationalist (Conservative) party General Tiburcio Carías Andino, the Honduran Liberal party was illegal. Under Carías' successor, José Gálvez, the party was allowed into the open once again. It appeared under new young leadership, pledged to carry out a broad program of economic and social reform. With the development of a labor movement, after 1954, the Liberals assumed the leadership of the trade unions. After considerable difficulty, the Liberal party won a general election in 1957, and its principal figure, Ramón Villeda Morales, became President of the Republic.

In Argentina the role of the Liberals was assumed by the Radical party. With the achievement of universal manhood suffrage and the secret ballot in 1916 the Radicals were able to elect Hipolito Irigoyen as President of Argentina. Because of Conservative control of Congress during the Irigoyen administration and the exceedingly moderate inclinations of his Radical successor, Marcelo T. de Alvear, the Radicals did little to change the economic and social status quo—their principal accomplishments were the establishment of democratic government and the organization of a nationalized petroleum industry.

The Radicals were overthrown in 1930 by a military *coup d'état,* and during the next twenty-eight years Argentina was ruled by a succession of dictatorships and semidictatorships, including the Perón regime. During this period the Radicals constituted the principal opposition party. Under Perón a schism appeared and the Left Wing, or "Intransigentes," advocated a program of economic nationalism and social reform that was not unlike that of Perón, except that it also advocated political democracy. After Perón's fall, the principal elements representing what we have called the Latin American social revolution gathered around the Intransigentes, and in 1958 the leader of this group, Arturo Frondizi, was elected President of the Republic. Although not carrying out all of the program on which he was elected, Frondizi did succeed in stimulating industrialization.

[Frondizi's decision to permit Peronista participation in the 1962 elections led to his ouster by a group of military leaders, demonstrating the continued appeal of Peronism, and threatening the future of the Intransigentes and of political democracy. The Communist Party of Argentina was barred from presenting candidates in elections in September, 1959. Its membership is estimated at approximately 50,000, and its reliable sympathizers at about 100,000. The PCA controls a number of front groups, notable among which is the Committee for Solidarity with the Cuban revolution. It has substantial, though not controlling, strength in the General Confederation of Labor and the principal student organization. The immediate future of the PCA appears to be tied to its relations with the resurgent Peronistas. There are Communists and sympathizers within the Peronista movement, and the movement is a chief target of Communist infiltration. Peronista leaders, on the other hand, use the threat of an alliance with the Communists in the effort to extract political concessions.—Ed.]

Other indigenous reform parties in Latin America have been patterned after European organizations. These include both Socialist and Christian Democratic groups. The principal Socialist parties are those of Argentina, Uruguay, Chile, Ecuador, Brazil, and Peru. All are relatively small, though the Chilean Socialists were for a time the third strongest of Chile's many parties. The Argentine and Uruguayan parties have been outstanding for the intellectual quality of their leadership and they have played an important role in popularizing ideas of social reform and labor legislation. In recent years most of these Socialist parties have leaned in a totalitarian direction.

There are Christian Democratic parties in Uruguay, Chile, Venezuela, Brazil, Argentina, Bolivia, and Peru. These, too, are relatively small, though the Venezuelan Christian Social party is the country's third largest. Their programs are similar to those of Europe, their social philosophy being based on the Papal Encyclicals Rerum Novarum and Quadregessimo Anno. Also like the European parties, they include a wide range of opinion.

More important than any of these parties as protagonists of the Latin American social revolution are those groups which are both relatively new and have not sought to copy any European models.

These include the Partido Peronista of Argentina, the Partido Tabalhista of Brazil, and a conglomeration of parties which may be called the national revolutionary parties.

Perón and Vargas, who established the Peronista and Trabalhista parties, respectively, were successful demagogues who sought the support of the working class to assure their tenure in power. Despite the different motives which impelled their actions, the effect was much the same in both cases. The advent of Getulio Vargas to power in Brazil in 1930 and Juan Domingo Perón in Argentina in 1945 marked the transfer of effective political power from the rural aristocracy to the middle- and working classes of the urban areas and set in motion a process of social and economic reform.

Both Vargas and Perón carried out programs of economic nationalism, extending protection to manufacturing industries with the aid of government funds. Both established extensive social security systems and enacted broad labor legislation. Perón gave great encouragement to the spread of the trade unions, though he submitted them to his close personal control. Vargas substituted a state-dominated labor movement for the small but independent unions which had existed before he established his dictatorship.

Vargas and Perón shared one other characteristic—neither was a democrat. Between 1937 and 1945 Vargas attempted to establish a totalitarian corporate state. Perón, though he might well have presided over a democratic regime, chose to be a dictator, and during his nine years as president moved slowly but unremittingly toward the establishment of a totalitarian regime.

In contrast to the regimes of Perón and Vargas, the national revolutionary parties are strong advocates of democracy. Among these are: the Aprista party of Peru, the Democratic Action party of Venezuela, the National Liberation party of Costa Rica, the Popular Democratic party of Puerto Rico, the National Revolutionary Movement of Bolivia, the Autentico and Ortodoxo parties in Cuba, and the Febrerista party of Paraguay.

These parties recognize a bond of fraternity among themselves, but they are true products of the Latin American environment.

They have developed as a result of events within their respective countries, and they speak the language of the people of those countries. Their programs, therefore, differ somewhat, depending upon the local circumstances, though they are similar in general.

All of these parties are somewhat nationalistic. They advocate the defense of native manufacturing industry and government participation in economic development. They are not opposed to foreign investment, though they think that such investment should be limited to certain parts of the economy, and should occur under conditions laid down by the national governments. They are in favor of agrarian reform, tailored to suit the local circumstances, social security, labor legislation, and a strong trade union movement. Finally, then, they are democratic.

In this context, one should also note the party which for three decades has controlled the government of Mexico. Now called the Partido Revolucionario Institucional, it has had a program embodying agrarian reform, industrialization, and labor and social legislation—the principal achievements of the Mexican Revolution. It has not been closely associated with any other revolutionary parties in Latin America, although in recent years it has moved closer to the group which we have called the "national revolutionaries."

Impact of the Indigenous Parties on the Communists

One fact stands out clearly about the relationships between the Communists and the indigenous parties: where the latter are successful, the former are not. On the other hand, where the indigenous parties falter, or where they do not develop, the Communists are the chief beneficiaries. There are several reasons why this is so.

First of all, the Communists and indigenous parties appeal to the same groups in the population. Although the Communists claim to be the unique spokesmen for the industrial working class, and the indigenous parties the spokesmen for several classes—the industrial workers, the peasants and the middle classes—they both in fact seek their supporters principally among the industrial wage workers, the white-collar workers, the peasants, and the intellectuals.

In the second place, the type of appeal of the Communists and the indigenous social reform parties is frequently similar on many points. Both call for changes in existing class relationships, such as agrarian reform, the introduction of collective bargaining and mass education. Both say they are for political democracy. Particularly in recent years, the Communists have sought to outdo the indigenous parties in their protestations of concern for the national sovereignty of their respective countries.

Hence, the two types of political parties are direct rivals. When one of them is successful, it is likely to cut off the possibilities of progress of the other. A number of instances can be cited to indicate that this has, in fact, been the pattern in the past.

In Venezuela and Peru the Aprista and Democratic Action parties have effectively blocked the growth of the Communists. Founded in 1931 the Aprista party immediately became the country's major political organization and the most important force in the trade-union and peasant movements. The Communists, although they acquired some popular support in the southern areas of Puno and Cuzco, were never able to become a major party. Their attempts have made them allies of three dictators—Sanchez Cerro, Prado, and Odría—who worked with the Communists in an attempt to develop a popular force which could confront the outlawed and persecuted Apristas.

In Venezuela the Democratic Action party became the country's largest political group in the early 1940's. It achieved power in 1945 and during the next three years carried out an extensive program of encouraging economic development and social reform, which consolidated its popularity. The dictatorial regime which took over in 1948 worked with one faction of the Communists for the same purpose that the Peruvian dictators worked with their local Communists. However, Democratic Action emerged once again from the Perez Jiménez dictatorship when it was overthrown in January 1958 as the country's majority party. Although the

Communists had benefited from the dictatorship, they were unable to seize control of the labor movement from Democratic Action or convert themselves into a major factor in the country's politics. APRA strength and appeal was demonstrated in their 1961 election, the party polling approximately one-third of the total vote and winning the election. When military leaders intervened to prevent APRA from taking office, the future of APRA and Peruvian democracy appeared uncertain.

In Costa Rica and Puerto Rico, indigenous social reform parties stunted the growth of the Communists. Between 1940 and 1948 the Costa Rican Communists won control of the labor movement, elected several members of the party to congress, and achieved considerable popular influence, through their alliance with the governments of the time. However, in 1948, José Figueres led a revolutionary civil war when President Teodoro Picado attempted to cancel the results of an election. Figueres then organized the National Liberation party, which assumed leadership of Costa Rican social reform forces. Although the Communists were by no means destroyed, they were reduced to a comparatively minor element in the country's political life.

In Puerto Rico during the 1930's the Communists profited from the decline of the Socialist party, which had formerly dominated the island's labor movement and had been the principal expression of popular discontent. The Communists became a leading factor in the trade-union movement and rapidly gained political support as well. However, their growth was cut short by the rise of the Popular Democratic party of Luis Muñoz-Marín which won the election of 1940 and has dominated Puerto Rican politics ever since. Under its leadership an extensive program of industrialization was undertaken as were many other reforms, and by 1958 the Puerto Rican Communist party was virtually defunct.

Finally, we may note the case of Mexico. Although a Communist party has existed there since the early 1920's, it has never been able to become an important political group. The reason for this is that the Mexicans have had their own revolution, which antedates the Russian Bolshevik Revolution. The Communists' appeal to follow the Soviet path has had little response in Mexico. Although the Communists have aroused some sympathy in Mexico through their attack on United States "imperialism" they have by no means had a monopoly on this issue and it has been an insufficient basis on which to build a strong popular party.

In contrast to these instances, we may note three Latin American countries in which the failure of the indigenous parties has spelled the success (albeit a moderate one) of the Communists, namely, in Chile, Guatemala, and Cuba.

During the middle 1930's the Socialist party in Chile, as we have noted, was making rapid headway. It dominated the organized labor movement, was growing in strength with each new election and was the real spokesman for the urban wage working class. However, in December 1938, the Socialists entered the Popular Front government of President Pedro Aguirre Cerda. This was a critical political error which exposed the weaknesses of the party's leadership. Too many of its top figures became involved in public schisms which have bedeviled the Socialists ever since. With each split the Socialists grew weaker, and as the Socialists declined, the Communists grew. The Communists were finally able to portray themselves more or less successfully as the only genuine spokesman for the Left.

The tragedy of the revolution in Guatemala which began in 1944 and ended, at least temporarily, with the overthrow of President Arbenz ten years later, lay in the lack of an ideological party of the democratic Left. Although numerous parties appeared, they all were dedicated to the personal fortunes of one or another leader. No politician was strong or farsighted enough to develop a party which could become the real spokesman for the revolutionary movement—for agrarian reform, economic development, social legislation, trade unionism—and so differentiate their program from the aims and objectives of the Communists.

The Guatemalan Communists established themselves solidly by getting control of a sizable segment of the labor movement. They showed their usefulness to the revolutionary government in 1949 by mobilizing their supporters to help defeat an uprising within the army. When Colonel Jacobo Arbenz became president, in 1952, the Communists found that they had the new chief executive's ear. The Communists' image of themselves as sincere and loyal supporters of the revolution was reinforced by the endorsement of the President. When Arbenz was overthrown in 1954, the Communists were on the verge of getting full control of the Guatemalan revolution.

The third case is that of Cuba, where in the 1940's the Autentico party, a national revolutionary group, won the support of the great majority of the workers and peasants of the island. However, when the Autentico party came to power, it betrayed the hopes of those who had supported it. Its leaders proved to be exceedingly corrupt, it failed to carry out its former program and finally, in 1952, it lost its power by *coup d'état* without even a fight. As a result of the failure of the Autenticos, the program of democratic social revolution in Cuba was seriously discredited, and this paved the way for Fidel Castro's betrayal of the very revolution he had led.

Attitude of Communists Toward the Indigenous Parties

The attitude of the Latin American Communists towards the indigenous social reform parties has varied with the changes in the political line of the international Communist apparatus. During the 1920's there were various alterations of the Communists' attitude, from sectarian opposition to attempted United Fronts, depending upon the momentary whims of the Comintern. During the Third Period the Latin American Communists, in line with their confrères elsewhere, were violent in their attacks on the Socialist and national revolutionary parties, as well as on such groups as the Radicals and Liberals, labeling them "social fascists" and proclaiming them worse "enemies of the working class" than the real fascists.

Then during the Popular Front period the Latin American Communists sought to form alliances with the indigenous social reform groups, though for the most part these groups refused alliances with the Communists. After another short period of isolation during the months of the Nazi-Soviet Pact, the Communists again sought *rapprochement* with the forces of the democratic Left.

Since World War II, the Communist attitude toward the indigenous social reform groups has been highly flexible. It has depended in part upon the local circumstances and the position of the indigenous parties themselves, though the Communists have always kept in mind their primary loyalty to the Soviet Union and their enmity towards the United States in determining their attitude. We have already noted that, in the case of some countries controlled by dictatorships, Communist flexibility went so far as to allowing a policy of two parties, one favorable to the dictatorship, one trying to make an alliance with the social reform party fighting the dictatorship. This was the case in Argentina, Peru, and Venezuela.

Four cases of Communist behavior toward indigenous social reform parties over the years should be noted: Cuba, Puerto Rico, Chile, and Brazil. In the first two instances, Communist behavior resulted in their own defeat, in the other two it has won them a considerable degree of success. All four countries are important in illustrating the relationships between the two types of parties.

The Communists were allies of Fulgencio Batista from 1938 to 1944, who was dictator from 1938 to 1940 and president of the Republic between 1940 and 1944. They formed part of Batista's so-called Democratic Socialist Coalition, and had two members of his Cabinet as ministers without portfolio. Although Batista assured the Communists of control of the country's labor movement, he allowed honest elections in 1944. The Autentico party won these elections, and their leader, Dr. Ramón Grau San Martin, became president.

With the election of Dr. Grau, the Communists feared loss of their privileged position, particularly in the labor movement. They threatened the new president with a general strike if he attempted to dislodge them from control of organized labor. When Grau agreed to leave the Communists their control in the unions, at least for a while, they reciprocated by backing Autentico candidates in the 1946 congressional elections. Autentico victory in these elections, together with a purge of the army, gave Grau San Martin solid control of the government, and his followers in the labor movement began to move against the Communists.

Seeking to maintain their control of the Confederacion de Trabajadores de Cuba when its fifth congress met in the summer of 1947, the Communists went so far as to assassinate one of the Autentico delegates to the congress. When the Autenticos aujourned the congress and the government appointed a committee to reconvene it sometime in the future, the Communists refused to cooperate with this committee, which resulted in Autentico and Communist elements in the labor movement holding separate congresses. The organization which emerged from the Autentico-controlled meeting was recognized by the government as the genuine Confederacion de Trabajadores de Cuba, and the Communists were soon reduced to a minor position in the Cuban labor movement. Having lost influence in organized labor, and lacking the support of friends in the government, the Communists lost virtually all their popular and electoral power, and finally, through their failure to poll the requisite number of votes, even their legal standing as a political party.

At the outbreak of hostilities in the Confederacion de Trabajadores de Cuba, the Communists began a violent campaign against Autentico Labor leaders and against Grau San Martin's Minister of Labor, Carlos Prío Socarras, who had worked closely with his party associates in the trade union movement. The Communists labeled the Autentico CTC as the "CTK," substituting the initial for the word *krumiro*, which means "strikebreaker," for the final letter in the CTC initials. They denounced Prío as "Carlos Prío Machado Socarras," trying to associate his name with Gerardo Machado, a violently antilabor dictator of Cuba in the late 1920's and early 1930's. When Prío Socarras became president in 1948, they redoubled their campaigns against him.

Their concerted attack on the Autenticos was disastrous for the Communists. The fact was that their long record of collaboration with Batista's unpopular dictatorship had discredited them in spite of their apparent strength so long as Batista remained in command. The populace enthusiastically supported the Autenticos in 1944 and for several years thereafter, and by violently denouncing them the Communists put themselves in the political wilderness for more than a decade.

One can argue that the Communists had no alternative to their line of action against the Autenticos since the latter were determined to take control of the labor movement away from the Communists and to reduce their political influence in general. However, in other instances, if their general line called for it, the Communists in various Latin American countries have found it possible to remain almost slavishly friendly to politicians who were not only opposed to them but were actually persecuting them. For example in 1938, after Getulio Vargas had outlawed the Brazilian Communist party and put most of its leaders behind bars, the Brazilian Communist party followed the current "popular front" line by advocating a "national democratic front" including Vargas, ostensibly to fight the green-shirted Integralistas—whom Vargas by that time had reduced to political impotence.

There was undoubtedly another explanation for the vehemence of Communist opposition to the Autenticos inside and outside the labor movement in Cuba. This was the fact that the Autentico labor leaders took an outstanding part in establishing (in cooperation with the American Federation of Labor) a new continental labor organization to compete with the Communist dominated Confederacios de Trabajadores de America Latina (CTAL). Not only did the Autentico labor leaders cooperate with the AFL, but the Autentico governments maintained the most friendly relations with the United States during a period when Communist propaganda against the United States was reaching a crescendo.

A somewhat similar situation to that of Cuba was created by the Puerto Rican Communists' behavior toward the Popular Democratic Party of Puerto Rico and its leader, Luis Muñoz-Marín. Following the international Communist line of collaboration with the democratic Left during World War II, the Communists supported the PDP until after 1945, while trying to maintain the foothold which they had gained in the labor movement. However, once the war was over, and it became clear that Muñoz had given up his old ideal of independence for the island, the Communists turned savagely upon him. They became so violent in their attacks on Muñoz that they made an informal alliance with the terroristic Nationalist party which on various occasions attempted to kill Puerto Rican and continental public officials.

The Puerto Rican Communists' attacks upon Muñoz were even more futile than their Cuban comrades' assaults on the Autenticos, since Muñoz was overwhelmingly popular with the Puerto Rican people, winning almost every election for twenty years with a majority of two-thirds or more. With Muñoz' encouragement, the Communists were virtually purged from the labor movement and their political influence reduced to insignificance. Some Puerto Rican Communist leaders have since admitted to this writer that their blind opposition to Muñoz-Marín was the reason for the near disappearance of their party.

Chile and Brazil are examples of Communist success in their relations with indigenous social reform parties. They are important in illustrating conditions under which the Communists can penetrate and reduce indigenous parties to impotence.

The Communists bear a large part of the responsibility for the destruction of the Chilean Socialist Party as the principal spokesman for the democratic Left among the workers. The Chilean Socialists suffered from four weaknesses vis-à-vis the Communists: a tendency on the part of their leaders toward being prima donnas; these same leaders' yearning for Cabinet posts; their ideological confusion; and the fact that they operated in a political climate of extreme opportunism.

The Chilean Socialist party was organized in 1933 as a merger of a number of small Socialist groups, most of which had been organized around a particular leader. The rivalry among these "caudillos" was still acute when they came into power late in 1938, and broke out virulently when disagreements arose within the ranks concerning the party's role in the popular-front government. This rivalry was the principal cause of the serious divisions in the party which occurred in 1940, 1944, and 1948, and in lesser ways throughout the party's history.

These splits almost always occurred over two issues—the party's participation in the government of the day, and the party's relations with the Communists. The first issue arose from some of the party leaders' desire for ministerial posts and other jobs, a desire which they usually disguised as a belief that Socialist participation in the government was essential to the maintenance of a democratic regime in the republic. The second problem was created by a lack of ideological clarity, a chronic weakness of the Chilean Socialists which led them to seriously consider organic unity with the Communists both in 1944, and again fourteen years later in 1958.

The Communists, of course, have been consistent in encouraging the splits in the Socialist ranks. In 1940 they backed the official party against its dissidents, though later they shifted their position and absorbed the dissident Partido Socialista de Trabajadores. In 1944 they backed Marmaduque Grove's break from the majority of the party. In 1948 they began by backing the dissident Popular Socialist party, again shifting ground four years later and making a close political alliance with the opposite group.

In continually effecting these splits, the Communists have used the full force of their propaganda machine—to back the group they ostensibly support and to damn the one they allegedly oppose. They have played upon the prima donna attitudes of the various Socialist leaders, extolling and denouncing in their press and in propaganda those whom they were temporarily for or against.

There is considerable evidence that the Communists have had secret members within several of the quarreling Socialist groups. For one thing, the fact that they absorbed some of the Socialist factions over the years gives credence to this hypothesis.

The Socialists' lack of a consistent position on collaboration with the Communists has resulted from their ideological confusion. The Socialists have continually called themselves "Marxists" without having any clear conception of what Marxism is about, and have insisted on the label "Left Wing Socialists," although no Chilean Socialist group has ever sought affiliation with the Socialist International. This declared ideological purity has not prevented the Chilean Socialists from making alliances from time to time with everyone from extreme Right to extreme Left. They have made few if any serious studies of the real problems of their country. In recent years, one faction among them has characterized itself as "Leninist" and "Titoist," again with no serious consideration of the doctrinal positions of either Lenin or Tito.

The ideological uncertainty of the Chilean Socialists has moved them into the hands of the Communists. The latter have cleverly exploited the supposed divisions of Chilean political parties into "Left" and "Right" and played upon the Socialists' uneasiness at having a party in existence—the Communist Party—which was presumably further "Left" than they. Periodically, the Communists have been able to convince the Socialists that the only real way to be "Left" was to be in alliance with the Communists. Hence, in spite of occasional outbreaks of violent anti-Communist feeling in the Socialist ranks, and despite the fact that collaboration with the Communists in each case meant Socialist disaster, the Chilean Socialists have, more often than not, aligned themselves with the Communists.

The Socialists have also been maneuvered under Communist control through fear. Over the years, the Communists developed a tremendous propaganda apparatus, consisting of newspapers, career propaganda party members, and other media. This apparatus is turned full force on any politician who opposes the Communists, particularly any politician of the Left. There have been enough politicians destroyed in this way to make any Socialist leader hesitate before opposing the Communists and submitting himself to such attack. The Communist propaganda machine is all the more effective because no other left-wing group in Chile has been able to sustain for any length of time a daily newspaper with a wide circulation among the urban working class.

Finally, the Communists in Chile have had the advantage of possessing at all times a large, full-time staff. There are hundreds of full-time Communists working in the press, the trade-union movement, and in general political activity, with no occupation other than their work for the party. It is therefore possible for the Communists at a moment's notice to mobilize the forces of the party, always having other people available to carry on the day-to-day work of the trade unions and other organizations. Socialist politicians, on the other hand, both inside and outside the labor movement, have to earn their living, and can only engage in political or trade union work in their off hours. This fact is important in explaining Communist success in Chile.

The result of this has been the reduction of the Socialists' role from that of a major force in Chilean politics and a dominant element in the trade-union movement to that of a small political power, a power that is uncertain how much of its political strength is really its own and how much comes from the Communists.

The extreme opportunism characterizing Chilean politics has been a mixed blessing for the Communists. In regard to the temporary alliances, Chilean politics are amoral. At any moment the Cabinet may contain the most diverse elements of political opinion, and the political components of the administration's opposition are similarly various. Overnight shifts from bitter enmity to alliance, and vise versa, are commonplace. This has made it possible and expedient for the Communists to ally themselves not only with the Socialists and Radicals of the Left, but with such groups as the right-wing Liberal party, the Christian Democrats, and virtually every other party in the country. However, at the same time, this rapid changing of political alliances has made it impossible for the Communists to fully capitalize on any one of their many collaborations. Therefore, that the Communists have very nearly destroyed the Socialists as an effective political group has not brought the Communists themselves much nearer the center of political power.

[In the 1961 elections, the Communist Party of Chile had the first opportunity since 1947 to present a national candidate in its own name. In that election Communist, Socialist groups, National Democratic and National Vanguard parties formed an electoral alliance called the Popular Action Front. The Communist party polled 157,451 votes or 11.7 per cent of the total vote and won twenty seats, thereby demonstrating that its appeal extended considerably beyond its members (estimated at 18,000 to 20,000) and reliable sympathizers (estimated at about 5,000). The PCC dominates the major trade union federation—the Chilean Workers Central, but the influence and importance of this organization has greatly declined. The Committee for Defense of the Cuban Revolution is a principal front organization.—Ed.]

The Brazilian experience is not unlike that of Chile. After 1945 the principal indigenous social reform group in Brazil was the Partido Trabalhista, organized by the followers of Getulio Vargas in the latter days of his dictatorship. It had the support of the overwhelming majority of the urban workers with whom it is still popular. Founded as a personalist party to support Vargas, it has always had little ideological coherence. Its middle-rank leadership has fallen into the hands of politicians anxious to exploit the urban workers' lingering loyalty to Vargas and thereby gain positions in Congress, state governments, or other government posts. The party has been wracked with personal ambitions and each state and locality has its PTB "caudillo," all of whom are continually jockeying for positions and influence.

Like that of Chile, the political climate of Brazil is characterized by extreme opportunism. Most of the parties lack a clearly defined political program, and even those that ostensibly have one are not above sacrificing it for momentary political advantage. Alliances are easily formed and broken, and the Cabinet may at any moment contain the most bizarre confusion of political friends and enemies.

The Brazilian Communists have exploited this chaotic situation. In 1950 they supported Vargas for re-election as president, knowing that he was getting old, and hoping that by becoming "Getulistas" they would be able to get a hearing among his followers. When Vargas committed suicide in 1954, leaving letters behind in which he blamed his suicide on plots against him by "enemies of the workers" and "corrupters of the national sovereignty," the

Communists proclaimed themselves more Getulista than Getulio himself and hastened to try to gain sympathy among his followers.

The Communists have formed alliances with ambitious followers of Vargas both within the trade-union movement and within the Partido Trabalhista. They have encouraged the factionalism within the PTB and have undoubtedly infiltrated many of their own people into local organizations of the Vargas party. Only the loyalty of the majority of the workers to the memory of Vargas, and their memory of his long-time opposition to Communism, along with the convictions of a minority of the trade union and PTB leaders, stand in the way of Communist domination of the rank and file trade unions and the Partido Trabalhista Brasileiro.

[The Brazilian Communist party has an estimated 25,000 to 40,000 members and, in spite of a poor showing in the 1958 congressional elections, has influence over important sectors of society. They retain a significant minority position in the labor movement and control the principal national student organizations. The loose, unideological character of the major political parties make them susceptible to Communist penetration. The Brazilian Labor party of "Jongo" Goulart is rather heavily infiltrated. The PCB attempts to surmount its own limited appeal by running its members on the tickets of other parties.—Ed.]

In both Chile and Brazil, the Communists since World War II have laid constant emphasis on nationalism, directing their arguments against the United States. They have avidly grasped any action or inaction on the part of the United States government or by individual North Americans turning it into one more fact to defend their thesis that the United States was a constant and imminent menace to these countries' national sovereignty. These arguments have had more effect in Chile and Brazil than in many other Latin American countries because these countries have had no well-organized indigenous social reform party with a well-thought-out position concerning its relations with the United States. The Communists have been able to exploit the vague "anti-imperialism" of the Chilean Socialists (and other parties), and of the Brazilian Trabalhistas. The Communists have been successful in carrying this argument to absurd extremes only because there was no other party to offer a more reasonable nationalist program.

The cases presented here demonstrate several points concerning relations between the Communists and the indigenous social reform parties. First, the Communists have been thwarted by the indigenous parties where these have had a clear ideology and a meaningful program and were themselves clear on the differences between themselves and the Communists. Second, the Communists have made headway in destroying the indigenous social reform parties where the following three conditions have existed: (1) lack of ideological clarity; (2) excessive personalism among the leaders of the indigenous social reform group; and (3) a general political milieu of widespread opportunism.

Conclusions Concerning Communists and Indigenous Social Reform Parties

What conclusions can be drawn from the study of the relations between the Communists and indigenous social reformers in Latin America? It seems that there are seven major conclusions which stand out as those from which one may derive an important lesson with regard to policy.

First of all, one cannot understand contemporary Latin America unless one sees that the area is undergoing a fundamental social revolution. It is experiencing a transformation brought about by the impact of industrialization, the growth of nationalism, and political events in other parts of the world. This trend toward change has become inevitable. However, the ultimate question as to whether the Latin American social revolution is to take the path towards the full development of political democracy or is to end up in totalitarianism can be influenced by people in both parts of the hemisphere.

Second, it is clear that the traditional type of Latin American military distatorship is worse than useless as a means of influencing the future development of Latin America toward democracy

rather than totalitarianism. Not only are the dictatorships themselves the very negation of democracy, but they frequently work
with the Communists and other totalitarians. Even when the dictatorships do not work with the totalitarians, they tend to confuse
the differences between their Communists and non-Communist
opponents which results in a strengthening of the Communists,
who are generally more adept at underground activities than are
the democratic groups.

Third, the Latin American Communists, who are one of a number of different groups which have sought to give political expression to the Latin American social revolution, are integral members
of the international Communist movement. Anyone who looks
upon them as "mere agrarian reformers" or "harmless" is either
deluding himself or purposely misleading others.

Fourth, Communists compete with other groups for the leadership of the Latin American social revolution. Some of these other
groups have emerged from the traditional Latin American parties
of the nineteenth century; others have sought to follow political
philosophies which have already gained currency in Europe. Most
important are those political parties which have grown out of the
events transpiring in the Latin American countries themselves—
those we have labeled the national revolutionary parties.

In the fifth place, it is these indigenous social reform groups
which are best equipped to confront the Communists. They compete with them for the same clientele; they offer to the peasants,
industrial workers, middle-class people, and intellectuals of Latin
America the same kind of hope which the Communists seek to inspire. The significant difference, of course, is that the indigenous
parties have some prospect of bringing this hope to fruition and
of doing so by establishing a firm foundation for political democracy, unlike the Communists who use the hopes of the masses as
a vehicle through which to establish totalitarianism. The effectiveness of the indigenous social reform groups as an antidote to the
Communists is shown in a number of countries where they have
either prevented the Communists from ever becoming a strong
force in local politics or have thwarted the Communists after the

latter have already gained some influence and importance. On the other hand, when the indigenous social reform groups have failed to develop, this has tended to strengthen the Communists, as has been amply demonstrated in Guatemala, Chile, and Brazil.

Sixth, the Latin American Communists' attitude toward the indigenous social reform groups has varied from time to time in conformity with the political line of the international Communist apparatus. Since World War II the Communist attitude has been more flexible than in the past, depending a good deal on local circumstances, though it has always been subject to the necessities of Soviet foreign policy. During this last period since World War II the Communists have stressed the arguments of nationalism, social reform, and the fight against particular dictatorships.

Seventh, the Communists' dealings with the indigenous social reform parties have been most successful when the indigenous parties have lacked ideological clarity, have been subject to excessive personalism in their leadership, and have operated in a political milieu of exaggerated opportunism, with frequently shifting political alliances.

5

Conflict and Consensus in the United Nations

THE U.S. AND THE U.S.S.R. IN THE U.N.

Charles Burton Marshall

■ For more than half a century, non-Communists have grappled with the sense that the disciplined Communist is a different sort of man, with distinctive ways of perceiving, valuing, and behaving. A small library of studies has been written by non-Communists in their effort to comprehend a type of human behavior so different from traditional patterns that it can be understood only by painstaking intellectual analysis. A legion of former Communists has provided maps to guide the uninitiated across the frontiers and into the interior of the distinctive political culture of the Communist movement. The psychology, semantics, philosophy, patterns of socialization, history, and ethics of the movement have been analyzed in the effort to penetrate the dynamics of this culture. The effort was not superfluous.

Where basic assumptions and values are shared, empathy and intuition may be relied upon to understand the behavior of others. Where they are not shared, empathy, which is based on projection, is a pitfall for unwary, the source of most problems in cross cultural communication. From anthropology, psychology, and experience we have learned that human behavior can be correctly interpreted only in the context of the assumptions and expectations of the actor, and that these are a function of his total culture and character, and cannot be understood apart from them. To the Communist, an American rolling mill may be perceived as an instrument of exploitation and aggression; a monument to American materialism; a Soviet rolling mill, on the contrary, may be seen as a lyric three-dimensional embodiment of progress and justice.

The disparity between non-Communist and Communist modes of perceiving, knowing, and valuing has consequences of great importance for relations between the Communist and non-Communist worlds.

In the language of game theory, Communists and non-Communists are like opponents playing different games by different rules on the same board. The United States, the nations of Western Europe, and many other countries are involved in a game which looks toward the resolution of conflict by the partial accommodation of the interests of all parties. The achievement of a stable equilibrium—called peace—is its goal. This game conceives the opponent as a fundamentally "reasonable man" with limited objectives, oriented to compromise, ready to discuss issues on their merits, to play by rules, and to obey the referee. Communist leaders, on the other hand, play a game which looks toward the resolution of conflict by the defeat and absorption of the enemy. This game conceives the opponent as a mortal enemy, bent on annihilation, eternally aggressive and treacherous. The only rule of this game is the rule of the jungle: survival and victory by all available means. There is no referee. The world is the board.

Significant portions of the game are played out at the United Nations. In the following essay, Charles Burton Marshall examines the confrontation of the United States and the U.S.S.R., at the U.N. in the light of the assumptions, expectations and goals each brings to the encounter. He is particularly interested in the consequences of the "presence of a super-power with a deeply engrained 'two camp' view in a one-world organization." (The phrase is Alexander Dallin's.) Mr. Marshall brings wide knowledge and practical experience to the problem. Currently a Research Associate at the Washington Center for Foreign Policy Research, he served under President Truman as a member of the Policy Planning Staff of the U. S. Department of State. He is the author of The Limits of Foreign Policy, and of numerous articles on foreign affairs. ∎

Alexander counted among his achievements the gathering of the world together under one rule after extending domination over a span less than that of South America. The Romans thought of themselves as approaching the limits with an empire about equal to present Indonesia in scope. The ancient dream of organizing the world through conquest testifies to the circumscription of geography in those epochs. In any event, the idea of organizing the world through subordination of its parts to one center of authority differs from that of organizing it through free association among juridically equal components. This latter notion had to await the emergence of modern nation states. So long as such states were phenomena exclusively or preponderantly European and so long as power in world affairs remained concentrated in the same area, the notion of world organization was reflected in various schemes for institutions of ordered accommodation among Europe's rulerships —academic projects dreamed up by such figures as William Penn, the Abbe de St. Pierre, Jean Jacques Rousseau, Jeremy Bentham, and Immanuel Kant and poetic speculations such as Tennyson's. As an undertaking pertinent to the policies of governments, world organization has less than a half century of continuity—brought to life in the circumstances of World War I, given form in the Treaty of Versailles, and recast as the United Nations in 1945. In age as an active political idea, it is among the newest.

Here the concern is with the place of the world organization in the policies of two governments, the great adversary powers of the contemporary world scene, namely the United States and the Soviet Union. The approach is one emphasizing the effect on the world organization of trends and forces having sources outside it— as distinct from an approach emphasizing the forms of the organization. In formal terms, the world organization has developed so far in two stages—the League of Nations and then its successor, the United Nations. From a standpoint emphasizing the play of politics rather than the function of form, the League went through four distinct stages, and the United Nations has experienced three and now confronts an issue over entering a fourth. It would be appropriate to consider the whole development as a succession of seven Leagues and a possibility of yet another.

The first phase of the League proper might be called the Wilsonian phase reflecting the idea of permanent participation by the United States with other powers, especially those of Europe, in keeping constant watch over the problems of order, stability, and peace. The American President did not precisely invent the idea —though his name was graven on a tablet at Geneva as the founder. It had been talked about unofficially for some years. Lord Grey, the British Foreign Minister, broached it first as a policy proposition in the summer weeks of 1914 during the vain efforts to head off the outbreak of war. The concept took hold among sectors of public opinion first in Great Britain and then in the United States. Woodrow Wilson put behind it the force of his personality and office. Not as a matter of proof but at least a reasonable speculation, the League would scarcely have materialized otherwise. To this extent it is just to refer to Wilson as the founder.

Justice to the proponent's practical sense requires mention of a linkage, in intention if not in form, between the League project and a collateral treaty anticipating the North Atlantic Treaty by thirty years in committing the United States explicitly to the security of Western Europe—an undertaking put aside after the Senate's rejection of the League. Thus Wilson, however much pressed to it, at least came to recognize need of a foundation in regional security for a projection onto a world scale of the premises of a democratic and constitutional order. In his estimate, moreover, realization of the project would be worth a high price in compromise and expediency with respect to other considerations. The imperfections could all be corrected in due time after establishment of a framework of constant, open interchange. Communication was a key to reason in world political relations. Community would be discovered through discourse. Rivalries would eventuate into accommodation if the parties would but hear the issues out—given a framework of obligations and principles to which all were plighted.

Germany, too, would be brought into the conclave—though this, instead of being immediate on the return of formal peace as at first projected, came to be deferred until after a period for re-habilitation. Save for a few exceptions, the door otherwise was to be left open widely. The most significant exclusion was that of Soviet Russia, a new revolutionary power nursing an expectation of creating a world order in another pattern, imagining itself as destined to be the model maker of a world organization, and scornful and hostile toward the emerging League as an instrument of its adversaries marked for early failure and bound to be superseded when the dream of world revolution should come true. It was a case of mutual antipathy.

The League coming into reality differed in a signal respect from the Wilsonian project—a difference such as to make the League basically different from what had been planned. The withholding of United States participation was the obvious factor making the difference. The organization took shape on a basis of a hegemony of the European victor powers—a hegemony too limited, fragile, and doubtful to serve the purpose for long. This was the League in its second phase.

A third phase began in 1924—the phase of the Locarno Pact signaling reconciliation between the European victor powers and defeated Germany. This brought the League to the height of its promise. Its tenth anniversary in 1929 was the occasion for a great array of congratulatory speeches, hopeful essays, and assured books hailing the apparent fact of the League's having overcome its initial disabilities. It seemed to be succeeding in making do without United States collaboration. It appeared to be making a place for itself as the instrument of a concord wider than that of the victor powers. While by no means exclusively European, it remained a Europe-centered institution, but Europe still enjoyed ascendancy in world affairs and seemed for the moment to have achieved a durable basis for collaboration almost as wide as the celebrated concert of European powers of the preceding century.

During this phase both the United States and the Soviet Union, while maintaining formal aloofness, took tentative steps toward collaboration in work of the League, especially with respect to disarmament. The United States moved a long way from the attitude characteristic of an earlier time when communications from League headquarters were left unanswered. The Soviet Union modified its earlier approach of discount and diatribe. This mellowing of aloofness by both powers at least implicitly added to the brightness of the time.

The hopefulness of the broader prospect was of short duration. Just when it ended is difficult to say. The Great Depression of 1929 and subsequent years and the related rush into economic antarchy revealed the basic weakness of the European hegemony. The durability of German cooperativeness with the victors appeared increasingly dubious. The earlier hopes lapsed with the collapse of the Weimar Republic and the reversion of Germany to militant defiance—a course already undertaken by Japan, whose example in withdrawing from the League Germany followed in the same year of 1933.

With Germany and Japan off on paths of intransigence and Italy veering in a like direction, the League entered a fourth phase, coincident roughly with the vogue of the United Front in European politics and marked by ambiguous approaches to cooperation between the Western European powers and the Soviet Union —ambiguous because each side in the ventures had fingers crossed and each suspected how it was with the other. For Soviet Russia the development brought transient vindication. It entered the League in 1934, not at its own request but on the bidding of the organization from which it had been proscribed. For a few years, represented at Geneva by Maxim Litvinov, it was among all governments the most vocal and active advocate of collective security —at least in discourse and probably in other respects, for the Soviet regime was sensible of its infirmities, alert to resurgent German aggressiveness, and anxious to stave off danger.

The year 1936 marked for all practical purposes the end of gestures toward collaboration between the Soviet Union and the West in the League—the year when things began definitely to go to pieces, the year of the reoccupation of the Rhineland and the abrogation of the Locarno Pact, of Italy's official annexation of Ethiopia and of the League's ignominious recision of sanctions placed against Italy for aggression there, of the outbreak of Spain's Civil War, of the formation of the Rome-Berlin Axis, and of the German-Japanese anti-Comintern pact. It was a year of foreboding also with respect to intensification of the purge within the ruling Communist party within the Soviet Union—a circumstance bringing into grave question the Soviet Union's internal strength as a factor bearing on its reliability in international affairs.

This last point has relevance to evaluation of the respective roles of the Soviet Union and the Western European powers in the breakdown of European security and the advance toward war. Basing judgment solely or primarily on declaratory policies uttered at Geneva may bring one to a highly affirmative appraisal of Soviet policy. Soviet attitudes on countering Axis aggression were unequivocal, while those of the Western powers were halting. In his generally authoritative *History of the League of Nations*, F. P. Walters thus comes to a high estimate of the Soviet approach with blame clearly falling to the Western powers for failing to take at face value and acting on the Soviet proffers of cooperation in defense. Implicitly, by this version, things would have turned out well and the debacle have been avoided if the Western parties to Locarno had made other assessments and joined hands with the Soviet Union. One is liable to fall into fallacy by accepting declarations in an international forum as conclusive. The West's statesmen had reason enough to be wary of the Soviet Union's solidity and reluctant to bring Soviet weight to bear in Central Europe. The course they elected turned out badly. This does not prove the alternative to be better. What confronted them was a dilemma. History is full of examples of getting caught between a reef and a vortex.

In any event, after 1936 the eclipse of the League never really lifted even briefly. Collaboration in security between the West and Soviet Russia became a dead letter. Geneva became less and less a place for making great decisions or even attempting them—an institution where important affairs were watched, occasionally commented on, but not dealt with seriously. The center of events moved elsewhere—to Nyon, Berchtesgaden, Munich, and then to

Moscow itself for the signing of the Hitler-Stalin Pact, which opened the way to World War II and the partition of Poland. The League had but one more decision within its capability—that a negative one. In December 1939 its Council declared the Soviet Union no longer a member—an action of symbolic punishment for the Soviet Union's attact on Finland. It was the sole instance of expulsion of a member in the League's unhappy and futile history and a last act of clearing up an anomaly, before the League itself went into caretaker status for the duration of the renewed World War.

The League had begun with forty-one member states. Cumulatively over twenty years the members totaled sixty-four. By 1939 forty-three remained—four of these being countries actually under annexation and only nominally participating. The European component of membership totaled sixteen at the outset, rose cumulatively to twenty-eight, and declined to a final twenty. The Latin American group began at fifteen, rose cumulatively to twenty-one, and declined to nine. The Asian members began at five, rose cumulatively to eight, and ended at seven. The African states began at three and rose to four. The balance consisted of three British dominions, two in the South Pacific, and one in North Africa. Non-European participation was proportionally even less in interest and influence than in numbers. In sum, the League never really succeeded in fulfilling the design of a world organization. Through much of its practical life, and especially toward the end, the League was characterized by instability of membership—both a cause and symptom of its weakness.

It is a commonplace to describe the pervasive effect of World War II as a transformation in the pattern of power in world affairs. The transformation was worked in many ways. Some countries were depleted by efforts beyond reasonable capacity; some suffered social disintegration under enemy occupation; some experienced the ordeal of being fought over once and again; some were brought low by defeat. The broad consequence was a draining away of capacity to achieve. Power being relative, what is lost by some passes to others. The United States and the Soviet Union were the receivers—the two major nations to emerge aggrandized in power. The first was stronger even in absolute terms than before the war. The second was certainly stronger in a relative sense despite huge losses in an absolute measure. Large portions of the Soviet land were still devastated. Its economic situation was precarious in the utmost. It had sustained huge losses in manpower. Its place in the world, nevertheless, was aggrandized by the abstract factor of prestige in having won through in the bitterest and most extensive fighting of the war and by the concrete factor of positions occupied by Soviet forces in the wake of retreating and collapsing Axis armies.

The central question bearing on the prospect for world tranquility thenceforth involved the future relationship between the two new major powers. In the circumstances, the question of a resumption of effort in world organization—and the form for it to take—lay with these two as with no others. Each, in distinct ways, was deeply affected in its approach to the question by experience and recollections related to the League, in its various phases.

With the United States, a primary consideration was a fault of conscience over having forsaken the League. That act set the precedent of being cavalier about League membership—an example all too widely copied later on. The withholding which fated the League to remain a mainly European institution had been an American action. Advocates of the League, Wilson pre-eminent among them, had based their case on the essentiality of a strong League to preservation of peace and the essentiality of United States participation to a strong League. With the United States' strength withheld, the League had remained feeble and unfulfilled, world war was renewed and the United States was again drawn in—a sequence seemingly corroborative of the warnings disregarded by public opinion and other forces of American politics at the time of the decision to stand aloof.

This argument from experience was neither empirically demonstrable nor logically conclusive. No one could ever know whether United States participation in the League would have made a determining difference between peace and renewal of war. Perhaps the forgotten treaty on Western European security was even more important among might-have-beens. The collapse of the structure of peace might in any case have been an inevitable consequence of the economic debacle following 1929—a set of circumstances to which the question of United States membership in the League had little bearing. Such conjectures were beside the point, however. After two decades, the predictions of dire consequences of the United States default seemed amply confirmed on the face of the evidence. The record suggested a set of compelling syllogisms regarding United States participation in world organization, henceforth.

On the second opportunity, United States public opinion was amply affirmative. This time no party issue was posed. In the prevailing mood, the United States was to outdo all others in devotion to the renewed cause. The undertaking was plighted in the Atlantic Charter even before the entry into belligerency. This time the planning effort for organizing peace began virtually with the onset of hostilities. The act of organizing was not to be postponed until the sequel but persevered in to completion even in the course of war. The organization, though a successor to the League and modeled after it in many particulars, was to represent a new start juridically and to be rooted in, and to derive its name from, the coalition of powers against the Axis.

Naming it the United Nations was a triumph of public relations, perhaps unconsciously contrived. Unity was explicit in the title. Unity means concord; and concord, peace. The tendency would be to foreclose argument in regard to issues arising over courses set in the emerging organization. Such a psychological advantage would surely not have obtained if it had been called the Assorted Nations, the Various Nations, or even the Assembled Nations.

The chosen name reflected, moreover, an assumption—at least a hope—of a continuation in the sequel to hostilities of the sharing of purposes taken to characterize wartime efforts against common foes. The official as well as the public disposition at the time was to overconstrue community of purpose and, as a corollary, to discount divergencies among the wartime collaborators. The differences among them, while not obscured, were certainly not highlighted. It is human nature to make the best of an ally while confronting still unvanquished enemies, and it should not be amazing to find human nature reflected in foreign policy. Policy, moreover, must be grounded on hope. The hope of finding a basis for working things out between the two powers of pre-eminent importance to the chances of peace had rational roots. As Inis Claude, Jr., has pointed out in his *Swords into Plowshares*, what was assumed was not an infallible prospect of postwar cooperation between the great powers but its indispensability to a peaceful order. Circumstances of the time rather than perfectionism of hindsight provide the best perspective for judging United States policy in that phase.

International as the frame of the new organization was to be, it was an American project in essential aspects. The thought— echoing Wilson—that realization of the project might be worth some compromises along the way was strictly an American attitude. One can scarcely imagine the Russians withholding their weight on an issue in hope of promoting thereby the achievement of a new world organization. Americans might entertain the idea —again echoing Wilson—that any imperfection necessarily acquiesced in could all be adjusted in the long run within the framework of the organization, but for Russians, to have acted on such a premise would scarcely be imaginable. Irked over Russian obdurateness, the President could, as he did, warn the Soviet Foreign Minister that the United States might change its mind about wanting Soviet participation. Surely the Russian official was in no position to hint at the retaliatory possibility of excluding the United States.

With the Soviet Union it was a case of going along with a project of others' devising. It did go along, notwithstanding rumors persisting to the last minute, of a design to stand aside from the conference at San Francisco, where the Charter was put into final form and signed. The idea of Soviet reluctance to join was to prove a durable myth. It presumably stemmed from Marshal

Stalin's intermittant professions of velleity and doubt—made with intent to elicit concessions as a price for the Soviet Union's consenting to embrace an opportunity which it is scarcely conceivable it would have renounced in any event. On this score, President Truman was surely nearer correct than his predecessor. The Russians must have been in a mood to be deterred by a prospect of being kept out rather than requiring to be humored into going along. Going along, however, did not entail identity as to understanding and purpose. This circumstance, discernible at the time and amply demonstrated since, gives rise to a question whether the Soviet Union was devious or sincere in the action—a question worth dwelling upon with care.

As an American Secretary of State was to put the matter sixteen years later, the Soviet Union, while having signed and ratified the Charter, never really concurred in it. In Leland Goodrich's telling phrase, the Soviet Union made its subscription to the Charter subject to a unilateral amendment entertained in its own intentions. The amendment, if the term applies, was of a most basic character. On one occasion—it happened to be at the Danube Conference in 1948—the Soviet Foreign Minister proposed what he called a procedural amendment: to insert a *not* before every verb in a draft under consideration. The reservation regarding the Charter entertained in the Soviet view might seem to be of that sort, involving mental insertion of a negative into some of the propositions fundamental to the document, at least as those propositions were understood by the proponents.

Care is called for in applying this notion of a mental reservation. One may too easily construe intended deceptiveness from Soviet discourse and actions. Moreover, the assumption may mislead one into unsubstantiable hopes. To assume mental reservations on the Russians' part in regard to the Charter implies their recognition of the authentic meaning, colored by preference for knowingly substituting an invalid interpretation as a basis for playing a double game to serve their own ends. From this assumption there seems to flow a possibility of the Russians' some day owning to error, confessing to having known what was right all along, and promising to desist from further waywardness. These things will happen when shrimps whistle. Individuals and groups with divergent concepts of meaning and truth are likely to regard each other as prevaricators even when doing their respective best to be sincere. In any dialogue, it is important to recognize linkage between sense of truth and grasp of reality as these are revealed in terms. To attribute untruthfulness to a person having hallucinations and reporting the presence of objects not actually at hand is no more appropriate than his counter attribution of the same malign quality to someone denying their presence—notwithstanding the question of validity as between their respective views. An Englishman using "billion" where we would say "trillion" no more intends to deceive us than do we him in saying "billion" for his "milliard." This injunction against construing deceptiveness from deviant usage of terms applies to international dialogues in general and to that with the Soviet Union in particular. The point to comprehend is that Soviet discourse does not necessarily involve flouting of truth in interpreting and using terms differently from us, asserting as real things which we do not discern, and denying matters of which we are certain.

Such differences are not likely to be manifest in relation merely to tangibles. They may not emerge in any dialogue about values, purposes, and principles as abstractions only. They are almost inevitable, however, in relation to any question linking tangibles and abstractions—as political dialogue essentially does.

I have heard individuals of scientific bent remark on the harmony prevailing between themselves and Russian counterparts in interchanges confined within the limits of a precise, verifiable common discipline and construe therefrom an idea of rendering all issues negotiable by translating them into terms of the mutual specialty. On the other hand, I have heard idealists comment upon the community of ultimate goals entertained by the two political societies concerned—both the United States and the Soviet Union affirming justice, progress, peace, and other such abstract goods. The conclusion drawn was that apparently intractable political issues might be resolved by concentrating on final desiderata.

Such simple, hopeful propositions are correct enough on a basis of inadequate premises. It is invariably futile, however, to suggest alleviating a difficulty of combination by reducing the problem to one term, as one does in proposing to solve political issues by treating them as if they were of some other sort. The rub is that politics—meant here in its broadest, most dignified sense—involves not merely tangibles or ultimate and indisputable goods. It involves linking the one sort of thing to the other in courses of action. It embraces not merely means or merely ends but means and ends. The focus of politics is what to do to promote the good society. Its issues do not impinge so long as talk is directed merely to the self-evident goodness of a good society or to things to do without reference to their effects in retarding or forwarding realization of one concept or another of such society. Means take on another dimension of value when linked to ends. Ends cease to be mere abstractions when linked to means. Then it is that issues are quickened and complicated by what one calls political characteristics.

Persistent differences with the Soviet Union within the United Nations, as elsewhere, have been in this realm of combining means and ends—not over questions of means or ends pure and simple. Soviet divergence from our views about implementing the Charter does not signify Soviet dissimulation in signing and ratifying it or even Soviet cynicism about its high purposes. It is indicative rather of a discrepant view of what the ends involve in relation to means. The discrepancy rises from basic differences about reality, the relation of will to history, and so on. Consideration of what this implies as to limits of usefulness of discussion as an avenue to solution of issues may be deferred for the moment. The focus here is on questions of Soviet motivation and sincerity in going along with the Charter.

It is unnecessary to account for the affirmative action by negative or subsidiary explanations—a presumed anxiety to avoid diplomatic isolation and to widen contacts, recollection first of long exclusion and then of punitive expulsion from the League and a linked desire for vindication, or reassurance due to the titling of the organization after a wartime collaboration of proved convenience. Beyond such marginal considerations, the Russians in all probability heartily accepted the Charter as they understood it in a frame of understanding cognate with a world outlook, a view of history known as Marxism-Leninism.

World politics, according to this outlook, inherently polarizes around two sets of opposed purposes. Since 1917, when the state of Russia was taken over by those adhering to the Communist conception of world socialist revolution, the Soviet Union has been one of the essential poles. This is so because it is the exemplar and agent of, an ineluctable truth of historic development, in the view of its proponents. The opposite pole, at any stage, has represented whatever outlooks, interests, and purposes were deviant from and opposed to those of the Soviet Union. The polarized situation in a world thus divided into a Communist camp and that of the others is taken not to be merely an object of preference, a working of policy, but an ineluctable characteristic of historic development. At some junctures the division into two camps may be blurred by the presence of third forces not identified explicitly with the Soviet Union or its adversaries. In some phases, interests and purposes may tend to overlap as between the Soviet Union and others not under its control or aligned with it. These are temporary situations—mere passing exceptions to a general course, breathing spells in historic progression. What seems aberrant to us is normal in the Soviet view, and vice versa.

An idea pervading the Soviet outlook is a total claim on the future. The law underlying the Soviet conception of what is rightful and what is not is taken as a law of history. It is conceived of as ordaining the universal triumph of Communist interests and purposes. Those interests and purposes are asserted to have an exclusive access to legitimacy, and all other interests and purposes are regarded as deviant and illegitimate. Peace to the Soviet regime, as it would to anyone else, means a legitimate order free of violence. Since in the Soviet view, however, legitimacy stands for whatever favors Communist interests and purposes, peace therefore stands for a nonviolent situation favorable to those interests and purposes. Whatever tends otherwise is by definition deviant in the direction of war. Peace, then, besides entailing an absence of war, means essentially a situation free of impediment to Communist purposes. To promote peace thus necessarily, in this view, entails frustrating all interests and outlooks standing aside from or opposed to those of the Soviet Union. Progress is defined from a similar set of premises. The same is true of justice. World affairs —interpreted in terms of a quest of these abstractions—are seen as a struggle between the Soviet Union and its adversaries. The conflict is regarded as one between ultimately irreconcilable opposites.

In Alexander Dallin's apt summation, the "presence of a superpower with a deeply engrained 'two-camp' view in a 'one-world' organization presents a challenging problem." With respect to this problem, as with other difficulties rising from the combination in the Soviet Union of great scope and power with an adherence to irreconcilability, some persons seek a hopeful way out by postulating a doubt of the Soviet rulers' belief in their own stated theory of history. The phrase "believe in" stands for the mind's function in ascribing some quality to an object. To test the phrase in a particular context requires filling in the attribute. Thus the quality concerned in believing in a weather report differs from that pertaining to belief in free enterprise, and that involved in believing in a religious doctrine differs from that pertaining to belief in, say, the integrity of a friend. Those hopefully skeptical of the Soviet rulers' belief in their own asserted dogma are usually at a loss when called upon to specify the qualities supposed to be inwardly withheld or when asked to explain in what, as an alternative, the Soviet rulers are supposed to believe. Clearly enough, those in the Soviet rulership do accept and use their assumptions as a framework for interpreting realities.

How, then, can this be squared with believing in the Charter? The problem of squaring would present no difficulty to one habituated to dialectic. The Charter and the pertinent organization are viewed in the special perspectives of Marxism-Leninism. Their reality is accepted. They are to be interpreted or participated in as may befit Soviet interests. In these senses they are believed in just as are the state system, the institutions of bilateral diplomacy, the pattern of world trade, or any other frame of action on the world scene. The dogma is not a basis for denying or withdrawing from a differentiated world but a way of coming to grips with it, interpreting it, and acting on it. To have subscribed to the Charter in a way involving abandonment of basic framework for interpreting political reality would have been beyond the capability of minds attuned to such dogma. To have accepted the Charter as a summation of final principles governing international relations in keeping with our premises and professions would have entailed their putting aside their own way of viewing the world and taking unto themselves outlooks of quite another sort. Such renunciation, such a reversal of habits of thought sometimes accompanies religious conversion and may sometimes occur in consequence of purely intellectual persuasion, but to have expected it of the Russians as an act of political accommodation was simply unrealistic. The idea of Soviet mental reservations regarding the Charter thus misses a point. It was not a case of withholding some part of their minds. It was a case of giving adherence consistent with their dialectical way of thinking. That some Americans assumed otherwise—and that some still look hopefully for evidences of transformation—is evidence of the innocence of pragmatic minds when confronted with dogmatic resoluteness.

The Russians, moreover, have remained true to the Charter in their fashion. That is to say, they have fitted its meanings into their outlook on politics. In their own way, they have regarded it as an instrument for peace—but with an approach quite different, as the power situation and the circumstances of power are different, from the necessitous time of the Soviet Union's attempts at leadership in collective security at Geneva during the United Front period when Moscow was anxious for allies. In the United Nations, as elsewhere, peace pure and simple is seldom at issue. Either side in any confrontation is most likely to wish to prevail without violence. Issues turn rather on the conditions of peace. As one should expect, the Soviet regime has sought to interpret and invoke the Charter in a way to promote conditions tending toward triumph of its own outlook, interests, and purposes and to impede, as it could, the fostering of an order based on any differentiated concept of legitimacy—that is to say, peace on other terms. The endeavor has been constant. Methods have been elastic—adapting to conditions prevailing at one phase or another in the organization's course.

A brief account to distinguish among these phases is appropriate. The first phase was that of the United Nations as projected in plans at Dumbarton Oaks and confirmed at the San Francisco Conference. In the chronicle of world organization in relation to political forces rather than documents and forms, this might be considered the fifth League, with a character derived from conditions and suppositions pertaining to the wartime coalition. That coalition had had five principal members. They varied widely in relative importance. As to two of them, major status was more a recollection or a hope than a current fact. Whatever the gradations among them, the five became the permanent hierarchs of the reincarnated and revamped world organization. Their collective authority was to be shared in a Security Council with seven other governments serving in rotation on election by the member states at large in a General Assembly. Subject only to a requirement of support from two among the seven adjuncts, the permanent five would be arbiters of legitimacy on questions of peace and war. A requirement of unanimity among the five reserved control to each of them, namely, the United States, the United Kingdom, France, the Republic of China, and the Soviet Union —an arrangement theoretically advantageous to each but peculiarly so to the Soviet Union as the single one with a concept of legitimacy antithetic to all the others.

As the fact of intransigent singularity prevailed over assumptions of concord, the Security Council became a center of inaction from the start. Its effectiveness has revived sporadically under special circumstances aligning the Soviet Union's *ad hoc* interests with others, but in respect of the primacy of the Security Council the United Nations as originally designed can scarcely be said to have materialized—a result generally recounted as a tale of frustration, though not so by the Soviet Union, still devoted to the primacy and exclusiveness of the Security Council on the grave questions of peace and war.

Not the hoped-for harmony among the five great juridic equals but the hegemonic position of the United States was the main political circumstance affecting the United Nations as it emerged into reality. The components of the position were many—among them a productive plant protected by distance from the impact of war and indeed greatly expanded by the war effort to form an unrivaled source of supply, transport capabilities both relatively and absolutely greater than ever before despite wartime attrition, unimpaired resources for credit, and a temporary monopoly of nuclear capability. These elements of ascendancy, long in development, were coming into full play about the time of the end of hostilities. The need of using this ascendancy on behalf of national policy came into reluctant recognition with mounting evidences of the Soviet Union's true purposes in Eastern and Central Europe, the Eastern Mediterranean, Iran, and East Asia, in Soviet performance in the United Nations, and in attitudes of Moscow-oriented Communist parties around the globe.

In this phase the United States turned significantly to frames of action outside the United Nations. It renounced the United Nations Relief and Rehabilitation Administration as a channel of assistance abroad—thereby recovering control of its aid as an instrument of policy. It moved on to imaginative undertakings for bolstering Greece and Turkey against Communist penetration and for the economic rehabilitation of Western and Central Europe. It adopted a program for military strengthening of areas under Communist pressure. As a matter of high importance, the United States turned to the creation of structures of collaboration for security apart from the United Nations—first with the Organization of American States and then notably with the North Atlantic Treaty Organization, an updated counterpart of Wilson's abandoned project to contract the United States into the security of Western Europe. As at Locarno a generation before, Germany, so much of it as was politically accessible, was brought into the security arrangement—now in concrete form rather than being an expression of intentions on paper. *Rapprochement* was established with the other erstwhile principal enemy, Japan.

United States hegemony was operative during this second phase within as well as outside the United Nations. The main events revolved around Korea. The United States turned to the General Assembly, first, to try to bring about the reunification of the country divided along the 38th parallel by the Soviet and United States occupations and second, to set up a frame of legitimate government in the southern part as a prelude to the withdrawal of United States forces. On June 25, 1950, forces of the Soviet-oriented Northern part attacked the Republic of South Korea. The United States spearheaded resistance carried out under the United Nations emblem and authorization.

In the first instance the United Nations aegis was granted by the Security Council—thanks to the Soviet Union's inability to impede with veto because of absence in a purported huff over an earlier decision against transferring China's franchise from the refugee regime on Formosa to the Communist regime now ensconced on the mainland. The absence has often been attributed to inadvertence—an implausible explanation quite at variance with the substantiated premise of long preparation for the attack on South Korea. The opportunity for veto missed on purpose—a miscalculation rather than oversight. Copies, later captured, of operational plans in Korea gave a clue; success in the attack was expected to be so prompt as to foreclose riposte even if the idea should be entertained. The Soviet Union must have wished to save itself the unnecessary embarrassment of vetoing an action supposedly futile in any case. Probably no riposte, even a futile one, was expected. This view was implicit in a discourse some months later by the Soviet Foreign Minister to a neutral diplomat. His theme was American perfidy. The United States had withdrawn its forces from Korea without leaving in their stead so much as a detachment with a flag. It had created only minimal military strength among the South Koreans. It had no pledge of defense.

It had conveyed responsibility to the United Nations—something scarcely compatible with serious intentions, according to the spokesman. The United States had suffered its forces within reach to go slack on household duties. It had dawdled on economic aid to South Korea. Short of an open invitation, it was hard to imagine clearer signals for forces from the north to clear up the anomaly of a divided Korea, said Vyshinsky, but the United States had responded to the resulting attempt by making a war of it and summoning the United Nations to its side. The account closed with sharp observations about inconsistency and irresponsibility.

With the Russian return on August 1 blocking further use of the Security Council as a channel for United Nations authority in the Korean action, the United States led the way in asserting a substitute authority in the General Assembly. An alternative way was conceivable, that of carrying the Korean action to conclusion without further color of United Nations authorization and in company with such partners as might choose to see the enterprise through—an awkward course involving risk of diplomatic isolation and loss of moral advantages implicit in having the United Nations identity. These difficulties appeared forbidding. By the letter of the Charter, the Assembly could not command but only commend in such matters—and this by affirmation of two-thirds of the members voting. In essence, the view according the General Assembly the desired authority tried to rise above literalness to construe the United Nations as a body politic and the General Assembly, by virtue of being the plenary group of such an organic institution, as appropriately and inherently empowered to act in event of the Security Council's being incapacitated by procedure. This conception of the United Nations as an organic entity and of the General Assembly as its capstone and as a body politic has been the kernel of the enduring central issue ranging the United States and the Soviet Union on opposite sides thenceforth.

Details regarding subsequent use of the Assembly as a source of symbols of legitimacy in the Korean experience may be elided here. The parliamentary device for shifting issues of war and peace from a blocked Security Council to the Assembly did serve to preserve a United Nations color to the operations. It was employed again to produce a resolution "endorsing all appropriate steps to ensure conditions of stability throughout Korea" coincident with the fateful carrying of military operations north of the 38th parallel. An adequate majority for a resolution condemning aggression was pressed forth in the sequel to Chinese Communist interposition. Eventually, after more than two years of exasperating battle and toilsome negotiations, hostilities were brought to abeyance, with the Chinese still holding the positions gained by the action labeled as aggression and with the United Nations and the United States, here interchangeable, willing to settle for a standoff. This set a baleful precedent for interpreting stalemates as achievements. The foul-up over moving into North Korea and the subsequent complication of issues by the Chinese entry had helped induce another development within the United Nations—the neutralist trend—with India as bellwether.

The second phase in development of the United Nations—that of United States ascendancy and the direct confrontation of Communist power—corresponded approximately to the tenure of Trygve Lie as Secretary General. The beginning of a third phase coincided more or less with Dag Hammarskjold's succession in 1953.

This is not to imply a cause-and-effect relationship beyond the circumstance of the second Secretary General's celebrated talents and energy, characteristics conducive to accentuation of his office —a main trend of the period. A companion trend was a growing vogue of neutralism—its exponents prefer to call it nonalignment —within the organization. This in turn related to far-reaching changes in the membership concomitant with the rapid decline of the colonial order and the proliferation of new states in the close of the 1950's and the opening of the decade of the '60's. All of these developments bore closely upon adaptations in the approaches both of the United States and the Soviet Union to the world organization. The complex of changing circumstances makes it not amiss to think of the period as that of the seventh League.

A comment on neutralism, or nonalignment, as a phenomenon of the period is fitting. Neutralism is distinguishable from neutrality as abstract nouns ending in *ism* are generally distinguishable from cognate terms ending in *ity*—as for example, moralism differs from morality or nationalism from nationality. The distinctions derive from differing degrees of self-consciousness, zeal, and desire to project. Neutrality denotes a policy of standing aside and withholding one's own power from the determination of outcomes. Neutralism is a way of pitching in, exercising power, and seeking scope—in sum, a cause. Like neutrality, however, it has to have a referrent. About either abstraction a pertinent question is: with respect to what?

The new governments expanding in numbers within the United Nations in recent years are not indifferent on issues in general. They tend to be thoroughly committed, thoroughly aligned, on issues counted important to themselves. Their assumption of nonalignment pertains to a complex set of problems antedating their existence as national entities. These governments had no hand in their making. The problems involve questions of power and strategy foreign to their backgrounds. The understandable response is to wish to override them, to get them out of the way, to bring to the forefront of concern causes rooted in their more limited experience and attuned to their ambitions. Neutralism is not a way of standing in the wings but a way of pushing to the center of the stage. It generally reflects not a simple meekness but the sort of meekness expectant of inheriting the earth. A spokesman for one of the new African governments stated the case in a speech in the fifteenth General Assembly. Put in compressed form, his line of thought equated newness with inexperience, inexperience with innocence, innocence with purity, purity with righteousness, righteousness with rightness, and rightness with moral title to determine what should count in the world.

The cause typically closest to the hearts of new governments burgeoning in the United Nations is anticolonialism—an attitude having affinity to anti-imperialism in terms of which the Soviet Union articulates its distrust, grievances, and ambitions toward the non-Communist world. On the other hand, the new states generally incline—at least in some parts of their discourse—toward viewing the United Nations as a body politic, attributing to it corporateness, a general will of its own, an authority inherent in the structure, a capacity to ordain beyond the strict letter of the Charter. It would be excessive to credit them with absolute consistency in this respect. Their endorsement of this view of the organization depends in some degree on their appraisal of the issue at hand in relation to their interests. In the degree of their adherence to the view, however, they tend to support the theory of the organization advocated by the United States rather than that maintained by the Soviet Union.

The stalemated outcome of the United Nations' military endeavor in Korea bears symbolic significance for the subsequent approach of the United States in relation to the organization increasingly weighted toward nonalignment. For a season this government voiced objections to the trend—exemplified in the late Secretary of State John Foster Dulles' abjuration of neutralism as immoral. The attitude still shows through in American discourse from time to time, but the policy of the Government accepts, even as it came to accept in Mr. Dulles' tenure, neutralism as a force to be recognized as legitimate and to be turned to useful purposes where possible. In exceptional cases, as in the Soviet attack on Hungary in 1956, a requisite majority may be generated in favor of an expression of disapproval, as distinguished from action. In the main, the United States has settled for an attitude of "if you can't help me, then please don't help that bear." United States policy has discerned in the United Nations, gravitating toward a neutralist stance, a considerable utility in providing buffers between the great adversaries in the confrontation called the cold war. This form of usefulness was exemplified in the United Nations interpositions first in the Suez crisis of 1956, then in the Lebanon crisis of 1958, and again in the Congo crisis of 1960 and forward.

This concept has involved emphasis on two parts of the organization—the General Assembly as a collectivity preponderantly desirous of peace and the Secretary General as the executive arm of a discerned world community and an instrument of what has come to be called preventive diplomacy. A concept of an executive authority presupposes existence of some corporate entity or body politic on behalf of which to exercise such authority. The Charter contains no reference to executive authority. In Dag Hammarskjold's case, such power was implicit in style, and the style was the man. Having a Secretary General with endowments for ministerial initiative fitting for a premier encouraged assumptions of the existence of an underlying body politic. In recent years the concept of executive authority in the Secretariat has appeared increasingly in United States discourse about the United Nations, and a like assumption of executive power was articulated in statements by the late Mr. Hammarskjold in the closing part of his tenure. In Karl Mannheim's perceptive generalization in *Ideology and Utopia*, "The fundamental tendency of all bureaucratic thought is to turn all problems of politics into problems of administration." In the shift of emphasis toward the United Nations secretariat in this phase, the broad tendency remarked upon by Mannheim was abetted by a felt need for finding a path around political cleavages within the representative bodies of the organization. It was a case of enlarging administrative scope and construing executive attributes not on a basis of political consensus but in place of it— a reflection more of what is missing than of what is present in the world organization considered as a body politic.

As for the Soviet Union, its approach to the United Nations has appeared more subtle and resilient from 1953 onward. This change in tactics has sometimes been accounted for as a result of the passing of Josef Stalin and the advent of more flexible and resourceful leadership in Nikita Khrushchev, more inclined to take initiatives to mold opinion and court favor in the exterior world. This personifying interpretation is probably too simple. It overlooks a number of important collateral circumstances. One of these circumstances was that economic recovery, accompanying political stabilization, and progress in the Atlantic alliance had gradually made Central and Western Europe less subject to pressures of the palpable sort previously exercised by the Soviet Union. A second circumstance was the progressive modification of political relationships through the world with the breakup of empire and the emergence of numbers of new states, presenting both new problems and new opportunities for Soviet policy. An accompanying circumstance was the Soviet Union's success in getting over the worst of the tasks of recovery from the ravages of World War II and generating some capability for competing with the United States in economic assistance to the emerging countries. In other respects, too, the ascendancy once enjoyed by the United States —so important as a factor underlying its challenged but unrivaled leadership within the United Nations in the preceding phase —had eroded. With progress in economic recovery elsewhere, exigency for United States assistance had lessened or ceased. To some extent amenability to leadership eased off with dependency for aid. Perhaps most importantly of all, United States monopoly in nuclear weapons was fading out.

The Soviet Union has never abated its juridic objections to the use of the General Assembly as arbiter on questions of legitimacy concerning peace and war. It has stuck to the letter of the Charter assigning authority in such concerns to the Security Council, subject to the Soviet Union's negative control as one of the permanent members. It has opposed consistently all tendencies to treat the United Nations as a body politic endowed with a mystique of inherent authority. In the Communist view the realization of a world community must be reserved for the time, still asserted to be within view and drawing closer, of a general triumph of the Communist outlook, purposes, and interests in world affairs. Only the Marxist-Leninist outlook has real legitimacy, in this view. Only a gathering of nations harnessed to this dogma could amount to a legitimate community by this tenet. A group of governments gathered together under the Charter's principles can be only a contingent rather than a final expression of the idea of community. Expression of executive power emanating from such a gathering is a presumption, unwarranted by the law of the Charter or the facts of historic development, in this view.

At the same time, the Soviet approach has been resilient with respect to dealing with the drifts and realities. The Communist leaders of eighty-one countries meeting in Moscow in the autumn of 1960, Nikita Khrushchev addressing Communist organizations of the Soviet Union in January of the following year, and the Twenty-second Party Congress in the next autumn all made articulate the Communist abjuration of neutralism, asserting a historic obligation and destiny of all nations to come at last into the Communist fold. This has not stood in the way of taking all possible advantage of the neutralist trend, exploiting it for support with customary Communist phrases inveighing against imperialism. While standing against the idea of inherent corporate authority in the General Assembly and the Secretariat, the Soviet Union has been intent upon ensuring against a possibility of having a requisite majority in the Assembly and the capacities of the Secretaryship brought to bear against Communist purposes and interests. This much it wants—the assurance that lies in being able always to count the amenability of one-third plus one of the Assembly. Beyond that, Soviet policy aspires to pluralize the Secretary Generalship and to make its powers contingent upon agreement among three elements representing, respectively, Communist interests, avowedly non-Communist interests, and neutralism, thus to subject the office to the negative control that operates with respect to the Security Council.

This last proposition—commonly called the troika—projects another phase in world organization, a sort of eighth League. The proposition was formulated by the Soviet Union after dynamic events in the Congo for a time brought the late Secretary General athwart the line of Soviet purposes and interests. It was articulated vehemently by Premier Khrushchev at the General Assembly in 1960 but put in abeyance when the Soviet Union agreed, late in 1961, after long delay, to the selection of U Thant of Burma to fill out the term left unfinished by Dag Hammarskjold's death. The issue still hangs over the United Nations in its seventeenth year, counterpart in chronology to the year 1936 in the life of the predecessor organization.

The seventeenth year since origin finds the United Nations on surer footing, in certain measurable respects, than the League was twenty-six years before. The act of belonging has settled on the members. The fad—so troublesome in the League—of quitting under the spur of pique or convenience has not been manifested. Perturbation has occasionally led one member government or another to mutter about getting out, but none has ever given effect to the threat beyond ostentatious withdrawal of delegates from sessions. Stability of membership and, even more importantly, the burgeoning of new states attending the decline of the colonial order give the organization scope of membership never approached by the predecessor, though comparison is less impressive, because of the absence of the mainland Chinese, when made on a basis of proportions of world population spoken for. Bureaucracy has proliferated beyond anything dreamed of in League days. Magnitude of physical plant and bustle of activity exceed the experience of the predecessor. Yet the issue arising from projection into the United Nations of two antithetic sets of ideas concerning its future and the courses of world politics hangs over the world organization.

There remains something to be said about putting the issue in perspective. The issue tends to take on an appearance of compelling importance because it reflects contrasting basic ideas between a Soviet government disposed to interpret all world affairs in light of its dialectic and a United States inclined to see the United Nations as a reflection on a larger screen of some elements of national experience in the development of its federal system. The constitutional doctrine of implied powers has a loose counterpart in efforts to construe greater scope for the world organization. The American tradition of executive authority, including the constitutional doctrine of inherent power, has a psychological link to current interpretations of the role of the Secretary General.

One cannot dismiss as wholly illusory the urge to visualize a true body politic representing a world community. Success in any such course must depend less on logic than on what events may produce. If enough governments and peoples should be persuaded to accept and to abide by certain premises of public conduct expressed in the Charter and properly interpreted, then the idea will work—a conclusion pre-empted by use of the word *enough*. The rub is that *enough* would have to include the Soviet Union and, of course, Communist China as well in order to amount to a world community transcending the present divisions.

Even in face of the reality, significance, and depth of these divisions, it is appealing to some to fashion hopes of accommodation of more modest dimension—perhaps a community effective at least as to issues outside zones of confrontation between the major antagonists. How this might be done has been dwelt upon by Inis Claude, Jr., in an essay in a book titled *The United States and the United Nations*. It is scarcely fitting to describe Professor Claude as an enthusiast for his idea. "I am not sanguine about our prospects for convincing the Soviets in these matters," he says realistically. Nevertheless, he postulates a possibility of persuading the Soviet Union to greater amenability with respect to issues in such marginal situations. In dealing with such instances, he points out, "The Organization may (a) take pro-Western action; (b) take impartial, neutralizing action; (c) take no action at all; or (d) take pro-Soviet action. In general, our preference runs like this: A-B-C-D. The Soviet preference . . . runs in reverse: d, c, b, a." He takes for granted the incompatibility between the two sides of the confrontation with respect to extremes in the orders of preference. He focuses instead on the importance of the middle members—b and c. Much could be accomplished, he argues, by getting the Soviet Union to accept our order of preference, placing neutralizing action ahead of no action. The avenue recommended is that of "persuading the Soviet leaders that they have a stake in preventing the Cold War from getting so desperately out of hand that it might precipitate World War III, and in convincing them that the United Nations can function impartially in forestalling such aggravation . . ."

The formula for abatement is based upon an interpretation of the confrontation as delimited rather than pervasive—an undemonstrated assumption. It also assumes that issues in marginal areas, if such areas exist, are significant as to the danger of letting the cold war get out of hand. This seems to make them at once both marginal and central. These points of doubt, however, may be put aside for something more basic. The suggested approach entails persuading the Soviet Union to concede impartiality and authority to a consensus beyond its control—thereby giving up on the essence of its dialectical view of world affairs. This, seems to me, to amount to alleviating problems of the cold war by construing them out of existence. What I should regard as most useful and important in Professor Claude's views is the idea of influencing the Soviet rulers by pressing upon their minds the follies and penalties of letting matters get out of hand. In this respect, he enters upon sound ground and puts our relationships to the adversary and to the United Nations into good perspective.

It is difficult for Americans, whether for or against it, to see the United Nations in proportion. This is so merely because of its physical presence. It stands far larger in the public life of the United States than in that of any other country. Its activities are concentrated at the originating terminals of United States communications—press, radio, and TV. This can be said of no other country. Its delegates congregate in our midst. The debates resound in our ears as in no others. In so far as it is a forum of propaganda, it acts upon Americans as on no others. The responsibilities of being host fall peculiarly upon this government. Concerning no other government would one be likely to hear, as here, references to a team of ambassadors operating at the United Nations. These circumstances add to the apparent dimensions of importance. It becomes easy to imagine the fateful questions all being centered at Forty-second Street and First Avenue.

The tendency is abetted by a disposition both of apologists and of critics to attribute more, for good or ill, to United Nations authorship than warranted by reality. Just as two decades ago it was easy to attribute immense evil consequences to the simple fact of our having stood aloof from the League, so now it comes easy to imagine that the world situation is either as bad as it is or else not a whole lot worse solely because of the existence of the United Nations. The United Nations gets blamed for military frustration in Korea. Actually the choice of settling for a standoff was primarily an American choice taken, however reluctantly, in full account of all the factors. The United Nations is credited with having stemmed the Communist thrust in Korea. Symbolically this can be asserted. Actually the action depended on our own national will to meet the challenge when it arose. The United Nations is often praised for unique virtue in providing facilities for confidential diplomatic approaches—notably the contact leading up to the Korean armistice talks—implicitly as if such contacts would not otherwise be possible, or as if such things had not occurred innumerable times before the origin of world organization. The United Nations often is blamed for loosing floods of propaganda into channels of international politics and debasing the value of words in international affairs—tendencies well along before its creation and inherent in the development of modern communications. It is credited for having frustrated Communist designs in the Congo and having saved the world from something tantamount to the Spanish Civil War, whereas the determining factor seems clearly to have been logistical inaccessibility—a matter of enormous hindrance to the Russians in any case, given a will to contest them. It is praised for having brought about the surge of colonial peoples into independence and blamed for having thereby diluted the essence of responsibility—but through helping bring about too much independence too soon—none can demonstrate that the collapse of the imperial-colonial structure would not have occurred in any event. All this adds up to what Senator Henry M. Jackson has expressed as "a tendency to believe the UN makes more history than it really does."

Alexander Dallin's wise words are in point: ". . . too much must not be anticipated or asked of the United Nations. . . . The UN can be expected to alter neither the fundamental power relations among states nor the motives of their rulers." This being so, the world organization will continue to be affected by forces of politics beyond its scope and control rather than being the determinant of those forces. Thus it has been for the decades since the beginning of the experiment. Thus it is likely to be for the calculable future. There will still be occasion for heeding Nicolo Machiavelli's advice: "That deliverance is of no avail that does not depend upon yourself; those only are reliable, certain, and durable that depend on yourself and your valor."